# PSALM 83
## The Missing Prophecy Revealed

*How Israel Becomes
the **Next Mideast**
Superpower!*

Hezbollah

Iran

Iraq

Syria

Hamas

Jordan

Saudi Arabia

Muslim Brotherhood

Palestinians

Egypt

D1286073

## Bill Salus

Prepare for Psalm 83
Hezbollah
Iran
Iraq
Syria
Hamas
Jordan
Muslim Brotherhood
Saudi Arabia
Palestinians
Egypt

To Steve

# PSALM 83
## The Missing Prophecy Revealed

### How Israel Becomes the Next Mideast Super Power

# Bill Salus

Second Printing: February 2013

First printing: January 2013

For information contact:

**Prophecy Depot Ministries**

P.O. Box 5612

La Quinta, CA 92248

ISBN-10: 0988726025

ISBN-13: 978-0988726024

(All Bible verses are taken from the New King James Version, unless otherwise notated).

Cover and Interior by Brent Spurlock, Green Forest, AR

**Printed in the United States of America**

Please visit our website for other great titles:

**www.prophecydepot.com**

## ACKNOWLEDGEMENTS

Behold, God is my helper; The Lord is with those who uphold my life.
(Psalm 54:4, NKJV)

Heartfelt thanks to my wife, children, and grandchildren who inspired me to write this book. A further debt of gratitude is extended to all those below whom in one way or another, through prayer, encouragement, support, research, or otherwise, genuinely blessed this book.

Bob and Lynette Holmes, Brad Myers, Ladd Holton, Lynn and Dixie Wheeler, Jim Tetlow, Jim Fletcher, Brent Spurlock, Sean Osborne, Don Mercer, Yvonne Dimora, Olivia Smith, Dave Hart, Mike Fulmer, Kevin Lea, Alyn Lloyd.

Lastly, a special thanks to all of those who participated in my focus groups to determine the book's title and cover design.

Best reading regards,

Bill Salus

# CONTENTS

# Introduction

This book presents the reader with an abundance of prophetic information. It is a compilation of over eleven years of specific biblical examination that was prompted by the terrorist attacks on September 11, 2001. Initially some of this research was published in the summer of 2008 in my book *Isralestine, The Ancient Blueprints of the Future Middle East.*

*Isralestine* explored in significant detail, the prelude, episode, and aftermath of the epic Psalm 83 Arab-Israeli war, and hypothesized that Israel would win decisively and subsequently become a greater and safer Jewish state. The book also theorized that the Psalm 83 prophecy appears to be an imminent event that should find fulfillment before the infamous seven–year "Tribulation Period" commences. Moreover *Isralestine* explained why it was probably an entirely different event than the popularized prophecy described in Ezekiel 38 and 39 commonly called the Gog of Magog Invasion.

Due to *Isralestine's* comprehensive look at Psalm 83, which was a relatively unexplored prophecy up to that point, it caught the positive attention of many of today's top Bible scholars.

*"Isralestine answered Bible prophecy questions I have had for many years."*
Joseph Farah – World Net Daily

*"New invaluable insights to Middle East Bible prophecy."*
Dr. David Reagan – Lamb and Lion Ministries

*"A most important Bible prophecy book for our times."*
Chuck Missler – Koinonia House

*"A must read to understand Mideast Bible Prophecy."*
Jonathan Bernis – Jewish Voice Television Ministries

*"Bill's extensive research provides an important biblical understanding of key current-day events in the Middle East."*
William Koenig – World Watch Daily

*"Isralestine has greatly impacted my understanding of Middle East Bible prophecy."*
Erick Stakelbeck – Stakelbeck on Terror TV

*"I wish I would have written Isralestine."*
Dr. David Hocking – Hope for Today Ministries

*"Isralestine presents valid arguments."*
Dr. Arnold Fruchtenbaum – Ariel Ministries

*"Bill's in-depth study of Psalm 83 and related Scriptures provides vital information to understanding the end-times scenario."*
Jim Tetlow – bestselling author – Eternal Productions

*"Bill Salus presents a believable case in describing the prophecy in Psalm 83."*
Terry James –Co-founder of Rapture Ready and bestselling author

*"I'm convinced that Salus is correct about Psalm 83 as a Bible prophecy."*
Eric Barger – Take a Stand Ministries

*"Salus has discovered an amazing prophecy that has been hidden from most until now."*
Tom Horn – Raiders News Network and bestselling author

*"Isralestine points out that Psalm 83 may be why the Arab nations are largely absent from Ezekiel 38."*
Jacob Prasch – Moriel Ministries

*"In Isralestine, the distinguishing of a Psalm 83 war from the Ezekiel 38 war was enlightening".*

Gary Fisher - Lion of Judah Ministry

However, not everyone agreed with my Psalm 83 hypothesis that was presented in *Isralestine*. Some raised the following objections:

1.  Psalm 83 was merely an imprecatory prayer of lament concerning all of Israel's historic enemies.

2.  The Psalm found historical fulfillment in the Old Testament, namely in 2 Chronicles 20.

3.  The Psalm prophecy found fulfillment in the Arab - Israeli wars of 1948, and/ or 1967.

4.  Psalm 83 is not a separate prophecy but is one and the same with Ezekiel 38.

5.  Psalm 83 is part of the Armageddon scenario that finds fulfillment in the Tribulation Period.

This book attempts to address all of the above objections at various points within the text. When these objections were brought to my attention, I always took them to heart and seriously considered the feasibility of their interpretations. But after careful and prayerful deliberation, time and time again I found myself fastened to the *Isralestine* hypothesis. I discovered that their interpretations didn't adequately explain away the logic, which made so much sense when Psalm 83 was factored into the end time's equation. Now many agree with me, that Psalm 83 was the missing piece that completes the end time's prophetic puzzle.

Because so many new developments have occurred since the initial release of *Isralestine*, it is important to update the reader with the prophetic implications of current Middle East and world events. Recent events like those listed below, could have direct relationship with either the Psalm 83 or Ezekiel 38 prophecies;

•   The unexpected Arab Spring of 2011,

•   The removal of numerous long-standing Arab leaders that resulted, like Hosni Mubarak of Egypt, Muammar Gaddafi of Libya, Osama Bin Laden of Al-Qaeda, and many more,

- The rise of the Muslim Brotherhood in Egypt,

- The Syrian revolution,

- Iran's rapidly developing nuclear program,

- The Muslim attacks of US embassies in the Mideast and North Africa, at the end of 2012.

- The arming of Hezbollah with over 50,000 powerful rockets,

- And, the deployment of chemical weapons throughout Syria.

These are just a few of the recent indicators that strongly suggest that the climactic concluding Arab – Israeli war predicted in Psalm 83 is nearing the time of its final fulfillment.

In conclusion, this book includes research that is mostly new with some that is old. Moreover, important additional information has been authored that has not been gathered from either of my previous books, *Isralestine* and *Revelation Road*.

# ONE

# The Missing Prophetic Puzzle Piece

**"Ancient Book of Psalms Found in Irish Bog"**

*NBC News 7/25/06*

"This is really a miracle find," said Pat Wallace, director of the National Museum of Ireland.

**"Psalm in a bog' linked to Israel's current war"**

*World Net Daily July 26, 2006*

The summer of 2006 was a very prophetic year. The Psalm 83:7 *"Inhabitants of Lebanon,"* whose modern day equivalent could be the Hezbollah, were engaged in a regional war with Israel. These terrorists, identified as the *"Inhabitants of Tyre"* in the Psalm, launched approximately 4,000 rockets into northern Israel during this 34-day conflict, fought from July 12, to August 14, 2006. Meanwhile, on July 26, 2006, an ancient parchment, which just happened to be opened to Psalm 83, was discovered buried underneath Irish bog soil. The find was heralded as the Irish Dead Sea Scrolls discovery.

### "Irish Dead Sea Scrolls in bog"

*BBC July 26, 2006*

Was it coincidental or providential that this unearthing occurred two weeks into the Middle East conflict? Considering the fact that there are 150 Psalms, 1189 chapters, and over 31,000 verses in the Bible, and Psalm 83 is the only place in scripture where Israel and Hezbollah appear pinned against each other in a war prophecy.

Tattered and torn fragments of other scriptures were also uncovered, but Psalm 83 was generally legible after about a millennium of being buried underneath the muddy bog soil. The ancient document should have been destroyed by the construction bulldozer, or ruined from the centuries of burial, but the director of the National Museum of Ireland remarked, "It was remarkably well preserved," and "Nobody has found anything like this for centuries."[1]

At the very same time that the war was underway and the Psalm 83 bog find took place, I was authoring *Isralestine, The Ancient Blueprints of the Future Middle East*, which explores the prelude, battle, and aftermath of the epic Psalm 83 war. Was this timing also providential? I believe so, considering commentaries written about the potential prophetic nature of the Psalm were generally non-existent. Although some traditional commentaries were researched, very few of them interpreted the Psalm as a potential Bible prophecy. Yet, the Bible says the author of the Psalm was a Hebrew prophet, much like Isaiah, Jeremiah, and Ezekiel.

> "Moreover King Hezekiah and the leaders commanded the Levites to sing praise to the LORD with the words of David and of *Asaph the seer*. So they sang praises with gladness, and they bowed their heads and worshiped." (2 Chronicles 29:30, NKJV; emphasis added).

This 2 Chronicles 29:30 verse identifies Asaph, the author of Psalm 83, as a seer. The Hebrew word used is *chozeh,* and it can also be translated as, *a prophet* or *a beholder of vision*, according to *Strong's Hebrew and Greek Dictionaries*.[2]

The Irish bog discovery included about twenty pages of manuscript that represented about 15% of the book of Psalms. These highly illegible parchments require years of painstaking analysis before going on public display, and they were written in Latin. It is important to note that Psalm 83 in the Latin Vulgate translation is Psalm 82 in most modern English Bible translations. Due to this discrepancy, this fascinating discovery may not correlate with the Mideast war of 2006. However, it is worthy of an honorable mention and will hopefully pique the reader's interest in Psalm 83. Scriptures presented in this book strongly suggest that Psalm 83 is an important Bible prophecy for our time.

There is an abundance of prophetic content about the "end times" contained within the scriptures. Information that not only authenticates the sovereignty of God, the only true Author of prophecy, but is furthermore intended to prepare humanity for the times in which they live. The intent of this book is to explore Bible prophecies that receive little regard, which are extremely relevant today.

It is not difficult to find prophetic Christian commentaries written about the Rapture of the Church, whereby Jesus Christ returns "in the twinkling of an eye" to miraculously remove from the Earth millions, perhaps billions, of His true believers.[3] Nor are writings scarcely scattered upon the shelves of bookstores regarding the coming Russian- Iranian led confederate invasion of Israel, commonly referred to as the Magog Alliance.[4]

It is also easy to find exposition explaining the epic events of the Tribulation Period and the one-thousand-year Messianic Kingdom period to follow.[5] But is a chapter missing—a concealed matter in desperate need of being searched out? Is it a chapter unfolding before our eyes, yet remaining virtually unnoticed? In light of the events developing on the world scene these days, prophetic scriptures exist that command equal attention!

Indeed, this missing chapter is the critical component that completes the final piece of the prophetic puzzle. Until we understand it, the events listed above find themselves out of chronological sorts. Far too often, we sweep misunderstood prophecy into the final seven-year Tribulation Period. Though many significant events will manifest during that period, expositors would do well not to make that window of time the catchall closet for misunderstood prophecy.

The Bible tells of a time in the world's future when Israel amasses an "exceedingly great army." This army develops out of the need for national defense to protect against the continued advance of Arab aggression. At some point, this finely tuned military instrument unleashes deadly force against its aggressors to achieve a decisive victory. Because of this Israeli conquest over the inner circle of the core surrounding Arab populations of Palestinians, Hamas, Egyptians, the Muslim Brotherhood, Lebanese, Hezbollah, Syrians, Saudis, Al-Qaeda, and Jordanians, Israel's borders are enlarged, prosperity increases, and national stature is enhanced.

Israel as a nation experiences a condition of regional superiority, which enables it to dwell securely in an otherwise insecure neighborhood. The Jews still dispersed throughout the world at that time will flow back into their safe haven of Israel. With this influx of Jewish population, the Jews will exploit the resources of the conquered Arab territories and the people will be set to experience the "restoration of their fortunes."[6] At that time Israel will become one of the wealthiest nations in the world, perhaps the wealthiest of them all.

When Israel finds itself in this prosperous condition, the aforementioned prophetic events are set forth for their final fulfillment. This book explores the lines connecting the end-times, in order to locate the missing puzzle piece of Bible prophecy.

The appropriate time placement of this information enables Christians to intelligently answer the questions being asked of them in these days, and in so doing, bring glory to the sovereignty of God and the authority of His word. The terrorist events that occurred in New York on September 11, 2001, whereby the world witnessed the collapse of the Twin Towers, not only took America and the secular world by surprise, but it also caught the Church of Christ off guard. Catholics, Protestants, and the like were found wanting, wondering if these attacks and terrorism in general had biblical significance.

In essence, the puzzled world population imposed upon the Church the need to do its job and seriously search the scriptures for the appropriate answers. This book is a start in that direction. Passages populating these pages clearly evidence that the LORD did not forget to foretell the perils of our time.

The twentieth century Church should have predicted Jews would experience the horrifically grave circumstances of the Holocaust, and that from those dry bones conditions, the Jewish people would be restored into the Holy Land of Israel.[7] Furthermore, the Church should have known from scripture that part and parcel with the rebirth of the nation of Israel would come the protests of neighboring Arab nations. Modern history clearly evidences the occurrence of these events.

The Middle East mayhem that scripture clearly predicted is the present thorn in the world's side. Terrorism has become the by-product of this conflict, and has extended its ugly embrace deep into the international community. What the world fails to recognize is that divine foreign policy, established ages ago in Genesis 12:3, still exists, fully capable of resolving this most unfortunate form of misbehavior.

Now is the time for the Church to seize the opportunity and answer the questions on the hearts and minds of the masses. As of this book's writing, the world wages war against terror and wonders of its outcome. The reader will find God has not left the results of this episode in human history to random chance; rather, an end is in sight.

# TWO

# Can the Future of the Middle East be Known?

## *Includes an Overview of Psalm 83*

**"U.S. Officials Concerned Over What Follows Arab Spring"**

*Bloomberg 9/13/12*

**"Does the Bible Matter in the 21ˢᵗ Century?"**

*Fox Nation News 4/14/11*

**C**an the outcome of the Arab-Israeli conflict be known in advance? According to the prophet Isaiah, the answer is yes.

Remember the former things of old, for I am God, and there is no other; I am God, and there is none like Me, *declaring the end from the beginning, And from ancient times things that are not yet done*, saying, 'My counsel shall stand, and I will do all My pleasure,' (Isaiah 46:9-10; emphasis added).

Isaiah declares that only the Lord can foretell the future. It was the calling of the Hebrew prophets, like Isaiah, Jeremiah, Ezekiel, and more to inform of future events, and in so doing showcase the supreme sovereignty of their God. This book identifies a plethora of prophecies regarding the future of today's Arab-Israeli conflict, that when aligned together, seems to present a clearer picture of its foreseen conclusion.

What the world has witnessed in the Middle East over the past six decades appears to have been anticipated thousands of years in advance. Due to the spiritual significance of the Arab-Israeli struggle, it can be expected that the prophets had plenty of prophetic information to pen for our understandings about today's complex Middle East scenario.

The Arab Spring of 2011 has increasingly destabilized an already explosive situation in the region. Many Mideast pundits are concerned the Arab protests and revolts that led to shifts in the political landscapes of several predominately Muslim countries, will encourage the spread of pro-Palestinianism, anti-Semitism, and governance by Islamic Sharia law. As such, many familiar with the Psalm 83 war are wondering if the event is about to find final fulfillment.

## Overview of Psalm 83

Psalm 83 describes a climactic, concluding Arab-Israeli war that was prophesied by Asaph the seer, about three thousand years ago.[8] The actual text of the Psalm has been included for your reading convenience in the Appendix called "The Text of Psalm 83."

It is my firm assessment that the Psalm is more than an imprecatory prayer concerned with Israel's ancient enemies; I believe it also predicts a Middle East war that is now imminent. Geo-political events involving the Arab Spring of 2011, the Palestinian quest for statehood, and several decades of failed diplomatic efforts to swap Israeli land for Arab peace, has primed the populations listed in Psalm 83:6-8 to confederate against the Jewish state in direct fulfillment of this prophecy.

The Psalm identifies an inner-circle of Arab states that share common borders with modern-day Israel. This is in stark contrast to an outer-ring of nations listed in a separate coalition described in Ezekiel 38. Although some eschatologists attempt to merge the two prophetic episodes together, these appear to be two differing Middle East wars.

The Arab confederates of Psalm 83 form a collective strategic war plan to destroy Israel. Their ultimate goal is to eradicate the Jewish state and confiscate all the land it presently possesses. This would include the land captured by Israel in the Six-Day war of June, 1967.

Presently, most of the international community and the Arabs are pressuring the Israelis to forfeit much of this land, in order to form an independent Palestinian state. Psalm 83 suggests the Arabs will someday abandon diplomatic efforts and opt for war instead. Inuendos of this nature are already emanating out of Egypt by leaders within the Muslim Brotherhood, as the news headline below suggests.

### "Egypt considering violating peace treaty with Israel"

*World Net Daily – 8/15/12*

This will prove problematic for the Arabs because according to Genesis 15:18 the land in question belongs to the Israeli descendants of Abraham, Isaac, and Jacob, rather than the Arabs.

> "And God said to him, [Abraham's grandson Jacob] "Your name *is* Jacob; your name shall not be called Jacob anymore, but Israel shall be your name." So He called his name Israel. Also God said to him: "I *am* God Almighty. Be fruitful and multiply; a nation and a company of nations shall proceed from you, and kings shall come from your body. The land which I gave Abraham [in Genesis 15:18] and Isaac I give to you; and to your descendants after you I give this land." (Genesis 35:10-12).

Psalm 83 describes a blatant Arab attempt to confiscate this Promised Land. In various places this book provides Scriptural support attesting to the fact that the final Arab-Israeli war will be won by the Jews. The guiding principle to this understanding is found in Jeremiah 31.

> "Thus says the LORD, Who gives the sun for a light by day, The ordinances of the moon and the stars for a light by night, Who disturbs the sea, And its waves roar (The LORD of hosts is His name): "If those ordinances depart From before Me," says the LORD, "Then the seed of Israel shall also cease From being a nation before Me forever." Thus says the LORD: "If heaven above can be measured, And the foundations of the earth searched out beneath, I will also cast off all the seed of Israel For all that they have done," says the LORD." (Jeremiah 31:35-37)

Psalm 83:3-5, 12 informs that the Arabs will confederate for the explicit purposes of destroying Israel and capturing their Promised Land once and for all, something Jeremiah 31:35-37 says is utterly impossible. Unless the Arabs can alter the ordinances governing the universe, they will not succeed.

Currently, the Jewish people are repopulating this land in fulfillment of several Bible prophecies. The Jews are returning into the land after centuries of dispersion into the Gentile nations of the world. According to these prophecies this process appears to be irreversible. This appears to be the reason that the Jewish state is expanding, rather than contracting. This reality is attested to by the fact that the Arab-Israeli wars of 1948, 1967, and 1973 strengthened, rather than weakened the resolve of the Israelis. The Jews continue to make aliyah to Israel and nothing the Arabs have done to date has been able to prevent their return.

Thus, in a nutshell, Psalm 83 predicts that Israel's ancient Arab enemies, which happen to be Israel's most observable Arab foes today, will at some point in the future, confederate, form a war strategy to destroy the Jews and their state, eradicate the name of Israel forever, and confiscate the Promised Land.

According to connecting prophecies in Obadiah v. 18, Ezekiel 25:14, 37:10, Jeremiah 49:1-6, and elsewhere, the Israel Defense Forces (IDF) prevail in the Psalm 83 war. The war, its conclusion, and imposing aftermath affects are discussed throughout various portions of this book. As you read, understand, and apply these prophetic passages to Psalm 83, it is important to recognize that the Arabs are attempting to curse the Jews. As such, they must be cursed according to the divine foreign policy issued in Genesis 12:2-3.

> "I will make you (Abraham) a great nation; I will bless you And make your name great; And you shall be a blessing. I will bless those who bless you, And I will curse him who curses you; And in you all the families of the earth shall be blessed." (Genesis 12:2-3, NKJV; emphasis added).

Herein lies all Gentile foreign policy: those who bless Abraham will likewise be blessed, but those cursing him, will be cursed! It is commonly understood contextually, that these verses extrapolate from Abraham to his Hebrew descendants through the genealogies of Isaac, Jacob, and Jacob's twelve sons, who formed the twelve tribes of Israel. Hence, the Genesis 12:3 principle applies to the Jewish descendants of these twelve tribes today. Moreover, there is no valid reason to conclude that this Gentile foreign policy isn't still applicable.

At the time the Genesis 12:3 foreign policy was issued, the world was populated with people. Out from the masses, one was divinely called, and that was Abraham. In essence he became the first Hebrew, and many translate the word Hebrew to mean to pass over.[9] Hence, they regard it to mean the man who passed over. Abraham, which in the Hebrew language means, "father of multitudes," passed over from ungodly men, to become a man of God. The common understanding from that point forward was that humanity was comprised of Abraham and his Hebrew descendants, and everybody else called Gentiles.

The reason this is important to note is to confirm that the God of the Bible is a just God, with age-old Gentile foreign policy in place. He is not a God that renders divine judgment upon the undeserved. The Psalm 83 Arabs, by their own choice, ignore the foundational understandings contained in Jeremiah 31:35-37, and fundamental precepts in Genesis 12:3. They seek to destroy the Jews, which means they will extract lethal judgment upon themselves. Rather than pity their unenviable plight, it is better to warn them beforehand.

There are naysayers who don't believe Psalm 83 is a bona fide Bible prophecy. Some believe it is merely a prayer of lament. Others don't separate it out as a distinct Middle East war, apart from Ezekiel 38 or Armageddon. Many of the objections to my hypothesis that Psalm 83 is a distinct and imminent war have been encountered since the summer 2008 release of *Isralestine*—the initial edition of this book. These issues are addressed inside portions of the commentary and appendices of this book.

If one considers Psalm 83 to be a prayer and not a prophecy, then it is doubtful that they will raise the red flags of warning to the Arabs beforehand. Or, if someone doesn't believe the Psalm war is imminent, they may lack a sense of urgency to inform the Arabs to form an immediate exit strategy into a safe destination. As for me, I intend to send a clear message in this book, that the Arabs need to watch out, because it appears the war of Psalm 83 is about to occur and they are in imminent danger. The existential threat they pose to Israel actually reverses to become an existential threat to many Arabs involved in Psalm 83.

One can't be dogmatic about such matters, especially when there are some eschatologists that argue against Psalm 83 being a prophecy. But, due to the severity of the potential Arab-Israeli war, it is better to err on the side of safety, than to risk taking the chance that many of us are mistaken about the Psalm's prophetic implications. This is because the Psalm 83 war will result in a multitiude of Arab, and possibly Israeli, casualties as pointed out in the chapter called "Psalm 83 and the Prophets." Moreover, Americans need to support Israel's cause during this battle, which is a point that is explained in the chapter called, "America's Role in Psalm 83."

In retrospect the Arab Spring of 2011 appears to have primed the pot for the prophetic fulfillment of Psalm 83. At the time it was occurring many liberal pundits suggested that it was merely a youth bulge responding to the freedoms they were learning about over the Internet social networks like Facebook, YouTube, and Twitter. However, it is important to note a declaration made by Daniel the prophet.

> "Daniel answered and said: "Blessed be the name of God forever and ever, For wisdom and might are His. And *He changes the times and the seasons; He removes kings and raises up kings*; He gives wisdom to the wise And knowledge to those who have understanding." (Daniel 2:20-21; emphasis added).

One thing for certain about the Arab Spring of 2011: the seasons of change appear to have arrived in the Middle East. Moreover, Arab leaders like Zine al-Abedine Ben Ali of Tunisia, Hosni Mubarak of Egypt, Muammar Gaddafi of Libya, and Ali Abdullah Saleh of Yemen have been removed, making way for others to be raised up. Daniel attributes these types of sovereign events to the supernatural doings of the Lord.

Perhaps what is more concerning is not what leaders have been removed, but which ones remain in place at the time of authoring this book. Ayatollah Khameni, president Mahmoud Ahmadinejad of Iran, president Bashar Assad of Syria, Secretary General Hassan Nasrallah of Hezbollah, Hamas leaders Ismail Haniyeh and Khaled Meshaal, and Palestinan Authority president Mahmoud Abbas, just to name the predominant ones.    Additionally, now Egypt is being ruled by a new president, Mohammed Morsi, from the Muslim Brotherhood. It appears that this existing crop of Arab and Persian leaders could be among those that lead their countries and terrorist organizations into war with Israel.

# THREE

# When Diplomacy Ends, War Begins

**"Shadows loom over Middle East peace talks"**

*The National 10/9/09*

**"US: Crisis stage for Mideast peace process"**

*Xinhua News Agency 10/23/12*

**W**hen diplomacy fails war becomes the only remaining option. According to the prophecy of Psalm 83, this appears to be what finally eradicates the age old Arab–Israeli conflict. This climactic war will render all past political efforts to resolve the conflict null and void. It will demonstrate that two–state solutions, roadmap plans, and land for peace deals were unsuccessful because they didn't address the heart of the matter.

In the final analysis it will be blatantly clear that the Arabs didn't want peace with the Jews they wanted peace without the Jews. They didn't want two states with Palestinians and Jews living side by side, they wanted only one more Arab state called Palestine.

Since the time of the Madrid Conference in October, 1991, to the present, a long list of US presidents have pressured Israel to make concessions for peace with the Arabs in general, and Palestinians specifically. In his article called the Betrayal of Israel, end-times expert Dr. David Reagan writes:

"Our nation's betrayal of Israel began in 1990 when the Communist government of Russia decided to open its doors to allow Jews to emigrate to
Israel. . .Israel's Prime Minister, Yitzhak Shamir, applied to the World Bank for
a loan of $10 billion to cope with the needs of the refugees. He was told
that the loan would be granted only if the United States would guarantee
it. When he then turned to the first Bush Administration, he was told that
the guarantee would be supplied only if he agreed to start negotiating with
the Palestinians. This resulted in the Madrid Conference in October of 1991.
In short, we forced Israel to start down the suicidal path of trading land for
peace."[10]

Since George H. W. Bush, each consecutive president has followed in the same
vain footsteps, adding additional pressure along the way.

## October of 1991

US President George H. Bush invited Israel, Syria, Lebanon, Jordan, Egypt, and the
Palestinians to a conference in Madrid, Spain. The goal was to model a broader Arab-
Israeli peace patterned after the Egyptian-Israel treaty made in 1979. However, Prime
Minister Shamir's plans for the $10 billion in US loan guarantees included expanding
Jewish settlements in order to facilitate the influx of Jews flowing into Israel. The
Arabs vehemently opposed Israeli settlement expansion, putting Bush in a precarious
geopolitical tug-of-war.

The Arabs began questioning America's role as Mideast mediator at the time.
This troubled George H. Bush, because he had achieved high political marks for his
handling of Operation Desert Storm against Saddam Hussein, in Iraq earlier that year.
For many, Bush's behavior at the time signaled the pro-Israel Ronald Reagan years had
ended. As the list of failed attempts made by his successor's evidence below, their
suspicions proved correct.

## July of 2000

US President Bill Clinton hosted the Middle East Peace Summit at Camp David.
Unsuccessfully, he attempted to negotiate a final settlement status to end the Pales-
tinian/Israeli conflict with Israeli Prime Minister Ehud Barak, and Palestinian Authority
President Yasser Arafat. PM Barak was willing to concede land for peace. He generously
offered to return about ninety percent of the West Bank to the Palestinians. His offer
was rejected indignantly by Yasser Arafat. It was at that point many Israelis, liberal and
conservative, began to question the true intentions of the Palestinians. It appeared
Arafat wanted all, rather than part, of Israel.

## April of 2003

US President George W. Bush issued his three-phased Performance-Based Road-map Plan to a Permanent 2-State Solution to the Israeli-Palestinian conflict. Bush's plan amounted to another land-for-peace deal, that didn't resolve the Middle East conflict. Phase one, calling for the cessation of Palestinian Terror, never got accomplished. His plan still sits on the shelf collecting dust.

## September of 2010

US President Barack Obama hosted a meeting with Middle East leaders and foreign dignitaries. Former Egyptian President Hosni Mubarak, Jordan's King Abdullah II, Israeli Prime Minister Benjamin Netanyahu, Palestinian Authority President Mahmoud Abbas, and Quartet representatives Toni Blair and Hillary Clinton were all in attendance. Obama hosted this conference in order to jump-start direct peace talks between the Israelis and Palestinians. It didn't work, and by the end of that same year, all hopes for Mideast peace had again collapsed.

## May of 2011

US President Barack Obama called upon Israel to forfeit lands acquired as a result of their victory over Jordan, Egypt, and Syria in the Six-Day war in June of 1967. It was another desperate American attempt to pressure Israel into a land-for-peace deal to resolve the Mideast conflict.

Just days after Obama's preposterous "real estate request," Israeli Prime Minister Benjamin Netanyahu declared before the US Congress, in a historic moment, that Israel would not comply with President Obama's wishes. He said Israel refused to give up the land it acquired in 1967, and furthermore specified the following:

- Jerusalem *will* be the undivided capital of the Jewish State,

- Millions of Palestinian refugees *won't* be returning inside Israel,

- The Palestinians *must* recognize Israel's right to exist as the sovereign Jewish State,

- The Hamas – Fatah unity agreement of 2011 *must* be abolished,

- Palestinian unilateral attempts at statehood through the United Nations *must* cease,

- Israel maintains the *right* to defensible borders,

- The Israeli demographic population changes since 1967 *must* be accepted, and

- Israel *will* monitor Palestinian organizations and operations for national security purposes.[11]

Simply stated, the summation of Netanyahu's declarations suggests that land-for-peace deals are over. They have run their two-decade course, to no avail. They have proven to be "fruitless" efforts, and Israel no longer possesses the luxury of pursuing the land-for-peace path further. This is because during the four presidential periods identified above, Israel's enemies have become armed and dangerous. They now possess the weapons and manpower to accomplish the mandate of Psalm 83:4, which is to destroy the Jewish state so that the name of Israel will be remembered no more.

By now it should become obvious to the spectator that diplomacy in the Mideast has failed and in the process America, apart from Israel's Arab enemies, has done more to pressure Israel to divide the Promised Land than any other country, since Israel became a nation on May 14, 1948. The futile efforts of these US Administrations have potentially put Americans in harm's way, according to prophecies like these below.

> "I will also gather all nations, And bring them down to the Valley of Jehoshaphat; And I will enter into judgment with them there On account of My people, My heritage Israel, Whom they have scattered among the nations; They have also divided up My land." (Joel 3:2).

> "And it shall happen in that day that I will make Jerusalem a very heavy stone for all peoples; all who would heave it away [divide the land] will surely be cut in pieces, though all nations of the earth are gathered against it." (Zechariah 12:3).

Although these prophecies are specifically addressing judgments that occur within the trib-period during the Armageddon Campaign, they should be a warning to Americans today. Suffice it to say, the Lord does not take kindly to those nations seeking to divide the Promised Land, or tear Jerusalem away from Jewish sovereignty. The overriding, divine rule-of-thumb is determined by Genesis 12:3, for America and all countries. This passage promises blessings to the nations that support Israel and curses those whose actions adversely affect the Jewish state.

Americans should recognize that the sun now sets on the British Empire. There was a time when it couldn't because British sovereignty extended into Australia, Asia,

Africa, India, South America, and North America. However, when the British failed to implement Lord Balfour's declaration of 1917, which called for the restoration of the Jewish state, the sun began setting on one country after another as the empire collapsed. The US presidential time line of meddling in Mideast matters above, explains why Americans over the past two decades have witnessed the sun begin to set on its superpower status. (The statements in this paragraph are explored in detail in the chapter called, "America's Role in Psalm 83").

# FOUR

# The Mideast Stage is Set for the Apocalyptic Wars

**"If NATO Attacks, Syria Will Fire Missiles Into Tel Aviv"**

*Jerusalem Post – 10/4/11*

**"Nasrallah warns of regional war if Iran, Syria attacked"**

*YNET News 11/11/11*

A t the time of writing this chapter an estimated 45,000 or more Syrians have been killed as result of the ongoing Syrian revolution. This death toll surpasses the massacres of Hama in 1982 when a young sixteen year old Bashar al-Assad witnessed his father, Hafez al-Assad kill approximately10,000 to 20,000 of his Syrian countrymen. But, that was then and this is now, and the stakes to the detriment of the entire region are much higher. The Mideast has never been more volatile and an epic war could commence at any time.

In October of 2011, Syrian President Bashar al-Assad threatened to attack Tel Aviv with missiles if the NATO alliance intervened on behalf of the Syrian protesters.[12] At the time his comments were made, only an estimated 3,000 Syrian protesters had been killed by his Alawite regime. NATO intervention in Libya a few months prior to Assad's statement had led to the toppling of Libyan President Muammar Gaddafi, causing Assad grave concern that he could be ousted similarly. Graphic images of Gaddafi with a bullet hole in his head undoubtedly prompted Assad's continued warnings to NATO and threats against Israel.

Included inside his initial threat, the Syrian president stated that he would call on Hezbollah to launch a simultaneous missile attack into Tel Aviv, and for Iran to prevent US and European warships from entering into the Persian Gulf. Israel's response to Assad's threats was to retaliate against the Syrian capital of Damascus.

Presently, Israel is concerned about such a multi-front offensive, and regularly conducts civilian defense drills called "Turning Point," as a preparatory measure. Many Israelis possess personal gas masks, and know the location of nearby bomb shelters in case such an attack occurs.

Syrian Scud D missiles are a grave concern of Israel's. White House correspondent Bill Koenig, of www.watch.org, informed me at the end of 2009 that Syria was reported to have the most advanced Scud missiles in the world, including Scud B,C and D missiles. Many US lawmakers believe Scuds were transferred to Hezbollah from Syria in early 2010. The Washington Times reported on 4/22/2010 that the Senate Select Committee on Intelligence Chairman Dianne Feinstein, California Democrat, told Agence France-Presse, "I believe there is a likelihood that there are Scuds that Hezbollah has in Lebanon. A high likelihood."[13]

### "Defected Syrian general: Damascus planned to send chemical weapons to Hezbollah"

*Times of Israel 11/4/12*

In addition to Scuds, many analysts believe that chemical weapons exist in Syria's and Hezbollah's arsenals. Syria is believed to have the third largest chemical weapons arsenal in the world.[14] The Kuwaiti newspaper Al-Siyasa revealed this in March of 2009.[15] Moreover, Georges Sada, one of Saddam Hussein's top generals, confirms that, in addition to Syria's own chemical weapons, many of Iraq's weapons of mass destruction were transported into Syria before the Iraqi dictator was toppled.[16]

Although the Bible doesn't specifically predict a chemical weapons attack targeted against Tel Aviv, it does prophesy about several end-time's Israeli war prophecies. Those wars, along with many other Bible prophecies, are the subject of this book and also my *Revelation Road* end-times book series. Because these predicted attacks are coming, and these dangerous weapons already adorn the arsenals of the attackers, it is possible that they will be utilized during the coming conflicts.

These conflicts could be coming soon, in light of increased regional instability brought about by the Arab Spring of 2011. Almost every affected Middle Eastern or North African country is involved in either Psalm 83 or Ezekiel 38. Liberal pundits hope that democracies will spring up across the region as a result of all the Arab unrest, however, apart from Israel, democracies haven't characterized the Middle East. Historically, power shifts in the region have occurred through revolutions, assassinations, rigged elections, or combinations thereof. The fact of the matter is that these are predominately Anti-Semitic Muslim populations that support the Palestinian plight. When it is all said and done, it is likely that these populations will oppose Israel and support the quest for a Palestinian state. If this turns out to be the case, the wars of Psalm 83 and Ezekiel 38 may occur soon, sequentially, and without much delay between.

Ultimately after Psalm 83 and Ezekiel 38, the battle staged in the Armageddon campaign caps off all the Middle East wars predicted to occur upon this present earth. The Armageddon battle is fought between Christ and all the remaining armies of the world, led by the Antichrist. Revelation 19:11-21, in connection with Isaiah 63:1-6, teaches that Christ will prevail over the Antichrist and his armies. 2 Thessalonians says the lawless Antichrist will be no match for the mere brightness of Christ's coming.

> "And then the lawless one will be revealed, whom the Lord will consume with the breath of His mouth and destroy with the brightness of His coming." (2 Thessalonians 2:8).

There are ten members in Psalm 83 and nine different populations in Ezekiel 38. Comparatively, there are about 195 countries in the world at present.[17] If the Psalm 83 and Ezekiel 38 armies are destroyed, that still leaves about 176 countries left in the aftermath to align with the Antichrist against Israel, in Armageddon.

Psalm 83, the final Arab-Israeli war, and Isaiah 17, the destruction of Damascus, Syria are thoroughly discussed in this book. The Ezekiel 38-39 Russian-Iranian led invasion of Israel and the campaign of Armageddon are given a modicum of coverage in this book, but are both going to be addressed more exhaustively in The *Revelation Road* novel / commentary book series.

However, Isaiah 17, Psalm 83, Ezekiel 38-39, and the Armageddon battle, may not be the only major Middle East showdowns yet to come. Other apocalyptic episodes, like a preliminary confrontation between Israel and Iran, seem to occur in the Fertile Crescent, as well. Jeremiah 49:34-39 suggests that Iran, as Elam, appears in another end time Middle East military confrontation. More information about Jeremiah's Elamite prophecies are explored in this book in the chapter called, "Iran's Double Jeopardy in the End Times."

# Psalm 83 or Ezekiel 38 What's the Next Middle East News Headline?

**"Israel Building Fence Along West Bank"**

*CNN 6/18/02*

**"Israel Builds Security Wall Along Lebanese Border"**

*Israel National News 4/30/12*

**"Israel to build security barrier on border with Egypt"**

*Telegraph 1/11/10*

Current Middle East events seem to be setting the stage for the final fulfillment of the Israeli War prophecies of Psalm 83 and Ezekiel 38-39. Throughout much of 2010, Turkey distanced itself from Israel. This moved many to the edge of their seats, thinking that Ezekiel 38 was an imminent event, because it meant that Turkey and Iran, both members of the Ezekiel 38 coalition, shared a common enmity toward Israel.

Certainly, there is just cause to consider the Ezekiel 38-39 prophecy in light of Turkish and Iranian anti-Israel sentiment; but, what about Egyptians, the Muslim Brotherhood, Lebanese, Hezbollah, Syrians, Hamas, Saudis,

Jordanians, Iraqis, and the Palestinian refugees? They are also at odds with Israel to one degree or another. Curiously, Ezekiel 38 describes nine distinct populations by their ancient names, including Russia, Iran, Turkey, Libya, and several others, but omits these Arab countries and terrorist organizations.

In light of the fact that these omitted populations are presently among Israel's most observable enemies, some of those teaching that Ezekiel 38 is impending have attempted to identify them in Ezekiel 38:6 among the many peoples with thee of the Ezekiel 38 Magog confederacy. However, there are three potential problems with this line of teaching.

1. Hezbollah, Syria, Hamas and the Palestinians along with the Egyptians, Saudis, and Jordanians are identified in a distinctly different Israeli War prophecy described in Psalm 83. The Psalm lists ten entirely separate members not included among the Ezekiel 38:1-6 invaders. Thus, it is probable they are not the "many peoples with thee" in Ezekiel 38:6, but are "many peoples *distinct from thee*" not listed in Ezekiel 38 among the invaders.

2. The hordes of Ezekiel 38 invaders must cross over much of the land possessed by these Psalm 83 nations and territories inhabited by the terrorist populations in order to invade the nation of Israel. This beckons the question: why aren't these nations, terrorists, or refugees specifically listed among the Ezekiel 38 invaders?

3. Most importantly, Ezekiel 38 identifies nine specific invading populations, but oddly doesn't mention any of the Psalm 83 Arab confederates among them. This conspicuous omission makes no sense when you consider that Ezekiel references all of the Psalm 83 members numerous times elsewhere throughout his prophetic book.

Case in point: Ezekiel lists Tyre twelve times. Tyre is a member of Psalm 83, and likely represents the Hezbollah today. He alludes to Philistia or Philistines four times. They are probably the Hamas. Edom or the Edomites are referenced seven times. Asaph, the author of Psalm 83, calls them the tents of Edom and I interpret that as today's Palestinian refugees. The other Psalm 83 members like, Moab or Moabites, Ammon or Ammonites, Amalakites, Egyptians, Assyrians, Gebal (Lebanon), and the Saudis under the ancient banners of Dedan or the Ishmaelites, are also referenced elsewhere in the book of Ezekiel. In fact, all together the above Psalm 83 confederates are mentioned eighty-nine times by Ezekiel within his forty-eight chapters.

Not one of those eighty-nine "enlisted" references shows up in Ezekiel 38-39, with the exception of a potential Saudi contingent represented by Dedan, in Ezekiel 38:13. But in this instance, Dedan appears to abstain from enlisting with the Ezekiel invaders.

This suggests they want no further part in an invasion of Israel. Ezekiel 25:13 declares many in Dedan will be killed in a war, which appears to be the result of the Psalm 83 war. If so, this could be the reason they apparently opt-out of the Ezekiel invasion.

I believe the glaring omission of the Psalm 83 Arab confederates from the Ezekiel 38 list of invaders suggests they are not part of the Ezekiel 38-39 invasion. It is highly possible that they are defeated prior to the Ezekiel 38-39 Israeli War prophecy. Listed below are a few of the reasons I believe Psalm 83 precedes Ezekiel 38.

Ezekiel 38:8-13 mandates that Israel must be dwelling securely, without walls, bars, or gates, and in the center of the land, probably alluding to the Genesis 15:18 landmass. This point about Israel dwelling securely is so important that much of the latter part of this chapter is devoted to this topic. Additionally, the Jewish state must be in receipt of great spoil. In my estimation, Israel today is not fulfilling these prerequisite conditions.

Israel is unable to dwell securely as a result of their surrounding Psalm 83 hostile Arab neighbors. Walls, bars, and gates exist in Israel today in order to protect them from being terrorized by certain members of the Psalm 83 confederates, such as Hamas, Hezbollah, and the Palestinians in general. Additionally, the goal of the Ezekiel 38 invaders is to destroy Israel and take their plunder and great spoils. Israel doesn't presently appear to possess all of the great spoil that Russia and their coalition will someday covet.

However, in the aftermath of an Israeli conquest over the Psalm 83 confederates all of the above requirements could easily be met. A safe-dwelling Israel could temporarily emerge. Arab spoils of war could be had, additional territory annexed, and walls, bars, and gates could be swiftly taken down.

Another important distinction between the prophecies of Ezekiel 38 and Psalm 83 is found in their differing motives. Psalm 83:12 declares that the Arab confederates want to destroy Israel in order to take over the Promised Land. Ezekiel 38:12-13 states the Ezekiel invaders will seek to destroy the Jewish state and confiscate plunder and great spoil.

Also an important difference between Psalm 83 and Ezekiel 38 may be understood by identifying the purpose of the exceedingly great army of Ezekiel 37:10. The Ezekiel invaders are destroyed divinely, but the Psalm 83 Arab confederates appear to be defeated by the Israel Defense Forces according, to Ezekiel 25:14, Obadiah v. 18, and elsewhere.

Interestingly, an exceedingly great army of Israel is mentioned in Ezekiel 37:10. This reference seemingly segues into the Ezekiel 38-39 prophecy. Logically, a reader might assume this army plays an instrumental role in the war of Ezekiel 38 because it's identified in the chapter that precedes it. However, Ezekiel 38:18-39:6 teaches that this army plays little to no part in Ezekiel's invasion. These verses specify that the Lord divinely defeats the Ezekiel invaders. There is no mention of an Israeli army, apart from perhaps playing a role in the burying of the dead soldiers for seven months, and the burning of the enemies weapons for seven years. (Ezekiel 39:9-16).

The Ezekiel 37:10 army is the subject of the chapter in this book called "Israel's Exceedingly Great Army." This amazing army appears to be the tool empowered by God to defeat the Psalm 83 Arab confederacy. If so, the fact that the army of Ezekiel 37:10 is referenced prior to the Ezekiel 38-39 war passages infers that chronologically Psalm 83 precedes Ezekiel 38. In the chapter called "The Ezekiel 35 – Psalm 83 Connection," I point out that the wars of Ezekiel 35 and Psalm 83 appear to be one and the same. For more information about the exceedingly great army of Ezekiel 37:10, you can also refer to the appendix called, "Is Ezekiel's Army About to Face Off with the Arabs?"

## Ezekiel 38 Has Preconditions Still Outstanding

The fact that Israel today does not meet all of the requirements identified in Ezekiel 38:8-13 means that Ezekiel 38 still has preconditions. A Bible prophecy cannot be considered imminent until all the prophetic prerequisites are met.

> ""After many days you will be visited. In the *latter years* you will come into the land of those brought back from the sword and gathered from many people *on the mountains of Israel*, which had long been desolate; they were brought out of the nations, and now all of them *dwell safely*. You will ascend, coming like a storm, covering the land like a cloud, you and all your troops and many peoples with you." Thus says the Lord GOD: "On that day it shall come to pass that thoughts will arise in your mind, and you will make an evil plan: You will say, 'I will go up against a land of *unwalled villages*; I will go to a *peaceful people*, who *dwell safely*, all of them dwelling *without walls, and having neither bars nor gates*'—to take plunder and to take booty, to stretch out your hand against the waste places that are again inhabited, and against a people gathered from the nations, who have acquired livestock and goods, who *dwell in the midst of the land*. Sheba, Dedan, the merchants of Tarshish, and all their young lions will say to you, 'Have you come *to take plunder*? Have you gathered your army to take booty, to carry away silver and gold, to take away livestock and goods, *to take great plunder*?" (Ezekiel 38:8-13, NKJV; emphasis added).

These Ezekiel passages specify the following:

1.  Israelis must be regathered from the nations in the latter years into a re-established sovereign Jewish state.

2.  Jews will be brought back from the sword, to dwell in the midst (center) of the land, which had long been desolate.

3.  Israelis must be a peaceful people dwelling securely at the time.

4.  Israel's security is characterized by the absence of walls, bars and gates.

5.  The nation possesses an abundance of gold and silver, and has acquired livestock (agricultural) and (commercial) goods.

6.  The Jewish state is in possession of great plunder and booty.

These Ezekiel passages begin by stating that the Jews will be regathered from the nations of the world to the "mountains of Israel." This does not imply that all Jews will migrate into the mountainous areas of Israel; rather, it alludes to the Jewish people forming a sovereign state. Although the Bible often refers to mountains in a literal, geographical sense, it may also allude to the leadership or government of a nation in the typological sense. In this instance, the inference is an independent Jewish entity over which a sovereign government presides.[18] Since this government is associated with "the mountains of Israel," we can safely surmise that the location of this restored sovereign Jewish state is Israel.

Moreover, the Jews are coming out from persecution into a desolate land. This was the case after the persecution of the holocaust. The Jews returned after experiencing a genocidal attempt by the Nazis into a land that had been predominantly desolate for centuries. Mark Twain visited Israel in 1867, and published his impressions in Innocents Abroad. He described a desolate country—devoid of both vegetation and human population:

> "A desolate country whose soil is rich enough, but is given over wholly to weeds… a silent mournful expanse…. a desolation…. we never saw a human being on the whole route…. hardly a tree or shrub anywhere. Even the olive tree and the cactus, those fast friends of a worthless soil, had almost deserted the country."[19]

Furthermore, the prophet depicts the Jewish people as dwelling in a condition of security. Ezekiel declares that the Israelis are "a peaceful people who dwell safely (yashab betach), all of them dwelling without walls."

This means that as a nation they "all" "dwell safely." He uses the Hebrew words Yashab Betach three times in Ezekiel 38:8, 11, and 14 to highlight this point.[20] The Bible uses these Hebrew words in tandem elsewhere in the Old Testament, to identify the sovereign State of Israel dwelling in a condition of military security.[21] Ezekiel's description of a nation dwelling without walls, bars, nor gates, also emphasizes a genuine condition of national security.

Throughout time, humans constructed fortified walls to prevent enemy intrusions and to enforce separation between two diverse population groups. The Chinese built the Great Wall around 200 BC to protect China's northern borders from intruders. The Germans erected the Berlin wall in 1961 in order to separate the Communistic political system of the East from the capitalism spreading in the West.

Likewise, Israel has today constructed its own fortified wall intended to prevent the terrorist element of the Palestinian population from intruding into Israel proper. This wall reaches up to twenty-five feet and is projected to span at least 403 miles upon completion. As such, Israel today is not "a nation dwelling without walls" as described in Ezekiel 38:11.

Note that Ezekiel references "a people gathered from the nations, who have acquired livestock and goods." Israel acquires livestock, representing agricultural wealth, and goods, representing commercial wealth. This condition of restored fortune will resemble the period of Israel's history around 1000 BC, when King Solomon reigned over the nation.[22] As was the case then, Israel will become one of the wealthiest—if not the wealthiest—of the world's nations. In his next verse, Ezekiel informs us that Israel's restored fortune is what the Russian-Iranian-led coalition aspires to attain. Sheba and Dedan, which likely represent the modern nations of Yemen and Saudi Arabia, along with other merchant and military populations, question the coalitions motivation and in so doing enlighten us as to its true intention.

> Sheba, Dedan, the merchants of Tarshish, and all their young lions will say to you, "Have you come to take plunder? Have you gathered your army to take booty, to carry away silver and gold, to take away livestock and goods, to take great plunder?" (Ezek. 38:13, NKJV).

The Russian-Iranian coalition targets the livestock, goods, and other "great plunder" acquired by Israel. That Israel possesses great plunder further emphasizes the idea of a wealthy nation. The present international political prescription for Israel to accomplish the conditions listed above, is to make sweeping political and real estate concessions with the Palestinians and their Arab cohorts. In return, Israel expects international security assistance and acceptance by more members of the Arab League for the right to exist as a sovereign Jewish State. However, this international solution is not biblically supported.

The Bible appears to suggest that the nation of Israel accomplishes these "prerequisite" conditions via a military solution. The Israeli Defense Forces will become engaged in a serious regional conflict. In victory, they will become primed for the future events of the Russian-Iranian coalition destined to form against them. Turning back a few pages from the Ezekiel passages quoted above to Ezekiel Chapter 28, we discover that God will come to the defense of Israel. These passages inform us when Israel will dwell securely.

> "And there shall no longer be a pricking brier or a painful thorn for the house of Israel from *among all who are around them, who despise them*. Then they shall know that I *am* the LORD GOD. Thus says the LORD GOD: "When I have gathered the house of Israel from the peoples among whom they are scattered, and am hallowed in them in the sight of the Gentiles, then they will dwell in their own land which I gave to My servant Jacob. And they will dwell safely there, build houses, and plant vineyards; yes, they will dwell securely, when I execute judgments on all those around them who despise them. Then they shall know that I *am* the LORD their God." (Ezek. 28:24–26, NKJV; emphasis added)

Simply paraphrased: "Yes, they will dwell securely (yashab betach), when I (God) execute judgments on all those (Arab nations) around them who despise them." Ezekiel reminds us that the national security Israel so desperately seeks today occurs via the judgments executed "on all those around them who despise them."

Surprisingly, "all those (Arab nations) around them who despise" the emerging Jewish State of Israel, are conspicuously absent from the Gog of Magog coalition. Unlike the Psalm 83 Arab states, not one of the Ezekiel invaders shares common borders with Israel. Why not? This particular question has longed baffled many prophecy buffs, because the Arab nations surrounding the Jewish state are Israel's most observable enemies, and they clearly represent "all those around them who despise them."

The adversaries of Israel, identified in Psalm 83, will seek to cut the Jews off from being a nation by forming their own coalition. Unfortunately for them, their fate is described in Ezekiel 28:24–26 as "all those around them who despise them." They are those upon whom God will execute devastating judgments prior to the formation of the Russian-Iranian coalition. But how will these judgments be executed? The answer to this question is one of the central themes of this book. The IDF will become an "exceedingly great army," and defeat the surrounding enemies of Israel that despise the Jewish state!

We can safely presume that the execution of the judgments upon the surrounding Psalm 83 nations, those countries that despise Israel, will occur before the Gog of Magog coalition forms. We deduce this by recollecting that the Russian-Iranian led coalition will attempt to invade a militarily secure Israel. This condition of security becomes a reality only subsequent to the judgments executed upon the surrounding Psalm 83 nations.

Some people believe the secure Israel that the Ezekiel invaders attack results when the Antichrist confirms the seven-year peace treaty with Israel in Daniel 9:26-27. Although Israel will temporarily become secure at that time, this is probably a subsequent period of national security for the Jewish state. This is because the seven-year treaty begins the seven years of tribulation, i.e Daniel's Seventieth Week," and the Gog of Magog invasion seemingly precedes this period. I qualify this statement in the chapter called "Psalm 83 and the Prophets," by explaining the timing of Ezekiel 38.

Additionally, the Israel that becomes a peaceful people dwelling securely in Ezekiel 38:8, 11, 14, seems to obtain this peace and safety in the strict interpretation of the Hebrew words "yashab betach." Tandem biblical uses of these words found in Ezekiel 28:26, and Deuteronomy 12:10, describe a condition of national security that is obtained militarily, rather than politically.

Because of the judgments executed upon the Arabs who despise Israel, the Jewish state will attain the autonomy required to set the stage for the Ezekiel 38 invasion. The world will be forced to internationally esteem Israel as the sovereign Jewish State, and the Arab-Israeli conflict we witness today, will finally be resolved. As such, Israel will be a nation of peace achieved via their military might. It is the "exceedingly great army" of Israel foretold in Ezekiel 37:10 that is the instrumental tool utilized in the execution of the judgments against the surrounding Arab nations. In the aftermath of their IDF victory, the Jewish State will probably seize some conquered Arab territory, and exploit vast amounts of the Arab spoils of war. Israel will then resemble the Israel described in Ezekiel 38:8-13.

Before further developing the theme of the Israeli conquest "on those around them who despise them," let us first appreciate the reason for the restoration of the nation Israel as the Jewish state, which occurred May 14, 1948. Many people, including numerous Christians that subscribe to "Replacement Theology, believe the existence of Israel is the result of a UN moral obligation to the Jews after the horrendous holocaust event. However, Israel's existence is a miraculous fulfillment of several Bible prophecies. One of the evidences of this is the Ezekiel 38 prophecy. The Lord intends to use this most massive Mideast invasion of all time, to uphold His holy name through Israel and the Israelis, so that mankind will recognize that He is the Holy One in Israel. We are told this in the verses below.

> "So I [God] will make *My holy name* known in the midst of My people Israel, and I will not *let them* profane My holy name anymore. Then the nations shall know that I am the LORD, the Holy One in Israel. Surely it is coming, and it shall be done," says the LORD GOD. "This *is* the day of which I have spoken." (Ezek. 39:7–8, NKJV; emphasis added)

With the exclusive divine help of their God Jehovah, the Jews defeat the Gog of Magog coalition during the events described in Ezekiel 38:18-39:6. Then in Ezekiel

39:7 we see that through these events, God makes His "holy name" known to all the rest of the world nations. Similarly, in Ezekiel 36:22–24 we learn that the Restoration of the Nation Israel as the Jewish State serves the same greater purpose.

> "Therefore say to the house of Israel, "Thus says the LORD GOD: 'I do not do *this* for your sake, O house of Israel, but for *My holy name's* sake, which you have profaned among the nations wherever you went. And I will sanctify *My great name*, which has been profaned among the nations, which you have profaned in their midst; and *the nations shall know* that *I am the LORD*,' says the LORD GOD, '*when I am hallowed in you* before their eyes. For I will take you from among the nations, gather you out of all countries, and bring you into your own land.'" (Ezek. 36:22–24, NKJV; emphasis added)

Furthermore, it is noteworthy that God intends to be "hallowed" by the Jewish people in the sight of the international community. The Hebrew word for "hallowed" is qadash, and it is the same word utilized in Ezekiel 36:23 and Ezekiel 28:25, concerning Israel's enemies that despise them. In both instances, it emphatically highlights the restoration of the sovereign Jewish state of Israel as an epic and holy event.

Miraculously, in modern history the call of Zionism has tugged adamantly upon the hearts of the Jewish people, who for centuries lived dispersed throughout the nations of the world. Israel became a nation in 1948, and the Jewish people have responded to the Zionistic inclination implanted within them, both individually and corporately. Many of them have answered the sacred call, and have migrated back into the land that 1,878 years prior had bid them a hostile farewell.

Yes, the Jews have returned and "all those (predominantly Arabs) around them who despise them" have attempted to prevent the prescribed process. Therefore, I invite you to reread Ezekiel 28:24–26 with this hallowed understanding.

What we can glean from all of this is that God is presently preparing to make His Holy Name known throughout the nations of the world. He is gathering the Jewish people and forming them into an exceedingly great army. The execution of judgments on many Arabs will be a humbling and hallowing event in the world's future history. Gentiles will consider the Jews, the Jewish sovereign state, and most importantly, the holy name of their God Jehovah.

The Ezekiel invasion required the existence of the "Chosen People", and their possession of the "Promised Land." These are both critical components of the unconditional Abrahamic Covenant. When the Lord divinely defeats the Gog of Magog invasion, He can whole-heartedly declare that He is the covenant-making, promise-keeping LORD; the Holy One in Israel!

What the world is currently witnessing in the theater of the Middle East is the stage being set for the marquee event, whereby the holy name of God features prominently before the international audience. The Arab-Israeli conflict, the Arab

Spring, the rise of the Muslim Brotherhood in Egypt, the Iranian nuclear concerns, Turkey's newfound disdain toward Israel, and many other events are but opening acts in God's grand show.

Due to the strengthening relationship between Russia and Iran, prophetic scholars are rightfully discerning the world's nearness to the fulfillment of the events described in Ezekiel 38 and 39. They will indeed occur soon, however, not necessarily next. Prior to this, the nation of Israel must display sovereignty, peace, security, and fortune. "All those around them who despise them" presently oppose these four conditions.

The LORD will soon execute judgments upon these enemies! These judgments will be fashioned in the manner prescribed by God, who is presently poised to sanctify His Holy Name. Approximately four-thousand years ago, God spelled out His international foreign policy through Abraham, as contained in Genesis 12:3 He promises blessings to those who bless the Jewish descendants of Abraham, and curses those who curse them.

The same recipe for Jewish disaster that the surrounding Arab nations concoct will be redirected against them in like fashion. This punishment will highlight the curse-for-curse-in-kind component of the Abrahamic Covenant.[23] The Arab Kingdom will come against the Jewish Kingdom in an apparent fulfillment of the prophecy of Jesus Christ.

> "For nation will rise against nation, and [Arab] *kingdom against* [Jewish] *kingdom*. And there will be famines, pestilences, and Earthquakes in various places. All these *are* the beginning of sorrows." (Matthew 24:7–8, NKJV; emphasis added)

In World War I and World War II, nation rose against nation. This set the stage for the restoration of the nation Israel and the reestablishment of the Jewish Kingdom. The Arab nations bordering Israel have proven their dissatisfaction with the re-emergence of the Jewish Kingdom in their area of the world. They will ultimately confederate in the fulfillment of Psalm 83, and, in that unified condition will represent the sentiment of the broader Arab Kingdom. They [the Arab Kingdom] have said, "Come, and let us cut them off from being a nation, That the name of Israel [the Jewish Kingdom] may be remembered no more." (Psa. 83:4, NKJV)

When the Jewish Kingdom prevails militarily over the Arab Kingdom, the fulfillment of Ezekiel 28:24–26 will occur, as God executes the "judgments on all those around them who despise them." The deliverance of these devastating judgments via the mighty means of the Jewish Kingdom will display that the divine foreign policy contained in the ancient decree of the Abrahamic Covenant is still effectually intact. The Abrahamic Covenant will, at that time, nullify all incompatible international foreign policy relating to the Arab- Israeli conflict.

After digesting this information, the reader might consider that there is indeed a God, and that His name is holy. Enormous events on a David-and-Goliath scale continue to unfold in the Middle East and directly affect our daily lives. Terrorism, primarily born from Middle East mayhem, has extended its ugly embrace around our lives. Try carrying a tube of toothpaste onto an airplane. It has become a major ordeal as tight airport security has become unavoidable. Who among us would have foreseen that a basic element of personal hygiene would become an advanced tactical weapon in the arsenal of terrorism?

Now is the perfect time to consider the significance of the reestablishment of Israel, Jesus Christ (the Jew who claimed to be the Messiah and the Son of God), and the holy name of God, our Heavenly Father. Let us continue to delve into the Bible to discover more about the days in which we live. Let us be active participants in keeping His book in its rightful position at the top of the best-seller list.

In conclusion, the fulfillment of a Bible prophecy mandates that the episode meets the prophetic description of the event entirely and exactly. There can be no overlooking even the slightest detail given. The growing tendency among eschatologists to recognize that current Mideast events are stage setting for the coming Psalm 83 and Ezekiel 38 wars is to be commended. However, newspaper exegesis can often cause us to overlook significant prophetic details, and should be avoided.

Perhaps Ezekiel 38 will come soon and precede Psalm 83, but it is doubtful. There are ten members listed in Psalm 83 that are not listed in Ezekiel 38. These ten represent Israel's most observable modern-day enemies, since becoming a nation in 1948. For the plethora of reasons explained in this chapter, I don't believe Ezekiel 38 is an imminent event. However, I do believe Psalm 83 could be the next prophetic Mideast news headline.

# SIX

# Israel's Exceedingly Great Army

So I prophesied as He commanded me, and breath came into them, and they lived, and stood upon their feet, an exceedingly great army. – Ezek.37:10,nkjv

## "IDF Preparing for War on Several Fronts"

*Israel National News 7/11/12*

## "Only 'the nuclear option' can work against Iran, former IDF chief says"

*The Times of Israel 11/11/12*

Ezekiel 37:10 informs us that Israel, rising from a seemingly helpless fate, will establish for itself an "exceedingly great army." The Jews will change from victims to victors, from destroyed to destroyers, and from hunted to hunters. Today we witness the doors to the Holy Land, which approximately 2000 years ago bid them a hostile farewell, re-opening. One by one, they come home to Israel. With the Holocaust behind them and their ancient enemies before them, they arrive with one eye on the farm and the other on the fight.

The Jewish army rises to power to fulfill a specific purpose found within the prophetic plan of God. The outline below chronicles the events scheduled to occur as foretold by the prophets:

1. God gathers the Jews into the land of Israel from the four corners of the Earth.

2. Jews rebuild ruins and inhabit formerly abandoned cities.

3. They meet with Arab resistance.

4. Israel establishes an army in self-defense.

5. Surrounding Arab nations form a confederacy.

6. The confederacy plots to destroy Israel.

7. War starts between the confederacy and Israel.

8. Israel regains the title "My people Israel."

9. Israel decisively defeats the confederacy.

10. Israel takes prisoners of war.

11. The region is reshaped.

12. Israel expands its borders, and becomes a "Greater Israel."

13. Israel dwells securely in the land.

14. Israel has become an "exceedingly great army."

15. This segment of the plan of God is fulfilled!

A primary purpose of this prophetic period is casting judgment upon the animosity established in ancient times toward the promises God made to Abraham. Long ago, Hagar, Ishmael, Esau, Moab, and Ammon formed adversarial attitudes toward God and His covenantal promises. Throughout the years that followed, their descendants perpetuated this hatred and propelled this disposition across the region. Other historical enemies of Israel found it favorable to embrace this attitude. In time, this "ancient hatred" became cleverly enveloped into a religion, known as Islam. This ancient Arab hatred is discussed in detail in the chapter called, "The Ancient Arab Hatred of the Jews."

## 1. God gathers the Jews into the land of Israel

This gathering is foretold in numerous scriptures, just a few of which I will list. This present Aliyah process, whereby the world is witnessing the immigration of world Jewry back into the land of Israel, is the fulfillment of this gathering.[24]

> For I will take you from among the nations, gather you out of all countries, and bring you into your own land. (Ezek. 36:24, NKJV)

> Therefore prophesy and say to them, "Thus says the LORD GOD: 'Behold, O My people, I will open your graves and cause you to come up from your graves, and bring you into the land of Israel.'" (Ezek. 37:12, NKJV)

These passages from the prophet Ezekiel describe in detail the return of the Jews to the Holy Land. He declares that the Jewish people will come out from "among the nations," alluding to the fact that the Jewish people were dispersed worldwide. Secondly, God is rescuing these returning Jews from a horrifically grave Holocaust-type condition.

> "It shall come to pass in that day *That* the LORD shall set His hand again *the second time* To recover the remnant of His people who are left, From Assyria and Egypt, From Pathros and Cush, From Elam and Shinar, From Hamath and the islands of the sea. He will set up a banner for the nations, And will assemble the outcasts of Israel, And gather together the dispersed of Judah *From the four corners of the Earth.*" (Isa. 11:11–12, NKJV; emphasis added)

Isaiah informs us the LORD will set His hand a second time to recover the remnant of His people from "the four corners of the Earth." To set "His hand" refers to an event that occurs because of divine orchestration. In this instance, God takes the responsibility to ensure the survival and return of a remnant of Jewish people. Isaiah declares that it is "a second time;" there is no third, fourth, or fifth occurrence referenced in scripture, making the second time both significant and final. There are theories as to what constitutes the first and the second times, and they are further discussed in my book called *Isralestine, The Ancient Blueprints of the Future Middle East* inside the chapter called "The Second Time: A Jewish Sequel." Isaiah's use of the four corners idea signifies that the extent of the gathering is worldwide..

> "That the LORD your God will bring you back from captivity, and have compassion on you, and gather you again [a second final time] from all the nations where the LORD your God has scattered you. If *any* of you are driven out to the farthest *parts* under heaven, from there the LORD your God will gather you, and from there He will bring you. Then the LORD your God will

bring you to the land which your fathers possessed, and you shall possess it. *He will prosper you* [Jews] and multiply you more than your fathers." (Deut. 30:3–5, NKJV; emphasis added)

This Deuteronomy passage prescribes not only the worldwide gathering, but also the restoration of Jewish fortunes. This is another purpose for the rise of the exceedingly great army. This army will be instrumental in the recapture of the real estate of the Promised Land, and as such, the inherit resources and wealth therein. This booty seemingly becomes part of the great plunder the Ezekiel 38 invaders covet.

## 2. They rebuild ruins and inhabit formerly abandoned cities

During the dispersion period, the cities of Israel were forsaken and reduced to ruins. Cultural landmarks were laid to waste. Surrounding nations swallowed the country from every side, and in so doing gave themselves the land promised to Abraham and his descendants, the Jewish people. The prophet Ezekiel presaged this scenario over 2,500 years ago.

> "And you, son of man, prophesy to the mountains of Israel, and say, "O mountains of Israel, hear the word of the LORD! Thus says the LORD GOD: 'Because the enemy has said of you, "Aha! The ancient heights have become our possession,"" therefore prophesy, and say, "Thus says the LORD GOD: 'Because *they made you desolate and swallowed you up on every side*, so that you became the possession of the rest of the nations, and you are taken up by the lips of talkers and slandered by the people therefore, O mountains of Israel, hear the word of the LORD GOD!" Thus says the LORD GOD to the mountains, the hills, the rivers, the valleys, the desolate wastes, and the cities that have been forsaken, which became plunder and mockery to the rest of the nations all around therefore thus says the LORD GOD: "Surely I have spoken in My burning jealousy against *the rest of the nations and against all Edom*, who gave *My land* to themselves as a possession, with wholehearted joy and spiteful minds, in order to plunder its open country." (Ezek. 36:1–5, NKJV; emphasis added)

The key phrases in these scriptures are the "rest of the nations all around," "all Edom," "My land," and "they made you desolate and swallowed you up on every side." The surrounding Arab nations, including Edom, took full advantage of the land of Israel while the Jewish people were reduced to absentee owners during their centuries of worldwide dispersion. In essence, they homesteaded the Holy Land. Edom is the subject of the chapter called "Who-domites? Who are the Edomites Today."

At the heart of the conflict in the Middle East today is this Holy Land. The return of the Jew has meant the eviction of Arab trespassers. Many have become homeless refugees, and the surrounding nations from which their ancestors came have not facilitated their return. Israel seeks acceptance among these nations for the mere right to exist as a nation. In order for these nations to concede this right, they must forfeit much of what they consider their real estate holdings in the Holy Land of Israel. "They have not conceded," nor will they, according to the prophecy of Psalm 83, apart from the Israeli conquest over them.

The Arab trespassers expect to extract a heavy price for this real estate, and until they receive this ransom, they systematically terrorize the Holy Land. Ultimately, scripture suggests that whether or not the price is honored, Jews will remain the victims of the ancient hatred infecting the region. [25] Regardless of the formidable opposition awaiting the Jewish people upon their return to the land of Israel, from their trespassing Arab neighbors Ezekiel further prophesies that the cities shall be reclaimed and the ruins rebuilt.

> "But you, O mountains of Israel, you shall shoot forth your branches and yield your fruit to *My people Israel, for they are about to come.* For indeed I am for you, and I will turn to you, and you shall be tilled and sown. I will multiply men upon you, all the house of Israel, all of it; and *the cities shall be inhabited and the ruins rebuilt.*" (Ezek. 36:8–10; NKJV, emphasis added)

## 3. They meet with resistance in the region

Enemies unsuccessfully advanced major assaults against Israel in 1948, 1956, 1967, and 1973. Additional regional conflicts occurred from the north in 1982 and 2006 in Lebanon, and from the southwest in Gaza in 2008-2009. Islamic nations have embraced the unconventional method of terror as an alternative to all of these failed attempts at conventional warfare. Scripture suggested this would be the case.

> "*The terror you* [Edom–Palestinian Refugees] *inspire* and the pride of your heart have deceived you, you who live in the clefts of the rock, who hold the height of the hill. Although you make your nest as high as the eagle's, from there I will bring you down, says the LORD." (Jer. 49:16, NRSV; emphasis added)[26]

> "I have heard the reproach of Moab [Central Jordan], And the insults of the people of Ammon [Northern Jordan], With which *they have reproached My people* [Israel]*, And made arrogant threats against their borders.*" (Zeph. 2:8, NKJV; emphasis added)

> "Thus says the LORD GOD: "Because the enemy has said of you [Israel], 'Aha! The ancient heights have become our possession,'" (Ezek. 36:2, NKJV)

"Thus says the Lord GOD: "Because of what Edom [Southern Jordan] did against the house of Judah, by taking vengeance, and has greatly offended by avenging itself on them." (Ezek. 25:12, NKJV)

*"For violence against your* [Esau] brother Jacob [Israel], Shame shall cover you, And you shall be cut off forever." (Obad. 1:10, NKJV; emphasis added)

"Because you have had an ancient hatred, and have shed the blood of the children of Israel by the power of the sword at the time of their calamity, when *their iniquity came to an end.*" (Ezek. 35:5, NKJV; emphasis added)

As a people, the Jews had been led apostate by their leaders leading up to and during the first advent of Christ. This resulted in the national rejection of Christ as their Messiah. This national and unpardonable sin detailed in Matthew 12:24–31 was the iniquity referenced by Ezekiel, an iniquity that ended with the Holocaust. This event was the climactic, catastrophic event that concluded the discipline of the Jewish people. From the point of Israel's national rejection of Christ forward, in fulfillment of Hosea 1:9–10, the title "My people Israel" began to slip away from the Jews, as Christ turned His future efforts toward both Jew and Gentile. He began speaking in Parables in Matthew 13, evidencing His ministerial turnabout.

The Hebrew word for iniquity is avon, and is first used in Genesis 4:13 with regard to the punishment of Cain for the shedding of his brother Abel's blood. Hebrews 12:24 declares that a better blood than Abel's was shed upon the cross.

"To Jesus the Mediator of the new covenant, and to the blood of sprinkling that speaks better things than *that of* Abel." (Heb. 12:24, NKJV)

All the guilt for the righteous bloodshed, even Abel's, was to be measured against the Jewish generation present at the time of the first coming of Christ. The client nation the world knew for the longest time as "My people Israel" had become a brood of vipers. The Jewish leadership were likened to serpents who would ultimately shed the blood of Christ like their fathers before them shed the blood of the prophets who foretold of Christ.

"Therefore you are witnesses against yourselves that you are sons of those who murdered the prophets. *Fill up, then, the measure of your fathers' guilt.* Serpents, brood of vipers! How can you escape the condemnation of hell? Therefore, indeed, I send you prophets, wise men, and scribes: *some* of them you will kill and crucify, and *some* of them you will scourge in your synagogues and persecute from city to city, *that on you may come all the righteous blood shed on the Earth, from the blood of righteous Abel to the blood of Zechariah,* son of Berechiah, whom you murdered between the temple and the altar.

Assuredly, *I say to you, all these things will come upon this generation."* (Matt. 23:31–36, NKJV; emphasis added)

The connection of brother spilling brother's blood and receiving avon, or punishment, for it is as follows: Cain was Abel's older brother. Cain was jealous of Abel's fellowship with God, because his works were evil and Abel's works were righteous. As such, Cain spilled the blood of his brother. For this Cain received avon:[27]

> "And Cain said to the LORD, "My punishment *is* greater than I can bear! Surely You have driven me out this day from the face of the ground; I shall be hidden from Your face; I shall be a fugitive and a vagabond on the Earth, and it will happen *that* anyone who finds me will kill me." (Gen. 4:13–14, NKJV)

Likewise, His Jewish brethren—playing the role of jealous older brother—spilled the blood of Christ. Their ways and deeds were evil like Cain's, and the works of Christ were righteous like Abel. Their sacrificial offerings, much like those of Cain, fell short of God's acceptance in that they lacked true repentance. Their Mosaic law, which they had reduced to a condition of hypocrisy, eventually passed away and was replaced by the better "New Covenant."[28] Christ was, and still remains, a Jew. He therefore justifiably considers the Jewish people His brethren.[29]

> "So I scattered them [The Jews] among the nations, and they were dispersed throughout the countries; *I judged them* according to their *ways* and their *deeds*." (Ezek. 36:19, NKJV; emphasis added)

As punishment, the LORD drove Cain out from the face of the ground. Similarly, the avon of the Jewish people were driven from the face of the land of Israel. Cain became a fugitive and a vagabond on the Earth, always under threat of persecution. "I shall be a fugitive and a vagabond on the Earth, and it will happen that anyone who finds me will kill me."[30] We can make a comparison to the Jewish people during their centuries of worldwide dispersion. Some glaring examples of Jewish persecution during the dispersion period were the Spanish expulsion of 1492 and the Holocaust, concluding in 1945.

Lastly, Cain complained, "I shall be hidden from Your face." This was the like predicament of the Jewish people; they became "not my people," seemingly hidden from the face of God.[31] Ezekiel 36:19 informs us that the Jewish people have been judged. They have been judged severely for "their (avon) iniquity," and though they remain in the national condition of unbelief in the Messiah, God is moving forward with His prophetic program.

## 4. Israel establishes an army in self-defense

Israel has become a sharpened military instrument as a result of the Arab assaults against them. Its army has arisen, unbeknownst to the masses, in preparation for the fulfillment of the sworn oath of God foretold by Ezekiel.

> "Therefore thus says the LORD GOD: "I have raised My hand in *an oath* that surely the nations that are around you [Israel] shall bear their own shame." (Ezek. 36:7, NKJV; emphasis added)

By way of review, God had Ezekiel prophesy that the Jews would find themselves in a grave-like condition; this was fulfilled 24 centuries later at the time of the Holocaust. Prior to Ezekiel, Isaiah 11:11 had informed them that they would be restored as a people and brought back into the land of Israel a second time, of which the first phase is ongoing today.

God also had Ezekiel declare that the land upon which the Jews were to return was swallowed up and homesteaded by the surrounding Arab nations "all around." As a result, the land of Israel bore the shame of those neighboring Arab nations:

> "Therefore prophesy concerning the land of Israel, and say to the mountains, the hills, the rivers, and the valleys, "Thus says the LORD GOD: 'Behold, I have spoken in My jealousy and My fury, because you have *borne the shame of the nations*.'" (Ezek. 36:6, NKJV; emphasis added)

God raises His hand in a powerful  oath to reverse the direction of shame placed upon Israel. He declares through Ezekiel: "Surely the nations that are around you shall bear their own shame." God will execute the shame of those hostile Arab nations that "are around" Israel in compliance with the curse-for-curse-in-kind clause inscribed in Genesis 12:3.

This clause is the historically proven foreign policy procedure of God toward the Gentile nations. The reversal of shame will involve the shedding of Arab blood, as they are guilty of shedding Jewish blood. It will involve placing portions of Arab lands under Jewish sovereignty, as they had done to the land of Israel, and it will involve the taking of the spoils of war. The condition the Jewish people find themselves enjoying subsequent to these things above is what the Magog alliance appears to be after according to Ezekiel 38:8-13. (Refer to these verses in the appendix called, "The Text of Psalm 83 and Ezekiel 38:1-39:20.").

These Ezekiel 38 excerpts summarize well the point of Israel's condition prior to this Russian-Iranian Magog advance. "In the latter years those brought out of the nations, a peaceful people, who dwell safely, the waste places that are again inhabited, a people who have acquired great plunder."This point was previously explained in the chapter called "Psalm 83 or Ezekiel 38: What's the Next Mideast News Headline?"

This condition partly results from the Israeli Conquest over the Psalm 83 confederacy, of the surrounding Arab nations. Sheba and Dedan, which are ancient cities most likely representing the countries of Yemen and Saudi Arabia, seem to be acknowledging the great plunder Israel has acquired through the defeat of these Arab nations. They, along with the young merchants of Tarshish, appear to abstain from enjoining themselves with the Russian-Iranian-Turkish Magog alliance.

As pointed out in the chapter called "Psalm 83 or Ezekiel 38: What's the Next Mideast News Headline?" the Psalm 83 confederate Arab nations are absent from the Russian-Iranian alliance. Some commentators have found it interesting that Palestinians, Lebanese, Syrians, Jordanians, Saudis, Iraqis, and Egyptians, who are presently the most observable opponents of the Jewish state, appear to opt out of this advance. The logical explanation for their transparency would be their prior defeat at the hands of Israel's exceedingly great army.

Further on in this book we find passages that appear to depict these Arab peoples displaced from their homelands. Many of their citizens are killed, displaced, or captured and placed in internment camps. The exceedingly great army of Israel seizes their land, livestock, and wealth. Israel, no longer living under Arab threat, becomes a peaceful state dwelling in unwalled villages in the latter years.

Presently there is little doubt among any nation in the region or the world as to which Middle Eastern nation is most militarily dominant. It is Israel, who has promptly risen to this position of prowess. They have had to—their survival as a nation depended upon their ability to fight off numerous Arab assaults. It is becoming increasingly clear that Israel has rapidly been fashioned into the military instrument prophesied about in Ezekiel 37:10. All that stands between them and the title an "exceedingly great army" is the Israeli Conquest over the Psalm 83:6–8 Arab confederacy.

## 5. The surrounding Arab nations form a confederacy

Lebanon to the north, Syria to the northeast, Jordan to the east, Saudi Arabia to the southeast, Gaza to the west, and the Sinai Peninsula and Egypt to the south all number themselves among the confederacy.Hints of this confederacy surfaced during the Arab advances against Israel in 1948, 1956, 1967, and 1973. However, none of these fits the description of the final fulfillment of the Psalm 83:1–8 prophecy.

## 6. The confederacy plots to destroy the nation Israel

To date, the general consensus among these nations and terrorist organizations is to reject Israel's right to exist. Moreover, the international community has been unable to resolve the Arab-Israeli conflict diplomatically, and probably won't be able to do much more at this point. Perhaps, on a longshot, the international community will succeed in forcing these nations to accept Israel's right to exist, but at some point, probably soon, these nations will assemble into a confederacy whose mandate is nothing less than the extermination of the Jewish people and the recapture of the Holy Land of Israel.

> They have said, "Come, and let us cut them off from *being* a nation, That the name of Israel may be remembered no more." For they have consulted together with one consent; They form a confederacy against You...(Psa. 83:4–5, NKJV; emphasis added) Who said, "Let us take for ourselves the pastures of God for a possession." (Psa. 83:12, NKJV).

These Psalm 83 nations will confederate in an attempt to promote the spread and dominance of Islam, the destruction of the Jewish people and their religion, and of course the possession of the property of Israel with all of its recently rebuilt ruins and revitalized interests.

## 7. War breaks out in the Middle East between the confederacy and Israel

Soon to come is a major and devastating war in the Middle East between the confederacy of Psalm 83:5–8 and the exceedingly great army of Israel. The previous Arab advances against Israel will be child's play compared to this final confederate attempt.

> "Therefore behold, the days are coming," says the LORD, "That I will cause to be heard *an alarm of war* In Rabbah [Amman, Jordan] of the Ammonites; It shall be a desolate mound, And her villages shall be burned with fire. *Then Israel shall take possession* of his inheritance," says the LORD. (Jer. 49:2, NKJV; emphasis added)

> "Behold, he [the confederacy of Esau] shall come up like a lion from the floodplain of the Jordan Against the dwelling place of the strong [the army of Israel]; But I will suddenly make him [Esau] run away from her [Israel]." (Jer. 49:19, NKJV, abbreviated)

> "Flee, turn back, dwell in the depths, O inhabitants of Dedan [Saudi Arabia]! For I will bring the calamity of Esau [Southern Jordan] upon him [Esau's descendants], The time that I will punish him." (Jer. 49:8, NKJV)

These three scriptures, along with many more scattered throughout this book, point to a Middle-Eastern war that many Bible scholars do not appear to recognize is coming. Among those who do, many place its occurrence in the final seven-year tribulation period—I respectfully disagree. This event will occur soon, well in Advance of both the Russian-Iranian Magog invasion and the seventieth week of Daniel (i.e., the Tribulation). During the Tribulation Period, this army, having previously won the acclaimed title of being exceedingly great, will be sidelined for the first three-and-one-half years while a false and temporary peace accord is confirmed.[32] Then, in the second three-and-one-half years, this army is defeated, and the Jews flee Israel for safety elsewhere, as the Antichrist advances in an attempt to destroy them.[33]

## 8. Israel regains the title "My people Israel"

Somewhere, in the midst of events listed in this chapter, the Jewish State of Israel rises to its former status as the "Client Nation," chosen of God. When this occurs, the nation will again be identified as "My people Israel". The next chapter is dedicated to describe the significance of this national name-changing event. The compilation of scriptures contained in the following chapter encourages the placement of this episode here chronologically. I reference it now to introduce the topic, but defer to the forthcoming My People Israel chapter for further details.

## 9. Israel decisively defeats the confederacy

The army of Israel will defeat the Psalm 83 confederacy, and as a result God will fulfill the oath He made in Ezekiel 36:7. The confederacy of Arab nations will be humiliated for their attempt to expire the Jewish race. Historians will record their failed attempts alongside those of Hitler at the time of the Holocaust, and Pharaoh at the time of the Hebrew Exodus out of Egypt. Additionally the divine foreign policy contained in the Genesis 12:3 clause of the Abrahamic covenant, will be demonstrated again to the watchful eyes of humanity. The passages below pertain to the Israeli conquest over their ancient enemies.

> "The house of Jacob shall be a fire, And the house of Joseph a flame; But the house of Esau shall be stubble; They shall kindle them and devour them, And no survivor shall remain of the house of Esau, For the LORD has spoken." (Obad. 1:18, NKJV)

Israel, represented by the house of Jacob and Joseph reduces Southern Jordan, which is represented by Esau, to rubble. This defeat is thorough leaving no survivor. Then your mighty men, O Teman, shall be dismayed, To the end that everyone from the mountains of Esau May be cut off by slaughter. (Obad. 1:9, NKJV)

Obadiah 1:9 describes the soldiers of Teman, which was an important city in Edom, as having been slaughtered. This emphasizes the severity of Israel's defeat over the Palestinian descendants of Edom. Teman's modern equivalent may be Taiwan, about 3 miles (5 km) east of Petra. However, Teman and the mountains of Esau appear to be representative of the entire region of Edom in this passage.[34]

> "Therefore thus says the LORD GOD: "I will also stretch out My hand against Edom, cut off man and beast from it, and make it desolate from Teman; Dedan [Saudi Arabia] shall fall by the sword. I will lay My vengeance on Edom by the hand of My people Israel [Israeli Defense Force I.D.F.], that they may do in Edom according to My anger and according to My fury; and they shall know My vengeance," says the LORD GOD." (Ezek. 2513–14, NKJV)

The same hand that God lifted up in a sworn oath in Ezekiel 36:7, he will stretch out in order to lift up the great army of Israel. This army will execute God's revenge against the Arabs who attack the Jews and, in so doing, assault the Abrahamic covenant. This war extends into Saudi Arabia, as the army of Israel advances beyond the Southern border of Jordan into northwest Saudi Arabia, represented by Dedan.

> "Therefore hear the counsel of the LORD that He has taken against Edom, And His purposes that He has proposed against the inhabitants of Teman: Surely the least of the flock shall draw them out; Surely He shall make their dwelling places desolate with them. The Earth shakes at the noise of their fall; At the cry its noise is heard at the Red Sea." (Jer. 49:20–21 NKJV)

The results are devastating for the descendants of Esau; even the least of the Jews possesses dominance over them, or draws them out. This is a possible reference to the capture process resulting from the military defeat. Israel will take prisoners of war. The noise refers to this war and all of its thundering sounds. This war does not limit its battleground to southern Jordan, but extends as far south as the Red Sea. This places the confederate members of Saudi Arabia, Southern Jordan, and Egypt within its scope. Jeremiah says the Earth shakes at the sound of their fall. This shows the magnitude of the affect that the Israeli Conquest over the Arab nations will have upon the international community. The Hebrew word used is "raash," which reflects the trembling experienced during a devastating earthquake and its aftershocks.

> "But I have made Esau bare; I have uncovered his secret places, And he shall not be able to hide himself. *His descendants are plundered*, His brethren *and his neighbors*, And he is no more." (Jer. 49:10, NKJV; emphasis added)

Israel makes barren the territory of southern Jordan because of this war. The Israelis plunder the descendants of Esau and his genealogy appears to end. The Jews also plunder the neighboring confederate nations involved in the conflict.

"He will set up a banner for the nations, And will assemble the outcasts of Israel, And gather together the dispersed of Judah From the four corners of the Earth. Also the envy of Ephraim shall depart, And *the adversaries of Judah shall be cut off;* Ephraim shall not envy Judah, And Judah shall not harass Ephraim. But *they shall fly down upon* the shoulder of the Philistines toward the west; Together they shall *plunder* the *people of the East;* They shall lay their hand on Edom and Moab; And the people of Ammon shall obey them." (Isa. 11:12–14, NKJV; emphasis added)

The army of Israel will cut off its confederate adversaries, and then come down upon the Gaza territory. In continuing their conquest, they plunder the people of the East, which, according to its first scriptural usage in Genesis 29:1, would be Syria. They then lay their hands on all of Jordan, causing its capitol to fall under Jewish sovereignty. Ammon represents northern Jordan, the location of the capital city of Amman. Isaiah says the people of Ammon shall obey them, depicting the surrender of Jordanian sovereignty.

"The burden against Damascus. Behold, Damascus will cease from *being* a city, And it will be a ruinous heap." (Isa. 17:1, NKJV)

The city with the longest standing history of civilian habitation will be extinguished. It, like much of Jordan, will be reduced to rubble.[35] Presently, almost every known Middle Eastern terrorist organization has representation in Damascus. Soon, they will have none. How fitting that the city most adversarial to the nation of Israel will cease to exist. The destruction of Damascus is so important that this book devotes two chapters to this topic.

"Against Damascus. "Hamath and Arpad are shamed, For they have heard bad news. They are fainthearted; There is trouble on the sea; It cannot be quiet. Damascus has grown feeble; She turns to flee, And fear has seized her. Anguish and sorrows have taken her like a woman in labor. Why is the city of praise [Jerusalem] not deserted, the city of My joy? Therefore her young men shall fall in her [Damascus] streets, And all the *men of war* shall be cut off in that day," says the LORD of hosts." (Jer. 49:23–26 NKJV; emphasis added)

"In that day, Egypt will be like women, and will be afraid and fear because of the waving of the hand of the LORD of hosts, which He waves over it. And the land of *Judah will be a terror to Egypt;* everyone who makes mention of it will be afraid in himself, because of the counsel of the LORD of hosts which He has determined against it." (Isa. 19:16–17, NKJV; emphasis added)

Even Egypt will be in the sights of the exceedingly great army of Israel. The picture Isaiah aptly portrays is that of a fragile, unarmed female fighting a skilled male warrior wielding a mighty sword. The woman is frightened as the warrior waves his sword in the air. Like Damascus, prophecies concerning Egypt are equally as important, and therefore, two chapters explaining Egypt's future are included in this book.

## 10. Israel takes prisoners of war

"Wail, O Heshbon, for Ai is plundered! Cry, you daughters of Rabbah, Gird yourselves with sackcloth! Lament and run to and fro by the walls; For Milcom shall go into captivity With his priests and his princes together…But afterward I will bring back The captives of the people of Ammon," says the LORD." (Jer. 49:3,6, NKJV)

"Woe to you, O Moab! The people of Chemosh perish; For your sons have been taken captive, And your daughters captive. Yet I will bring back the captives of Moab In the latter days," says the LORD. Thus far is the judgment of Moab." (Jer. 48:46–47, NKJV)

Leave your fatherless children [descendants of Esau], I will preserve them alive; And let your widows trust in Me. (Jer. 49:11, NKJV)

Israel will establish future detention camps in the regions of Southern Lebanon and the Negev. Israel is accustomed to imprisoning known Palestinian terrorists. This process will greatly intensify as Israel captures prisoners of war from the various Psalm 83 confederate nations.

"And the captives of this host of the children of Israel *Shall possess the land* of the Canaanites As far as Zarephath. The captives of Jerusalem who are in Sepharad Shall possess the cities of the South." (Oba. 1:20, NKJV).

The captivity of Milcom, the Ammonite god, and Chemosh, the Moabite god, may have interesting ramifications. Presently, the god served by most Jordanians is Allah. The Islamic faith emerged subsequent to the writings of these prophecies. Islam put under a monotheistic umbrella the polytheistic practices of the Arabs in the region. Estimates that as many as 360 various gods celebrated by the Arabs in the Middle East were packaged into one god named Allah. Prophetic phrases like Milcom shall go into captivity, and Chemosh perish, may imply the diminished scale of Islam, at least in the Middle East. And, the instrument of this dimishment would appear to be the IDF.

"This they shall have for their pride, Because they have reproached and made arrogant threats Against the people of the LORD of hosts. The LORD *will be* awesome to them, For *He will reduce to nothing all the gods of the Earth*; *People* shall worship Him, Each one from his place, Indeed all the shores of the nations." (Zeph. 2:10–11, NKJV; emphasis added)

*(More on this topic is explained in the chapter called, "Psalm 83 and the Prophets.")*

## 11 . The region is reshaped

Due to the magnified scope of Israel's military campaign, the region will experience severe damage. Israel will levy a series of decisive blows, and gain sovereignty over much of the Middle East. In the passages below, Syria, Jordan, and the Gaza Strip come under serious attack, and what were once thriving cities or territories become desolate wastelands. Supporting scriptures are located in Isaiah 17:1, Jeremiah 49:2, 10, Zephaniah 2:4.

## 12 . Israel expands its borders

The result of a military conquest is sovereignty over the affected territories. This rule of thumb appears to apply in this case. Israel will begin to resemble the tribal territories about 3,000 years ago when Solomon was king.

> "The South shall possess the mountains of Esau (southern Jordan), and the Lowland shall possess Philistia (Gaza Strip). They shall possess the fields of Ephraim and the fields of Samaria (West Bank). Benjamin shall possess Gilead (West Bank & Golan Heights)." (Obad. 1:19, NKJV)

The Negev will possess Southern Jordan, and the lowland of Judah will possess the Gaza Strip and the southern parts of the West Bank. Northern Israel will possess the northern part of the West Bank, the Golan Heights, much of northern Jordan, and southern Syria. Alluding to Jordan, Jeremiah 49:2 declares "Then Israel shall take possession of his inheritance," says the LORD.

Much of modern-day Jordan was once part of the inheritance of Israel. The tribes of East Manasseh, Gad, Benjamin, and Reuben, once possessed land that is presently under Jordanian Sovereignty.

> In that day five cities in the land of Egypt will speak the language of Canaan [Hebrew] and swear by the LORD of hosts; one will be called the City of Destruction. In that day there will be an altar to the LORD in the midst of the land of Egypt, and a pillar to the LORD at its border. (Isa. 19:18–19, NKJV)

Isaiah appears to suggest that the Expansion of Israeli sovereignty in the region will burden even Egypt to some degree. Five Hebrew speaking cities will develop in the land of Egypt. In the center of the country, an altar will be erected to Jehovah, and at the border, a pillar will be erected to the God of the Jews. The altar may be built to offer sacrifices to Jehovah, which was often the scene in the days of old when Mosaic Law was operative.

## 13 . Israel dwells securely in the land

Israel is elevated to a condition of regional superiority due to their decisive victory over the confederacy of the surrounding Arab nations. As such, they dwell securely in the Middle East for a time, a point already detailed in the chapter "Psalm 83 or Ezekiel 38: What's is the Next Middle East News Headline."[36]

## 14. Israel becomes an exceedingly great army

"So I prophesied as He commanded me, and breath came into them, and they lived, and stood upon their feet, an exceedingly great army." (Ezek. 37:10, NKJV)

Undeniably, the result of all the events outlined in this chapter earns Israel the right to classify its defense force (IDF), as an "exceedingly great army." To genuinely achieve such a title, it is required that the army delivers a decisive victory in a full-scale war. The Psalm 83 confederate advance against tiny Israel will be considered by the international community a full-scale war. Repeating Jeremiah 49:21: The Earth shakes at the noise of their fall; At the cry its noise is heard at the Red Sea.

Some have suggested that Ezekiel 37:10 refers to a great multitude, rather than an exceedingly great army. I argue against the great multitude interpretation, and explain why this verse alludes to an army, in the appendice called "Is Ezekiel's Army About to Face Off with the Arabs?"

## 15 . God fulfills this segment of His plan

Again, the purpose of this segment was to judge the animosity established in ancient times and perpetuated through the ages to the covenantal promises God gave to Abraham. The Psalm 83 confederate advance is a direct assault against the Abrahamic covenant. It is an attempt to kill the Jewish people and confiscate the land of Israel. The preservation of both are critical elements contained within the covenant.

Furthermore, if the enemies of the Jews succeeded in exterminating them, there would be no remnant left to fulfill the mandate of the second coming of Christ, which is the Jewish remnant to repent and beckon His return.[37] Likewise, the return of the

Messiah fulfills the Davidic aspects of the covenant and the New Covenant, which is an amplification of the entire Abrahamic covenant. God promised Abraham a people, a place, and an eternal throne; unfortunately for the Arab confederacy, the survival of this covenant is non-negotiable.

# SEVEN

# My People Israel

**"State of Israel is Born "**

*The Palestine Post 5/16/48*

**"'Catholic Cleric: Jesus Cancelled Biblical 'Chosen People''**

*Israel National News 10/24/10*

"The Creator's promise that the Land of Israel is for Jews is no
longer valid, a Catholic synod said, but added "The Word of
the Lord is eternal"'.

G od formally recognized the descendants of Abraham, Isaac, and
Jacob in scripture as His people in Exodus 3:7. God declared: "I
have surely seen the oppression of my people who are in Egypt."[38] More
than three-hundred years had passed after the death of Jacob, and God,
in remembrance of His covenant with Abraham, put the world on notice
that these people were "My people."

Not long before, Pharaoh of Egypt had attempted to weaken God's
people with his campaign to kill their newborn male children.[39] This act,
along with his stepped-up enslavement of the Jews, provoked the contents of the Abrahamic Covenant into enactment as per Genesis 12:2-3.
The historical events that followed evidenced the supremacy of God and
His faithfulness to His covenant with Abraham. Everything subsequently

fashioned by Pharaoh to harm God's people boomeranged back to harm Pharaoh and his people in a like manner.

The world saw that these, the descendants of Abraham, Isaac, and Jacob, were the people of God. Nothing could suppress their supreme God from fulfilling His unconditional covenant custom made for Abraham and his descendants, the Jews.

> "For you *are* a holy people to the LORD your God; the LORD your God has chosen you to be a people for Himself, a special treasure above all the peoples on the face of the Earth. The LORD did not set His love on you nor choose you because you were more in number than any other people, for you were the least of all peoples; but because the LORD loves you, and *because He would keep the oath which He swore to your fathers,* the LORD has brought you out with a mighty hand, and redeemed you from the house of bondage, from the hand of Pharaoh king of Egypt." (Deut. 7:6–8, NKJV; emphasis added)

These passages from Deuteronomy adequately describe the preferred client-nation status once bestowed upon Israel. They were the least of all peoples, but because God loved them and swore an oath to their patriarchal fathers Abraham, Isaac, and Jacob, they would one day become a holy people. They would be the chosen people of God, treasured above all the peoples on Earth. People throughout the world would come to know them as "My people Israel."

As we study the history of the Jewish people, we see a continual love-hate relationship toward God developed amongst their culture throughout time. When they were in love with God they were obedient to His callings and were blessed accordingly. They were mighty and prosperous, and the land of Israel produced bountifully. However, when they were indifferent toward God and had digressed into idolatrous practices, God severely disciplined them. Jewish leadership misdirected the nation, the military experienced defeat, rain did not fall in due season, and the land failed to produce.

Several Old Testament passages remind us that their dominant tendency was to be fickle, rather than faithful to their calling as the client nation.[40] As such, God gave official notice through Hosea the prophet that a time would arrive whereby the client nation Israel would become "not my people," and would be stripped of their coveted "My people Israel" title.[41] The ramifications of the fulfillment of this prophecy were staggering! Humans could question the very character of God's covenant-making capabilities if indeed God disinherited the true descendants of Abraham, Isaac, and Jacob.

> Then the Angel of the LORD called to Abraham a second time out of heaven, and said: *"By Myself I have sworn*, says the LORD, because you have done this

thing, and have not withheld your son [Isaac], your only *son* [not Ishmael]— blessing I will bless you, and multiplying *I will multiply your descendants as the stars* of the heaven *and as the sand* which *is* on the seashore; and your descendants shall possess the gate of their enemies. In *your seed* all the nations of the Earth shall be blessed, *because you have obeyed My voice.*" (Gen. 22:15–18, NKJV; emphasis added)

The Angel of the LORD, which scholars commonly teach to be an Old Testament reference to a "Christophony" of the pre-incarnate Jesus Christ, tells Abraham that God has sworn by nothing less than His own righteous character that because Abraham obeyed God, Abraham's descendants would multiply without end. In those days, the numerical equivalent to infinity was the innumerable number of the stars of heaven or the grains of sand on the seashore.

This scripture offers no opt-out clause. God based this sworn oath to multiply the descendants of Abraham upon an obedient act of Abraham "because you have done this thing, and have not withheld your son, your only son," and no matter how many the disobedient acts of his descendants that followed may have been, this promise was understood to be irreversible. Moreover, Genesis 15:8-21 clearly evidences that the Lord made an unconditional covenant with Abraham.

The question then arises: Could it be that the multiplication of Abraham's descendants will never cease, but unlike their father Abraham, they as a people might reach a point of hardening or callousness toward God? Those who recognized the contents of the Abrahamic covenant could not conclude this definitively, because through one of his descendants, his "seed," all the nations of the Earth were to be blessed. The prophecies concerning the seed of Abraham pertain to the Messiah, Jesus Christ, and pass through the loins of Abraham (Gen. 22:18), Isaac (Gen. 26:4), and Jacob (Gen. 28:14).

To the spectator, it would appear as though God had indeed painted Himself into a corner by Hosea's prophecy. Hosea declares that the God of Abraham will at some point cease to be the God of Abraham's descendants, the Jewish people.

Now when she had weaned Lo-Ruhamah, she conceived and bore a son. Then *God* said: "Call his name Lo-Ammi, For you *are not My people*, And I will not be your *God*." (Hosea 1:8–9, NKJV; emphasis added)

Then, almost in the next breath, Hosea quotes the multiplication of Abraham's descendants clause:

Yet the number of the children of *Israel Shall be as the sand of the sea*, Which cannot be measured or numbered. And it shall come to pass In the place where it was said to them, "You *are* not My people," *There* it shall be said to them, "*You are* sons of the living God." (Hosea 1:10, NKJV; emphasis added)

There appeared to be an identity crisis in the making: on the one hand, Jews were the blessed "My people Israel," because God swore an oath to Abraham. On the other, because as a people they generally disobeyed God, He would disqualify them at some point from that coveted title. They would be known as "not My people," though they would never face ultimate extermination as they were still promised to multiply without end. Lastly, as a nation the LORD would classify them as "sons of the living God."

What was happening here? It was as if the Jewish people were playing Russian Roulette with their heritage. How was this turn of events prophetically scheduled to occur? To understand this better, it is important to go back historically to the point whereby "My people Israel" became "not My people."

Though Hosea 1:9–10 speaks of a time when Israel would be reclassified as "not My people," this declassification did not find final fulfillment during Hosea's time, whose ministry spanned from 750 to 725 BC. Rather, it was a prophecy of events to come. The title "My people Israel" continued to apply even during the time of the prophet Jeremiah, whose ministry began in the thirteenth year of Josiah (628 BC). They continued to hold the title even during the Babylonian captivity, evidenced by the fact that Daniel was still prophesying from within Babylon during that period.

It is not plausible to think that the Jewish people lost this coveted title during the post-exilic period after the Babylonian captivity, which ended in 536 BC, as they were instructed in the Old Testament book of Nehemiah to return to their home-land Israel and rebuild their temple in Jerusalem. During that time, God was still communicating with His people of Israel through the post-exilic prophets Haggai, Zechariah, and Malachi. Even up to the time of the first advent of Christ, they were still operating in the official capacity of "My people Israel," as evidenced by the fact that John the Baptist, also a Jewish prophet, continued to disseminate prophecy.

For over seven-hundred years, the inference inherent in this Prophecy should have haunted the Jews. Then came "the seed," Christ. Until that point, the Jews continually wondered when they would become "not My people." What generation would be stripped from the responsibilities of the adoption, the glory, the covenants, the giving of the law, the service of God, and the promises given by God to Abraham, Isaac, and Jacob?[42] All these were appointed to the people of God, "My people Israel."

Could it be that Gentiles would someday replace the Jews in God's eyes? As preposterous as the thought appeared, Old Testament prophecies familiar to the Jews spoke of the Messiah being a light to the Gentiles.(Isaiah 42:6, 49:6, and 60:3).

This is an important area of study, because the assumption within the preponderance of the Church today is that this was exactly what happened. Many believe that God is done with the Jew, and that the Jewish people are no longer "My people Israel." They believe that the Jew has no further place within the overall prophetic plan of God. They surmise that the Church has replaced them as the people of God. Estimates tell us this dangerous misconception, known as Replacement Theology, is held by as much as 85 percent of the visible Church.

We must now look at when the nation of Israel lost its coveted title. God finally fulfilled his prophecy in the generation that rejected Christ (Matt. 12:24). This was when the nation Israel committed the unpardonable sin—the denial of Christ as Messiah based on demon possession. From that time forward the title began to wane, and beginning in AD 70 and continuing into the centuries of worldwide dispersion that followed, the Jews assumed the title "not My people."

The fulfillment of Hosea's prophecy had finally come, and the Abrahamic covenant hung in the balance . Would God abandon the covenant He made with Abraham and, in so doing, disinherit Abraham's children, the Jewish people? Perhaps He would replace the true descendants of Abraham with Gentiles. It would be highly unlikely He would choose the former, because to abandon an unconditional covenant would be to defame His own character as the true God over all creation. One can bet that Satan and his fallen angels packed the theater at that time to see God work His way out of this quandary.

The answer everyone awaited finally came in one of the eight mysteries of the New Testament (a mystery is the revealing of information in the New Testament that hadn't been disclosed in the Old Testament). Years later, Paul resolved the dilemma by introducing the mystery.

> So that you may not claim to be wiser than you are, brothers and sisters, I want you to understand this mystery: *a hardening has come upon part of Israel*, until the full number of the Gentiles has come in. (Rom. 11:25, NRSV; emphasis added)

It was no mystery that Israel would become hardened. After all, they would eventually become so calloused that they would become "not My people." Neither was it a mystery that God would call a full number of Gentiles to be saved.[43] However, it was indeed a mystery that "not all Jews" would be classified as "not My people."

God's surprise was keeping the Abrahamic covenant in tact by holding onto a believing faction of the Jews as the true descendants of Abraham. These believing Jews never assumed the title "not My people." They were simply reclassified from "My people Israel," to "My people the Church." Hence, we must now touch upon a second of the New Testament's mysteries, the fellowship mystery.

> By which, when you read, you may understand my knowledge in the mystery of Christ, which in other ages was not made known to the sons of men,

as it has now been revealed by the Spirit to His holy apostles and prophets: *that the Gentiles should be fellow heirs, of the same body*, and partakers [with the believing Jews] of His promise in Christ [the seed of Abraham] through the gospel. (Eph. 3:4–6, NKJV; emphasis added)

We therefore understand that "God is not done with the Jew" as the apostle Paul so aptly asserted in Romans Chapters 9–11. Paul specifically reminds us in Romans 9:25–26 of what Hosea 1:9–10 disclosed.

As He says also in Hosea: "I will [yet again] call them My people [Israel], who were not my people, And her beloved, who was not beloved. And it shall come to pass in the place where it was said to them, 'You are not My people,' There they shall be called sons of the living God." (Rom. 9:25–26 NKJV)

We see that, as He promised their father Abraham, God will never be done with the Jews.[44] Though the greater part of the client nation, the hardened part, was temporarily stripped of the coveted title "My people Israel," until the full number of Gentiles has come in, the Jews were never erased entirely from God's last will and testament. In addition to being heirs of the unconditional Abrahamic covenant, they will be the recipients of numerous Old and New Testament end-time prophecies yet to occur.

The hardness or blindness of the nation of Israel will end after "the fullness of the Gentiles has come in" (Rom. 11:26). Furthermore, we know that ultimately "all Israel will be saved." The national salvation of Israel occurs with the second coming of Christ, and from that point forward, all of Israel remains saved throughout the Messianic Kingdom. It is at that point that the world comes to know them as "sons of the living God." Yet several scriptures inform us that before this happens, the Jewish people will go from their present "not My people" status, to their former world-renowned title "My people Israel."

We need, then, to determine when the Jewish people, who are presently "not My people," become "My people Israel." Ezekiel wrote several prophecies clearly identifying the Jewish nation in advance of the second coming of Christ as "My people Israel."

But you, O mountains of Israel, you shall shoot forth your branches and yield your fruit to My people Israel, for they are about to come. For indeed I *am* for you, and I will turn to you, and you shall be tilled and sown. I will multiply men upon you, all the house of Israel, all of it; and the cities shall be inhabited and the ruins rebuilt. I will multiply upon you man and beast; and they shall increase and bear young; I will make you inhabited as in former times, and do better *for you* than at your beginnings. Then you shall know

that I *am* the LORD. Yes, I will cause men to walk on you, My people Israel;
they shall take possession of you, and you shall be their inheritance; no
more shall you bereave them *of children.* (Ezek. 36:8–12, NKJV)

Ezekiel 36:8–12 re-introduces the Jewish people as "My people Israel." Twice
within these passages they are referred to this way. The first usage suggests they
have returned to God's favor even before their return to the land of Israel in 1948.
Ezekiel writes: "For they are about to come." The second usage portrays the Jewish
people as walking upon the Holy Land of Israel, in full possession of it.

The Hebrew words translated as "about to come" are qarab bo, and can also
be translated as "draw near to attain." The first Ezekiel usage may imply that the
Jewish people, formerly recognized as "My people Israel," but better known in their
dispersion as "not My people," draw near, to re-attain their client-nation status. The
second usage, however, makes clear that when Israel takes possession of the land
and the land becomes their inheritance, their God once again recognizes them as
"My people Israel."

Describing the gathering, Ezekiel also uses the phrase "all the house of Israel, all
of it," alluding to two things: first, that the gathering would be worldwide and, secondly, that the Jewish people would no longer be a divided kingdom as in the times
between the Northern Kingdom (Samaria) and the Southern Kingdom (Judah). This
is a point also prophesied in Isaiah 11:12–13 and Ezekiel 37:15–22.

To date, it is at least clear that the Jewish people have drawn near to attain
full autonomy over the Promised Land . We can also surmise that they are a united
people, no longer dividing allegiance to a northern or southern kingdom. The land
is productive, the Jewish people are reproductive, and the cities are inhabited as in
former times. It is debatable, however, as to whether or not they fully possess the
land, a critical condition that must be in place when the Jews once again are seen
as "My people Israel."

Another Ezekiel passage describes the Jewish people as an extension of God's
hand in judgment against Arabs. This passage likewise identifies the Jews as "My
people Israel" in advance of the second coming of Christ.

"I will lay My vengeance on Edom [Southern Jordan] by the hand of My
people Israel, that they may do in Edom according to My anger and according to My fury; and they shall know My vengeance," says the LORD GOD.
(Ezek. 25:14,NKJV)

In a major campaign to extinguish all the Jewish people, Edom forms a confederacy with the other Arab nations that presently border the land of Israel. The Bible
describes this confederacy and their campaign in Psalm 83:1–8, 12. The judgment
Ezekiel describes is, in part, God's response to this confederate effort. The Arabs

come against the Jewish people at a time when they are gathering back into the land and have become, or will soon again become, known as "My people Israel."

When the Psalm 83 campaign finally arrives on the world scene, the Jewish people will rise up and rain God's vengeance upon Edom according to His anger and fury. After this Israeli Conquest, the Jewish people will walk in full possession of more of the land. At that point, if not before, they will undoubtedly be again classified as "My people Israel."

> "I have heard the reproach of Moab, And the insults of the people of Ammon, With which they have reproached My people, And made arrogant threats against their borders. Therefore, as I live," Says the LORD of hosts, the God of Israel, "Surely Moab shall be like Sodom, And the people of Ammon like Gomorrah— Overrun with weeds and saltpits, And a perpetual desolation. The residue of My people shall plunder them, And the remnant of My people shall possess them." (Zeph. 2:8–9, NKJV)

The execution of vengeance extends beyond Edom into Ammon and Moab. Thus, all of modern-day Jordan will be vanquished by Israel. Ammon and Moab are enlisted members, along with Edom, in the Psalm 83 confederacy. As this book points out, this will be in addition to the confederate territories of Lebanon, Syria, Saudi Arabia, Egypt, West Bank, and the Gaza Strip, who will all come under some form of military domination from Israel's exceedingly great army.

The point here is that, as it was during the early campaigns of "My people the Hebrews," the exodus from Egypt, and the migration into the Promised Land, God will endow the present Jewish generation with the strong arm of His might. All present Arab attempts against the successful return of the Hebrews into the Holy Land, and the reclamation of their coveted title "My people Israel" are beyond futile; they will prove to be fatal. Present Arab aggressions provoke the providential protection with well-known historical Hebrew precedent. Soon the world will experience the Jews coming into possession of much of the Promised Land through the strength of the exceedingly great army prophesied in Ezekiel 37:10.

Subsequent to the fulfillment of Ezekiel 25:14, "The Israeli Conquest," the Russian-Iranian Magog alliance described in Ezekiel 38 and 39 will confront the Jewish people. The world will know the Jews by this time as "My people Israel." Ezekiel 38:14, 16, and Ezekiel 39:7 also refer to the Jewish people as "My people Israel." God endows the Jewish people with this title at a time when He has re-gathered them from the nations back into the land of Israel in the latter years.

One might justifiably question the whereabouts of the church at this time. If Israel is at some point again called "My people Israel," then where on Earth are "My people the Church?" The church is thought to be the people of God in these days; could it be they will be raptured on or near the time of Israel regaining their client nation status? After all, the Church came into being around the same time Israel lost their favored-nation status.

Perhaps the answer to this question comes in the understanding of what Paul meant by the term "fullness of the Gentiles." Expositors like Adam Clarke, Warren Wiersbe, and many more believe Paul meant this to represent the Gentile believers during the Church age, i.e., the Bride of Christ.[45] They advocate that when the rapture occurs, the "fullness of the Gentiles" has come in. As such, the stage begins to set for the LORD to save all of Israel. However, we know that all of Israel will not be saved for at least seven years, a period which encompasses the "Seventieth Week of Daniel," i.e., the "Tribulation." It will actually be longer than seven years, because it is not the rapture that will set the seven-year clock ticking; rather, it is the signing of the false covenant by Israel, confirmed by the Antichrist.[46]

So we are left to wonder what occurs between the time of the rapture, if that is when the "fullness of the Gentiles has come in," and the end of the Tribulation Period whereby "all Israel shall be saved." Many things happen, but for the purposes of this study, we are concerned with the reclassification of the client nation status to "My people Israel." This gap between the rapture and the tribulation period is explored in my trilogy book series. The first book called "Revelation Road, Hope Beyond the Horizon" is already published.

During that window of time, Israel will be restored to its client nation status. They will be "My people Israel." There appears to be some time correlation between the calling out of the 144,000 Jewish witnesses of Revelation 7:1–8 and the reinstatement of the "My people Israel" title. These are clearly Jews called to the service of God. They come on the scene at a very interesting time and represent Israel again in a preferred national condition. They are clearly identified genealogically from their ancestral Jewish tribes, and the ordering of the usage of their tribal names, though puzzling, may have ministerial meaning.

The Bible calls these 144,000 Jews "the servants of our God" in Revelation 7:3. They receive their ministry after the Church is raptured. According to many, the simple interpretation of Revelation 2 and 3 represents the Church on Earth, and Revelation 4 and 5 represents the Church, raptured and residing in heaven. Revelation 7 starts with the Greek words "meta tauta," interpreted in English as "after these things." After the summation of events of the Church age on Earth and the rapture of the Church, the events of Revelation 7 occur. This adds credence to the fact that, if the "fullness of the Gentiles" is the Church, then the fullness of the Gentiles has been completed and it is time for "My people Israel" to again take front-and-center stage as God's people.

For the most part, all Jewish tribal genealogical records were destroyed in AD 70, yet a Revelation 7:5–8 prophetic event still to occur distinctly identifies the emergence of twelve thousand members from each of their twelve ancestral tribes.[47] This is not a random selection; rather, God orchestrated it and ordained it by the angel having the "seal of the living God." It is not an accident that there are not 11,999 from one tribe and 12,001 from another. There are exactly 12,000 from each tribe sealed for service. From these specifics, we can assume God is administering His Earthly program once again through the Jewish people. This safely suggests that these Jews are not "My people the Church," which by this time have likely been raptured. Rather, they represent a significant component within "My people Israel."

These 144,000 servants minister after the Church age, and should therefore be very familiar with the gospel and the mystery of fellowship quoted earlier from Ephesians 3:4–6. Thus, they would know—and therefore teach—that salvation now comes through faith in Christ and not the Mosaic Law. They also teach that it is God's will that Gentiles should be partakers along with the Jews through the gospel. With this understanding, we can interpret the possible ministerial message within the ordering of the names of the twelve tribes in Revelation 7:5–8.

- of the tribe of *Judah* twelve thousand *were* sealed;

- of the tribe of *Reuben* twelve thousand *were* sealed;

- of the tribe of *Gad* twelve thousand *were* sealed;

- of the tribe of *Asher* twelve thousand *were* sealed;

- of the tribe of *Naphtali* twelve thousand *were* sealed;

- of the tribe of *Manasseh* twelve thousand *were* sealed;

- of the tribe of *Simeon* twelve thousand *were* sealed;

- of the tribe of *Levi* twelve thousand *were* sealed;

- of the tribe of *Issachar* twelve thousand *were* sealed;

- of the tribe of *Zebulun* twelve thousand *were* sealed;

- of the tribe of *Joseph* twelve thousand *were* sealed;

- of the tribe of *Benjamin* twelve thousand *were* sealed.
  (Rev. 7:5–8, NKJV; emphasis added)

The names of the twelve tribes are listed in this non-chronological order, perhaps to describe the ministerial purposes of the 144,000 Hebrew Christian witnesses of Revelation 7:5–8. Normally, the Bible lists descendants in the chronological order of their birth. However, the apostle John lists these tribes out of order, apparently giving us insight into the ministry of these witnesses.

The tribe of Judah is listed first in Revelation 7:5, however, in birth order, Judah was the fourth son. Similarly, the Bible lists the other tribes out of order in Revelation 7:5–8. An astute student of the Word watches for these abnormalities within the scriptures and, as such, is always encouraged to dig deeper in order to discover what the Holy Spirit intends for him or her to understand relative to the text.

## The Meanings of the Names:

Judah (Praise God), Reuben (behold a son), Gad (good fortune), Asher (happiness), Naphtali (my wrestling), Manasseh (God has caused me to forget), Simeon (hearing), Levi (joining or adhesion), Issachar (God hath given me my hire, or man for hire), Zebulun (elevated or elevated dwelling), Joseph (adding or increaser), Benjamin (son of the right hand).

## The Message of the Names:

Praise God! Behold! a son of good fortune and happiness. My wrestling God has caused me to forget. Hearing of our joining, God hath given me my hire and elevated dwelling increased by the son of the right hand.

Inherent in these oddly ordered names, appears to be the ministerial message of the 144,000 witnesses. Their "Mission Statement" should read as follows:

> "Praise God for the gospel of Christ, a Son of good fortune and happiness. My struggle with sin and the Mosaic Law, God has caused me to forget. Hearing of the mystery of our grafting in with the Gentiles,[48] God has reinstated me into an elevated position of ministry once again, and is increasing those being saved through Christ, the Son of the right hand."
>
> These are the ones who were not defiled with women, for they are virgins. These are the ones who follow the Lamb wherever He goes. These were redeemed from *among* men, being firstfruits to God and to the Lamb. And in their mouth was found no deceit, for they are without fault before the throne of God. (Rev. 14:4–5, NKJV; emphasis added)

These 144,000 servants become "firstfruits to God and to the Lamb," (Jesus Christ),[49] suggesting that after the rapture the subsequent dispensation has the 144,000 as its firstfruits. This further suggests that at that time God will again administer His sovereign program through "My people Israel." These 144,000 servants likely represent the first crop of harvested souls subsequent to the Rapture of the Church. They are the first of many saved souls which were foretold to follow the sudden disappearance of the Christian Church. These saved souls are identified in Revelation 7:9–17, and elsewhere.

## Firstfruits

The choice examples of a crop harvested first and dedicated to God. In accordance with Mosaic law, individual Israelites brought to the house of the LORD "the first (that is, 'the best') of the firstfruits of thy land." (Ex. 23:19; 34:26)[50]

# EIGHT

# The Future for America in Bible Prophecy

**"Texas Megachurch Pastor Says Obama Will 'Pave Way' for Antichrist"**

*The Christian Post 11/8/12*

**"U.S. economy on schedule to crash March 2014"**

*The Washington Times 10/25/12*

**"America is Vulnerable to an Electromagnetic Pulse Attack"**

*Human Events 6/29/09*

It is highly possible that the biblical wars of Psalm 83 and Ezekiel 38 will adversely affect America. This chapter takes a look at the Future for America according to Bible prophecy. Below are some of the topics that will be covered in this chapter.

*Topics Covered: Will Terrorist's Attack America Again? Islamic Extremists Identify America as the Great Satan; America Slips from Superpower Status, According to Bible Experts; The Primary Views About America's Location in the Bible; America Experiences Divine Remedial Judgments; If Remedial Warnings Go Unheeded, Divine Judgment Results*

## Will Terrorist's Attack America Again?

Suicide bombers, airplane bombers, bus bombers, shoe bombers, and underwear bombers sit atop a developing list of modern-day methods of terrorism. One of the latest ill-conceived terror tactics is explosive breast implants in females.

### "Bosom bombers: Women have explosive breast implants"

*World Net Daily 2/1/10*

"Bosom bombers," writes Joseph Farah, the founder of World Net Daily.[51] He states in his shocking article, that Muslim doctors trained at leading UK hospitals are fitting female Al-Qaeda suicide bombers with lethal explosives in techniques similar to breast enhancement surgery.

Because Al-Qaeda toppled the twin towers, Richard Reid smuggled triacetone triperoxide in his shoes, and Umar Farouk Abdulmutallab stitched a bomb into his under-britches, far too often Americans get groped by the Transportation Security Administration (TSA) at airports. Strict security measures seem like a minor price to pay to fly from point A to point B safely, but will it ever cease? Osama Bin Laden and his high ranking cohort, Anwar al-Awlaki, have both been assassinated; shouldn't the Department of Homeland Security (DOHS), which was established in response to the September 11 attacks, be shut down? That would save the struggling US economy about $100 billion dollars per year.[52]

Of course not; the DOHS should remain intact; the threat of terror has not subsided since Bin Laden's and al-Awlaki's death. In fact, the list of terror tactics above is almost laughable when compared to the sophisticated threats Americans may face in the future. In the novel portion in my book called *Revelation Road, Hope Beyond the Horizon*, I hypothesis the occurrence of a high-level, multi-pronged terror attack that puts the United States on virtual lock-down! Dirty Bombs in multiple major ballpark stadiums, widespread wilderness wildfires, and suicide bomb attacks in Jewish Synagogues all across America, all happening at the same time. These are just possible examples of what could someday occur in America.

National threats like electromagnetic pulse (EMP) attacks, tactical nuclear weapons explosions in high profile places, and suicide germ bombers are of grave concern to the DOHS. In July 2011, the New York Police Department (NYPD) began testing a new technology intended to detect and thwart "dirty bombs."[53] The NYPD established a command center in lower Manhattan to monitor 2,000 mobile radiation detectors carried by officers each day around the city. Each day NYPD officers carry radiation detectors! That is a troubling reality.

Subsequently, during the weekend of the ten year anniversary of September 11, in September 2011, the NYPD was canvassing the streets of Times Square looking for cars containing potential dirty bombs. Fortunately, the credible Al-Qaeda terror threat they were acting upon turned out to be a false alert.[54]

Imagine several dozen imbedded jihadist cells intentionally infected with some incurable germ virus, roaming about densely populated city streets, purposing to create a widespread apocalyptic plague. These suicidal maniacs don't particularly care what poison they pick as long as it transports them to Jannah, the Muslim heaven, upon death. According to their misguided thinking, the more death and destruction they cause, the greater assurance they have of being received by Allah.

This type of plague campaign could be carried on undetected until it's too late, and hundreds of thousands of Americans are quarantined across the United States. Remember the H1N1 influenza virus scare, also called the "Swine Flu," in 2009? The US Centers for Disease Control (CDC), and World Health Organization (WHO) both elevated it to be a public safety emergency of pandemic proportions.[55] The British government ordered 90 million swine flu vaccines as a precaution.[56] At that time it equated to more vaccinations than citizens in the UK.[57] In Japan, Japanese citizens donned facial protection, causing the Japanese Trend Shop to sell out of surgical masks.[58]

Although the swine flu threat has temporarily subsided, there are other deadly diseases like ebola, bubonic plague, cholera, and typhoid fever to be concerned with, just to name a few.[59] Deadly famines and pestilences occur in the end times, according to Revelation 6:8, 18:8, and Matthew 24:7. When, why, how, and where these biblical catastrophes occur, may or may not be related to a terrorizing germ war within America, but the prospect for such a terrorist-induced plague exists today. It is at least plausible to think that an attack on America could serve as a trigger for a chain-reaction around the globe, thus fulfilling the prophecies concerning last days' plagues.

America could again become a target of terror for several reasons:

- Islamic extremists call America's the Great Satan,

- America seems to slip from superpower status, according to the Bible, and

- America is already experiencing divine remedial judgments.

## Islamic Extremists Identify America as the Great Satan

America is commonly called the Great Satan by many Muslim leaders and clerics. The term, first coined by former Iranian Ayatollah Khomeini in a November 5, 1979, speech, has resonated throughout many Mideast and world mosques ever since.[60] American freedoms of worship, speech, woman's rights, and more stand in strict contrast to rigid Sharia laws in many Islamic countries. Additionally, our nation's support for Israel, who many Muslims identify as the "little Satan," further fuels fundamentalist Islamic hatred toward America.

The goal of Islam is to conquer the world. Muslim's are called to convert, subjugate, or destroy non-Muslims. The holy book of Islam, known as the Qur'an, instructs Muslims that they are not to wage war with unbelievers until they are first preached to. But, if then they don't convert, they are to be fought.[61]

Below are a couple of Islamic scriptures that express this truth:

"Slay the idolaters wherever ye find them, and take them captive, and besiege them, and prepare for them each ambush. But if they repent and establish worship and pay the poor-due, then leave their way free. Lo! Allah is Forgiving, Merciful." (Qur'an 9:5). The "poor-due" in this verse is *zakat*, which is one of the Five Pillars of Islam, and regulates religious tithes.

"Fight those who believe not in Allah nor the Last Day, nor hold that forbidden which hath been forbidden by Allah and His Messenger, nor acknowledge the religion of Truth, (even if they are) of the People of the Book, (Jews and Christians) until they pay the Jizya with willing submission, and feel themselves subdued" (Qur'an 9:29). The *jizya* was a tax inflicted upon non-believers.[62]

As long as Muslim extremists exist, employ tactics of terror, and consider America as Satan, Americans are subject to future terrorist attacks. Perhaps some devastating terror attack affects America, dethroning it from its superpower status.

## America Slips from Superpower Status, According to Bible Experts

Many Christian Americans are wondering if the United States can be identified in Bible prophecy. Seldom do my colleagues or I escape a question-and-answer session at a prophecy conference without being asked, "What is America's future according to prophecy?" This question is on the minds of many for three primary reasons:

- America is rapidly becoming less Christian,

- It's difficult to locate America in the Bible, and

- It's obvious that humanity is living in the last days.

When these three factors are all considered, one logically surmises that America's departure from the Lord in these last days brings forth divine judgment upon the United States, and that's why it's difficult to discover the USA in the Bible.

Fortunately, several respected prophetic voices have been burdened to research and write on this subject over the past couple years; Dr. Mark Hitchcock wrote *The Late Great United States*, Dr. David Reagan revised *America the Beautiful*, his third edition, and Terry James authored *The American Apocalypse*. All three books impart invaluable information related to the subject. I've had the privilege to interview each of these individuals over the radio about their books, and can report both good and bad news as a result.

The good news is that the three experts generally agree about America's future. Conversely, the bad news is that the news is not necessarily good for Americans. They all agree that America is hard to locate in the Bible, and if it is identified it's probably not represented as a superpower.

Presuming America can even be found in the Bible, why is the world's greatest ever super-power, the United States of America, hard to locate in Scripture? The Bible lists countries, cities, and locations throughout its pages; Israel is listed approximately 2,302 times. Even the tiny Gaza Strip area, which encompasses approximately 140 square miles, is listed about forty-four times under Gaza, Philistia, or the land of the Philistines. But, where is America? How many times is it listed in the Scriptures?

## *The Primary Views About America's Location in the Bible*

Listed below are some prevalent views suggesting America can be located in the Bible. America could be identified:

- as the unnamed nation of Isaiah 18,

- as the Babylon of Revelation 18:9-11,

- within the ten lost tribes of Israel,

- the great eagle of Revelation 12:13-17,

- amongst the young lions of Tarshish in Ezekiel 38:13, or

- within the Armageddon nations of Joel 3:2.

## America as the unnamed nation of Isaiah 18

> Woe to the land shadowed with *buzzing wings*, Which is *beyond the rivers* of Ethiopia, Which sends *ambassadors by sea*, Even in vessels of reed on the waters, saying, "Go, swift messengers, to a nation tall and smooth of skin, To *a people terrible* from their beginning onward, *A nation powerful* and treading down, *Whose land the rivers divide*." (Isaiah 18:1-2, NKJV; emphasis added.)

The buzz words causing some to consider America as this unnamed nation are, buzzing wings, beyond the rivers, ambassadors by sea, a people terrible, a nation powerful, land the rivers divide. The possible interpretations of these descriptions could be Americanized as follows:

- *Buzzing wings* – Advanced American commercial and military aircraft.

- *Beyond the rivers* (of Ethiopia) – America is far west of Ethiopia.

- *Ambassadors by sea* – Alludes to a great maritime and / or naval power, like America presently possesses. Because this armada floats on a sea beyond the rivers of Ethiopia, the Atlantic Ocean becomes a candidate for the sea described by Isaiah.

- *A people terrible* – Some translations, like the NASB and NIV, say "a people feared far and wide." America, as a superpower nation, is feared far and wide.

- *A nation powerful* – The United States military is ranked #1 in the world.

- *Whose land the rivers divide* – The United States has thousands of rivers; some say there are too many to count.

If only these two verses were considered when deciphering Isaiah 18, these above possible interpretations could identify America; however, contextually Isaiah 15-19 addresses burdens against regionally specific locations in the Middle East and Africa. Isaiah 15-16 is a burden against Moab (Jordan). Isaiah 17 is a burden against

Damascus, the capital of modern-day Syria. Isaiah 19 is concerned primarily with Egypt, and remotely with Israel and Assyria at the end of the chapter. Sandwiched in between is Isaiah 18 and the prophet appears to be addressing "Cush."

Cush, the son of Ham and grandson of Noah, settled west of the Red Sea. His descendants spread across the proximity of what are today the African countries of Egypt, Sudan, Ethiopia, and possibly Eritrea and Somalia. Therefore, imposing the name of America upon the unnamed nation of Isaiah 18 would appear to be a mistake.

## America as Babylon of Revelation 18:9-11

> The *kings of the earth* who *committed fornication* and *lived luxuriously* with her will weep and lament for her, when they see the *smoke of her burning*, *standing at a distance* for fear of her torment, saying, "Alas, alas, that *great city* Babylon, *that mighty city*! For in *one hour your judgment has come*." And the *merchants of the earth* will weep and mourn over her, for no one *buys their merchandise* anymore: (emphasis added)

This passage is filled with buzz-words likening end-times' Babylon to the United States of America. The theme is international commerce and the great city is supposedly New York, the iconic place of America's material abundance. Those advocating that America is identified in Revelation 18 have a field day with these verses, for a litany of reasons.

- Some suggest NYC because this American city is the central hub of global commerce.

- Babylon is represented as a "mighty city" similar to NYC.

- NYC is home to Wall Street and the World Trade Center (WTC).

- Babylon is a "harlot" in Revelation 17, and the Statue of Liberty in NYC is a *female*.

- When the WTC Twin Towers toppled, the "merchants of the earth mourned."

- The September 11th terrorist attacks suggested that "judgment" had come to America / Babylon.

- The towers toppled quickly, within "one hour" of each other.

- September 11 was a scene of "smoke" and "burning" witnessed by "standing at a distance."

To find America in Revelation 18 requires a lot of sensationalizing, as the list above demonstrates. Many mighty cities have come under siege over the past two millennia, since the apostle John inscribed this prophecy. In several instances, the same could have been thought about their disasters. For this and several other reasons it is difficult to conclude that the USA is identified as Babylon.

Revelation 18:11 concludes by saying "no one buys their merchandise anymore." Wall Street wasn't destroyed on September 11, 2011, and people are still buying and selling stocks and merchandise worldwide. Several remaining verses in Revelation 18 declare that Babylon's judgment is a permanent catastrophe.

Revelation 18:14 says all the materialism end-times Babylon characterizes can be found no more. Revelation 18:17 says all of her riches are brought to nothing. Revelation 18:19 says she is made desolate. Revelation 18:21 predicts that upon judgment, Babylon will not be found anymore. Revelation 18:23 says, "The light of a lamp shall not shine in you anymore, and the voice of bridegroom and bride shall not be heard in you anymore."

None of the declarations above can be said of New York City today. Additionally, Dr. Mark Hitchcock points out in the Late Great United States that Babylon appears about 265 times in the Bible by its actual or associated names, and almost always describes a literal location slightly west of the Euphrates in modern-day Iraq. The few exceptions are in Revelation 17 and in 1 Peter 5:13. In these instances it is believed Babylon represents Rome, rather than America.

## Within the ten lost tribes of Israel—(Anglo Israelism)

Some believe the ten lost tribes of Israel migrated throughout time into the UK and beyond into the USA. This theory is called British Israelism or Anglo Israelism. This hypothesis is rooted in the belief that the descendants of the ten Hebrew tribes of Reuben, Issachar, Zebulun, Dan, Naphtali, Gad, Asher, Ephraim, Manasseh, and Levi are primarily floundering about generally incognizant of their tribal identities in countries like America.

The brief background dates back to around 930 BC, when these ten tribes rejected Solomon's son Rehoboam as their king. They followed Jeroboam, who managed the laborers Solomon had conscripted for his huge building projects[63] instead, and in the process Israel became a divided kingdom. The split kingdom was generally identified as the northern kingdom of Israel, occupied by the ten tribes, and the southern kingdom of Judah, occupied by the remaining two tribes of Judah and Benjamin.

Both kingdoms were conquered at different intervals. Assyria conquered the northern kingdom in 722 BC, and Babylon conquered the southern kingdom around 586 BC. After the prophesied seventy years of Babylonian captivity, the tribes of Judah and Benjamin began making their way back into Israel.[64] However, tracking the migration of the ten tribes captured by the Assyrians has proven to be more difficult.

2,000 years ago, the Hebrews relied on handwritten records, rather than Facebook, to keep track of their tribal trees. These records were stored in the Jewish temple. In 70 AD, when the Romans destroyed the second Jewish temple, these important genealogical records were destroyed. Since there are no remaining accurate records readily available, the obvious conclusion the Anglo-Israelist draws is that America, being home to millions of Jews, must be where descendants of the ten lost tribes exist. Undoubtedly, there are Jews in America from an assortment of these ten tribes and genetic testing today is proving that.

A case in point is that of Bill Koenig, the founder of World Watch Daily. Recently Koenig, a red-blooded American citizen, discovered he was from the tribe of Levi. Bill recounted his story to me, how he was raised all his life thinking he was a Gentile, but his sudden love for Israel, after becoming a Christian, prompted him to trace his historical roots. Ultimately, Bill was genetically tested and found out that he wasn't a Gentile, but a Jew of Levite ancestry.

There are other Jews today finding themselves in Koenig's shoes. This is because at various points during the Diaspora, being a Jew was dangerously unpopular. For understandable reasons, many Jews shunned their natural identities over their 1,878 years of worldwide dispersion, between 70 – 1948 AD.

For instance, at the time of the Spanish Inquisition in the late 1400s, many Jews abandoned their heritages. They were coerced under duress to convert to Catholicism or be persecuted. Persecution often led to death or expulsion from Spain. Conversos and Marranos began springing up all over Spain. Conversos were true converts to Catholicism, but Marranos falsified their conversions. Some believe Christopher Columbus was a Jew, and that his three ships, the Pinta, Nina, and Santa Maria were filled with Jews attempting to flee persecution.[65]

During the Hitler holocaust, being a Jew in Europe turned out to be a death sentence for approximately six million Jews. It is believed that many Jews intentionally abandoned their heritage and became Gentile impostors, in order to escape Nazi extermination.[66]

The fact that Jews from the ten tribes of Israel may dwell in America, hardly clues us into America's future. Additionally, the ten tribes are not entirely lost, because passages like Ezra 7:7 tells us that many Levites migrated back to Israel after the Babylonian captivity. Furthermore, in the New Testament Luke 2:36 points out that the prophetess Anna was from the tribe of Asher. Also from the New Testament, it can be assumed that the assortment of Jews mentioned in the historical account of Acts 2 included members from the ten tribes.

Lastly, Revelation 7:1-8 informs us that the Lord has not lost track of the whereabouts of the ten tribes, as 12,000 members from each of those tribes show up in the end times among, the 144,000 Hebrew witnesses. However, the location of these ten tribes is not given, other than a clue that some angel from the "east" is instrumental in sealing these witnesses for service to the Lord. But typically, east is not a term identifying America, which exists far west of Israel today.

Although there are likely members from the ten tribes of Israel residing in America today, their identities are not entirely lost, and their existence in America does not preclude that the United States exists in the Bible. More importantly, identifying the whereabouts of these ten tribes hardly offers any invaluable insights into America's future.

## The Great Eagle of Revelation 12:13-17

Dr. David Reagan addresses this argument as follows:[67]

Another favorite passage for applied imagination is Revelation 12:13-17. These verses state that in the middle of the Tribulation God will provide a means of escape for the Jewish remnant in Israel. They will be carried into the wilderness to a hiding place on the "wings of a great eagle."

Some people have seized on this imagery to teach that the U.S., whose national symbol is the eagle, will supply the end time airlift that will save the Jewish remnant.

But the Bible is its own best interpreter. And when you look up the phrase, "wings of an eagle," you will find that it is the same one that God used in Exodus 19:4 to describe how He brought the Israelites out of Egypt. God is the eagle, not the United States (see Deuteronomy 32:11).

## Amongst the young lions of Tarshish, in Ezekiel 38:13

America appears to be identified in Bible prophecy as the young lions of Tarshish in Ezekiel 38:13. More and more respected eschatologists are beginning to believe Americans are these young lions. One of the best studies I have heard to date on this connection was delivered by Dr. David Hocking of Hope for Today Ministries. At the time, Dr. Hocking, Pastor Tom Hughes, and I were on a panel addressing questions about America in Bible prophecy on July 3, 2011. Hocking's teaching on the subject, and our overall program, can be viewed at this Internet link: http://www.ccsjonline. org/media/sunday-night/

Ezekiel 38:13 identifies a group of merchants of Tarshish and their young lions seemingly interested in conducting commerce with Israel. In stark contrast to Russia's coalition bent on wiping Israel off the map and confiscating great plunder, these merchants seemingly want to bless the Jewish State by participating in the spread of its prosperity. In my book called "*Revelation Road, Hope Beyond the Horizon,*" I point out how this may prove to be a positive development for America.

## Within the Armageddon nations of Joel 3:2

> For behold, in those days and at that time, when I bring back the captives of Judah and Jerusalem, I will also gather *all nations*, and bring them down to the Valley of Jehoshaphat; and I will enter into judgment with them there on account of My people, My heritage Israel, Whom they have scattered among the nations; they have also *divided up My land.* (Joel 3:1-2; emphasis added)

This passage says all nations existing on Earth at the time will be gathered for judgment in the Valley of Jehoshaphat. The judgment of all nations occurs at the end of the end times, in the Armageddon campaign, as per Revelation 16:14-16. As Joel 3:1-2 points out, the Jews will have been previously re-gathered from world nations, and those nations "have also divided up" God's land.

Since America is among all nations presently, the presumption is that America will be gathered alongside the other nations for judgment. The Jews are presently being re-gathered into Israel, and as pointed out in the commentary of chapter nine, The Final Arab – Israeli War, America is certainly guilty of attempting to pressure the Israelis to divide up their Promised Land.

## America Experiences Divine Remedial Judgments

One of the ways the Lord disciplines a nation is through remedial judgments, and giving them the political leadership they deserve. Israel's history is lined with good and bad kings that characterized the heart of the nation during their respective reigns. The goal of remedial judgments is to lead the affected nation to repentance and godliness. A classic historical example of this is found in the story of Nineveh. The prophet Jonah warned of Nineveh's imminent destruction, and it brought about a national repentance and a stay of execution for over 100 years, until the prophet Nahum proclaimed it subsequently.

Many end-times experts, including everyone mentioned in this chapter's commentary and myself, believe America is undergoing a period of remedial judgments.

Since the turn of the century several big events, like the terrorist attacks of September 11 (2001), three Mideast wars (Afghanistan, Iraq, and Libya), Hurricane Katrina and Rita (2005), the Mortgage Meltdown (2007), the collapse of major financial institutions (2008), the BP oil spill (2010), and record–breaking, Bible Belt tornado seasons (2011), Hurricane Sandy (2012), to name a few, have shaken the foundations of the United States. Additionally, political partisanship rose to an unprecedented high during the same periods.

Acts 17:26 declares the Lord establishes the times and boundaries of the nations. America appears to have been established for three primary purposes. First, as a Christian nation, America was established to become a beacon of Christianity for the nations.  Second, as a Christian nation, America was to become a safe-haven for the Jews during the Diaspora. Third, as a Christian nation, America was to be instrumental in the reestablishment of the nation Israel.

A careful tracking of history shows that America has fulfilled all three of its primary purposes. American Christian missionaries went forth into the nations and spread the gospel worldwide. Jews began arriving in America as far back as the 1600s, and more Jews ended up in America over time than anywhere else in the world. President Harry S. Truman was one of the primary world leaders used to reestablish the Jewish State in 1947-1948.

As a Christian nation, America accomplished all the above. However, in June, 2008, prior to being elected president of the United States, Barack Obama said the following about America's Christianity,

> "Whatever we once were, we're no longer a Christian nation. At least not just. We are also a Jewish nation, a Muslim nation, and a Buddhist nation, and a Hindu nation, and a nation of nonbelievers."[68]

Some pundits believe Barack Obama is the most anti-Israel, pro-abortion, and pro-homosexual president in American history. On January 20, 2009, did Americans inaugurate the president they deserved? One way to know is by honestly asking the following questions:

1. Has money become America's god?

2. Has greed become America's motivator?

3. Has America kicked God out of its schools?

4. Has America legalized abortion?

5. Has America become the moral polluter of the earth?

6.  Is America redefining the biblical meaning of marriage?

7.  Are American states beginning to approve of same-sex marriages?

If the honest answer to all the above questions is yes, then why wouldn't Americans be experiencing serious remedial judgments and receiving the rulers they deserve?

With respect to bullet number 6 above; below is a quote from the Huffington Post on the Internet, that evidences a dramatic shift in US policy regarded with marriage. It pertains to the Defense of Marriage Act (DOMA). DOMA defines marriage as the legal union of one man and one woman.[69]

> "In a major policy reversal, the Obama administration said Wednesday (February 23, 2011) it will no longer defend the constitutionality of a federal law banning recognition of same-sex marriage."

> "Attorney General Eric Holder said President Barack Obama has concluded that the administration cannot defend the federal law that defines marriage as only between a man and a woman. He noted that the congressional debate during passage of the Defense of Marriage Act 'contains numerous expressions reflecting moral disapproval of gays and lesbians and their intimate and family relationships—precisely the kind of stereotype-based thinking and animus the (Constitution's) Equal Protection Clause is designed to guard against.'"[70]

## The Bible defines marriage similar to DOMA.

> Therefore a man shall leave his father and mother and be joined to his wife, and they shall become one flesh. (Genesis 2:24)

This definition of marriage in the book of Genesis is confirmed by Christ, as in the gospel accounts of Matthew 19:5 and Mark 10:7, and elsewhere in the New Testament in Ephesians 5:31.

America has accomplished its three main purposes; and Israel is now in God's, not America's hands. Therefore, Americans need to repent of their immorality and stop pressuring Israel to divide its land. A fall from Christianity and failure to support Israel will evidence that America has stepped out of alignment with God's original intentions for the nation.

Two very famous historical figures echoed a timeless truth. First, about 2,000 years ago Jesus Christ said,

> If a kingdom is divided against itself, that kingdom cannot stand. And if a house is divided against itself, that house cannot stand. (Mark 3:24-25)

Subsequently on June 16, 1858, the then-Republican Senator Abraham Lincoln, thought to be a Christian, paraphrased Christ when he declared, "A house divided against itself cannot stand."

As it was during Lincoln's time, so it is again today in America; the nation is split over enslavement. Slaves to sin or bond-slaves to the Lord; that is the apropos question American Christians today must ask themselves.

America needs its own Nineveh moment and we are instructed in 2 Chronicles 7:14 how that can be brought about.

> If My people who are called by My name will humble themselves, and pray and seek My face, and turn from their wicked ways, then I will hear from heaven, and will forgive their sin and heal their land.

This passage states the Lord, not the politicians, possesses the ability to heal a nation's wounds. It declares the healing occurs as a direct result of God's people departing from wickedness in pursuit of godliness. Verses like this suggest American Christians can do more than call their congressman, or cast their vote at the ballot box; they can petition the Lord to respond favorably to their changed behavior.

However, on the flip-side, a country undergoing judgment beckons the question: why isn't God healing the land? Are His people pursuing wickedness rather than godliness?

## If Remedial Warnings Go Unheeded, Divine Judgment Results

The natural digression of God's interactions with a nation goes from blessings to remedial warnings, and finally to divine judgment if the warnings go unheeded. When a country finds favor with the Lord it is blessed, but when it falls from favor the nation undergoes disciplinary measures.

Since America is hard to locate in Bible prophecy, the possibility that America comes under divine judgment looms large. Dr. David Reagan points out in his book, and in his prophecy presentations about America, that several things could happen in a judgment sequence to the United States. Any one of the events listed below, or a combination of one or more, could occur as a form of judgment upon the nation.

- The rapture of the Christian church

- Economic collapse

- External nuclear attack, (including an electromagnetic pulse (EMP) attack)

- Internal terrorist attack

- Internal moral rot (Hedonism)

It is important to note that historically, dominant world empires usually fall from power within 200 to 250 years of their founding. At the time of the authoring of this book, America has existed for 236 years. Could the sun be about to set on America's superpower status? Is that why America is hard to find in the Bible?

# NINE

# America's Role in Psalm 83

**"Obama and Clinton to host Middle East peace talks in September"**

*USA Today 8/20/10*

**"Arabs reject Middle East peace talks without US plan"**

*BBC Middle East News 12/16/10*

*"Arab foreign ministers have rejected further Palestinian-Israeli peace talks without a "serious offer" from the US on ending the Middle East conflict."*

In August 2009, Prime Minister Netanyahu announced a ten-month settlement freeze on West Bank construction. It was approved and implemented on November 25, 2009. This good faith concession on Israel's part extended a favor to U.S. President Barack Obama, who like several of his presidential predecessors was pushing for a "two–state" Middle East peace plan between the Israelis and Palestinians. The Palestinians demanded, as a precondition to peace talks with Israel, a halt to construction of Jewish settlements within the West Bank. So as a good will gesture, Netanyahu complied.

Even though the Palestinians were generously granted their request, they neglected to seize the opportunity during the ten month period to begin peace talks with Israel. Likewise, neither did America because at the time President Obama, along with the U.S. Speaker of the House Nancy Pelosi, and Senate Majority Leader Harry Reid, were feverishly promoting their "Obamacare" health plan along with several other domestic policies, and jump starting peace negotiations between the Arabs and Jews apparently became a lesser priority.

As the freeze period neared its end, in a seeming act of desperation President Obama tried to jump start the peace talks by hosting several Middle East and world dignitaries in Washington on September 2, 2010. The list included Egypt's former president Hosni Mubarak, Israeli Prime Minister Benjamin Netanyahu, Palestinian Authority President Mahmoud Abbas, Former UK Prime Minister Tony Blair, and US Secretary of State Hillary Clinton. In the end analysis, this summit amounted to nothing more than an incomplete "Hail Mary pass," and the peace talks collapsed entirely before 2010 came to an end.

Subsequently, in lieu of direct peace talks with the Israelis, the Palestinians petitioned the United Nations for statehood. Their initial UN bid was vetoed by the United States, and from then, until the time of this book's publication, there is still no peace between the Israelis and the Palestinians. Moreover, considering that the Palestinians appear to be a lead member of Psalm 83, as the "tents of Edom," there probably won't be any peace treaty formed between them and Israel.

Why is America, among all the world nations, at the forefront of Mideast peace negotiations? One might think that France or the United Kingdom should assume the role as peace brokers considering that they were jointly sovereign over the area throughout the first half of the 20th Century after the fall of the Ottoman Empire in 1917. In spite of that, the mantle has clearly shifted to America, and as a result President Jimmy Carter brokered peace between Egypt and Israel in 1979, with President Bill Clinton following suit, negotiating peace between Jordan and Israel in 1994.

One probable reason that the Arabs and Jews look to America as the primary peace broker is because the United States is currently the world's greatest superpower nation, and one of the largest providers of foreign aid to both the Israelis and the Palestinians. Also, from Israel's perspective, the United States has historically been one of its greatest allies.

As pointed out in the chapter called "The Future for America in Bible Prophecy," the Lord has purposes for the establishment of the nations. This is specified in Acts 17:26 and elsewhere. America's world prominence was not achieved apart from the blessings of God, and therefore, America is beholding to God for its superpower accomplishments. Accordingly, the United States has been a beacon of Christianity to the world and a safe haven for the Jews. In fact; apart from Israel, there are presently more Jews residing in America than anywhere else in the world.

At least five million Jews live in the United States which is over ten times the amount of the next most populated nation of Jews, which is France. By estimated comparison, France has 483,500, Canada around 375,000, the UK about 292,000, followed by Russia with approximately 205,000.[71] Moreover, America was instrumental in the establishment of the nation of Israel on May 14, 1948 and has been the strongest supporter of Israel in the United Nations ever since.

As stated in the previous chapter, America, as generally viewed by much of the Arab and Muslim world, is so connected to Israel that former Ayatollah Khomeini called Israel 'the Little Satan,' and America 'the Great Satan' in 1979. These negative labels have been quoted by many Muslims ever since. The seeming inseparable bond between Israel and America is also the reason in September of 2012 that Egyptian President Mohammad Morsi suggested that Israel is responsible for much of the hatred of Washington in the Arab world. He also compared Egypt's obligation to Israel with America's obligation to the Palestinians.

When Morsi was asked about Egypt's peace treaty with Israel he made the following comments;

> "The US has "a special responsibility" to the Palestinians rooted in Washington's signing of the 1979 peace agreement between Israel and Egypt...Washington should help establish a Palestinian state in order to overcome anger directed towards it in the Arab world.... As long as peace and justice are not fulfilled for the Palestinians, then the [Camp David] treaty remains unfulfilled."[72]

## America Shoulders Great Responsibility in Psalm 83

The point was previously made, that the Lord has purposes for the nations and Christ said in Luke 12:48, "....For everyone to whom much is given, from him much will be required; and to whom much has been committed, of him they will ask the more." Unquestionably, America has been given much, and as such bears a proportional responsibility in the scheme of God's end times plan.

As pointed out throughout various points of this book, this divine plan includes the survival of the Jewish state of Israel. The Psalm 83 Arab confederacy clearly seeks to destroy the Jewish state and banish the name of Israel forever. This is problematic for Israelis and Arabs, but also for Americans.

For obvious reasons it's bad for the Israelis, but the reason it's bad for the Arabs is spelled out in Genesis 12:3. Attempting to destroy the Jews will provoke the Lord to curse the Arabs populations participating in Psalm 83. This chapter has already demonstrated the importance of the symbiotic relationship between Israel and

America, but understanding America's responsibility in relationship to the Psalm 83 war is explained below.

Neither the Psalm nor the related prophecies pointed out in this book concerning the Psalm; seem to identify America directly with the prophecy. However, the case will be made for America's indirect obligations, because of its superpower status, to continue as the staunchest supporter of Israel. The comparison between the United Kingdom's responsibilities in the reestablishment of Israel, to the United States duty toward Israel in the Psalm 83 war is posited below.

## Psalm 83—A Prophecy In Process

A Google search of "The Psalm 83 prophecy" on March 31, 2012 displayed 1,380,000 results. Another Google search on the same day under "The Psalm 83 war," uncovered 2,460,000 results. These numbers reflect approximately fifty-times as many results than there were in the same month 4 years prior. I recall that, because in 2008 when my book, *Isralestine the Ancient Blueprints of the Future Middle East* was published, I had attempted to find research over the Internet on these two subjects.

Psalm 83 is the central theme of *Isralestine*, and frankly, Internet research in these areas during that time was generally fruitless, which is one primary reason why the book unwittingly turned into an eight-year project, requiring countless hours of biblical study and extra-biblical historical research. At the time, most of the respected existing commentaries on the Psalm 83 war offered little more than poetic expositions. Fortunately, Dr. Arnold Fruchtenbaum, David Dolan, and Jack Kelley had previously written summarily about the prophetic possibilities of the Psalm, which presented me with some helpful insights.

So what is all the hype about Psalm 83? Why did the Google results increase exponentially over the past four years, from thousands to millions? I believe the increased numbers reflected a growing interest in the timely prophetic implications of the Psalm; especially after the Arab Spring that dominated much of the news in 2011.

Interestingly, some scholars suggest that Psalm 83 is simply an imprecatory prayer of lament concerning Israel's Arab enemies throughout time immemorial. Others like me believe it is a bona fide Bible prophecy. In the chapter called "Psalm 83 and the Prophets," and in an Internet article called "Psalm 83, What IT IS, and What it IS NOT," I attempt to dispel the possibility that the Psalm is merely a prayer. This article can be read at this Internet link: http://www.prophecydepot.net/2012/psalm-83-what-it-is-and-what-it-is-not-part-one/

The article, like this book, explains that the Psalm speaks about an Arab confederacy that forms for the explicit purposes of destroying Israel, and dispossessing the chosen people from their Promised Land, once and for all. If it is an imminent prophecy, this implies that the confederacy fights to destroy Israel, in order to replace it with one more Middle East Arab state, called Palestine.

Presuming the Psalm is indeed a prophecy as hypothesized in this book, there are diverse opinions among prophecy experts about the Psalm's timing. Some teach the prophecy was fulfilled historically in 2 Chronicles 20. This is generally a minority view that is refuted in the appendix called "Psalm 83—Has It Found Final Fulfillment?" Another minority view holds to the thinking that Psalm 83 occurs during Ezekiel 38. This argument is debated in the chapter called "Psalm 83 or Ezekiel 38: What's the Next Middle East News Headline?"

A final timeline argument is that the Psalm occurs during the final seven-year tribulation period. One of my favorite eschatologists, Dr. Arnold Fruchtenbaum, once held this view as expressed in his Footsteps of the Messiah book.[73] Dr. Fruchtenbaum, who also believes Psalm 83 is a prophecy, has seemingly reconsidered this view for the general reasons that are explained in my Internet article called "Is Psalm 83 a Great Tribulation Event." This article can be read at this Internet link:

*http://prophecydepot.blogspot.com/2009/12/is-psalm-83-great-tribulation-event. html*

In my estimation one nearby morning the world will wake to the world-changing Mideast war described in Psalm 83. The Psalm specified that six primary things needed to be in place before the major Middle East battle could begin.


1.   Israelis (Psalm 83:3),

2.   The Nation of Israel (Psalm 83:4, 12),

3.   An Israeli Defense Forces; the IDF (Psalm 83:9-11),

4.   Palestinian Refugees; i.e. *the tents of Edom* (Psalm 83:6),

5.   An Arab League (Psalm 83:6-8),

6.   An Arab Hatred of Israelis (Psalm 83:3).


Presently all six of these prerequisites are in place. Israelis became a reality when Israel was reborn as a nation on May 14, 1948. As evidenced by the Arab – Israeli wars of 1948, 1956, 1967, and 1973, the Hezbollah-Israel conflict of 2006, and the Hamas-Israel confrontation in 2009, an Arab hatred has been displayed ever since the Jewish state was reconceived.

The Palestinian refugees became a reality in the aftermath of the Israeli war of independence in 1948, as did the IDF that promptly formed to fight off the Arab aggression. With each subsequent war the IDF became a stronger army, apparently in fulfillment of Ezekiel 25:14, 37:10, and Obadiah 1:18.

Lastly, the Arab League was established in Cairo on March 22, 1945 before all the conflicts began. The Arab League includes each member identified within the Arab confederacy of Psalm 83. Apart from fragile peace treaties between Israel and Egypt, and Israel and Jordan, the Psalm prophecy, essentially, appears to be on the verge of fulfillment.

Many pundits believe that the Muslim Brotherhood leadership now dominant in Egypt will soon abrogate the 33 year old peace agreement with Israel. Should Egypt break peace with Israel, there are few that believe Jordan will covet the lone-wolf position of being the only remaining Arab state that possesses a peace accord with Israel. The legitimate concern is reflected in the adage; "As goes Egypt, so goes the rest of the Middle East."

Lacking a substantial peace accord with the most populated Arab state; Egypt, and one of the most moderate ones; Jordan, there is little that prevents Psalm 83 from finding fulfillment.

Similarly, as the rebirth of Israel was a prophecy in process, so is Psalm 83. On May 14, 1948 the world awoke to a new Jewish state, and avid Bible prophecy students shouldn't have been surprised about it at the time. Numerous prophecies like the ones listed below, all came to fruition on that infamous day.

- Ezekiel 36:22-24 – foretold that the Jews would be in spiritual unbelief at the time. It anticipated that world Jewry at large would be characterized by the same religious indifference that had overtaken their forefathers when the Diaspora began in 70 AD.

- Ezekiel 37:11-13 – predicted the Jews would come out of a holocaust scenario; *"Our bones are dry, our hope is lost, and we ourselves are cut off!"* (Ezek. 37:11).

- Isaiah 11:11 – informed that the Lord would regather the Jews into Israel from the nations a second time, there are no third, fourth, or fifth times found in scripture alerting that Israel today fulfills this prophecy. (Some believe this regathering has two phases; in unbelief, followed by belief. Thus, they tend to believe that the first phase is being fulfilled today, and the second phase is fulfilled by a faithful Jewish remnant at the end of the 7-year tribulation period).

- Ezekiel 38:8 – foretells that the regathering takes place in the "latter years," which is one reason why many eschatologists consider Israel as the super-sign of the end times.

- Ezekiel 39:21-29 – explains the rationale from the Lord's perspective of the Diaspora and the regathering of the Jews into Israel in the latter years.

These are just a few of the prophecies that predicted that someday the Jews would be regathered out of the nations of the world, to return back into their ancient homeland of Israel in the end times.

The process toward prophetic fulfillment of the rebirth of the nation Israel generally began around 1896 when Theodor Herzl published his book Der Judenstaat (Jewish State in German). He is considered to be the father of political Zionism. Herzl recognized that Anti-Semitism was rising throughout the world, and especially in Europe. He believed the only way the Jews could escape mounting world persecution was to, once again, have their own homeland.

Below is an interesting quote from his diary issued in 1897.

> "At Basle, I founded the Jewish State. If I said this out loud today, I would be answered by universal laughter. If not in 5 years, certainly in 50, everyone will know it."[74]

Dying approximately 7 years after writing this statement, he didn't realize how prophetic it was. Exactly 50 years later the United Nations passed resolution 181 in 1947, which called for the establishment of the Jewish state. Christians should have anticipated that Israel was about to become a nation by the start of the Zionist movement.

World War I was the next tip off that the nation Israel was about to be birthed. In the aftermath of the war, Lord Balfour of Britain issued a declaration calling for the establishment of a Jewish state in 1917. At the time Israel was appropriated land that would have encompassed modern-day Israel and Jordan. This land was well within the territory granted to the Jews through their patriarchal father Abraham, about four-thousand years ago, in Genesis 15:18. Britain had full license to implement this declaration, but failed to do so.

Britain's failure to act in accordance with what appears to have been God's explicit will, subjected the Jews to the atrocities of the holocaust, and apparently caused the imminent collapse of the British Empire. At the time there was a saying that "The Sun Never Sets on the British Empire," but today the sun always sets on the British Empire!

This is because, over the course of the following 7 decades, Britain relinquished sovereignty over almost all of its colonized territories. Presently, about 50 million people populate England and 62 million in the UK, in total.[75] There are about 20 million more Arabs living in Egypt than there are citizens of the UK. Compare these numbers to the British Empire during its heyday.

> "By 1922 the British Empire held sway over about 458 million people, one-fifth of the world's population at the time, and covered more than 33,700,000 km (13,012,000 sq. miles), almost a quarter of the Earth's total land area."[76]

Due to Britain's superpower status at the time, it had a proportionate responsibility in executing the plan of God. The reestablishment of Israel was at the center of that plan during the time of the British Empire reign. Britain's demise can likely be attributed corporately to the clause contained in Genesis 12:3 that curses those who curse the descendants of Abraham, Isaac, and Jacob. Again, Christians should have recognized, after World War I, that Israel would soon become reinstated as the Jewish state. Unfortunately today, the preponderance of Christianity in the UK is plagued by "Replacement Theology."

This erroneous theology, also called "Supersessionism," is the belief that the Lord is done with the Jew. This view presupposes that, because the Jewish leadership rejected Christ as the Messiah during His first advent, that the Lord has officially rejected the Jews. This theology generally advocates that all the unfulfilled prophecies and promises to Abraham's, Isaac's, and Jacob's direct Jewish descendants, have been forfeited over to the Christian Church. In essence, the Church has replaced Israel; theoretically it has become the new Israel. The problem with this view is that these promises were unconditionally granted to these Jewish patriarchs, and therefore, they cannot be abrogated from the Jews.

World War II was the final clue to the prophecy onlooker, that Israel was about to be rebirthed. As stated above, the UN General Assembly approved the Jewish State on November 29, 1947. With 33 yes votes, 13 no votes, and 10 abstentions the Jewish state was a done deal, and on May 14, 1948 the prophecies predicting the coming of Israel were fulfilled.

Guess what nations were among the 13 that voted no to UN resolution 181? They were most of the Psalm 83 nations; Lebanon, Saudi Arabia, Iraq, Syria, and Egypt. Hezbollah, Hamas, and the Palestinian refugees hadn't been created at the time to oppose the resolution, and Jordan didn't become an admitted UN member until December, 1955. Thus, Jordan's would-be no vote was unable to be counted!

Similar to the prophecies concerning the rebirth of Israel, Psalm 83 appears to be a prophecy in progress. Someday soon it will arrive; but for those of us who have been paying attention to the stage-setting signs, we realize that the Psalm prophecy has been over six decades in the making, and appears to be poised to happen soon!

In light of all the above clues, American's should recognize that the sun is beginning to set on the superpower status of the United States. The remedial judgments presented in the chapter called "The Future for America in Bible Prophecy," reinforce this reality. The modern day precedent for the decline of a superpower was established through the British Empire. Over the past two prior decades, American leadership has been cursing Israelis inadvertently, by forcing their leadership to trade God's land for Arab peace. This diplomacy is not working, and is the very thing that Joel 3:2 warns against; dividing God's land!

If America continues to travel down the political slippery slope of pressuring Israel to forfeit land for illusive peace, it flirts with the same fate of its British ally. The rise of the United States to superpower status seems to directly correlate with the severe decline of the British Empire. Not surprisingly, replacement theology in America is also on the increase. This is why American political leaders need to stop attempting to divide the Promised Land, and to staunchly support our best ally in the Middle East, Israel!

American attempts to shrink the size of Israel works against Israel's critical ability to defend itself. The Psalm 83 prophecy is currently in process, and one nearby morning the world will awake to missiles flying throughout the Middle East and the fulfillment of the Psalm 83 war.

## What is the U.S. Response to Psalm 83?

Thus far America's obligation to be Israel's stalwart shoulder of support has been explained, but what will America do when Psalm 83 finally finds fulfillment? If Psalm 83 is as imminent as it appears, then it would seem reasonably safe to presume that the U.S.A. would be drawn into the fray. But, is there any scriptural support for including America or any other nations in this Arab–Israeli war? The fact is, Psalm 83 doesn't specifically say, and in some respects seems to suggest otherwise.

Psalm 83:9-11 draws our attention to the historical battles in Judges 4–8. These ancient biblical accounts provide important clues about how the Lord intends to deal with the Arab confederacy of Psalm 83. Judges, chapters 6-8, inform us that the Midianites had oppressed the Israelites for seven years. Outmanned and outgunned by 400 to 1, Gideon took 300 warriors and destroyed 120,000 Midianites.[77] It appears as though no Israeli casualties resulted from Gideon's war against the Midianites. Furthermore, it doesn't seem that the Midianites ever oppressed the Israelites again.

The same holds true in the Israelite-Canaanite war described in Judges 4-5. The Canaanites oppressed the Israelites for twenty years. Subsequently, the Canaanites suffered a bitter defeat by Barak and the "IDF" of that time. There are no mentions of Israeli casualties of war reported as a result of that conflict either, nor are there any indications whether the Canaanites ever oppressed the Israelites again.

In both examples, the Israelites were operating under divine empowerment and protection. Additionally, both enemies of Israel were defeated from top to bottom. Even their kings, nobles, and princes were killed alongside their soldiers. Importantly, these particular enemies ceased to ever oppress the Israelites or their Promised Land again. The fact that the surrounding Arab countries and terrorist populations continue to oppress the Israelis strongly suggests that Psalm 83 has not found final fulfillment.

These Israeli military victories, which occurred only a century or two prior to the Psalmist's time, would certainly both be most memorable and logical events for Asaph to remind the Lord of concerning Psalm 83. But, even though Gideon's defeat of the Midianites and Barak's conquest of the Canaanites were miraculous accomplishments for the IDF of those days, they were not a single-handed, divine victory like when Pharaoh's army was swallowed up in the converging waters of the Red Sea.

Curiously, Asaph did not petition the Lord to defeat the Psalm 83 Arab confederacy similarly to the Egyptian army. Why not? The exodus episode was exemplary, because the defeat of Pharaoh's army at the time was by far Israel's most remarkable historical survival episode up to that point. Moreover, supernatural single-handed divine victories by the Lord are still forthcoming according to prophecies in Ezekiel 38:18–39:6 and Isaiah 63:1-6.

By petitioning the Lord to defeat the Psalm 83 Arab confederacy in the historical methods inscribed in Judges 4-8, Asaph is encouraging the divine empowerment of the IDF to victory. This is exactly what occurred in these epic Midianite and Canaanite battles. There was no IDF in existence at the time of the Exodus, but during the time of Judges there was, and today Israel possesses the number 10 world-ranked army. It has become a great army as a result of the various Arab – Israeli wars and regional skirmishes. Ezekiel 37:10 predicts it will become more than just a great army, but an "exceedingly great army."

Barring one exception, the Midianite and Canaanite wars of Judges 4-8 were waged exclusively by the IDF, without foreign military support. Jael, the wife of Heber the Kenite assisted Barack's IDF by assassinating the Canaanite General Sisera. The Kenites were a nomadic tribe that primarily resided in the southeastern hill country of Judah.[78]

> "Then Jael, Heber's wife, took a tent peg and took a hammer in her hand, and went softly to him and drove the peg into his temple, and it went down into the ground; for he was fast asleep and weary. So he died." (Judges 4:21, NKJV).

This one exception may scripturally suggest that there is some foreign military intervention in Psalm 83, but the preponderance of connecting prophecies included in this book, like Ezekiel 25:14, Obadiah 1:18, and Zephaniah 2:9, point to the IDF as the primary instrument utilized to defeat the Psalm 83 Arab confederacy. This was similarly the case in the Arab – Israeli wars of 1948, 1967, and 1973. In all of these wars the IDF had nominal foreign support, but still reigned victorious.

Presently, the Arabs oppress the Jews and want to dispossess them of their Promised Land. Ultimately, they will confederate in a final attempt to wipe Israel off the map. They will lose decisively, and like the Midianites and Canaanites, become incapable of ever oppressing Israel again. The inability of the surrounding Arab countries and terrorist populations to further oppress Israel, will indicate that the Psalm 83 prophecy has found final fulfillment.

## America's Lesson from Psalm 83

The defeat by the IDF of the Psalm 83 War would not only fulfill many of the prophecies included in this book, like the accolade of becoming an exceedingly great army, but would also demonstrate to the international community that the Lord's Gentile foreign policy spelled out in Genesis 12:3 is still operable.

The Psalm predicts that the Arabs confederate to cut the nation off, so that the name of Israel is forgotten forever. The only logical way this could be accomplished is militarily rather than politically. The Arabs confederate militarily to destroy the Jewish state, but in retaliation the IDF defeats the Arabs. This is why Psalm 83:9-11 petitions the Lord to defeat the confederacy by empowering the IDF.

The Arab attempt to curse the Jews militarily in the Psalm, boomerangs back and curses the Arab's militaries. This is a curse-for-curse-in-kind response that is part of Genesis 12:3. It is similar to when Pharaoh's army wanted to curse the Hebrews at the Red Sea during their Exodus from Egypt, but instead the Egyptian army was cursed by the converging waters of the Red Sea. Another example is when the Persian Haman wanted the Jew Mordecai hung at the gallows, but in reversal, Haman was hung at those gallows according to Esther 8:7.

The take-away lesson to America and the world in the aftermath of Psalm 83, as alluded to in the chapter called the "The Final Palestinian Farewell," is worth repeating here;

"The execution of tremendous fury and vengeance against the Palestinians, leaving none to carry on the lineage of Esau, will demonstrate to the world that if God did not spare the descendants of Jacob's own twin brother Esau, then any who seek to bring harm to the Jewish people will not escape the curse-for-curse-in-kind clause."

For more information I have a teaching video on this subject that can be viewed at this Internet link: *http://www.prophecydepot.net/2012/2012-nuclear-middle-east/*

# TEN

# Isralestine—God's Middle East Peace Plan

**"Obama Speech Backlash on Call to Reinstate 1967 Mideast Borders"**

*ABC News 5/19/11*

*"The United States believes that negotiations should result in two states, with permanent Palestinian borders with Israel, Jordan, and Egypt, and permanent Israeli borders with Palestine. The borders of Israel and Palestine should be based on the 1967 lines with mutually agreed swaps, so that secure and recognized borders are established for both states."* (President Barack Obama)

**"Netanyahu Rejects Obama's 1967 Border Proposal"**

*Fox Nation News 5/20/11*

*I*sralestine is a new word construct that was coined by the author, and was first used in his book of the same name, *Isralestine, The Ancient Blueprints of the Future Middle East*. Throughout the book, it is utilized in multiple ways to define present and future geopolitical concepts. Its usage in this chapter title is intended to illustrate the return of the Jewish people into the land of Palestine in fulfillment of biblical prophecy.

The ancient name of the territory was Israel; Palestine became a superseding name imposed upon the land by the Romans in 135 AD. Therefore, the Jewish State of Israel became re-established on land formerly recognized as Palestine. *Isralestine* merges the terms Israel and Palestine in an attempt to give the reader further insight into the subject matter of this chapter.

Since Israel became a nation on May, 14, 1948, the international community has been unable to resolve the ongoing conflict between Israel and the Palestinian refugees. The Palestinians and the Arab states that share common borders with the Jewish state, want Israel to trade land for peace. Most of the international community favors this idea, but Israel justifiably refuses to forfeit land because of legitimate concerns that it would make its national borders indefensible. This standoff will likely remain in a deadlock indefinitely, and it is not biblically supported.

We gain insight from Jeremiah that God already has His own Middle East peace plan in place. Over 2,500 years ago, God informed the Hebrew prophet that at the appointed time, the Jews would be re-established in the land of ancient Israel, regardless of how their Arab and Persian partners in the neighborhood feel about the matter. This chapter introduces God's Middle East peace plan issued in Jeremiah 12:14-17, but beforehand, reminds the reader that the existence of Israel today is a modern day miracle!

## *Israel, God's Modern-Day Miracle*

In fact, in this author's estimation, Israel's existence today is a greater miracle than the parting of the Red Sea during the Hebrew exodus from Egypt, for the reasons listed below. Certainly, parting the waters of the Red Sea long enough for an estimated two-million Hebrew refugees to pass through on dry ground, is no minor undertaking. In fact, no one has been able to accomplish such a miraculous feat since, but in order for Israel to exist today, the Lord had to:

- Destroy the Ottoman Empire, which ruled over the Mideast from 1517 to 1917. This occurred during World War I, when the Entente Powers of Russia, France, and the UK defeated the Central Powers consisting of the Ottoman, German, and Hungarian empires.

- Create a Zionistic inclination in Jews scattered worldwide. This began in the late nineteenth century, around the time Theodor Herzl published his book *Der Judenstaat,* the Jewish State in German in 1896. (Zionism is defined in the chapter called, "The Psalm 83 Report").

- Defeat the Nazi regime which attempted Jewish genocide in order to prevent the return of the Jews to their ancient homeland of Israel.

- Unite and empower the Allied Forces of the British Empire, the Union of Soviet Socialist Republic and the United States of America to stop Hitler's holocaust attempt.

- Reestablish the Arab and Persian States in order for many Arabs and Persians to vacate out of Israel: Afghanistan (1919), Egypt (1922), Saudi Arabia and Iraq (1932), Iran (1935), Lebanon (1943), and Syrian and Jordan (1946).

- Move the United Nations to legislate and approve the "Partition Plan of 1947," which called for the reestablishment of the Jewish State, so Jews could have a homeland again.

- Create and empower the Israel Defense Forces so that the Jews could survive Arab attempts in 1948, 1967, and 1973 to destroy the reestablished Jewish State.

- Preserve and prosper Israel, since the future Israel described in Ezekiel 38:8-13 turns out to be a very secure and prosperous Israel.

None of these eight sovereign achievements above could have been accomplished singlehandedly by the United Nations. They all required the Lord's divine providence in order for the Jewish state to exist today. As amazing as this miracle is, the preponderance of humanity, including many Christians, believe that the exisitance of Israel today is nothing more than the result of a UN moral obligation after the holocaust. They don't see God's conspicuous fingerprints all over the rebirth of the Jewish state. Several of the Bible prophecies pertaining to the regathering of the Jews into a rebirthed nation of Israel are contained in the chapter called, "America's Role in Psalm 83."

It's only fitting that Jeremiah would declare the following about the miracle of Israel today, considering that he is the prophet that issued God's Middle East peace plan.

> "Therefore behold, the days are coming," says the LORD, "that it shall no more be said, 'The LORD lives who brought up the children of Israel from the land of Egypt,' but, 'The LORD lives who brought up the children of Israel from the land of the north and from all the lands where He had driven them.' For I will bring them back into their land which I gave to their fathers. (Jer. 16:14-15, NKJV; emphasis added).

As you read the remainder of this chapter be duly informed, that in the end analysis, Israel will survive the coming Mideast wars of Psalm 83 and Ezekiel 38 according to Obadiah.

> "But on Mount Zion there shall be deliverance, And there shall be holiness; The house of Jacob [Israel] shall possess their possessions." (Obadiah 1:17, NKJV).

## The Isralestine Peace Plan

"Thus says the LORD: "Against all *My evil neighbors* who touch the inheritance which I have caused My people Israel to inherit—behold, *I will pluck them* [the Arabs] *out* of their [the Jews] land [Israel] and pluck out the house of Judah from among them [the surrounding Arab nations]. Then it shall be, after I have plucked them out, that I will return and have compassion on them and bring them back, everyone to his heritage and everyone [Jew and Arab] to his [respective] land. And it shall be, if they [the resettled Arabs] will learn carefully the ways of My people, to swear by My name, 'As the LORD lives,' as they taught My people to swear by Baal, then they shall be established in the midst of My people. But if they do not obey, I will utterly pluck up and destroy that nation," says the LORD." (Jer. 12:14–17, NKJV; emphasis added).

God proposes His own compassionate, peaceful sovereign solution to the potential regional problem of the return of the Jews into the Holy Land. He would cause the corridors to be open for the Arabs to leave the land destined to become the Jewish state and return to the lands of their ancestry. In addition, He would resettle the Jews out of the surrounding Arab nations, and bring the Jews back into their homeland Israel. As each ethnic group migrated they would vacate homes and jobs enabling the returning peoples economic opportunities, and in some cases already existing communities to inhabit. It had the makings of a perfect *Isralestine* plan.

These passages represent ancient blueprints, divinely designed to insure the successful return of the Jewish people back to the land of their heritage. God's Mideast peace plan took into consideration that there would be "evil neighbors" homesteading the holy land. He foreknew they would have to be relocated to make way for the return of the Jewish people. For the Jews it meant a regathering into a rebirthed nation called Israel. For the Arabs living in the new Israel, it meant a departure from from that land into their ancient homelands, and an abandonment of the term Palestine forever.

The Middle East conflict that confounds politicians today has not caught God off guard. Provisions were included in Jeremiah's prophecy for their future as well. They would be "plucked out" and escorted back to the lands of their ancestry. A fertile future awaited them, if they entreated their affections to Jehovah, the God of the Jews, and Architect of this Isralestine plan.

In apparent fulfillment of the Jeremiah 12:14–17 prophecy, there are millions of Arabs "plucked out" from the territory formerly recognized as Palestine. For over six decades, these uprooted Arabs have been unable to relocate to an alternative homeland. They have been reduced to refugee status because their Arab relatives have shut their national doors to them. These refugees remain strategically deployed by their Arab partners close to the borders of Israel.

These Arab nations have cleverly managed to shift the burden of responsibility for the relocation of these refugees into the lap of the international community—the same community that legislated the re-establishment of the nation Israel as the Jewish State, implemented in 1948. UNRWA, the United Nations Relief and Works Agency, was established May 1, 1950, to find a solution to the refugee problem. By not taking responsibility for absorbing Palestinian refugees into their societies, these Arab nations are in severe breach of God's Mideast peace plan. They have decided against worshipping Jeremiah's God, and implementing the ancient blueprints, specifically designed for the political architects of our time. This is a terrible mistake, which we will discuss at the conclusion of this chapter.

## Was There Divine International Intervention?

As we review the events leading to the restoration of the nation Israel, we see that the Lord implemented international efforts to facilitate this divine program. Shortly after the conclusion of World War I, the Middle East changed. In succession Egypt, Saudi Arabia, Iraq, Lebanon, and Syria, all received their independence after four hundred years of Turkish domination between 1517-1917. This began to pave the way for the return of Arab peoples back to their ancestral homelands.

Additionally, the League of Nations drafted the Balfour document in 1917. This document in its original draft referenced Palestine as the intended location for the re-establishment of the Jewish State. It conceded land east and west of the Jordan River for this specific purpose. This land mass represented all of modern-day Israel, and Jordan. This document would enable the Jewish people to come out of the neighboring nations and resettle into their own state. It appeared as though the world was unknowingly reorganizing the Middle East in fulfillment of Jeremiah's prophecy.

However, certain influential Arabs, due to their relationship with Britain, were able to convince the British to act unilaterally to separate the land east of the Jordan River out of the Jewish state and to place it into Arab sovereignty. In 1922, the land east of the Jordan River came to be called Transjordan, and fell under Arab rule. Britain relinquished its control over Transjordan on March 22, 1946. Today, we call Transjordan the Arab nation of Jordan.

Palestine, which in 1917 was to include approximately 46,000 square miles extending from the Mediterranean Sea on the West, Eastward to Iraq, and was intended to be the entire Jewish state as per the Balfour Document, fell to less than 9,000 square miles. It included only the land west of the Jordan River. The divine consequences of Britain's failure to implement the Balfour Declaration are discussed in the chapter called "America's Role in Psalm 83." This chapter reminds the reader that Britain is no longer a dominant world empire.

Then in 1947, United Nations General Assembly approved Resolution 181, which called for the establishment of a Jewish State. This "Partition Plan," was intended to establish the small notch of unclaimed land west of the Jordan River, into two co-existing states. They drafted it as a Two-State Solution intended to allow the Arabs and Jews to co-exist peacefully in their ancestral lands.

By May 14, 1948, when the Jewish state officially arrived, what was left of the approximately 46,000 square miles designed for them as per the international community back in 1917, was a meager small notch of land. Immediately in 1948, the nations of Egypt, Jordan, Syria, Lebanon, and Iraq attacked the tiny Jewish state. As such, they evidenced their true title given in the Jeremiah 12:14 prophecy "My evil neighbors."

The Arab disposition caused a suspension in the divine compassionate peaceful political approach, and forced God's military plan into effect. Still, the prophetic plan moved forward as the attackers instructed those Arabs residing within the tiny Jewish state to vacate temporarily, while their militaries could destroy the newly forming nation.

At the same time, the Jews in Arab lands were forced out of their jobs, homes and communities, leaving them no choice but to resettle in their ancient homeland Israel. Hence, the "pluck-out" process began, as the evil neighbors were routed out of Israel, and the Jews were uprooted from their century-old communities established in the neighboring Arab lands.

As we know, the Jewish state was not destroyed and, therefore, it became the burden of those neighboring Arab nations to assimilate these refugees into their lands. Henceforth, and continuing today, is the Palestinian refugee problem. Unlike the unsettled Arab crisis, which has burdened the United Nations for over six decades, the Jewish refugees have been welcomed and absorbed into Israeli society.

Even still God stated through Jeremiah that if these Arabs would "swear by My name," that they would "be established in the midst of My people." However, on the flip side, "if they do not obey," God "will utterly pluck up and destroy that nation." In other words, a peaceful co-existence could still occur in the region if these Arab nations would comply with God's holy program. But if they persist as "evil neighbors," they will provoke upon themselves their own destruction.

The use by Jeremiah of the words "pluck out," and "evil neighbors" gave prior indication that the resettling process would not be a cooperative effort. The Hebrew word for "pluck out" is nathash and its primary scriptural usages point to an involuntary uprooting of a people out of a land. Thus, we see that a two state solution is not a new concept. However, as time elapses and the ruins of Israel are rebuilt, the cities are inhabited, and the desolate wastes become prosperous places, these Arabs covet the land their ancestors homesteaded all the more.

That tiny, less than 13 percent of what remained of Palestine, now called Israel, is under constant threat of evil neighbors. The Arabs have been conducting their own plucking process. They are attempting to pluck out the client nation Israel, which is the apple of Gods eye according to Zechariah 2:8. In so doing, they seal their own fate: God "will utterly pluck up and destroy that nation!"

# ELEVEN

# Who-domites?

## *Who Are the Edomites Today?*

**"U.N.'s oldest refugee camps look at sensitive upgrades"**

*Reuters 5/9/12*

"Three generations of Palestinians displaced by the founding of Israel in 1948 know only life in U.N. refugee camps, going to schools beneath the blue-and-white U.N. flag and drawing their food stocks from U.N. warehouses."

The present conflict in the Middle East between the Israelis and Palestinians is proof positive that we are nearing the end of times. The Bible foretold the face off between these two ethnic groups to occur in the last days! Scripture informs us that it will be resolved through a sizeable regional war in the Middle East. This war is waged between Israel's exceedingly great army, and the Psalm 83 Arab confederacy. At the helm of this confederacy are the descendants from the ancient Edomites. In the process the IDF executes the vengeance of their God on the Palestinians and their coalition of Arab allies. The historical equivalents to the Palestinians, at least in part, are these ancient Edomites.

Regarding the Edomites, there are numerous scriptures in the Bible written by various prophets that predict their present participation in the

Middle East crisis. These prophecies, when appropriately discerned, present us with invaluable insights into the cause, details, duration, and resolve of the conflict at hand. As such, this prophetic information has direct and specific application to this present generation.

This chapter is committed to the study of the Edomites and boldly attempts to connect part of their genealogy to the modern-day ethnic group commonly referred to as the Palestinians. Unless you are a Middle East historian or an avid student of the Bible, you likely run the risk of not knowing whom the Edomites were and, therefore, what some of the Palestinian ancestry was. The Edomites have for the most part long been forgotten. However, they and their former homeland of Edom, which is modern-day Southern Jordan, fill many pages of end-times Bible prophecy.

## Who-domites?

- Did you know that in the last days scheduled for the Earth we presently occupy, the land of modern-day Southern Jordan, the ancient homeland of the Edomites, is the predetermined stage for the return of Jesus Christ and His face-off with the Antichrist and the armies participating in the campaign of Armageddon?[79]

- Did you know that before the Armageddon campaign, the Palestinians will enjoin the nations of Egypt, Saudi Arabia, Jordan, Syria, and Lebanon in a confederate attempt to extinguish the Jewish people, hoping to cause the name "Israel" to be "remembered no more?" (Psalm 83:1-8).

- Did you know that at least some of the Palestinian terrorists in the Middle East today are likely of Edomite descent? That's right. Contained within the Palestinian population of today resides a remnant of people who are of Edomite descent.

## Who are the Edomites?

Simply put, they are the descendants of Esau, the twin brother of the infamous Jacob of the Old Testament.[80] Jacob was later known as Israel, and from his twelve sons came the formation of the nation Israel. Likewise, the descendants of Esau formed the nation of Edom, from which comes the term Edomites.[81]

## Who are the Palestinians?

Palestinian is the ethnic label tossed about loosely in modern times to identify three primary predominately Arab groups of people: the Palestinians of the Gaza

Strip, the Palestinians of the West Bank, and the Palestinian Refugees. These groups inhabit the territories that most closely approach the borders of modern-day Israel, with pocket communities in the surrounding Arab nations. We generally understand that these three groups are comprised of a mixture of peoples who descend from various origins, one of these being traceable back to Esau, father of the Edomites.

Unlike the Jewish people, who all share a common lineage traceable to the biblical patriarchs of Abraham, Isaac, and Jacob, Palestinians have no such common historical lineage specifically linking them biologically to any distinct ethnicity. Their genealogies can be traced back to the Edomites, Egyptians, Assyrians, Philistines, Sidonians, Ammonites, Moabites, Yemenites, Saudi Arabians, Moroccans, Christians from Greece, Muslim Sherkas from Russia, and Muslims from Bosnia, just to name a few.[82]

It is unfortunate that the history books and encyclopedias of our time have generally lost track of the Edomites. However, the fact remains that if the Bible is correct, the Edomites will resurface and they and their former homeland will play parts in future world events.

We must consider  that when the prophecies of the Bible were written, the peoples and places subject to the prophecies were identified in accordance with their recognized titles at the time. For instance, should any pending prophecies regarding ancient Philistia be fulfilled in modern times, they could be referring to the Palestinians of the Gaza Strip. Likewise, prophecies regarding the Palestinians of the West Bank could find association with the Edomites. As pointed out further in this chapter, many Edomites migrated from Edom into Hebron, which is located in the modern-day West Bank.

Through time, titles often changed as epic events altered the course of ethnic and geographic history. For example, the Romans relabeled Israel the Land of Palaestina in AD 135 when they defeated the Bar Kokhba revolt. There are numerous unfulfilled prophecies in the Bible that concern Philistia, Edom and the Edomites. The Jewish prophets who described them at the time had no Palestinian labels to give further identification as to exactly which of the three Palestinian groups of our day would have specific application. These unfulfilled prophecies are of particular interest in modern times, as knowledgeable students of prophecy suspect that these prophecies will soon find their final fulfillment.

The premise we should now consider is that this ethnic Edomite group never officially ceased to exist; rather, they have apparently been existing for many centuries in the Middle East in general, and in the land of Israel and Southern Jordan more specifically. Though their identity has been mistaken, we must not overlook their ethnic reality.

Since the Bible predicts future events with 100 percent accuracy, we can recognize that a remnant of the Edomites still exists in some ethnic classification today. Though their identity at present is somewhat obscured, the fulfillment of the predicted events will clearly prove who the Edomites are and have been. As we study the prophecies regarding Edom and the Edomites we are forced to consider their close association with the Palestinians of today.

As you read the following three sections of scripture, you will notice Edom plays a significant role in each of them.

Do not keep silent, O God! Do not hold Your peace, And do not be still, O God! For behold, Your enemies make a tumult; And those who hate You have lifted up their head. They have taken crafty counsel against Your people, [The Jews] And consulted together against Your sheltered ones. They have said, "Come, and let us cut them off from *being* a nation, That the name of Israel may be remembered no more." For they have consulted together with one consent; They form a confederacy against You: The *tents of Edom* and the Ishmaelites; Moab and the Hagrites; Gebal, Ammon, and Amalek; Philistia with the inhabitants of Tyre; Assyria also has joined with them; They have helped the children of Lot. *Selah* (Psa. 83:1–8, NKJV; emphasis added)

Thus says the LORD GOD: "Because of what *Edom* did against the house of Judah by taking vengeance, and has greatly offended by avenging itself on them," therefore thus says the LORD GOD: "I will also stretch out My hand against *Edom*, cut off man [Palestinian] and beast from it, and make it desolate from Teman; Dedan [Saudi Arabia] shall fall by the sword. I will lay My vengeance on *Edom* by the hand of My people Israel, [The Jews] that they may do in *Edom* according to My anger and according to My fury; and they [Palestinians and the Saudi Arabians by association] shall know My vengeance," says the LORD GOD. (Ezek. 25:12–14, NKJV; emphasis added)

Come near, you nations, to hear; And heed, you people! Let the Earth hear, and all that is in it, The world and all things that come forth from it. For the indignation of the LORD *is* against all nations, And *His* fury against all their armies; [future campaign of Armageddon] He has utterly destroyed them, He has given them over to the slaughter. Also their slain shall be thrown out; Their stench shall rise from their corpses, And the mountains shall be melted with their blood. All the host of heaven shall be dissolved, And the heavens shall be rolled up like a scroll; All their host shall fall down As the leaf falls from the vine, And as *fruit* falling from a fig tree. For My sword shall be bathed in heaven; Indeed it shall come down on *Edom*, And on the people of My curse, for judgment. The sword of the LORD is filled with blood, It is made overflowing with fatness, With the blood of lambs and goats, With the fat of the kidneys of rams. For the LORD has a sacrifice in *Bozrah*, And *a great slaughter* in the land of *Edom*. (Isa. 34:1–6, NKJV; emphasis added)

These scriptures are just a few of the numerous end-time pieces of the prophetic puzzle, and they place either Edom or the Edomite people in the midst of the circumstances. The first piece, the prophecy of Psalm 83, references the "tents of Edom," which if it were fulfilled in modern times would be better translated as the "tents of Palestinians." Tents biblically represent a population assembled in refuge, and/or military encampments.

Tent communities housing Palestinians become instrumental to a confederate attempt with the nations of Egypt (Hagarenes) Saudi Arabia (Ishmaelites), Jordan (Moab and Ammon, the children of Lot), Syria and Iraq (Assyria), Lebanon (Tyre), and Gaza (Philistia).The explicit goal of this confederacy is the destruction of the nation Israel. Tent communities and military mindsets are well understood among the Palestinians. Presently, the world is witnessing glimpses of the Psalm 83:1–6 confederate scenario in its dangerous beginning stages as these Arab nations lend support to the Palestinians' fight against the nation of Israel.

**Fig. 1. Dheisha refugee camp, Bethlehem, West Bank 1949.**

*(Reproduced by permission from UNRWA. UNRWA photo, "Palestinian Refugees—Historical Photos," Badil.org, http://www.badil.org/Photos/history/Archive2/Photogallery/photo27847/real. htm [accessed 12/20/07].)*

***Fig. 2. Baqa'a refugee camp, Jordan, 1969.***

*(Reproduced by permission from UNRWA. UNRWA photo by Jay Nehmeh, "Photo Archive: Refugees' Condition," UN.org., http://www.un.org/unrwa/photos/archive/refugees/jordan.html [Accessed 12/20/07].)*

Resulting from this cursed confederate effort, the events of the second prophetic passage above regarding the Israeli Conquest over the "tents of Palestinians" as described in Ezekiel 25:12–14 occurs. This Jewish military effort extends beyond Edom, i.e., Southern Jordan, into at least Dedan, which is located in Northwestern Saudi Arabia. This conquest brings to a conclusion the Psalm 83 war effort and devastates most of what remains of the refugee Palestinian population. Furthermore, it transfers sovereignty of Southern Jordan over to the Jewish people.

This transfer of sovereignty leads to the third prophetic piece previously prescribed in Isaiah 34:1–6. Isaiah describes the "great slaughter in the land of Edom," which regards itself with the return of Jesus Christ to Edom in order to protect the faithful Jewish remnant. This Jewish contingency will be hiding in Bozrah as refugees who temporarily escaped the onslaught of the Antichrist. The Antichrist will be at that time involved in the final extermination attempt of the Jewish people, which climaxes in the campaign of Armageddon.[83]

The Bible predicts two pending judgments destined to occur in the territory of Edom. First the avenging of "My people Israel" against the Palestinians and their confederate member nations, and then subsequently the "great slaughter" by Jesus Christ of the Antichrist and his armies. The emphasis of this book is upon the first of the two pending judgments. The second judgment is entirely unrelated to the "tents of Palestinians."

In order to understand the connection between the Edomites and the Palestinians, one must trace the migration process of the Edomites into Israel over time, and likewise study the process of the name conversion of the land of "Israel," into the land of "Palestine." Yet even before this, it is important to explore the final fulfillment of two significant prophecies. These two prophecies play a crucial role in understanding how the land in question, developed into its disputed condition of today.

## The Two Palestinian Prophecies

Presently, the international community desperately seeks to position the Israelis and Palestinians side by side, in a peaceful co-existence. Did you know that these two groups, the Israelis and the Edomites, once successfully operated in a two-state solution of sorts? However, there were two prophecies written in ancient times that foretold of both Israel's and Edom's national decline, and at the time of the fulfillment of these two prophecies, their operational two-state solution disintegrated.

Hosea issued the first of the two prophecies, and Jeremiah along with Obadiah issued the second. Hosea declared that the Israelites would be declassified from "My people Israel," to "not My people," and Jeremiah and Obadiah predicted that the Edomites would become "small among the nations," and "despised among men."

## Israel

> Now when she weaned Lo-Ruhamah, she conceived and bore a son. Then *God* said: "Call his name Lo-Ammi, For you *are not My people*, And I will not be your *God*." (Hosea 1:8–9, NKJV; emphasis added).

## Edom

> I have heard tidings from the LORD, and a messenger has been sent among the nations: "Gather yourselves together and come against her, and rise up for battle!" *For behold, I will make you* [Edom] *small among the nations,* despised among men. (Jer. 49:14–15, RSV; emphasis added).

## Edom

> The vision of Obadiah. Thus says the LORD GOD concerning *Edom*: "We have heard tidings from the LORD, and a messenger has been sent among the nations: 'Rise up! Let us rise against her for battle!' *Behold, I will make you*

*small among the nations,* you shall be utterly despised." (Obad. 1:1–2, RSV; emphasis added).

In a twist of fate, the twin brothers, Jacob and Esau, would have their descendants share in a similar divine disciplinary action. The two historically infamous peoples, the Jews and the Edomites, would experience their national decline and at about the same time. Both ethnic groups find themselves conquered by the Roman Empire on or around AD 70 in what turns out to be the final fulfillment of these two important Bible prophecies.

Back then, these two populations co-existed semi-peacefully in a two-state solution of their own. The Jews inhabited Judea, and Samaria, which comprised the Northern and Southern kingdoms of Israel, and the Edomites occupied Idumea, and were known as the Idumeans, which was the Greek word for Edomites. Idumea-Edom encompassed land in Southern Israel, Northeastern Sinai, and Southwestern Jordan. The Jewish capitol was Jerusalem, and the central Idumean city was Hebron approximately 19 miles to the south. At the time of the Roman conquest, the Idumeans and Jews both practiced Judaism, evidencing a common bond between them.[84]

When the Romans conquered Jerusalem and destroyed the second Jewish temple in AD 70, they also fought against the Idumeans. According to the historian Josephus, many Idumeans were either killed, or sold into slavery, and ultimately about 40,000 remaining Idumeans were freed by Caesar to go wherever they desired enabling them to keep their ethnicity in tact.[85] Indeed, by AD 70 the LORD had made Edom/Idumea undeniably "small among the nations."

Maps depicting the layout of the region around AD 135 at the time of the Bar Kokhba Jewish revolt still recognized the existence of the territory of Idumea. As such, one might safely presume that Idumeans still resided in the subject land on or around AD 135.[86] This suggests that at least some of these 40,000 freed Idumeans continued to reside, and repopulate in the territory of Idumea.

To further understand the declassification of the Israelites to "not My people" it is important to read the chapter in this book called "My People Israel." For now it is important to recognize that the declassification of the Jews into "not My people" began at the rejection by the Jewish leadership of Jesus Christ, and found its final fulfillment in the destruction of Jerusalem and the second Jewish temple in AD 70 at the defeat by the Romans. Lastly, the assumption of the title "not My people" was not prophesied to be a permanent condition, and ultimately the Jews would be reclassified as "My people Israel," and furthermore "sons of the living God."[87]

Back to Edom becoming "made small among the nations," although it found fulfillment in AD 70 it will be made clear in this study that as a nation Edom experienced a gradual decline, which led to such a point whereby they slipped as an ethnic group from the pages of history.[88] If it were not for the end-times prophecies contained in the Bible regarding the restored Edomite element, there would be no further cause to remember them. They would be essentially extinguished, however the Bible suggests they have merely been "made small among the nations," and will resurface in that reduced national condition in a final confederate effort aimed at the destruction of the nation Israel.

Herein lies the problem; the Middle East conflict is the derivative of the descendants of these two former nations, attempting to reclaim the land of Israel-Palaestinia. This may seem an over-simplification of the matter; however, it is at the root of the conflict. Both formerly notorious nations who experienced their decline at the same-time and in the same-place, are attempting to pick up where they left off in AD 70. They are seeking to reestablish themselves now, again at the same time and in the same place. A recreation of sorts is occurring, and playing out in the Israel-Palestinian conflict.

When Israel became a nation again in 1948, the Palestinians essentially became a people. They became the refugees of Palestine because of the 1948 Arab-Israeli War. Up until that time, they were generally referred to as the Arabs of Palestine.[89] The surrounding Arab nations protested the reestablishment of the nation Israel, and confederated in a war effort against the returning Jewish people. They instructed the Arabs residing within Israel at the time, to vacate temporarily until the Jewish nation was destroyed, at which time these departing Arabs could return into the land.

Amongst the Arabs who left Israel at the time were those who had descended from Esau, i.e., the Edomites. History reports that the Jewish people were victorious, and these Edomites became numbered among the refugees of Palestine. Hence, at the time they became refugees residing in tents. The Edomites were essentially at the time the "tents of Palestine," or as they are called today, the Palestinian people. *(See photos of Palestinian Refugees, pages 107-108.)*

The present plight of the Palestinians is, in large part, the result of the failed Arab war against Israel, and therefore primarily the responsibility of the surrounding Arab nations. These Arab nations have done little to absorb and assimilate them into their lands, but have done much to use them as pawns against the developing nation of Israel. Hence, you have Israel aspiring to become "My people Israel" again, which is prophesied to successfully occur, and Edom wanting to become greater than the tents of Palestine, which will likely never occur!

Edom will never be great among the nations, as they were permanently "made small among the nations," and that is the best condition they will ever experience. In fact, because of their present attempt to curse the developing nation of Israel, the Edomites will be extinguished as a people. In other words, the Palestinians of today will likely never nationally ascend much beyond a refugee condition. At the time of publishing this book, the Palestinians are awaiting an approval from the United Nations for statehood. However, according to this prophecy a Palestinian state, should one be created, will be small among the nations.

## The Migration of the Edomites

The Edomites, later known as the Idumeans, became assimilated into the so-called Palestinians of today. This section studies the migratory path of the Edomites out of ancient Edom (present day Southern Jordan), into Southern Israel. It also explains the reasons for the migration, and in the end establishes the intelligent presumption that though history has lost sight of the Edomites ethnically, the Bible student can identify them today prophetically. They are an integral part of the present Palestinian population.

The ascent of the Edomites into the land of Israel officially began in 586 BC, which coincided with the destruction of Jerusalem by the Babylonians. At that time, the Edomites began to trespass into the land of Israel in large numbers, and began their homestead of the Holy Land with little to no Jewish, Philistian, Chaldean or Babylonian restriction. Hebron, which is located 19 miles south of Jerusalem, became their popular new frontier. Unlike Jerusalem, which was destroyed at the time, much of Hebron was still left in tact. Standing approximately 3,040 feet above sea level, and having been established as a city over 1,500 years earlier, it was considered prime property for the taking.

Coincidentally, about the same time a nomadic tribe known as the Nabateans began to migrate out of Arabia into Edom. They began to establish themselves alongside the Edomites, causing cultural and territorial conflicts, which played an instrumental part in this first wave of Edomite migration into Israel. Israel was the logical destination of Edomite relocation for the following reasons.

First, it was directly to the west of Edom with established routes of passage making it easy to enter. Second it was historically a more prosperous and resourceful land than Edom, which was primarily a place filled with unfertile deserts and jagged mountains. Thirdly, it was a land that the Edomites bore brotherly association with, in that their patriarch Esau was the twin brother of Jacob, who later bore the name Israel. They like their ancestral father Esau before them harbored a hatred of Israel and his descendants the Jews and quite possibly felt a form of restitution in their occupation of the land of Israel. Lastly, it was available for the taking, since the Babylonians had deported the Jews off into captivity.

Continued Edomite movement occurred over the fifth and fourth centuries BC into Southern Israel. Then, in 312 BC, the Seleucid King Antigonus, who had come to power when Alexander's empire was divided, conquered Edom. The last of the Edomites still held out in Edom at the time of the advance of Antigonus had to face the possibility of death by defeat or life by fleeing to Israel where they could find refuge with generations of relatives. Many chose to flee making it easier for Antigonus to prevail.

This episode in history caused a second major wave of Edomite migration into Hebron and greater Southern Israel. About that time, the Edomites were more commonly referred to by their Greek name, Idumeans. The territory of Southern Israel they inhabited, with its central city of Hebron, had come to be known as Idumea. Ultimately, the Nabateans annihilated Antigonus and his army, when they weighted themselves down with the plunder and booty of Edom, making them to slow to further fight.[90]

Hebron remained under Edomite/Idumean control until Judas Maccabeus retook the city under Jewish control in 164 BC. Thirty-eight years later, in 126 BC, history tells us the Edomites/Idumeans had to be re-conquered by the Jewish army, led by their prince and high priest John Hyrcanus.[91] The Edomites/Idumeans continued to rise up and rebel, causing Hyrcanus to put an end to their insurgency.

At that point, the Idumeans were forced to die, flee, or be proselytized into Judaism if they wanted to remain in the territory of Idumea, and/ or greater Judea. Many opted to stay rather than move back into their ancient homeland Edom, which still housed many Nabateans.

Then in 47 BC, Julius Caesar promoted the Idumean Antipater as procurator over Judea, Samaria, and Galilee, which in essence encompassed most all of the remaining Jewish kingdom. Ten years later in 37 BC, the Romans named Herod as the King over Israel. Herod was the son of Antipater, an Idumean, and his mother Nabatean. This evidences the point that the Edomites/Idumeans were well established in Israel, having over five centuries of prior history in Israel by the time of the first coming of the Messiah Jesus Christ. Mark 3:8 alludes to the territory of Idumea, further evidencing that the Idumeans were still around during the New Testament period.

Josephus the Jewish historian tells us that further Idumean interactions in Israel occurred up to and on through AD 70, at which time the Romans sacked Jerusalem and destroyed the second Jewish temple. He identifies them as a "a tumultuous and disorderly nation, always on the watch upon every motion, delighting in mutations; and upon your flattering them ever so little, and petitioning them, they soon take their arms, and put themselves into motion, and make haste to a battle, as if it were to a feast."[92]

Just prior to the sacking of Jerusalem by the Roman legions, led by Titus, the Idumeans joined the Jewish rebels led by John the Zealot, against the Orthodox Jews of the time.[93] All three groups, the Zealots, Idumeans, and the Orthodox Jews, were in fervor about the advancing Roman legions throughout the land, and as such, Israel was in a state of turmoil, which resulted in a civil war. About 20,000 Idumean infantry took part in the slaughter of many Orthodox Jews.[94]

After so doing, they repented and went back to what little, was left of their Idumean existence.[95] Shortly thereafter, the remaining Jews and Idumeans banded together against the Roman legions. Josephus goes on to say that the Idumeans were enlisted alongside the Jews in the fight.[96] As stated earlier, many Idumeans were either killed, sold into slavery, or enjoined among the forty thousand set free by Caesar.[97] These forty thousand Idumeans presumably attempted to reestablish the war torn territory of Idumea. Maps drafted as late as AD 135, at the time of the final Jewish revolt led by Bar Kokhba against the Roman occupation, still displayed Idumea giving it legitimacy as the nation of these Idumeans.

Thus, the  last traces of the Edomite/Idumean population residing in the land of modern-day Israel were approximately AD 135. From that point forward, further evidence of their ethnic whereabouts becomes scarce. As the next section reveals it was AD 135 when the Romans renamed the Land of Israel the Land of Palaestina, and as such, Idumea disappeared from future map, and the Idumeans fade from history.

## The Name Conversion of the Land

The name Palestine, which is the modern-day translation of the Latin term "Palaestina," the Arabic word "Filastin," and in Hebrew "Pelesheth" or sometimes spelled "Peleset" or "Peleshet," appears eight times in the Old Testament. The Romans renamed the land formerly known as Israel to the land of Palaestina in AD 135.

The original Hebrew word Pelesheth referred to the territory on the South West Coast of Israel, which the Philistines settled between 1200 and 1100 BC. These people had been driven out of Greece and the Aegean Islands around 1300 BC. They made their way down toward Egypt, and unsuccessfully attempted to invade Egypt around 1200 BC. Because of their defeat, they migrated up to the area generally referred to today as the Gaza Strip.[98] As such, this territory became known as Philistia, and was much more limited in landmass, than the Palestine of today. Ancient Philistia became established on territory belonging to the tribe of Judah.

When the Romans ended the Jewish revolt of "Bar Kokhba" around AD 135, they advanced the name "Palaestina" to describe the subject territory. The historical understanding of why the Romans implemented this name change was to blot out any vestiges of residual Jewish identity and interest in connection with the land. The story is told that "the Roman Procurator in charge of the Judean-Israel territories was so angry at the Jews for revolting that he called for his historians and asked them who were the worst enemies of the Jews in their past history. The scribes said, 'the Philistines.' Thus, the Procurator declared that Land of Israel would from then forward be called 'Philistia.'"[99] As referenced before, Palaestina is the Latin translation of Philistia, from which today we derive the word Palestine.

Bar Kokhba had about 200,000 men at his command, and in a final Jewish revolt, they recaptured Jerusalem and many strongholds and villages throughout the country.[100] This caused the Emperor Hadrian at the time to call legion upon legion of reinforcements to crush the Jewish insurgents. It is estimated that as many as 580,000 Romans and Jews were slain in this bloody revolt. Some Roman accounts suggest almost that many Jews alone were killed.[101]

This Bar Kokhba revolt was the final straw for the Jews as far as Hadrian was concerned; he purposed to stamp out Jewish nationalism entirely. Jewish traditions like circumcision, the Sabbath, and the reading of the "Mosaic Law" were forbidden.

He was determined to convert the war torn city of Jerusalem into a Roman colony. He changed the name from Jerusalem to Aelia Capitolina, and ordered the building of a temple to Jupiter, on the site where the second Jewish temple once stood. Lastly, he forbade any Jew, on pain of death to appear within site of the city.[102]

Though Palaestina was the name the Romans elected to use in AD 135, it was not the only name available to them at the time. Idumea, the Greek word for Edom, was still on the maps and could have likewise been used. The Idumeans/Edomites, still supported a population in Israel at the time in Hebron, and the surrounding areas near Jerusalem. The most logical explanations why the Romans opted not to name the region Idumea, are first that the Idumeans were most likely still practitioners of Judaism, the religion emperor Hadrian was attempting to vanquish, and secondly as such Idumea did not then rank as one of Israel's greatest historical enemies when compared against Philistia.

Regarding our study the point is not why the Romans chose the name Palaestina at the time; rather, it is the fact that there apparently were still Edomites/Idumeans residing in the land of Israel at the time of the renaming. The Edomites of old still had an ethnic identity well into the first and second centuries. However shortly thereafter they made their way off the pages of any further history.

The Bar Kokhba defeat only compounded the dilemmas of these two ethnic groups, the Jews and Edomites/Idumeans. It offered the necessary certainty that indeed the Jews were no longer the client nation, "My people Israel," and that the Edomites/Idumeans were made even more "small among the nations." Philistia, which had previously been an abandoned territorial name, became reinstated, and Idumea an established identity soon after the revival of Philistia became forgotten.

From that point, the land of Israel commenced to take on an entirely new identity. Around AD 390, the land of Palaestina broadened in scope to include three enlarged units: Prima, Secunda, and Tertia. These three units encompassed Judea, Samaria, the coast of Peraea, the Galilee, lower Jezreel Valley, regions east of the Galilee, Negev, Southern Jordan, and most of the Sinai.[103] The Edomite/Idumean remnant became further absorbed and harder to identify within these three units.

Arab rule over the area began around AD 635, and the Arab rulers back then divided the province into five districts, known as Junds, which were tribal corps. This period up to the tenth century was characterized by political upheavals, and several times the boundaries were readjusted. Around the tenth century, the division into Junds began to break down and the establishment of the Latin Kingdom of Jerusalem completed that process. Muslim control was re-established in the twelfth and thirteenth centuries, and the division into districts was reinstated, with boundaries that were frequently rewritten.

Around the end of the thirteenth century, Palestine comprised several of nine kingdoms of Syria, namely the Kingdoms of Gaza, Karak, Safad, and parts of the Kingdom of Damascus.[104] Then came the Turkish Ottoman Empire, which ruled over the land in question from 1517 to 1917. Their dominance was brought to an end at the conclusion of World War I, which evidenced that nation had begun to come against nation in accordance to the prophecy of Jesus Christ.[105]

Then in 1917, the Balfour Document was drafted which entirely broadened the scope of the land of Palestine. In its original draft, it incorporated most all of the Gaza, Israel, the West Bank, and modern-day Jordan, and this large landmass, approximately 46,000 square miles, was to be devoted to the Jewish State, i.e., Israel. However, by 1948, when the Jewish State became official, the Arabs had convinced the world, that only a small notch of land should be allotted to the returning Jewish people. Annexed out was modern-day Jordan, the West Bank, and the Gaza Strip.[106]  According to Genesis 15:18, this amount of land falls far short of the ultimate inheritance of Israel.

## Summary

In summary, the land in question during the 1,878 years of Jewish dispersion out of Israel and into the nations of the world, changed hands on several occasions. It experienced Roman, Christian, Arab, Turkish, and British rule, and the name Palestine, which Rome implemented in AD 135 was tossed, turned, shrank, and stretched in whichever way the dominant political influence decided at the time of its respective sovereignty. It went from the scope of ancient Philistia (Gaza Strip), down through the Sinai, up to Damascus, over toward the River Euphrates, and then in 1948 came back down in size to about 8,000 to 9,000 square miles which encompasses, Gaza, Israel, and the West Bank as defined today.

Palestine was essentially never officially recognized as a state or a nation; the terms were generally used loosely through the centuries to describe a territory with grossly undefined borders. However, in these times, the movement is to declare such a Palestinian state. This is because now there is a population group known as the Palestinians, and they have convinced the international community that they are deserving of such a state.

Today this population has definitely attained for themselves an ethnic identity, and as such have become a force to be reckoned with. Their general identity is founded in association with their refugee condition, and in that condition, they depict themselves, unlike "rebels without a cause," as "terrorists with a cause." Their move-ment is generally supported by the Muslim international influence, but is intrinsically lifted up by those Arab countries that most closely border the nation of Israel today. These Arab countries are the very same nations listed alongside the Palestinians in the forthcoming Psalm 83 confederacy. As stated in the beginning of this chapter, this confederacy is committed to the destruction of Israel and will surface in the end-times.

Perhaps we can glean a prophetic insight into the connection between the Edomites, later identified as the Idumeans, who today in many respects resemble the Palestinians and their tactics of terror.

*"The terror you* [Edomites–Idumeans–Palestinians] *inspire* and the pride of your heart have deceived you, you who live in the clefts of the rocks, who occupy the heights of the hill. Though you build your nest as high as the eagle's, from there I will bring you down," declares the LORD. "Edom will become an object of horror; all who pass by will be appalled and will scoff because of all its wounds." (Jer. 49:16–17 NIV; emphasis added)

The prophet Jeremiah speaks in the context of the end-times judgment predicted to come against Edom. Edom will become an "object of horror" due to the terror the Edomite population inspires. The word Jeremiah uses in the Hebrew is tiphletseth, and it is translated as a shuddering, horrific terror.[107] I devote an entire chapter to the study of terror in the Bible in my book *Isralestine*, in the chapter called "The End of Terror."

This gripping term is uniquely utilized only in this single instance in the entire Bible, yet it is the most descriptive word available in the ancient Hebrew language to identify the recently fashioned terrorism plaguing the nation Israel today. Back in Jeremiah's day there was warfare, ambush, and murder without cause, however Israel's enemies back then did not have the shuddering, horrific ability to strap explosives to themselves and take out not only themselves, but also large groups of Jews and/or Jewish supporters in one attempt.

The crimes of terror that were enacted on 9/11/2001 against America by the pro-Palestinian group Al-Qaeda put the world on alert that terrorism had become a bona fide method of warfare. What began in its fledgling stages in the Middle East had expanded its dangerous reach well into the international arena.

Presently, the world witnesses the "War on Terror" being waged against terrorist groups and the nations that sponsor them. The sizeable nations of Afghanistan and Iraq were promptly overturned for their sponsorship of terrorism. Their defeat evidences the international concern over the seriousness of the tiphletseth Jeremiah described. It is indeed a shuddering and horrific terror inspired by the Palestinians.

As this study suggests, the Edomites have a descendant population within the modern-day Palestinians. Therefore, this present behavior of the Palestinians, who inspire tactics of terror against the Jews in order to prevail over the land in question, is destined for judgment. This judgment is foretold to be delivered through the "exceedingly great army" of the nation Israel, and is described in Ezekiel 25:12–14 and Obadiah 1:18!

So then, is there any question today as to who the Edomites are? The Palestinians in part represent the Edomites in modern times. The terror that grips the Middle East is the result of their inspiration. It became a reality after the three conventional military attempts to destroy the nation Israel by the surrounding Arab nations in 1948, 1967, and 1973 failed. Terror is their relatively recently adopted attempt to accomplish the same aim, which is the destruction of the nation Israel. They have said, "Come, and let us cut them off from being a nation, That the name of Israel may be remembered no more." (Psa. 83:4, NKJV)

Terrorism will eventually give way to the fulfillment of the Psalm 83 prophecy, whereby the "Plight of the Palestinians," i.e., the "tents of Edom," in their final attempt to be made more than "small among the nations" causes them to confederate with the surrounding Arab nations that support their cause. One last Arab-Israeli war results, however this time, they will meet with the formidable "exceedingly great army" of Israel spoken of in Ezekiel 37:10. It is this great army that finally brings to conclusion the present conflict in the Middle East.

All political attempts presently on the table that struggle to resolve the tension between the Arabs and the Jews are at best a temporary salve, designed to make Israel less of a nation and the Palestinians into a nation. This goes against the grain of God, Who has previously decided that Israel will again be called "My people Israel," and that Edom has been permanently "made small among the nations"!

# TWELVE

# The Ancient Arab Hatred of the Jews

**"Palestinian kids raised for war"**

*World Net Daily 11/3/00*

"Taught to hate, kill Jews through 'Sesame Street'-type TV show."

**"Israel claims Palestinian leadership demonizes Jews, justifies violence, denies Israel's right to exist"**

*The Times of Israel 4/12/12*

The present hostilities experienced in the Middle East between the Arabs and Jews, can be traced to a disposition of hatred originating almost four thousand years ago. It was about that time, that the God of the Old Testament, made an unconditional covenant with the Jewish Patriarch Abraham.[108] Due to the inherent blessings contained within this covenant, the infamous Bible characters Hagar, Ishmael, Esau, Moab, and Ammon coveted the contents of this covenant. These jealous individuals and their descendants that followed came to hate the Hebrews, who were the heirs of this blessed covenant.

Throughout time, the neighboring Gentile peoples of the region found it advantageous to embrace rather than resist this adversarial disposition.

Ultimately, it evolved into a cleverly conceived religious package giving it license to unleash itself in a holy war. The Jihad, as it is often labeled, presently underway in the Middle East, finds its justification in Islam, but its roots in this longstanding hatred.

The Bible describes this disposition as an ancient hatred or in some translations a perpetual enmity. The two Hebrew words are olam ebah, and when used together they describe a condition stemming back long ago in ancient times, perpetuated throughout time, manifesting into hostility with no apparent end in sight.[109] They are only paired together in the entire Bible in the two passages listed below:

> Because you have had an ancient [olam] hatred [ebah], and have shed the blood of the children of Israel by the power of the sword at the time of their calamity, when their iniquity came to an end. (Ezek. 35:5, NKJV)

> Thus says the LORD GOD: "Because the Philistines dealt vengefully and took vengeance with a spiteful heart, to destroy because of the old [olam] hatred [ebah]." (Ezek. 25:15, NKJV)

The first passage refers contextually to Mount Seir located in Edom, which is the territory of Esau.[110] Today this area is known as Southern Jordan. In the Ezekiel 35:5 passage, we see that the hatred was had in the territory most closely associated with Esau. In the second passage of Ezekiel 25:5 we find that the Philistines embraced what was already preconditioned in Edom by Esau. Today what was formerly known as Philistia, the land of the Philistines, is now referred to as the Gaza Strip. In both scriptures, it is an enmity exhibited exclusively against the Jewish people.

The Bible teaches that this continuous and contagious disposition of hatred will evidence itself in a final showdown. It predicts a major war in the Middle East between those Arab nations that have refused to abandon the angered ancient attitude of their ancestors, and the Jews. It amounts to the final contest over the blessed contents contained within the Abrahamic covenant! The victor is finally exalted as the true heir apparent!

This study explores the roots of the hatred through biblical accounts centered on the main patriarchs of the modern-day Middle Eastern peoples. Much of the population in the region has their decent traceable back to the patriarchs contained within this study. These ancestors were notable characters on the world scene, from which several historical nations were born. These individuals were involved in significant events relative to the plan of God intended for the benefit of man. Therefore, their interactions proved to be consequential in the history and development of the Middle East. Their attitudes have remained alive in the region throughout time immemorial.

## Sarah vs. Hagar (The Root of the Hatred)

So he [Abraham, father of the Jews] went in to Hagar [Egyptian], and she con-ceived. And when she saw that she had conceived, her mistress [Sarah, mother of the Jews] became despised in her [Hagar's] eyes. Then Sarah said to Abram, "My wrong *be* upon you! I gave my maid into your embrace; and when she saw that she had conceived, I became despised in her eyes. The LORD judge between you and me." (Gen. 16:4–5, NKJV)

Sarah knew that God had previously promised Abraham a son, through whom a multitude of descendants would follow.[111] Genesis 16:2 informs us that Sarah possessed a barren womb. Because of her barrenness, she concluded that the promised heir would not come from her womb. In Genesis 16:3 we are told that Sarah in accordance with the legal custom of her day, gave her maidservant Hagar to Abraham to be his substitute wife in order that the child could be conceived, and the Abrahamic covenant advanced.

"In the legal custom of that day a barren woman could give her maid to her hus-band as a wife, and the child born of that union was regarded as the first wife's child. If the husband said to the slave-wife's son, 'You are my son,' then he was the adopted son and heir. So Sarah's suggestion was unobjectionable according to the customs of that time."[112]

Abraham likewise concluded it could not be Sarah's barren womb through which his descendants would come, and therefore acted in accordance with the legal custom of his day and took Hagar as a surrogate wife. Upon Hagar's conception, she became contemptuous toward Sarah. This contempt was in violation of Abraham and Sarah's plan. Hagar was merely to be a surrogate mother and was scheduled to forfeit her son to Sarah, the first wife.

Hagar's response from the human perspective of our day is understandable, how-ever at the time much more was at stake. The covenant God had previously made with Abraham may very well be what caused Hagar to despise Sarah. Hagar most probably understood the significance of Abraham, and therefore the purpose of her surrogacy in relationship to the covenant his God made with him.

Hagar should have understood that Abraham, as the recipient of the covenant, was promised a land, a nation, and the most prominent stature among men upon the Earth. God's foreign policy toward all other peoples residing upon the Earth was directly connected to their relationship with Abraham and his descendants. It is quite likely that Hagar's contempt toward Sarah was rooted in her coveting of the contents of the covenant.

No matter her motivation, the scripture goes on to tell that Abraham was clear on the custom of his day, and the covenant of his God. So Abram said to Sarah,

> "Indeed your maid *is* in your hand; do to her as you please." And when Sarah dealt harshly with her [Hagar], she fled from her presence. (Gen. 16:6, NKJV)

Sarah dealt harshly with Hagar with the permission of Abraham, because of Hagar's contempt for the covenant of God, the legal custom of their day, and her disdain toward Sarah her mistress. The severity of the harsh treatment caused Hagar to flee from Sarah's presence. When we ponder the significance of this entire episode, we can conclude that the roots of the ancient hatred may well begin here.

Furthermore, these roots are likely grounded in a jealous attitude toward the Abrahamic Covenant, as advanced by Hagar. Though Abraham and Sarah laughed at the prospect of Sarah ever conceiving a child out from her barren womb, this episode with Hagar was no laughing matter.[113] Abraham and Sarah were esteemed as the respondents to the covenant God made for the benefit of humankind. As such, the consequences of their actions relative to all of the contents of the covenant had the potential to cause disturbance within all of humanity, then and now.

Certainly, it was an unconditional covenant; however, Abraham and Sarah were its critical components. Similarly was the historical case of Adam and Eve in their Garden of Eden episode. Their mistake injected the sin nature into all of humanity. Abraham and Sarah's mistake involving Hagar appears to have injected the ancient hatred into the Middle East.

Due to the mistake by Adam, Jesus Christ "the Jew" was crucified to rectify the sin problem. Unfortunately, because of the ancient hatred, the Jews are being killed in the land of Israel today. Those Arabs terrorizing the Jews in Israel, whether consciously or unconsciously are in essence exhibiting the same attitude of coveting the contents of the Covenant, i.e., the land and prominence promised to Abraham and his Jewish descendants.

Scripture and history tells us that Hagar returned in submission to Sarah, but there is no evidence that her hatred toward Sarah was ever reversed. Abraham had paternal instincts of high regard for Hagar's son Ishmael, but it does not appear that Abraham ever officially accepted Ishmael in accordance with the legal custom as heir to the covenant. [114] Furthermore, many years later after the birth of Isaac out of Sarah's womb, at the time of his weaning we are told that this Ishmael scoffed at Isaac. Isaac was the true heir of the covenant in contrast to Ishmael.

> So the child [Isaac] grew and was weaned. And Abraham made a great feast on the same day that Isaac was weaned. And Sarah saw the son [Ishmael] of Hagar the Egyptian, whom she had borne to Abraham, scoffing. (Gen. 21:8–9, NKJV)

Again there arises a significant episode involving Sarah and Hagar revolving around the Abrahamic Covenant. For Ishmael to scoff at the miraculously born Isaac, who had come out of the formerly barren womb of the aged Sarah, indicated that there still existed an attitude of animosity over the contents of the covenant. Perhaps Ishmael exhibited an exclusive adversarial attitude toward Isaac; however, both Hagar and Ishmael were immediately forced to leave.

> Therefore she [Sarah] said to Abraham, "Cast out this bondwoman [Hagar] and her son [Ishmael]; for the son of this bondwoman shall not be heir with my son, *namely* with Isaac." (Gen. 21:10, NKJV)

What Sarah recognized was the enmity exhibited by Hagar, passed on through to her son Ishmael. Likewise, God confirmed this disposition developed in Ishmael.

> But God said to Abraham, "Do not let it be displeasing in your sight because of the lad or because of your bondwoman. Whatever Sarah has said to you, *listen to her* voice; for in Isaac your seed shall be called." (Gen. 21:12, NKJV; emphasis added)

God said to listen to her voice and "Cast out this bondwoman [Hagar] and her son [Ishmael]; for the son of this bondwoman shall not be heir with my son, namely with Isaac." These are the harshest of words, and represent Sarah and God's recognition of the severity of Ishmael's jealous attitude. This takes us back to the rightful attitude of Sarah in Genesis 16:6 at the time of the conception of Ishmael, whereby she dealt harshly with Hagar for this same adversarial attitude.

> So Abraham rose early in the morning, and took bread and a skin of water; and putting *it* on her shoulder, he gave *it* and the boy to Hagar, and sent her away. Then she departed and wandered in the Wilderness of Beersheba. (Gen. 21:14, NKJV)

God and Sarah told Abraham to cast out Hagar and Ishmael, so in obedience Abraham rose early and sent them away. Hagar wanders off into the wilderness and has her second divine encounter, this time with her son Ishmael present.[115] Ultimately, Hagar, an Egyptian, took for Ishmael an Egyptian bride.[116]

Thus, we see two powerful episodes whereby Sarah and Hagar are at odds with each other over the rightful heir to the Abrahamic Covenant. This argument still rages on between the three prominent religions of our time: Christianity, Judaism, and Islam. Christians and Jews believe that the covenant was passed on through Abraham, Isaac, and Jacob, whereas the Islamic holy book known as the Koran memorializes Ishmael in first position over Isaac.[117]

## Isaac vs. Ishmael

As previously stated, Isaac became the true heir of Abraham. This disqualified Ishmael, Abraham's first-born son, who according to the legal custom of that day should have been the rightful heir. The thing of greatest value to the rightful heir of Abraham was his covenant made by God between them.

Imagine the conditions of the first fourteen years of Ishmael's life, after which time Isaac arrived on the scene. Ishmael in his formative years was probably caught in this triangle of powerful emotions. Abraham exhibited paternal love to Ishmael his firstborn son, Hagar exhibited envy toward Sarah her mistress, and Sarah viewed Ishmael as her mistake for meddling with the Abrahamic Covenant. Is it any wonder that Ishmael scoffed at the weaning of Isaac? But scoffed indeed he did, and at a most important time in Isaac's life, his weaning. This scoffing was much more significant than a sibling squabble; otherwise, a simple disciplining would have been in order, rather than a casting-out.

Hagar and Ishmael, for a lack of a better descriptions, were players at that time on the world scene. They were elevated in stature due to their unique relationships with Abraham. The leadership of Egypt certainly knew of Abraham due to his previous encounter with Pharaoh, recorded in Genesis 12:10–20. Nine other most prominent kings in the region must also have come to know and revere Abraham.[118]

Therefore, the point to understand is that through Hagar and Ishmael this attitude of hatred was likely being spread among the elite circles in the region. The arguments against the rightful heir and the contents of the covenant were reaching foreign soil. After all Hagar and Ishmael could proudly boast that they were also involved in a covenant of their own personal interest. Ishmael was to be a "great nation!"

> Then the Angel of the LORD said to her, "I will multiply your [Hagar] descendants exceedingly, so that they shall not be counted for multitude." And the Angel of the LORD said to her: "Behold, you *are* with child, And you shall bear a son. You shall call his name Ishmael, Because the LORD has heard your affliction. He shall be a wild man; His hand *shall be* against every man, And every man's hand against him. And he shall dwell in the presence of all his brethren." (Gen. 16:10–12, NKJV)

> And as for Ishmael, I have heard you [Abraham]. Behold, I have blessed him, and will make him fruitful, and will multply him exceedingly. He shall beget twelve princes, and *I will make him a great nation*. (Gen. 17:20, NKJV, emphasis added)

> And God heard the voice of the lad. Then the angel of God called to Hagar out of heaven, and said to her, "What ails you, Hagar? Fear not, for God has heard the voice of the lad where he *is*. Arise, lift up the lad and hold him with your hand, for *I will make him* [Ishmael] *a great nation*." (Gen. 21:17–18, NKJV, emphasis added).

Ishmael went on to father twelve sons; he and his sons predominately settled in the Arabian territories. Thus, God fulfills this prophecy of the great nation in the manifestation of the nation of modern-day Saudi Arabia. The Psalm 83 confederacy section refers to them as the Ishmaelites.[119]

## Jacob vs. Esau

By the time Isaac and Rebecca had their twins Esau and Jacob, the disposition of hatred was advancing and infecting the Middle East region through the exploits of Hagar and Ishmael. The environment was a powerful incubator for the hatred Esau ultimately displayed toward his younger twin brother Jacob..

> So *Esau hated Jacob* because of the blessing with which his father blessed him [Jacob], and Esau said in his heart, "The days of mourning for my father are at hand; then *I will kill my brother Jacob.*" (Gen. 27:41, NKJV, emphasis added)

"Esau hated Jacob." This hatred was akin to the attitude already advanced by Uncle Ishmael and step-grandmother Hagar. Esau likewise came to covet the contents of the covenant. As the firstborn, it was his birthright to be the heir of the Abrahamic Covenant, not his twin brother Jacob. In Esau's estimation, the line of command was to be Abraham, Isaac, and Esau. A study of the interactions between Esau and Jacob give understanding into the development of Esau's hatred toward Jacob.

> Now Jacob cooked a stew; and Esau came in from the field, and he was weary. And Esau said to Jacob, "Please feed me with that same red stew, for I am weary." Therefore his name was called Edom. But Jacob said, "Sell me your birthright as of this day." And Esau said, "Look, I am about to die; so what is this birthright to me?" Then Jacob said, "Swear to me as of this day." So he swore to him, and sold his birthright to Jacob. And Jacob gave Esau bread and stew of lentils; then he ate and drank, arose, and went his way. Thus Esau despised *his* birthright. (Gen. 25:29–34, NKJV)

On the road to his hatred of Jacob, Esau first gave up his birthright for a short order of food. This episode evidenced his contempt for the contents of the covenant at the time. Ultimately, his nickname became Edom, which means red, in association with the red stew for which he sold his birthright to Jacob. Thus, "Esau despised his birthright." The Hebrew word for despised is bazah, a primitive root meaning to disesteem, despise, disdain, contemptible, think to scorn, or vile person.[120] At the time, Esau disesteemed the significance of the Abrahamic Covenant, which evidenced his lack of reverence for the God of his father Isaac, and his grandfather Abraham.[121]

By way of review, let us remember that the Abrahamic Covenant is the source of blessings toward all humankind. To Abraham and his descendants this promise was made; I will bless those who bless you, And I will curse him who curses you; And in you all the families of the Earth shall be blessed." (Gen. 12:13, NKJV)

Thus, Esau's disrespect for the contents of the covenant was an ultimate display of his disregard for humankind, its benefactor. As a consequence, the prophets Jeremiah and Obadiah would prophecy centuries later that the descendants of Esau would likewise in reversal be despised by men. Edom becoming small among the nations was discussed in great detail in the chapter called, "The Whodomites, Who are the Edomites Today."

> For indeed, I will make you [Edom] small among nations, Despised [bazah] among men. (Jer. 49:15, NKJV)

> Behold, I will make you [Edom] small among the nations; You shall be greatly despised [bazah]. (Obad. 1:2, NKJV)

The prophets use the Hebrew word bazah to describe the attitude among men toward the descendants of Esau. This prophecy likely depicts that Esau's disposition of enmity toward the contents of the covenant, was forwarded on through his descendants, as one would not expect God arbitrarily to advance a judgment well into the future generations without a cause. This enmity is explored further in the chapter called "Obadiah's Mysterious Vision."

Things go from bad to worse as the story goes regarding these brothers; before we study further it is important to preface the next event with the understanding that not only was Esau the firstborn, he was the preferred son of Isaac.

> So the boys grew. And Esau was a skillful hunter, a man of the field; but Jacob was a mild man, dwelling in tents. And Isaac loved Esau because he ate *of his* game, but Rebekah loved Jacob. (Gen. 25:27–28, NKJV)

This favoritism being displayed by Isaac toward Esau was in conflict with a prophecy that Rebekah had received from God. Rebekah realized that Jacob was destined to be the heir to the Abrahamic Covenant.

> But the children struggled together within her; and she said, "If *all is* well, why *am I like* this?" So she went to inquire of the LORD. And the LORD said to her: "Two nations *are* in your womb, Two peoples shall be separated from your body; *One* people shall be stronger than the other, And the older shall serve the younger." (Gen. 25:22–23, NKJV)

As Isaac's death drew near he was about to mistakenly pass on the blessings of the Abrahamic covenant to his firstborn Esau, rather than the appropriate recipient, Jacob.

Now it came to pass, when Isaac was old and his eyes were so dim that he could not see, that he called Esau his older son and said to him, "My son." And he answered him, "Here I am." Then he said, "Behold now, I am old. I do not know the day of my death. Now therefore, please take your weapons, your quiver and your bow, and go out to the field and hunt game for me. And make me savory food, such as I love, and bring *it* to me that I may eat, that my soul may bless you before I die." (Gen. 27:1–4, NKJV)

However, Rebekah convinced Jacob to deceive Isaac by impersonating Esau. It was her intent that the blessings would flow through Jacob, which was in line with the prophecy she had received from God that "the older shall serve the younger." Genesis 27 records the details of their conspiracy.

Some commentaries tend to exaggerate the point that this mother and son collaboration was a bit on the sinister side; however, the fact is that Isaac was already deceived as to whom the rightful recipient of the blessings should be. Isaac was about to bestow the blessings of the covenant to his preferred choice Esau the older, rather than Jacob the younger, God's chosen child. This would have been an enormous mistake, and therefore due to the severity of Isaac's foolishness in this matter, Rebekah and Jacob felt compelled to conspire in the manner that they did.

Centuries later, the Jewish prophet Malachi reinforced the fact that Rebekah was right-minded in her thinking. The contents of the Abrahamic covenant were indeed intended to flow through the loins of Jacob and his descendants. God preferred Jacob over Esau: The burden of the word of the LORD to Israel by Malachi. "I have loved you," says the LORD. "Yet you say, 'In what way have You loved us?' Was not Esau Jacob's brother?" Says the LORD. "Yet Jacob I have loved; But Esau I have hated, And laid waste his mountains and his heritage For the jackals of the wilderness." (Malachi 1:1–3, NKJV)

There is little doubt that Rebekah had previously informed Isaac of her prophecy that "the older shall serve the younger." Isaac should have recognized that it was Jacob and not Esau, who was to receive the blessings. Furthermore, one can suspect that Isaac had also been informed that Esau had previously sold his birthright to Jacob for a bowl of red (Edom) stew. In light of this information, it can be considered foolish for Isaac even to consider Esau, who had blatantly expressed his disregard toward the contents of the covenant, as the rightful heir to these all-important blessings.

Because of their successful collaboration, Jacob rightfully became the recipient of the blessings. As such, Esau came to hate Jacob and wanted to murder him as per Genesis 27:41. Harboring this attitude against Jacob, again displayed Esau's disrespect for the contents of the covenant, and his disregard for humankind. Like his uncle Ishmael before him, Esau likewise exhibited contempt toward the plan of God for the benefit of man, as Jacob's brother was supposed to adhere to the instructions in the verse below.

> Let peoples serve you [Jacob], And nations bow down to you. Be master over your brethren, And let your mother's sons [including Esau] bow down to you. Cursed *be* everyone who curses you, And blessed *be* those who bless you! (Gen. 27:29, NKJV)

Far from being excited about the prospects for his brother Jacob, the heir apparent as chosen by God to carry the torch of the Abrahamic Covenant, we are informed that:

> When Esau heard the words of his father, he cried with an exceedingly great and bitter cry, and said to his father, "Bless me—me also, O my father!" (Gen. 27:34, NKJV)

At this point we see Esau begin to covet the contents of the covenant: "Bless me—me also, O my father!"

> Then Isaac answered and said to Esau, "Indeed I have made him [Jacob] your master, and all his brethren I have given to him as servants; with grain and wine I have sustained him. What shall I do now for you, my son?" And Esau said to his father, "Have you only one blessing, my father? Bless me— me also, O my father!" And Esau lifted up his voice and wept. Then Isaac his father answered and said to him: "Behold, your dwelling shall be of the fatness of the Earth, And of the dew of heaven from above. By your sword you shall live, And you shall serve your brother; [Jacob] And it shall come to pass, when you become restless, That you shall break his yoke from your neck." So Esau hated Jacob because of the blessing with which his father blessed him, and Esau said in his heart, "The days of mourning for my father are at hand; then I will kill my brother Jacob." (Gen. 27:37–41, NKJV)

Isaac instructed Esau to serve Jacob, not to hate and desire to kill him. However, Esau, who had cried with "an exceedingly great and bitter cry," decided to deviate from the plan. In so doing, he evidence his lack of fellowship with the God of his father Isaac and his grandfather Abraham.

In his embittered state Esau goes to the clan of Ishmael and marries a daughter of Ishmael named Mahalath. Commentaries are mixed as to whether Esau did this in an attempt to please his father Isaac, or if he intended to be spiteful. Regardless of the motivation, the fact is that in so doing he entered into hostile territory, whereby the hatred harbored by Ishmael and his offspring was presumably well established. Esau married the daughter of a powerful figure, with a wellknown dislike for Isaac. It is probable that Mahalath fueled rather than extinguished the flame of Esau's bitterness toward his brother Jacob.

Esau saw that Isaac had blessed Jacob and sent him away to Padan Aram to take himself a wife from there, *and that* as he blessed him he gave him a charge, saying, "You shall not take a wife from the daughters of Canaan," and that Jacob had obeyed his father and his mother and had gone to Padan Aram. Also Esau saw that the daughters of Canaan did not please his father Isaac. So Esau went to Ishmael and took Mahalath the daughter of Ishmael, Abraham's son, the sister of Nebajoth, to be his wife in addition to the wives he had. (Gen. 28:6–9, NKJV)

Esau, like Ishmael, was also a big name on the Middle Eastern scene at the time. In accordance with the prophecy given to his mother Rebekah ("Two nations are in your womb"), a nation arose out from him, also.[122] Modern-day Southern Jordan, was formerly called Edom. This was the territory settled by Esau, and Edom became the nation that grew out of him.[123] Jacob, as heir to the Abrahamic Covenant which also promised the rise of a nation, became the nation Israel.

Hence, you have these three family members forming nations that border each other. As Ishmael (Saudi Arabia) and Esau (Edom/ Southern Jordan) formed their nations, they infused their hatred toward Jacob (Israel) into their cultures and descendants. As the nation of Edom formed, it advanced many aggressions against the Jewish people. For more detail, read the chapter in this book called "The Final Palestinian Farewell."

## Moab and Ammon: The Children of Abraham vs. the Children of Lot

The animosity that developed between Moab and Ammon, the children of Lot, toward the Jewish people can be understood, but its roots are more difficult to trace.[124] Unlike their relatives Hagar, Ishmael, and Esau, Moab and Ammon are not noted in the Bible as having any negative personal encounter with Abraham, Isaac, or Jacob. Though the lives of Moab and Ammon paralleled Ishmael and Isaac on the timeline, most of the adversarial activities between the Moabites and Ammonites in relationship to the Jews were manifested through their descendant's centuries after the deaths of Moab and Ammon.

There are several presumptions we can consider regarding the awareness of both Moab and Ammon:

1. They were familiar with the land boundaries Abraham appropriated to their father Lot (we study this episode later in this section).

2. They were familiar with the Abrahamic Covenant.

3.   They were familiar with their kinship with Ishmael and Isaac, and knew them, or at least knew of them personally.

4.   They had heard of the rivalries between Hagar and Sarah and Ishmael and Isaac.

5.   They were familiar with the hatred (*ebah*) developing in the entire region.

6.   They were also notable characters on the world scene during their time.

In time, the ancient hatred permeated into the Moabite and Ammonite cultures, and in Psalm 83 we are told that their descendants ultimately align themselves with the final Arab confederacy to be formed in the future against Israel. Furthermore, biblical accounts often find the descendants of Moab and Ammon acting out the olam ebah antagonistically toward the nation Israel. Interactions between the Moabites and Ammonites against the Jews often depict a dispute over the possession of certain parts of the Promised Land.[125] Considering the presumptions above, the historical biblical accounts, and the Psalm 83 prophecy, let us explore the development of the region in relationship to the land appropriated to Lot, which later formed into the territories named after his children, Moab and Ammon.

The tribal boundaries of Israel were established approximately four to five hundred years after the territories of Moab and Ammon became settled. These tribal boundaries of Israel penetrated eastward of the Jordan River, and abutted up to the previously established borders of Moab and Ammon.

## The Chain of Title

Perhaps a biblical search into the chain of title of these lands is a good starting point. The initial conveyance of the Land was to Abraham, and it was recorded in the Abrahamic Covenant.

> Now the LORD had said to Abraham: "Get out of your country, From your family and from your father's house, To a land that I will show you. I will make you a great nation; I will bless you And make your name great." (Gen. 12:1–2, NKJV)

The land in question at this point lacked description. Abraham, then known as Abram, moved in the direction of Canaan, which gives us our first clue as to the vicinity of the land promised to him.[126] Ultimately it was identified as the land between the River of Egypt and the River Euphrates.[127] However, beforehand, while the land was yet generally unidentified, a significant dispute, which is recorded in Genesis 13: 5-7, arose regarding the land between the herdsmen of Abram and the herdsmen of Lot, Abram's Nephew.[128]

So Abram said to Lot, "Please let there be no *strife* between you and me, and between my herdsmen and your herdsmen; for we *are* brethren. *Is* not the whole land before you? Please *separate* from me. If *you take* the left, then I will go to the right; or, if *you go* to the right, then I will go to the left." And Lot lifted his eyes and saw all the plain of Jordan, that it *was* well watered everywhere (before the LORD destroyed Sodom and Gomorrah) like the garden of the LORD, like the land of Egypt as you go toward Zoar. Then Lot chose for himself all the plain of Jordan, and Lot journeyed east. And they separated from each other. (Gen. 13:8-11, NKJV)

Abraham granted Lot the area eastward of Canann, referred to in the above passages as the plain of Jordan. This land later came to be known as Moab, and Ammon, named after the direct descendants of Lot. Today this territory best represents modern day Central and Northern Jordan.

Abram dwelt in the land of Canaan, and Lot dwelt in the cities of the plain and pitched *his* tent even as far as Sodom. But the men of Sodom *were* exceedingly wicked and sinful against the LORD. And the LORD said to Abram, after Lot had separated from him: "Lift your eyes now and look from the place where you are—northward, southward, eastward, and westward; for all the land which you see I give to you and your descendants forever." (Gen. 13:12–15, NKJV)

God told Abram to lift his eyes and look panoramically about him, and that all the surrounding land would become his and his descendants forever. Lot, apparently possessing the same panoramic view as Abram also lifted his eyes, and turned his focus to the fertile soil to the East of where they stood. This land, presumably also in the scope of Abram's view, was thus Abram's to keep or convey. Abram opted to appropriate this land to Lot and his herdsmen.

The territories that today best represent most of modern-day Israel and Northern and Central Jordan were then available at the discretion of Abram to be distributed. This ability of Abram to distribute the land evidenced that at least those subject portions were part of the Promised Land; otherwise, he would have lacked the ability to convey appropriately the title between the two of them.

So it was that Abraham settled west of the Jordan River (Israel), and Lot settled east of the Jordan (Northern and Central Jordan). Southern Jordan was eventually developed by Abraham's grandson Esau and became known as Edom. Historically, Central Jordan was territorially developed by the descendants of Moab, Lot's firstborn son, and Northern Jordan likewise developed by the descendants of his second son Ben Ammi.[129] The territory was identified as Ammon. Thus, the children of lot are better known biblically as Moab and Ammon.

This event gives the first official description of the Promised Land, and in the same instance depicts the first contest over the Promised Land in question. As stated previously in Genesis 13:7–8, "there was strife" between the herdsmen of Abram's livestock and the herdsmen of Lot's livestock. So Abram said to Lot, "Please let there be no strife between you and me and between my herdsmen and your herdsmen; for we are brethren."

In order to avoid further strife between them and their herdsmen over the coveted covenanted Promised Land, Abraham requests that Lot and his herdsmen depart.

> *Is* not the whole land before you? Please separate from me. If *you take* the left, then I will go to the right; or, if *you go* to the right, then I will go to the left. (Gen. 13:9, NKJV)

The second encounter of significant proportion was between the Hebrews and the Moabites, whereby the Jews were making their way out of Egypt back into the Promised Land via the Exodus route through Edom, Moab, and Ammon (modern-day Jordan). The Moabites were concerned that the Hebrews would overtake the territory of Moab and reclaim it back into their promised land.[130]

> By this point, it was understood that this land, which was situated between the River of Egypt and the river Euphrates, had in Genesis 15:18 (over four hundred years prior) been given by God back to Abraham and his Hebrew descendants. This meant the Hebrews returning to their Promised Land could reclaim Moab and Ammon.

The Hebrews in power exited Egypt and the leadership of Moab sought to curse them.[131] Thus, early on we see the descendents of Moab already harbored hostility toward the children of Abraham. Whereas the people of Moab harbored hatred toward the Jews, the Jews were taught early on that they were not to harm the land appropriated to the descendents of Lot. This respect for the land chosen by Lot caused the Hebrews to remember their history. They would be responsible to recall the dispute between the herdsmen of Abraham, and herdsmen of Lot, which eventuated in the separation of the land.[132]

> Then the LORD said to me [Moses], "Do not harass Moab, nor contend with them in battle, for I will not give you *any* of their land *as* a possession, because I have given Ar to the descendants of Lot *as* a possession." (Deut. 2:9, NKJV).

> And *when* you come near the people of Ammon, do not harass them or meddle with them, for I will not give you *any* of the land of the people of Ammon *as* a possession, because I have given it to the descendants of Lot *as* a possession.'" (Deut. 2:19, NKJV).

The next historical interaction between the children of Lot and the children of Israel was a story of conflict. Subsequently Moab and Ammon confederated in war against Israel and defeated it. Israel was under the sovereignty of Moab for approximately eighteen years.[133] Israel later regained their own sovereignty by defeating Moab, their enemy, killing about 10,000 of the stout men of Moab.[134]

The Bible records numerous conflicts that continued throughout time between Moab and Ammon against Israel. These encounters prove that early on the precedent had been clearly established; Moab and Ammon chose to embrace the ancient hatred spreading rampantly in the region. For the most part, Moab and Ammon considered Israel their enemy. They chose to serve their gods, rather than Jehovah, God of the Jews, the God who gave their patriarch Lot their prescribed lands.

The image below, called "The Family Feuds," connects the historic biblical accounts of the family rivalries.

## The Family Feuds

| | | | |
|---|---|---|---|
| **The Mothers** | Sarah vs. Hagar | HAGARENES | *Genesis 16 & 21* |
| **The Sons** | Isaac vs. Ishmael | ISHMAELITES | *Genesis 16, 17 & 21* |
| **The Twin Brothers** | Jacob vs. Esau | PALESTINIANS | *Genesis 25-28 & 32-33* |
| **The Cousins** | Israelites vs. Ammonites & Moabites | JORDANIANS | *Numbers 22- 25, Judges 3 & 10-11, 2 Kings 3, 2 Chron. 20* |
| **The Great Grand Kids** | Hebrews vs. Amalakites | AMALAKITES | *Numbers 14, Judges 3* |

**Fig. 3. The Family Feuds of the Patriarchs and Matriarchs.**
(*Created by Prophecy Depot Ministries.*)

Also contributing to the ancient hatred in the region were the plagues that came against Egypt. This devastating period in Egyptian history eventually led to the

Hebrew Exodus out of Egypt and into the Promised Land. These plagues cemented the ancient hatred firmly in place in Egypt. The Egyptians were already prone to hate the Hebrews from the disposition Hagar had introduced to them about five hundred years prior.

> "Because you have had an ancient [olam] hatred [ebah], and have shed the blood of the children of Israel by the power of the sword at the time of their calamity, when their iniquity came to an end, therefore, *as* I live," says the LORD GOD, "I will prepare you for blood, and blood shall pursue you; since you have not hated blood, therefore blood shall pursue you. Thus I will make Mount Seir most desolate, and cut off from it the one who leaves and the one who returns." (Ezek 35:5–7, NKJV)

This prophecy of Ezekiel tells the story. It points out that when the iniquity of the Jewish people had run its due course, those who harbored the ancient hatred still persisted in shedding Jewish blood. For this, those who persisted in the shedding of Jewish blood well beyond that point in time when the Jewish "iniquity came to an end" will see their own blood shed.

The inference is as follows: The iniquity of the Jews was the rejection of Jesus Christ; this evidenced their total apostasy as the client nation of their God Jehovah, i.e., "My people Israel." Subsequently, in AD 70 and wholly in AD 135, they were dispersed out of Israel into the nations of the world at large. This Jewish judgment "came to an end" as evidenced by the Holocaust episode in world history. In the aftermath, the Jewish people began to make their way back to their homeland Israel, and immediately met with "the power of the sword" upon their return. This hostile welcoming committee exhibited the "ancient hatred" (olam ebah).

It was not part of the prophetic program that upon the restoration of the nation Israel, whereby the Jewish people would return into their homeland, that the Arabs should shed Jewish blood. Therefore, in accordance with the curse-for-curse-in-kind clause contained within the Genesis 12:3 clause of the Abrahamic Covenant, these Arabs will experience the shedding of their own blood.

> I will prepare you [*Psalm 83 Arabs*] for blood, and blood shall pursue you; since you have not hated [*spilling Jewish*] blood, therefore blood shall pursue you. (Ezekiel 35:6, NKJV; emphasis added).

Though the Arabs who harbor the "ancient hatred" have made several confederate attempts in modern history to destroy the restored nation Israel, the one that issues the final farewell is described in Psalm 83. The confederate effort, expected to occur in the not-so-distant future, will finally provoke God to judge the "ancient hatred."

# THIRTEEN

# The Final Palestinian Farewell

## The Reprisal of Edom

**"Palestine 'ready to end all claims against Israel'"**

*The Telegraph 11/12/12*

"The Palestinians are ready to end all historic claims against Israel once they establish their state in the lands Israel occupied in the 1967 Middle East War, Palestinian President Mahmoud Abbas said on Sunday, addressing a long-standing Israeli demand."

**D**id you know the Bible has foretold for us the events that must occur in order to make an end of the present Israeli-Palestinian conflict? It predicted the arrival of the present Middle East predicament, and in keeping with its sovereign authority as the holy Word of God, dared to forecast its finality. This study focuses upon the reprisal of Edom, the expanse of which abruptly brings to a conclusion the ongoing Arab-Israeli conflict.

For the day of the LORD upon all the nations is near; As you have done, it shall be done to you; *Your reprisal shall return upon your own head.* (Obad. 1:15, NKJV; emphasis added)

This key passage, written by the Hebrew prophet Obadiah, speaks of a reprisal which returns upon the head of the descendants of Esau. Esau's descendants presently share ethnical representation within the Palestinians. This head blow knocks them down to the canvas and out for the count. It results in the final Palestinian farewell.

Though the world continues to cough up attempts at a political solution to the conflict, the Bible describes its end coming from events of an entirely different nature. "As you have done, it shall be done to you," alludes to a curse-for-curse-in-kind response. "Your reprisal shall return upon your own head," presents a boomerang affect, sending a blow back to the point of its origin.

By way of brief review, at this point you should recall the following:

1.  Esau was the twin brother of Jewish patriarch Jacob.[135]

2.  Esau was the founder of Edom, making him the father of the Edomites.[136]

3.  The Edomites initially inhabited what we today call Southern Jordan.

4.  They eventually migrated into Israel, maintaining a population in both places.

5.  They later assumed the Greek name Idumeans.

6.  A remnant of Esau's descendants resides within the Palestinians of today.

Digesting these facts, we can discern that Obadiah describes a judgment destined to debilitate the Palestinian people. Their mistreatment of the Jewish people, results in their own ethnical demise. It matters not what the world envisions, rather what has been written, is that which will indeed occur!

As previously mentioned, God established His Gentile foreign policy long ago in Genesis 12:1–3. Whether or not the Gentile would be blessed or cursed was directly related to his or her treatment, then and now, of Abraham and/or his descendants, the Jews. Though Abraham fathered several children, the context of the blessing or cursing clause finds its application through the patriarchal lineage of Abraham, Isaac, and Jacob, from who the Hebrew people came.[137]

Genesis 12:3 declares is "As you have done, (to Abraham or his descendants) it shall be done to you." Your reprisal, translated "your reward" in the King James Version, "shall return upon thine own head." This reprisal comes in strict accordance with the curse-for-curse-in-kind clause contained within the Abrahamic Covenant formulated approximately 4000 years ago. Unfortunately, Esau and his descendants, including the Palestinians, opted for the curse.

Before Obadiah issues the reprisal edict in Obadiah 1:15, he lists the crimes committed against Israel, by the Edomites, in Obadiah 1:10–14. We find a detailed explanation of these crimes in the Obadiah's Mysterious Vision chapter of this book.

Obadiah concludes in verse 15 with a devastating uppercut to the jawbone of the Palestinians: "As you have done, it shall be done to you; Your reprisal shall return upon your own head." This dreadful declaration is actually preceded by "For the day of the LORD upon all the nations is near;" which gives indication of the timing of the reprisal. The knockout punch to the Palestinians occurs prior to the "day of the LORD upon all the nations." This means the Arab-Israeli conflict will be concluded prior to the infamous seven-year Tribulation Period, otherwise known as Daniel's Seventieth Week.

As if the crimes committed in Obadiah 1:10–14 against the Jews, which occurred prior to the Holocaust, weren't horrific enough, the descendants of Esau picked up where they left off upon the return of the Jews back into the land of Israel, which commenced on May 14, 1948.[138] Ezekiel saw this subsequent misbehavior well in advance as per Ezekiel 35:5-6.

The international community continually complicates and confounds foreign policy, though God formatted it centuries ago in an utterly simplistic manner. How one interacts with the descendants of Abraham determines whether he or she is blessed or cursed. The world has no ability to override God's will in this matter. The descendants of Esau opted to curse the Jews by antagonizing them upon their restoration back into the land of Israel, thereby provoking upon themselves divine longstanding foreign policy of a similar negative nature.

An example of this foreign policy is a player on the international stage: Great Britain. When the famous Balfour Declartion was declared in 1917, Britain was a superpower, and had gained a significant hold on the Middle East. By 1939, however, anti-semitism had begun to assert itself in British politics, culminating in the infamous "White Paper," which limited Jewish immigration to Palestine (thus dooming many European Jews).

During the Oslo years, Great Britain has pressed Israel for concessions to the Palestinians, at the same time the country has been moving toward sharia compliance due to the number of radical Muslim clerics allowed to operate within the U.K. These incremental steps away from Israel not coincidentally parallel the twilight of the once-vaunted British Empire.

How ironic that at one time, Great Britain was led by men who believed the prophetic promises to the Jews. In our day, such a worldview is considered quaint at best, dangerous at worst. British religious leaders like Stephen Sizer are aggressive opponents of Zionism.

The return of the Jews back into the land of Israel was not an unknown prophetic phenomenon; many Jewish prophets had predicted its occurrence, even though, in the years just before World War II, such talk was scoffed at and laughed at. Among them Ezekiel actually foretold the condition from which the restoration would occur. He stated that they would come back into the land only after they, the Jews, would go through the horrifically grave conditions of the Holocaust.

> Then He said to me, "Son of man, these bones are *the whole house of Israel.* They indeed say, *'Our bones are dry, our hope is lost, and we ourselves are cut off!'* Therefore prophesy and say to them, 'Thus says the LORD GOD: "Behold, O My people, I will open your graves and *cause you to come up from your graves, and bring you into the land of Israel.* Then you shall know that I am the LORD, when I have opened your graves, O My people, and brought you up from your graves."'" (Ezek. 37:11–13, NKJV; emphasis added)

Imagine experiencing these grave events and then returning to your ancient homeland, only to be greeted with continued hostility. Indeed, that is what occurred; the descendants of Esau, alongside the other ancient Arab enemies of Israel, immediately protested the return of the Jews. In 1948, Egypt, Jordan, Syria, Lebanon, Saudi Arabia, and Iraq attacked the tiny Jewish state.[139] More of the same followed in 1956, 1967, and 1973 as the Arabs continued to war against the reformation of the nation Israel. Meanwhile, the descendants of Esau diminished into a refugee condition, out from which Palestinian guerilla forces arose to engage in various stages of the conflict.

Can this behavior be excused and continue without a reprisal? According to Obadiah, it will not be excused but be brought to an end! He declares that a great price will be extracted for the punishment the Palestinians, and their Arab cohorts continue to inflict upon the Jewish people.

## The Two Judgments upon Edom

Throughout this book, we reference the two judgments that come upon Edom. These two judgments are episodes extremely relevant to the understanding of end-times Bible prophecy. Because of these two judgments, Edom finds itself desolated, a wilderness unsuitable for human habitation.

The reprisal of Edom referenced by Obadiah regards itself with the first of the two. Though the reprisal brings a degree of damage to the territory of Edom, which is modern-day Southern Jordan, it is primarily a military campaign regarded with bringing a cessation to the perpetual enmity forwarded against the Jewish people by the Edomite descendants of Esau.

The reprisal of Edom extends beyond the ethnical boundaries of the Edomites and encompasses even those Arab cohorts who, throughout time, have embraced this enmity established long ago. Collectively these populations will confederate in one final and massive Arab attempt to destroy the nation Israel. (Psalm 83:4-8).

This confederacy will have for its lead member the "tents of Edom," thereby making them one, if not the primary, representative of this coalition.[140] Therefore, we can understand scriptures associated with the first judgment of Edom in the broader context of their collective effect upon the surrounding Arab nations assembled in the Psalm 83 confederacy. In direct correlation to this confederate effort aimed entirely at Israel's annihilation comes the issuance of the divine response, which of course is the reprisal. Not withstanding, numerous scriptures specifically target individual judgments at these Arab nations that occur concurrently during the time of the reprisal of Edom.

What needs to be recognized is that the Edomite descendants of Esau, have throughout time, never thoroughly abandoned the enmity established long ago by Esau toward his twin brother Jacob, the patriarch of the Jewish people. In fact, this ancient hatred quoted earlier from Ezekiel 35:5 is at the center of the Arab-Israeli conflict. The primary nations listed in Psalm 83:6–8 that will confederate alongside the tents of Edom, are Saudi Arabia, Jordan, Egypt, Lebanon, and Syria.

This is how this prophetic information translates in real-time application. The Edomites of old have a remnant of descendants amalgamated within the so-called Palestinians. Therefore, when the Bible speaks of the Edomites in reference to unfulfilled prophecy, it finds its closest association with their modern-day equivalent, the Palestinians. Thus, the "tents of Edom" are none other than the tent-like communities occupied by the Palestinians. It is important to note that tent-communities have historically been a big component of the tribal nature of many Arab peoples; remember that Muammar Guaddafi, the assassinated president of Libya, who was a huge anti-Semite, once lived in tents in the Libyan deserts. Even today there are dozens of nomadic and semi-nomadic Bedouin tribes residing in North Africa and the Middle East.[141]

The Bible uses tents descriptively to represent either refugee communities or military encampments. Today both scenarios find application— there are millions of displaced Palestinian refugees, including the Hamas terrorist group, and contained therein are millions opposed to the restoration of the Jewish nation of Israel. This opposition has developed a military mindset and has manifested into the ongoing struggle the world witnesses daily in the Middle East. Even the so-called "Right of Return" of the Palestinian refugees is another unconventional weapon used by the Arabs to try to destroy Israel. This bodes well within the PLO's "Phased Plan" adopted by Yasser Arafat in 1974. As the quotes below evidence, the return of millions of Palestinian refugees into Israel proper would greatly facilitate this 3-phased plan.

## The PLO's "Phased Plan"[142]

"In the October 1973 Yom Kippur War, the Arab states launched a surprise attack against Israel on the holiest day of the Jewish calendar. Once again they tried to eliminate Israel, further motivated this time by the desire to redeem their honor after their major defeat in the 1967 Six-Day War. Though Israel was initially caught off guard, it then regrouped and repelled the Arab attack, but not before incurring heavy casualties. The war convinced the Arabs that they would not be able to destroy Israel militarily within its post-1967 boundaries. Thus they embarked upon a new three-stage strategy for Israel's destruction, embodied in the PLO's 1974 decision commonly known as the Phased Plan (the text of which is below).

## The plan in brief:

1. Through the "armed struggle" (i.e., terrorism), to establish an "independent combatant national authority" over any territory that is "liberated" from Israeli rule. (Article 2)

2. To continue the struggle against Israel, using the territory of the national authority as a base of operations. (Article 4)

3. To provoke an all-out war in which Israel's Arab neighbors destroy it entirely ("liberate all Palestinian territory"). (Article 8)

*Today, the Phased Plan remains relevant. Speaking just after the 1993 revelation of the Israel-PLO accord, PLO Chairman Yasser Arafat announced that the historic agreement "will be a basis for an independent Palestinian state in accordance with the Palestine National Council resolution issued in 1974.... The PNC resolution issued in 1974 calls for the establishment of a national authority on any part of Palestinian soil from which Israel withdraws or which is liberated." (Radio Monte Carlo, 1 September 1993).*[143]

The plight of the Palestinians, whereby they seek to antagonize the restoration of the Jewish nation Israel, has become endearing to the surrounding Arab nations listed in Psalm 83:6–8. Their Arab ancestors, much like the Edomites, have harbored hatred toward the Jewish people throughout time. The plight of the Palestinians banners their common concerns regarding the restoration of the nation Israel as the Jewish state.

The fulfillment of Psalm 83 looms somewhere in the not-so-distant future, at which point the reprisal of Edom will result. This animosity toward the restoration of the nation Israel as the Jewish state, spearheaded by the Palestinians and applauded by the Arabs, will not subside, as it is too deeply rooted in its ancient origins. It will rear its ugly head in fulfillment of Psalm 83, at which time all the dastardly deeds of the Edomites throughout time immemorial will receive their reward! "Your reprisal shall return upon your own head."

Hence, we have the first of the two final judgments regarding the territory of Edom. The first judgment is executed via the means of the "exceedingly great army" of Israel. The world is witnessing the emergence of this army in these present times. This is the promise of reward to Edom that God made through the prophets:

> For the day of the LORD upon all the nations *is* near; As you have done, it shall be done to you; Your reprisal shall return upon your own head...The house of Jacob shall be a fire, And the house of Joseph a flame; But the house of Esau *shall be* stubble; They shall kindle them and devour them, And no survivor shall *remain* of the house of Esau," [The Final Palestinian Farewell] For the LORD has spoken. (Obad. 1:15, NKJV; Obad; 1:18, NKJV)

> "I will lay My vengeance on Edom by the hand of My people Israel, [IDF] that they may do in Edom according to My anger and according to My fury; and they shall know My vengeance," says the LORD GOD. (Ezek. 25:14, NKJV)

Edom can look forward to experiencing first hand the vengeance of God. It will become very familiar with His anger and fury, and ultimately "no survivor shall remain of the house of Esau!" This will be a catastrophic reprisal, and will essentially decimate the Palestinians at the time. As stated earlier, the expanse of the devastation extends deep into the collaborating Arab populations.

Whereas the Jewish people are instrumental in the execution of the first judgment destined for Edom, the second judgment concerns an entirely different campaign and is not delivered by the Jewish people, but by the Jewish individual Jesus Christ! This distinction is discussed further in the appendix called, "Those Surrounding Israel to be Devoured."

> For My [the Messianic person's] sword shall be bathed in heaven; Indeed it shall come down on Edom, And on the people of My curse, for judgment. [Antichrist and his armies] The sword of the LORD is filled with blood, It is made overflowing with fatness, With the blood of lambs and goats, With the

fat of the kidneys of rams. For the LORD has a sacrifice in Bozrah, And a great slaughter in the land of Edom. (Isa. 34:5–6, NKJV)

Who *is* this who comes from Edom, With dyed garments from Bozrah. This *One who is* glorious in His apparel, Traveling in the greatness of His strength? "I who speak in righteousness, mighty to save." [the Messianic person] Why *is* Your apparel red, And Your garments like one who treads in the winepress? "I have trodden the winepress alone, And from the peoples no one *was* with Me. [single handedly] For I have trodden them in My anger, And trampled them in My fury; Their blood is sprinkled upon My garments, And I have stained all My robes." (Isa. 63:1–3, NKJV)

These two sections of scripture quoted from Isaiah evidence that Edom will be the site of the final blood bath between Jesus Christ and the Antichrist and his armies. He single handedly conquers this enemy group in its entirety, trodding over them like one "who treads in the winepress." Edom will be the location of "a great slaughter."

The second judgment has nothing to do with the Palestinians per se, but has everything to do with the second coming of Jesus Christ. The Palestinian issue will have been resolved because of the reprisal of Edom prior to the second coming of Christ! Remember that the first judgment of Edom occurs when "the day of the LORD upon all the nations is near!"[144] The second judgment occurs subsequently when the day of the LORD upon all the nations is here.

For *it is* the day of the LORD'S vengeance, The year of recompense for the cause of Zion. (Isa. 34:8, NKJV)

For the day of vengeance *is* in My heart, And the year of My redeemed has come [recompense for the cause of Zion]. (Isa. 63:4, NKJV)

These passages from Isaiah 34 and 63 inform us that the timing of the Messiah, who comes to Edom and treads the winepress and gets blood sprinkled upon His garments at the time of the sacrifice in Bozrah, also referred to as the great slaughter in the land of Edom, is not when the day of the LORD is near, but rather when the day of the LORD has come. "It is the day of the LORD'S vengeance!"

This distinction is important in that it helps to clear up the common confusion taught from many prophetic pulpits, that the seven-year peace treaty between the Antichrist and the Jewish people has something to do with the current Arab-Israeli conflict in the Middle East. The seven-year pact made between the Jews and the Antichrist probably has absolutely nothing to do with the plight of the Palestinians. That conflict concludes in advance of the day of the LORD. The Jews will have already conquered the Arabs, who will be generally subservient under Israeli sovereignty.

It is not Arabs and Jews who make the seven-year treaty, but it is Antichrist and Jews, with the partial purpose of neutralizing the strengthening empowerment of the nation Israel. The Jews will have conquered the Psalm 83 confederacy, expanded their borders and sovereignty well into Arab territory, and become regionally superior as a result. Additionally, they will have become further esteemed by the events described in Ezekiel 38 and 39, whereby God divinely devastates the larger coalition of Russia, Iran, Libya, Ethiopia, and others. It is the episode that God has ordained through the Jewish people to uphold once again His Holy Name. (Ezekiel 38:16-39:7).

By the time the Antichrist drums up the seven-year treaty proposal, the Jewish people and the land of Israel will be operating from a position of extreme empowerment. This treaty may have nothing to do with stopping Palestinian terrorism and bringing peace to the Middle East, as we think of it these days. The Antichrist forwards this treaty in an attempt to neutralize the stature of the Jewish people, and their God, Who has once again made His holy name known through the client nation Israel, or "My people Israel."

The true content that is probably written upon the false covenant is a subject that I tackle in greater detail within the *Revelation Road* book series. In that series I approach the subject by:

1. Dispelling erroneous teaching on the false covenant,

2. Depicting the geopolitical conditions of the Mideast, and the world at the time,

3. Pointing out what the pertinent Bible verses declare.

## The Results of the Two Judgments Upon Edom

Scripture does not lack adequate description of the devastation resulting from the two judgments upon Edom. Below are numerous passages we can identify with either the first or the second judgment. The verses below suggest that the territory of ancient Edom (Southern Jordan), will witness some of the worst destruction the world has ever known.

As you read the following passages, you can generally determine whether the judgment is associated with the first or second judgment. The first judgment primarily affects the Palestinian people and some general war-torn territory in ancient Edom, whereas the second has little or nothing to do with the Edomites, but everything to do with the ancient territory of Edom. The second judgment permanently adversely affects the land of Southern Jordan.

The burden of the word of the LORD to Israel by Malachi [Malachi 450 BC].[145]

"I have loved you," says the LORD. "Yet you say, 'In what way have You loved us?'*Was* not Esau Jacob's brother?" [Esau and Jacob were twinbrothers] Says the LORD . "Yet Jacob I have loved; [Jacob fathered the Jewish nation] But Esau I have hated, [Esau fathered the Edomites represented by the Palestinians] And laid waste his mountains and his heritage For the jackals of the wilderness." Even though Edom has said, "We have been impoverished, [in fulfillment of Bible prophecy][146] But we will return and build the desolate places," Thus says the LORD of hosts: "They may build, but I will throw down [The Reprisal of Edom] They shall be called the Territory of Wickedness, And the people against whom the LORD will have indignation forever. Your eyes shall see, And you shall say, 'The LORD is magnified beyond the border of Israel.'" (Malachi 1:1–5 NKJV).

Egypt shall be a desolation, And Edom a desolate wilderness, Because of violence *against* the people of Judah, For they have shed innocent blood in their land. But Judah shall abide forever, And Jerusalem from generation to generation. (Joel 3:19–20, NKJV)

(Egypt will be a desolation for forty years, but Edom will be a desolate wilderness throughout the entire 1000-year Messianic kingdom. This is explained in the chapter called. "Egypt's Desolation, Deportation, and Conversion.")

Flee, turn back, dwell in the depths, O inhabitants of Dedan! [Saudi Arabia] For I will bring the calamity of Esau upon him, The time *that* I will punish him. [The Reprisal of Edom] If grape-gatherers came to you, Would they not leave *some* gleaning grapes? If thieves by night, Would they not destroy until they have enough? But I have made Esau bare; I have uncovered his secret places, And he shall not be able to hide himself. His descendants are plundered, [Palestinians] His brethren and his neighbors, [Surrounding Arab Nations] And he *is* no more [The "Final Palestinian Farewell" resulting from the first judgment]. (Jer. 49:8–10, NKJV; emphasis added)

"Will I not in that day," says the LORD, "Even destroy the wise *men* from Edom, And understanding from the mountains of Esau? Then your mighty men, O Teman, shall be dismayed, To the end that everyone from the mountains of Esau May be cut off by slaughter. [The Reprisal of Edom] For violence against your brother Jacob, [As you have done it shall be done to you] Shame shall cover you, [Your reprisal shall return upon your own head.] And you shall be cut off forever." (Obad. 1:8–10 NKJV; emphasis added)

Therefore hear the counsel of the LORD that He has taken against Edom, And His purposes that He has proposed against the inhabitants of Teman: Surely the least of the flock shall draw them out; Surely He shall make their dwelling places desolate with them. The Earth shakes at the noise of their fall; [The noise and shaking result from the war] At the cry its noise is heard at the Red Sea. [The battle cry extends to the Red Sea] Behold, He shall come up and fly like the eagle, And spread His wings over Bozrah; The heart of the mighty men of Edom in that day shall be Like the heart of a woman in birth pangs. [Resulting from the first judgment] (Jer. 49:20–22, NKJV)

"I see Him, but not now; I behold Him, but not near; A Star [Messianic Person] shall come out of Jacob; A Scepter shall rise out of Israel, And batter the brow of Moab [Central Jordan], And destroy all the sons of tumult. "And Edom shall be a possession [Israel expands its borders and sovereignty]; Seir [Southern Jordan] also, his enemies, shall be a possession [resulting from the first judgment], While Israel does valiantly. Out of Jacob One shall have dominion, And destroy the remains of the city. (Num. 24:17–19, NKJV; emphasis added)

Its [Edom's] streams shall be turned into pitch [resulting from the second judgment], And its dust into brimstone; Its land shall become burning pitch. It shall not be quenched night or day; Its smoke shall ascend forever. From generation to generation it shall lie waste; No one shall pass through it [Southern Jordan] forever and ever. But the pelican and the porcupine shall possess it, Also the owl and the raven shall dwell in it. And He shall stretch out over it. The line of confusion and the stones of emptiness. They shall call its nobles to the kingdom, But none *shall be* there, and all its princes shall be nothing. And thorns shall come up in its palaces, Nettles and brambles in its fortresses; It shall be a habitation of jackals, A courtyard for ostriches. The wild beasts of the desert shall also meet with the jackals, And the wild goat shall bleat to its companion; Also the night creature shall rest there, And find for herself a place of rest. (Isa. 34:9–14, NKJV; emphasis added)

"Edom also shall be an astonishment; Everyone who goes by it will be astonished And will hiss at all its plagues. As in the overthrow of Sodom and Gomorrah And their neighbors," says the LORD, "No one shall remain there, Nor shall a son of man dwell in it." (Jer. 49:17–18, NKJV)

Thus says the LORD GOD: "The whole Earth will rejoice when I make you desolate. As you rejoiced because the inheritance of the house of Israel was desolate, so I will do to you; you shall be desolate, O Mount Seir, as well as all of Edom—all of it! Then they shall know that I *am* the LORD.: (Ezek. 35:14–15, NKJV; emphasis added)

Therefore thus says the LORD GOD: "I have raised My hand in an oath that surely the nations [Psalm 83 confederates] that *are* around you [Israel] shall bear their own shame. [Resulting from the first judgment] (Ezek. 36:7, NKJV; emphasis added)

Thus says the LORD: "For three transgressions of Edom, and for four, I will not turn away its *punishment,* Because he pursued his brother [Israel] with the sword, And cast off all pity; His anger tore perpetually, And he kept his wrath forever. But I will send a fire upon Teman, Which shall devour the palaces of Bozrah [resulting from the first judgment]." (Amos 1:11–12, NKJV; emphasis added)

## Summary

God intends the reprisal of Edom to severely affect the Middle East and leave a lasting impression upon all the inhabitants of the world. It will serve in the future as an echo of God's past and present foreign policy. "As you have done it shall be done to you," appropriately describes the curse-for-curse-in-kind clause of the Abrahamic Covenant.

The fact that the timing of the reprisal of Edom occurs when "the day of the LORD upon all the nations is near" is a call to caution for the world population that the end of life on Earth at that time will also be near. It will be a call to remembrance that God blesses and curses in relationship to the treatment or mistreatment of Abraham or his descendants. At the time of the reprisal, the Jewish people will again be classified as "My people Israel," and as such, the Gentiles should carefully consider their behavior toward the nation Israel.

The execution of tremendous fury and vengeance against the Palestinians, leaving none to carry on the lineage of Esau, will demonstrate to the world that if God did not spare the descendants of Jacob's own twin brother Esau, then any who seek to bring harm to the Jewish people will not escape the curse-for-curse-in-kind clause.

It is understandable that the descendants of Esau should be dealt with harshly, in that they among all peoples should have shown brotherly affection toward the Jewish people. After all, Jacob, the patriarch of the Jewish people, was the twin brother of Esau, patriarch of the Edomites.

In contrast to Jacob, who was promised descendants, a homeland, and a King forever, his twin brother Esau will have none of this. The first judgment against Edom eliminates all of Esau's descendants, including any would-be kings, and the second judgment leaves Esau's homeland unsuitable for human habitation. Indeed, one will have to consider the brevity of the Abrahamic Covenant when they think about the contrasting fates of the twin bothers Jacob and Esau.

> "The house of Jacob (Israel) shall be a fire, And the house of Joseph (Israel) a flame; But the house of Esau (Edomites / Palestinians) *shall be* stubble; They shall kindle them and devour them, And no survivor shall *remain* of the house of Esau," For the LORD has spoken. (Obadiah 1:18, NKJV; emphasis added).

# FOURTEEN

# Psalm 83 and the Prophets

**"Israel says '79 rockets fired at it from Gaza"**

*Reuters October, 24, 2012*

**"Israel Asks Egypt to Remove Tanks From Sinai"**

*New York Times August 21, 2012*

## Is Psalm 83 a Prayer, Prophecy, or Both?

Although I believe that Psalm 83 is both an imprecatory prayer and a Bible prophecy, there are some who favor the view that the Psalm is merely a prayer. Widely respected pastor and Bible prophecy expert Dr. Mark Hitchcock leans in this direction. In a chapter titled, "What About the Psalm 83 War?" in his book called *"Middle East Burning,"* he non-dogmatically posits this view. After professionally presenting the *Isralestine* hypothesis, and the potential connections between Psalm 83 and Ezekiel 38, Dr. Hitchock writes;

*"We have to remember that the Psalms were written long before the prophets began to write and give specific prophecies concerning the nations. The prophets are where we look to find detailed information concerning the various world*

*powers and end time events"....... "While I like Bill Salus and appreciate the diligent work he has done in setting forth the thesis for a separate Psalm 83 war, I don't see a separate Psalm 83 war taking place before the Tribulation occurs. While there will be wars and rumor of wars and nation rising against nation in the end times, I believe Scripture points to two major wars involving Israel during the last days- the Gog of Magog war during the first half of the Tribulation and the battle of Armageddon at the culmination of the Tribulation."[147]*

Although I normally agree with the teaching of my friend Mark Hitchcock, I respectfully disagree with his views of the Psalm, and the timing of Ezekiel 38 in the first half of the Tribulation. However, I do agree that the "prophets are where we look to find detailed information concerning the various world powers and end time events." Fortunately, it appears as though the prophets did provide important additional information to the Psalm 83 prophecy. But, before identifying the pertinent prophecies of the major and minor prophets, I will explain why I believe the Gog of Magog invasion of Ezekiel 38 – 39 is probably a Pre-Tribulation event.

## Ezekiel 38-39 is probably a Pre-Tribulation Event

In fifty-two highly descriptive passages, the prophet Ezekiel predicts that nine populations named Gomer, Meshech, Tubal, Persia, Magog, Togarmah, Put, Libya, and Cush will invade Israel in the "latter years." The general consensus among many end time's experts today is that these ancient populations identify the modern day countries of Russia and its Southern Steppes, along with Turkey, Iran, Tunisia, Morocco, Libya, Ethiopia, Sudan, Somalia, and perhaps even Germany. This is a prophecy that many Bible prophecy experts are expecting to find final fulfillment in the near future. I agree that this prophecy is very near to finding its fulfillment, but I don't believe it is next. In my estimation Psalm 83 precedes Ezekiel 38, and that both prophecies find Pre-Tribulation fulfillments. More about this prophecy is explored in the chapter called "Psalm 83 or Ezekiel 38: What's the Next Middle East News Headline?"

Fortunately, the Lord intervenes on Israel's behalf and divinely defeats this formidable Gog of Magog coalition according to Ezekiel 38:18-39:6. Subsequently, the nation of Israel embarks upon national campaigns to bury the enemy corpses, and concurrently harnesses the energy from the weapons of these defeated invaders.

"Then those who dwell in the cities of Israel will go out and set on fire and burn the weapons, both the shields and bucklers, the bows and arrows, the javelins and spears; and they will make fires with them for seven years. They will not take wood from the field nor cut down *any* from the forests, because they will make fires with the weapons; and they will plunder those who plundered them, and pillage those who pillaged them," says the Lord GOD." (Ezekiel 39:9-10, NKJV).

These Ezekiel verses suggest that Israel will possess the know-how to convert the advanced enemy weapons of mass destruction possessed by the Ezekiel 38 invaders into fuel, perhaps for heating, electricity, and other related energy needs. Israelis appear to utilize these weapons for energy consumption for a period of seven-years. This will be no problem during the peaceful first half of the tribulation, but not likely during the perilous second half, because Jews will be fleeing for their lives, rather than harnessing this energy.

Concerning the separation point between the first and second halves of the Tribulation Period, Christ warned the Israelis in Matthew 24:15-22 that they should flee for their lives when they witness the "abomination of desolation," because that signaled a period of "Great Tribulation" was coming. This abominable event occurs at the mid-point of the Tribulation period.

> "Therefore when you see the *'abomination of desolation,'* spoken of by Daniel the prophet, standing in the holy place" (whoever reads, let him understand), "then let those who are in Judea flee to the mountains. Let him who is on the housetop not go down to take anything out of his house. And let him who is in the field not go back to get his clothes. But woe to those who are pregnant and to those who are nursing babies in those days! And pray that your flight may not be in winter or on the Sabbath. For then there will be great tribulation, such as has not been since the beginning of the world until this time, no, nor ever shall be. And unless those days were shortened, no flesh would be saved; but for the elect's sake those days will be shortened." (Matthew 24:15-22, NKJV).

These Matthew 24 verses are part of the reason the second half of the Tribulation is commonly called the Great Tribulation. It stands to reason that if Christ instructs Israelis to flee immediately for safety at the midpoint of the Tribulation period that the refugees won't be stopping along the way to convert anymore of these weapons in the process.

Therefore, many scholars suggest that Ezekiel 38 and 39 must conclude, not commence, no later than three and one-half years before the seven-years of tribulation even begins. This allows the Jews seven full years to burn the weapons before they begin fleeing for their lives. Realistically, it will probably take approximately a year to even collect, dismantle, and covert the weapons cache prior to that. It's even possible that there are more than seven years' worth of weapons available for fuel consumption, but the conversion process abruptly halts at the midpoint of the Tribulation when the abomination of desolation occurs.

Here's how this could break down incrementally in real time. Allow about one year for the Ezekiel 38 battle to occur and the weapons to be converted. Remember, assembling a coalition and mobilizing an invasion of the scope described in Ezekiel

38 is no twenty-four hour undertaking. Then consider an additional seven-year span to burn the weapons. And lastly, add in the final three and one-half years of Great Tribulation, for a total of eleven and one-half years.

If this hypothesis is correct, this means that at least (underscore at least because it's probably going to be longer) that from the time the Ezekiel 38 invasion begins until the second coming of Christ to set up His kingdom, there should exist at least eleven and one-half more years. I could be more technical on the timing, because Daniel 12:11-12 adds an additional seventy-five days to the equation. His infamous 'Seventieth Week' ends, and then the two and one-half month interval kicks in, at which time some Bible prophecy experts suggest that the sheep and goat judgment of Matthew 25:32-46 takes place."[148]

In summary, some scholars teach that little or no time separates the Gog of Magog invasion from the Tribulation period, and others believe the invasion actually occurs during the Tribulation. I agree with those that teach the Ezekiel 38 invasion must conclude at least three and one-half years before the seven-years of tribulation commences. After the Ezekiel invasion Israel may have more than seven-years of weapons supply for energy consumption. They could have ten or more years for all we know. But one thing seems almost certain, that at the mid-point of the Tribulation period when the genocidal campaign of the Antichrist is in full swing, Israelis appear to be fleeing for their lives rather than converting enemy weapons into sources of fuel for energy.

## Psalm 83 and the Major and Minor Prophets

Many of the prophecies written about by the Major and Minor prophets, that I believe find application to Psalm 83 have already been presented throughout various parts of this book, but for the purposes of the point of this chapter, some may be repeated. In *Revelation Road, Hope Beyond the Horizon*, one way I approach this subject is by identifying the Arab casualties and prisoners of war that seem to result from being defeated in Psalm 83. Below are portions of the *Revelation Road* commentary concerning this subject.

Several Scriptures suggest the Arabs will suffer severely from their bitter defeat. Numerous Arab refugees, prisoners of war (POWs), deaths, and injuries can be expected. As you read about the Arab losses, be reminded that the Lord so loves everyone that He desires that none should perish. That's the gospel message of John 3:16 and the reason Jesus Christ, the only begotten son of God, died sacrificially and rose again for all sinners; Arabs, Jews, and all of humanity alike. Proverbs 8:31 states that the Lord rejoices in His inhabited world and delights in mankind.

Therefore, it is clear that the Lord's "druthers" are to have a personal relationship with the Arabs through the sacrificial blood of Jesus Christ, rather than witness their demise during Psalm 83. But, He has longstanding divine foreign policy in place, as outlined in Genesis 12:3. This policy mandates the cursing of those who oppress Abraham and his Israelite descendants; i.e., the Jews today. Psalm 109:17 confirms this by stating, "As he [the Arabs in the case of Psalm 83] loved cursing, so let it come to him; As he did not delight in blessing, so let it be far from him."

The Psalm 83 Arab confederates "love cursing" Israel. According the Ezekiel 35:5 and Ezekiel 25:15, the Arab hatred toward the Jews is deeply steeped in ancient roots. The very mission of the confederacy in Psalm 83:4 is the total destruction of the Jewish State, that "the name Israel be remembered no more."

Psalm 68:30b says, "Scatter the peoples who delight in war." Scattering often occurs as a result of war. The citizens are reduced to refugees, and the soldiers become POWs. This inhibits them from waging further war, and hopefully humbles them and inclines them to the God of the victors, which in the case of Psalm 83 is the Lord Jehovah of the Bible.

"Scattering the peoples who delight in war" to the end that they incline themselves toward the Lord, is what the Psalmist appears to request:

> "O my God, make them like the whirling dust, Like the chaff before the wind!" (Psalm 83:13)

Whirling dust and chaff blown about by the wind is a picture of dispersion. Then in the last verse, after he requests in Psalm 83:13-17 that the Arab confederates become shamed, and made like the whirling dust and the chaff before the wind, and as the flame that sets the mountains on fire, he closes with the following imprecation:

> "That they [the Arab confederates] may know that You, whose name alone is the LORD, Are the Most High over all the earth. (Psalm 83:18).

In the case of the Jordanians (Moab and Ammon, in Psalm 83), that's what happens, according to the Jeremiah prophecies below. Remnants of Moabites and Ammonites will survive and someday realize that the Lord is the "Most High over the earth." As a result these remnants will be with Christ in the Messianic kingdom.

> "Woe to you, O Moab! The people of Chemosh [former Moabite god, now replaced by Allah] perish; For your sons have been taken captive, And your daughters captive. "Yet I will bring back the captives [POWs and refugees] of Moab In the latter days," says the LORD. Thus far is the judgment of Moab. (Jeremiah 48:46-47, NKJV; emphasis added).

> "Behold, I will bring fear upon you," Says the Lord GOD of hosts, "From all those who are around you; You shall be driven out, [scattered] everyone headlong, And no one will gather those who wander off. But afterward I will bring back

The captives [POWs and refugees] of the people of Ammon," says the LORD. Thus says the LORD of hosts. (Jeremiah 49:5-6, NKJV; emphasis added).

Moab and Ammon were the children of Lot, Abraham's nephew. In Psalm 83 they are depicted as one of the weaker military members taking part in the Arab confederacy. We know this, because the Psalmist declares,

"Assyria also has joined with them; They have helped the children [Moab and Ammon] of Lot. *Selah.*" (Psalm 83:8)

The Hebrew word for helped used by Asaph here is zeroa, and in this instance it suggests Assyria shoulders much of Jordan's military burden, or otherwise attempts to compensate for the general insufficiencies of the Jordanian Armed Forces (JAF). Whereas the other members of Psalm 83 have world-class armies, the JAF doesn't even rank within the military top forty.[149] The primary function of the JAF is to prevent the overthrow of the ruling Hashemite Kingdom. They have performed well against the PLO in the past, but miserably against Israel in their 1948, 1967, and 1973 wars.

Jeremiah says fear comes upon Jordan from all around. Those around Jordan today are Israel to the west, Hezbollah to the northwest, Syria to the north, Iraq to the east, and Saudi Arabia to the south. All of the above, including Jordan, are part of Psalm 83. Assyria, at the time of the Psalm's issuance, was comprised of parts of modern-day Syria and Iraq.

The above suggests that Jordan gets drawn into the Psalm 83 conflict and at some point witnesses fearful events on all sides of its borders. Interestingly, Jordan's King Hussein I was pressured by Egyptian president Gamal Abdel Nasser to join in the 1967 Arab-Israeli war. Damascus, which ceases to be a city according to Isaiah 17:1, is 109 miles north of Amman, Jordan. The destruction of Damascus could be one of the reasons fear befalls Jordan. Jordan is clearly an enemy confederate member against Israel, but whether they are a voluntary or involuntary member is uncertain. At present, Jordan possesses a fragile peace treaty with Israel, but that will be abandoned when Jordan enlists in Psalm 83.

## Arab War Casualties from Psalm 83

There appear to be hordes of Arab casualties resulting from Psalm 83. Before identifying several more supporting Scriptures that deal with the Arab loss of life and associated sufferings, please be informed that Dr. Arnold Fruchtenbaum provides important information in his Footsteps of the Messiah (revised edition) book approaching this subject from a somewhat different angle, when he writes about the Arab States in Bible prophecy. He points out how the Arabs are dealt with for their aversion to Israel either through occupation, destruction, or conversion.[150]

Listed below are some of the Scriptures that I believe identify the Arab casualties suffered as the apparent result of the Psalm 83 war.

## The Killed and Wounded Arabs of Psalm 83

- *Jordan* – Primarily alluding to passages about Ammon, Moab, and Edom. Ammon represents modern-day northern Jordan, Moab—central Jordan, and Edom—southern Jordan. Ezekiel 25:13, and Ezekiel 25:9-10; Jeremiah 48:8,42, and 49:2; Isaiah 15:4; and Amos 2:2-3.

- *Egypt* – Isaiah 19:18; and Ezekiel 29:5,8, and 30:4,8. (*These Ezekiel verses could be part of Egypt's third judgment by the Antichrist as written about in the chapter called "Egypt's Desolation, Deportation, and Conversion."*)

- *Syria* – Isaiah 17:1,9, 14; Jeremiah 49:26-27; and possibly Amos 1:3-5.

  (*Note: Psalm 83:8 identifies Assyria (Assur) rather than Syria (Aram). So some prophecies concerning Syria, as in Isaiah 17, could occur independently from Psalm 83. But it is the author's opinion that Isaiah 17 will occur during Psalm 83 or at least in the close proximity of time to Psalm 83*).

- *Saudi Arabia* – Ezekiel 25:13, primarily alluding to passages about Dedan, which is modern–day northwestern Saudi Arabia. The Saudis are represented under the banner of the Ishmaelites in Psalm 83:6.

- *Palestinians* – Primarily alluding to passages about Gaza, Philistia, Philistines, and the Edomites. Jeremiah 49:10; Ezekiel 25:16; and Obadiah v.18.

- *Lebanon* – Primarily alluding to passages about Tyre and Sidon. Ezekiel 28:13; Amos 1:10; and Joel 3:4 (possibly).

## The Arab POWs and Refugees from Psalm 83

- *Jordan* – Isaiah 11:14; Jeremiah 48:7, 44-47, 49:3, 5-6; Ezekiel 25:3-4; and Amos 1:15.

- *Egypt* – Ezekiel 29:12-13. (This may be more related to the desolation by the Antichrist in Daniel 11:42-43 as per the chapter in this book called *"Egypt's Desolation, Deportation, and Conversion."*)

- *Syria* – Isaiah 17:3, 9, 11:16; and Amos 1:5.

- *Saudi Arabia*- Jeremiah 49:8.

- *Palestinians* – Jeremiah 49:11, 20; Obadiah vv. 19-20; and Amos 1:8.

- *Lebanon* – Obadiah v. 19 alludes to captives as far as Zarephath, which would be located in modern-day southwestern Lebanon.


All of the above correlating verses to the Arab countries and / or terrorist populations are what the author believes may find potential application to Psalm 83. These verses along with the others included throughout this book, and the ones below appear to evidence that Psalm 83 was clearly alluded to by the Major and Minor prophets.

This book lays down the gauntlet to all those who suggest that the Major and Minor prophets never referenced Psalm 83. Now it is up to these scholars to disprove that the plethora of prophetic verses provided won't apply to Psalm 83. If they are unable do so, then they should be willing to admit that at least several of the Major and Minor prophets prophesied about Psalm 83.

Perhaps, some of the dozens of prophecies included in this book, that are thought to be associated with Psalm 83, apply to differing epic events. However, if even half of these predictions apply, which at the risk of redundancy the author has clearly connected to Psalm 83, then it provides sufficient proof that this specific Psalm is also a bona fide prophecy.

To the author's best knowledge, this book has identified more prophetic verses that appear to be related to Psalm 83 than any other published work regarding this subject to date. Granted Ezekiel 38-39 offer fifty-two passages of extremely detailed, and important prophetic information. However, in reality this is a generous statement, because Ezekiel 39:23-29 are generally exclusive verses, which explain the Lord's overall sovereign plan to use Israel as His modus operandi, as a witness to the Gentile nations of the world. Thus, this means that Ezekiel 38-39 provides forty-five applicable verses, rather than fifty two.

Comparatively, this book identifies nearly 150 verses that appear to apply to the Psalm 83 prophecy. These include prophecies from the Major Prophets including Jeremiah, Ezekiel, and Isaiah, as well as the Minor Prophets consisting of Obadiah, Zephaniah, and Zechariah. Remember that Asaph, the author of Psalm 83, is also a prophet as per 2 Chronicles 29:30. Below are just a few examples of the many passages relating to the Psalm 83 prophecy. This extensive list doesn't include the prophecies in Amos 1:1-15, which might also find application with Psalm 83.

- Psalm 83:1-18....................................... (18 verses)

- Jeremiah 49:1-29, 12:14-17...................... (32 verses)

- Ezekiel 25:12-17, 28:24-26, 35:1-36:7, 37:10 (32 verses)

- Isaiah 17:1-14, 19:1-18, 11:14................... (35 verses)

- Obadiah 1:1-21....................................... (21 verses)

- Zephaniah 2:4-11.................................... (8 verses)

- Zechariah 12:2, 5-6................................ (3 verses)

## The Israeli Conquest

"But *they (the IDF)* shall fly down upon the shoulder of the Philistines toward the west; Together *they* shall plunder the people of the East [Haran, N. Syria Gen 29:1–5]; *They* shall lay their hand on Edom and Moab; And the people of Ammon shall obey *them*." (Isaiah 11:14, NKJV; emphasis added)

These are telling prophetic phrases, "they shall fly down," "they shall plunder," "They shall lay their hand on Edom and Moab," "And the people of Ammon shall obey them." Isaiah declares that "they, they, They, and them," are the IDF and IAF. The identity of who's doing the flying down, plundering, and laying their hand on modern day Jordan is depicted in Isaiah 11:11, which informs us that it's the regathered Jews in Israel. An army and air force is required for any nation to fly down, plunder, and lay hands on another country.

Moreover Isaiah 11:12-14 announces that "they, they, They, and them" are no longer a divided kingdom fighting amongst each other; rather, "they, they, They, and them," become engaged in a serious regional conflict against Gaza, Syria, and Jordan. Gaza, Syria, and Jordan are three members in the Psalm 83:6–8 confederacies. Since this Psalm 83 prophecy is not yet fulfilled, and requires a non-divided kingdom of Israel in order to be fulfilled, we can surmise that the nation Israel united today, meets this requirement.

Isaiah 11:14 alludes to Syria as "the people of the East." This can be determined by referring back to the first biblical usage of "the people of the East," which is found in Genesis 29:1–5. It alludes to people Jacob met who were from Haran. The same Hebrew words are used in both scriptural instances "the people" (ben) "of the East" (qedem).[151]

"So Jacob went on his journey and came to the land of the people [*ben*] of the East [*qedem*]. And he looked, and saw a well in the field; and behold, there *were* three flocks of sheep lying by it; for out of that well they watered the flocks. A large stone *was* on the well's mouth. Now all the flocks would be gathered there; and they would roll the stone from the well's mouth, water the sheep, and put the stone back in its place on the well's mouth. And Jacob said to them, "My brethren, where *are* you from?" And they said, "*We are from Haran.*" Then he said to them, "Do you know Laban the son of Nahor?" And they said, "We know him." (Gen. 29:1–5, NKJV; emphasis added)

Jacob sojourns out of the land of Canaan, which best represents Israel proper today, in an attempt to locate his future wife. He goes to Haran, which would today be located in modern-day northern Syria. Therefore, by association Isaiah appears to be informing his readers that Northern Syria is scheduled for plundering. A comparative study between Isaiah 11:14 and Isaiah 17 suggests that the extent of the Israeli assault against Syria, reaches from the southernmost to the northern most boundaries of the Syrian nation.

Although Isaiah 11:13 has been previously quoted in this book, it bears repeating because it states, "Also the envy of Ephraim shall depart, And the adversaries of Judah shall be cut off; Ephraim shall not envy Judah, And Judah shall not harass Ephraim." We see today in the midst of the Middle East conflict that no such enmity between Judah and Ephraim exists. The "envy" of old, which caused the kingdom to divide into two, has departed as foretold by Isaiah. Israel is a united kingdom today, attempting to survive the clear and present danger of the "perpetual enmity" described in Ezekiel 35:5, of the surrounding Arab nations.

The fact that Isaiah 11:14 predicts that the IDF "shall lay their hand on Edom" is significant because Edom experiences two end-time judgment sequences, first by the IDF, and then second by Christ at His Second Coming. Ultimately Edom, like Babylon, is rendered desolate throughout the 1000 year messianic kingdom period. Joel 3:19 says Edom will be a "desolate wilderness" during that period, "Because of violence against the people of Judah". The violence of the "tents of Edom" in Psalm 83 probably plays a huge part in Edom's two judgments.

The important point is that the IDF will not be laying its hands on Edom when it is a desolate wilderness. In this desolated condition, the territory of Edom, which is modern-day Southern Jordan, will offer the Jews nothing of desire upon which to lay their hands except thorns and thistles. Furthermore, the hand of the Jews, i.e., their military, will be disbanded on or about the commencement point of the kingdom period according to Micah 4:3, because the swords of the nations will be beaten into plowshares. The IDF will not be flying down, plundering, or laying their hands upon anything at that time, except for accomplishing the ministerial instructions given to them from the Messiah.

Whereas, the IDF will not exploit Edom in the Kingdom, "They shall lay their hand on Edom," prior to the commencement of the Kingdom period. It is prophesied in Ezekiel 25:12–17, and Obadiah 1:18, and various other scriptures, that the Israeli military will successfully execute the vengeance of the LORD against the Palestinians and their cohorts listed in Psalm 83:6–8, the fulfillment of which seemingly places Jewish sovereignty over Edom. This would account for the availability of Edom (Petra, Jordan) to become the final place of refuge for the faithful Jewish remnant.

The faithful Jewish remnant is the end-times generation of Jews, who survive the devastating antics of the Antichrist during the heavily prophesied Tribulation Period. This period, also referred to in scripture as the "time of Jacobs trouble," "the Day of the LORD," and "Daniel's Seventieth Week," just to name a few, is characterized by the most severe Holocaust attempt against the Jews in their history. It will vastly overshadow the Holocaust of the Jews by Hitler and the Germans.

## Zephaniah's Call to Caution

Another chapter in *Isralestine* that connected the IDF with Psalm 83 is called "Zephaniah's Call to Caution." Zephaniah 2 presents pertinent related Psalm 83 prophecies much like Isaiah 11. Chapter 2 of Zephaniah delivers a powerful message to the meek of the earth, but it also dedicates a major portion toward activities that appear to occur at the time of the Israeli Conquest over the Psalm 83 confederated Arab armies. He alludes to Jewish victories over the Palestinians and Jordanians. These two contemporary groups are generally, but not exclusively, comprised of the descendant peoples from Philistia, Moab, Ammon, and Edom.[152]

These four historical ethnicities are enlisted in the Psalm 83:5–8 Arab confederacy, destined to attack Israel. Zephaniah foretells a time when the peoples of Philistia, Moab, and Ammon, i.e., the modern-day Palestinians and Jordanians, will be found guilty of homesteading the Holy Land. Their borders presently penetrate into the Gaza Strip, the West Bank, and border the Golan Heights, which Joshua 1:3-4 and Genesis 15:18 tells us will ultimately be territories deeded to the Jewish people.

In a nutshell, the Zephaniah 2 sets the stage as follows: The Jews return into the land of Israel, before the Tribulation, in a condition of unbelief (Zeph. 2:1-2), and conquer the Arab alliance, represented in part, by the Palestinians and Jordanians (Zeph. 2:3-4, 8-9). As a result, Israeli fortunes are greatly enhanced as they come into possession of the plunder and spoils of war (Zeph. 2:6-7, 9). In the process, Allah is greatly reduced as a god figure, and Islam is adversely affected (Zeph. 2:11).

Importantly, Zephaniah 2:2 points out that these above events occur before the day of the LORD arrives, which is the period most associated with the expiration date of the Earth in its present condition of existence, i.e., the Tribulation Period. He prophesies all of the above for the primary purpose of invoking the "meek of the Earth" into the worship of God (Zeph. 2:1-3).

## "Gaza shall be deserted, and Arab homes evacuated"

After Zephaniah's introductory call to caution to the "meek of the Earth" in chapter two, he proceeds to introduce the devastating effects that fall upon the Arab confederate members, Philistia, Moab, and Ammon. In so doing, he carries on with his theme that the Jewish people are gathering into the land of Israel, and that, in the process their fortunes are being restored. The modern-day equivalent of these Arab groups, are the Palestinians of the Gaza, the Palestinians of the West Bank, and the Jordanians of Northern and Central Jordan.

These specific Arab populations currently present themselves as formidable obstacles to the stretching out territorially of the returning Jews. As we read the words of Zephaniah, it becomes clear that these Arabs are considered trespassers and as such, they will be forcibly evicted before the Day of the LORD arrives. He outlines a series of conditions that will occur because of the Israeli victory over the Palestinians and Jordanians. The reason for this prophetic material is to serve as a "call to caution" to the "meek of the Earth."

> "Seek the LORD, all you humble of the land, who do his commands; seek righteousness, seek humility; perhaps you may be hidden on the day of the LORD'S wrath. For *Gaza* shall be *deserted*, and *Ashkelon* shall become *a desolation*; *Ashdod's people* shall be *driven out* at noon, and *Ekron* shall be *uprooted*. Ah, inhabitants of the seacoast, you nation of the Cherethites! The word of *the LORD is against you, O Canaan, land of the Philistines*; and I will destroy you until no inhabitant is left." (Zephaniah 2:3–5 NRSV; emphasis added).

Zephaniah describes a coming destruction that devastates several cities of ancient Philistia. Philistia is an enlisted member of the Psalm 83 Arab confederacy, which will advance against Israel, but will be destroyed by the IDF. Gaza, Ashkelon, Ashdod, and Ekron were four of the five prominent historical cities, known as the Pentapolis.[153]

Zephaniah prophesies of a future time when Gaza will be deserted, Ashkelon desolated, the people of Ashdod driven out, and Ekron uprooted. The lesson will be for that generation which experiences these four cities residing in those specific conditions that the day of the LORD is to shortly follow. This should cause the "meek of the Earth" to redeem the time and seek righteousness, humility, and to continue to uphold the justice of the LORD. The goal is that they may increase in number and many more might be hidden from the day of the LORD.

> "Seek the LORD, all you meek of the earth, Who have upheld His justice. Seek righteousness, seek humility. It may be that you will be hidden In the day of the LORD'S anger." (Zephaniah 2:3, NKJV).

Many are the commentaries that suggest prophesies regarding Philistia have already found their final fulfillment, and that the Philistines have become an ethnicity gone extinct. Though it may be difficult today to trace any residue of the ancient Philistines, the territory of Philistia is clearly identified in end-times prophecy through Psalm 83. Therefore, if what Zephaniah declares about these four cities should occur in the present or near future, it would likely find its closest association with the Palestinians of the Gaza area.

By Zephaniah's ordering of events, we are also caused to conclude that this prophecy regarding the desertion of Gaza, desolating of Ashkelon, driving out of Ashdod, and the uprooting of Ekron, is destined to occur sometime after the commencement of this present Jewish return back into the land of Israel, and yet before the day of the LORD. As such, it seems that this prophecy has yet to find its final fulfillment.

The Gaza of today is a coastal strip of land that the Palestinian Refugees occupy, and believe to be part of their heritage. However, long before there were Palestinians or even Philistines, this land was allotted to the tribe of Judah. Historically it was Jewish territory. Presently, it serves in part as a launch site for various types of short-range rockets aimed toward Jewish civilian targets in Israel. By no stretch of the imagination is Gaza deserted at the time of the writing of this chapter. Gaza is seeking to enlarge its borders into a connected Palestinian state with the West Bank.

> "And you, O seacoast, shall be *pastures, meadows for shepherds and folds for flocks*. The seacoast shall become the possession of the remnant of the house of Judah, on which they shall pasture, and in the houses of Ashkelon they shall lie down at evening. *For the LORD their God will be mindful of them and restore their fortunes.* (Zephaniah 2:6–7 NRSV; emphasis added).

We are further told that after Gaza is deserted, Ashkelon desolated, Ashdod driven out, Ekron uprooted, and no Palestinian inhabitants reside along the Southwestern seacoast of Israel, that this coastal territory will become the possession of the Jewish people. The territory will be for Israeli "pastures, meadows for shepherds, folds for flocks," rather than Hamas missile launch sites. The vacated houses of Ashkelon will provide shelter for the shepherds and their flocks. Presently, Gaza is not deserted; rather, it is home to the Hamas terrorist organization. Ashkelon and Ashdod are modern-day cities under Jewish jurisdiction.

Ekron today is most likely known as Tel Miqne, located approximately 23 miles southwest of Jerusalem. It has been the site of numerous noteworthy excavations in recent times, but is not today a city in its scope that is comparable to Gaza, Ashkelon, or Ashdod. Therefore, it will be up to the "meek of the Earth" to constantly observe the events that unfold in these Mediterranean seacoast areas, to see how this prophecy sets up and plays out.

Presently, this area is undergoing a serious "Land for Peace" struggle between the Palestinians and the Israelis. The final frontier, as to which group dominates over which territories, is not yet determined. At some point, however, the prophecy of Zephaniah will take place, Gaza will be deserted, and the houses of Ashkelon will be where the remnant of the house of Judah will lie down at evening time. It is interesting that a scenario has already occurred in modern history relative to Ashkelon, which might prove insightful. It is known as the Israeli National Master Plan of June 1949.

> "The Israeli national master plan of June 1949 designed Al Majdal as the site for a regional urban center of 20,000 people. Mass repopulation of the vacated Arab houses by Jewish immigrants or demobilised soldiers began in July 1949 and by December the Jewish population had increased to 2,500. During 1949, the town was renamed Migdal Gaza, and then Migdal Gad. Soon afterwards it became Migdal Ashkelon. In 1953 the nearby neighborhood of Afridar was incorporated and the current name Ashkelon was adopted. By 1961, Ashkelon ranked 18th amongst Israeli urban centers with a population of 24,000."[154]

It is doubtful the Israeli National Master Plan of June 1949 represents the final fulfillment of Zephaniah's prophecy that "Ashkelon shall become a desolation (to the Arabs)," "and in the houses of Ashkelon they (Jews) shall lie down at evening." However, at the very least, it suggests a Jewish mindset that is willing to occupy homes evacuated by Arabs.

## Repossessing Jordan, the Golan Heights, and the West Bank

Now Zephaniah shifts his attention to the modern-day nation of Jordan. He refers to this territory through the usage of the ancient names of Moab and Ammon. Upon the return of the Jews into the Promised Land, the people of Jordan are guilty of two things: they commit anti-Semitic acts against the Jewish people, and they trespass in on the eastern and northeastern borders of the traditional tribal territories of Israel.

> "I have heard *the taunts of Moab and the revilings of the Ammonites,* how they have *taunted my people* [Israel] *and made boasts against their territory.* Therefore, as I live, says the LORD of hosts, the God of Israel, Moab shall become like Sodom and the Ammonites like Gomorrah, a land possessed by nettles and salt pits, and a waste forever. *The remnant of my people* [Israel] *shall plunder them, and the survivors of my nation shall possess them.* (Zephaniah 2:8–9 NRSV; emphasis added).

Jeremiah the prophet, whose ministry briefly overlapped with Zephaniah's, also expounds upon this trespassing of the Ammonites into the Jewish tribal territory of

Gad. He foretells, as does Zephaniah, of the forcible eviction of the Arabs by the Jews, and the subsequent Israeli repossession of the land in question.

> "Against *the Ammonites*. Thus says the LORD: "Has Israel no sons? Has he no heir? Why *then* does Milcom *inherit Gad*, And *his people dwell in its cities?* Therefore behold, the days are coming," says the LORD, "That I will cause to be heard an alarm of war In Rabbah of the Ammonites; It shall be a desolate mound, And her villages shall be burned with fire.[155] *Then Israel shall take possession of his inheritance*," says the LORD. (Jeremiah 49:1–2 NKJV; emphasis added).

Jeremiah asks the Jordanians; "Has Israel no sons? Has he no heir?" The answer is obvious: of course Israel has descendants—they are repopulating the Holy Land in our day! He goes on to ask, then why are Jordanians trespassing in the Holy Land, which long ago was deeded to the Twelve Tribes of Israel, i.e., the twelve sons of Jacob? Gad was one of the twelve sons of Israel. Jeremiah's rhetorical question is extremely apropos, considering that it finds it's prophetic relevance in the aftermath of the Nazi Holocaust.

Therefore, Jeremiah emphasizes the similar point of Zephaniah, that for the Jordanian thievery of the Holy Land, at the time of the return of the Jew back into the land of Israel the Jordanians will come under military conflict. Because of military defeat over the Arab populations that occupy the land in question, Israel will inherit more Promised Land. This fits in fulfillment with the prophecy to restore some of the fortunes of the Jewish people prior to the "Day of the LORD."

Once upon a time, Ammon and Moab were legitimately appropriated the territories to the East of the allotted territories of the Twelve Tribes.[156] The Hebrews were taught to respect the territorial divides. However, at present the descendants of Ammon and Moab do not respect the boundaries established of old, and the prophets afore mentioned suggest that the Jordanians and the Palestinians will suffer the curse-for-curse-in-kind consequence contained in the Genesis 12:3 clause of the Abrahamic Covenant for their homesteading of the Holy Land.

Technically speaking, it may be that the Golan Heights, the West Bank, and the Gaza Strip are under the spotlight of the prophetic theater. These territories reside well within the borders of the land formerly possessed by the Twelve Tribes of Israel. Terms like Palestinians, and Jordanians were not available to Zephaniah at the time of his prophetic writings; thus, the "meek of the Earth" must extrapolate the times of their signs as they traverse through these periods of Middle Eastern territorial mayhem.

The point is clear! Unintended Arab parties are presently occupying prime property. Real estate in Israel comes at no small price tag, and yet today, it is given away hastily to the Arabs, in exchange for an elusive peace. There is a seesaw, back-and-forth battle for possession of the Promised Land that has plagued the region and burdened the international community since May 14, 1948, when Israel was restored as the Jewish nation. The Jews generally want to maintain the borders established after the Six-Day War of June 1967, and the Arabs would like to re-establish pre-1948 borders.

Scriptures already included in this study, once again listed below, do not allow for assimilation of the Holy Land into Arab control. A point, soon forthcoming, will find the Arabs displaced from the territories once allotted to the Twelve Tribes of Israel.

> For the LORD their God will be mindful of them and restore their fortunes. (Zeph. 2:7).

> "Then Israel shall take possession of his inheritance," says the LORD. (Jer. 49:2).

> The remnant of my people [Israel] shall plunder them, and the survivors of my nation shall possess them. (Zeph. 2:9).

These scriptures, and many more like them, line the prophetic pages of the Bible. The point is clear, that God's plan for the Jewish people will move forward on schedule, and He will restore unto them their fortunes. Part of this portfolio is the precious real estate of the Twelve Tribes of Israel. God deeded this land ages ago to Abraham and his descendants.

> "And the LORD said to Abram, after Lot had separated from him: "Lift your eyes now and look from the place where you are—northward, southward, eastward, and westward; for *all the land which you see I give to you and your descendants forever.* And I will make your descendants as the dust of the Earth; so that if a man could number the dust of the Earth, *then* your descendants also could be numbered. Arise, walk in the land through its length and its width, *for I give it to you.*" (Genesis 13:14–17, NKJV; emphasis added).

The Jews came into realization of much of this land after they had been delivered out of the four-hundred years of captivity in Egypt. Joshua led them in numerous battles as they marched as a people back into the Promised Land, and from a condition of victory, he distributed the land to the Twelve Tribes of Israel.

> "So Joshua took the whole land, according to all that the LORD had said to Moses; and Joshua gave it as an inheritance to Israel according to their divisions by their tribes. Then the land rested from war. (Joshua 11:23, NKJV).

Similarly, today the Jews return from hundreds of years of worldwide captivity, and they will retake some of the same territories, and probably more in the process of restoring their fortunes. As it was at the time of Abraham, so it remains today: Israeli real estate is a possession deemed to be of great value. A quick query on the Internet regarding the price tag of real estate for sale in Israel today finds many properties priced well over one-million dollars. However, more than just an expensive price tag, real estate provides shelter, productivity, defensibility and more to its possessor. When God says He will be "mindful of them and restore their fortunes," one must indeed consider real estate as an important part of this national wealth.

The fact remains intact that the land in question is God's, to deed to whom He so chooses, and He has not chosen to bequeath it to the Arabs, who presently seek to seize it from the Jews. After the Jews are finished with the political attempts to resolve the issue, they will ultimately conclude that the land does not belong to the Arabs, but that it is theirs for the taking and that it can only be regained via the means of military conflict. When the "meek of the Earth" experience this magnificent episode, they need to "seek the LORD" with all fervor and redeem the time for the salvation and protection of their loved ones.

## Summary of Zephaniah

In conclusion, the time is at hand to consider Zephaniah's call to caution. At the time of this writing, the reformation of the nation Israel is underway. A strong, wealthy Jewish nation is on the horizon. Don't be surprised to see the Israeli Defense Force evict the Hamas from ancient Philistia, and the other terrorist entities out of the coming Greater Israel, or what I like to call Isralestine. Gaza will soon be deserted, serving as an end-time sign that the "day of the LORD'S" anger is shortly to follow.

Wherever the place and whenever the time, it is wise to keep a watchful eye on the events revolving around Isralestine. The LORD desires that the meek of the Earth be duly informed, so that they may get right with Him, in order to be hidden from the disturbing events destined to befall the inhabitants of the Earth during the day of the LORD.

At the request of the LORD, Zephaniah inscribed centuries ago this invaluable prophetic information in Chapter 2 of his book, for you, the "meek of the Earth." He said that the Jewish people would re-gather in their ancient homeland and that they would do so in a condition of unbelief. Then he describes the Jews overcoming the Palestinians and their Arab cohorts, thereby taking back territory once belonging to their twelve tribal ancestors. This event brings with it a severe blow to the religion of Islam, the religion of the defeated Arabs. Jewish fortunes are enormously increased and then it appears that Russia is lured into forming the Gog of Magog coalition and coming after the great booty Israel possesses Ezekiel 38:13.

All of the above has been foretold by Zephaniah, as well as among other Old Testament Jewish prophets, in order that the "meek of the Earth" would be called to caution as they witnessed the unfolding of these specific events. This select population group, upon witnessing all of the above, can then be certain that the day of the LORD draws near, and that they are to seek the righteousness of Christ, in order that they may "be hidden, In the day of the LORD'S anger."

> "For the day of the LORD upon all the nations *is* near; As you (Edomites / Palestinians) have done, (to Israel) it shall be done to you; Your reprisal shall return upon your own head." (Obadiah 1:15, NKJV; emphasis added).

It's important for the "meek of the earth" to consider what Christ instructed about being "hidden" during the day of the LORD;

> "Watch therefore, and pray always that you may be counted worthy to escape all these things that will come to pass, and to stand before the Son of Man." (Luke 21:36, NKJV).

# FIFTEEN

# The Psalm 83 Report

**"Egypt Islamist vows global caliphate in Jerusalem"**

*Jerusalem Post 5/08/12*

"The capital of the United States of the Arabs will be Jerusalem, preacher tells thousands at (Muslim) Brotherhood rally."

**"Israeli Foreign Ministry: U.S. ignored Arab radicalization"**

*Haaretz News 9/16/12*

"Foreign Ministry official on signs of 'radicalization' in Arab world: 'We knew what was happening, but the Americans preferred to find excuses."

The *Psalm 83 Report* is an attempt to further understand what God intends to do about the Arabs plans in Psalm 83:4 to destroy the Jewish state. According to Ezekiel 39:7, the Lord promises to uphold His holy name through the existence of the Jewish people. Therefore, it is reasonable to presume that God will not sit by idly and allow the Arab confederacy to destroy Israel. It is also realistic to believe that the Lord will issue a detailed prophetic report about how the Psalm 83 genocidal attempt will be thwarted. To preface this assertion, let me quote what the Jewish prophet Amos said about 2,760 years ago:

> Surely the LORD GOD does nothing, Unless He reveals His secret to His servants the prophets. (Amos 3:7, NKJV)

From this Amos declaration, we can be certain that an event of the magnitude of the Psalm 83 scenario will not go without a report. If God intends to do something to stop this Arab onslaught, He will certainly reference His plans somewhere through the writing of "His servants the prophets." Even the Psalmist requests such a report in the very first verse. He beseeches the Lord to not keep silent about this important matter.

> Do not keep silent, O God! Do not hold Your peace, And do not be still, O God! (Psa. 83:1, NKJV),

Although we get some clues from Asaph's petitions in Psalm 83:9-18 about how Israel survives this amazing Arab advance, the body of the Psalm 83 report is primarily contained in Jeremiah 49, and Obadiah 1. Many interesting similarities exist between these prophecies. Both prophets receive parallel messages. The Hebrew words they both use for hearing their reports is "shama," "shemuah," which used together can be translated as the attentive listening to a newsworthy proclamation.[157]

## The Report

> I have heard [shama] a message [shemuah] from the LORD, And an ambassador has been sent to the nations: "Gather together, come against her, And rise up to battle!" (Jer. 49:14, NKJV)

> The vision of Obadiah. Thus says the LORD GOD concerning Edom (We have heard [shama] a report [shemuah] from the LORD, And a messenger has been sent among the nations, saying, "Arise, and let us rise up against her for battle"). (Obad. 1:1, NKJV)

Comprehensive studies of Jeremiah 49:1-27, and Obadiah 1:1-21 are critical to the understanding of the Psalm 83 Report. These studies further develop the theme of the

Israeli Conquest over these confederate nations. The chapter called, "Obadiah's Mysterious Vision," presents a comprehensive commentary on his 21 verses. This study picks up in Jeremiah 49:7 and regards itself with Edom, the apparent lead member of the confederacy. Edom is the first member mentioned in Psalm 83:6–8 of the ten-member alliance.

Similar to the credits at the end of a movie, whereby the star's name is displayed before the supporting cast and crew, whenever a nation is listed first in the Bible it often identifies it as the star of the show. Furthermore, information delivered through the prophets about the lead member is generally understood to find some correlation with the other enjoining member nations. In Edom's case, this principle applies. Unfortunately, this star of the show turns out to be the villain rather than the victor.

In this instance, Edom is referred to as "the tents of Edom" in Psalm 83:6. This implies that at the time of the fulfillment of the Psalm 83 prophecy, Edom will resemble an assemblage of refugees in tents, a military encampment, or both. For our purposes, we will intelligently presume the both scenario. Upon entering into the Arab confederacy, Edom will be refugees, who have assembled themselves into a militia or army.

Here is how this is could be understood presently: "the tents of Edom," labeled as such by Asaph centuries before there were ever Palestinian refugees, are indeed these refugees.[158] These Palestinian refugees are the stars of the show! The plight of these refugees becomes the thread that unites these Arab nations and ignites them into the ten-member confederacy of Psalm 83.

## Palestinianism

A good neologism for the plight of the Palestinian refugees is "Palestinianism," which is an emerging term representing the common brotherhood, that continues to develop between the Palestinians, and those Islamic nations that support their struggle for autonomy. The term was coined by Egyptian-born author Bat Yeor, a pioneer in the study of Dhimmitude and Jihadist tactics.[159] Bat Yeor defined Palestinianism in her book Eurabia: The Euro-Arab Axis as follows:

> *"Palestinianism condenses jihadist values. It promotes the destruction of Israel, the denial of Hebrew biblical history and hence Christianity. It preaches Islamic replacement theology and the Arabization and Islamization of the Holy Land's biblical archeology."*

Throughout history, these Arabs often fought each other, yet in this century, their empathy for the Palestinian refugees has served to unite them in the common cause of Palestinianism. This also evidences their collective hatred of Zionism. Remember that the battle cry of the Psalm 83 confederacy is the destruction of the nation Israel.

## Zionism[160]

In stark contrast to Palestinianism is the movement founded by the Viennese Jewish journalist Theodor Herzl, called "Zionism." Hertzl argued in his 1896 book Der Judenstaat (The Jewish State), that the best way of avoiding anti-Semitism in Europe was to create an independent Jewish state in Palestine. Zionism was named after Mount Zion in Jerusalem, a symbol of the Jewish homeland since the Babylonian captivity in the sixth century BC. The movement culminated in the birth of the state of Israel in 1948.

## Palestinianism vs. Zionism

Palestinianism paired with Zionism becomes a recipe for disaster. These two philosophies cannot coexist in the Middle East. Zionism calls for a Jewish state and Palestinianism promotes the denial and ultimate destruction of any such state; indeed, the Arabs have often referred to the Jewish state as a "cancer" in their midst. The Jews feel compelled to migrate into Israel because of Zionism, and the Arabs attempt to deny them that right.

The makings for the coming Middle East War comes down to the ideological clash between Palestinianism verses Zionism. The tents of Edom get their Arab cohorts to sympathize with the continuing saga of their prolonged refugee status. One of the reasons they feel sorry for these Palestinian souls is that the Arabs never appropriately assimilated these displaced refugees back into their respective lands. These Palestinians were instructed by the surrounding Arab nations temporarily to vacate Israel in 1948, under the premise that the Arabs would destroy the newly forming Jewish state. The Arabs lost, and their miscalculation created the Palestinian refugees, also known as "tents of Edom."[161]

The pages of history advocate adversities amongst these Arabs. At no time in the past were all ten members of Psalm 83:6–8 ever sincerely united in a common cause. However, this trend began to change with the invention of Islam in the seventh century. Islam served to unite the Arabs ideologically. They began to embrace similar holy days, places, and practices, and slowly the longstanding issues that once divided them started to erode.

Probably the most notable attempt at Arab unity came in 1945 with the formation of the Arab League. They married up together for two primary purposes; first to promote independence for Arab States, and secondly to prevent the formation of an independent Jewish State. They achieved their first goal of becoming autonomous Arab States promptly, as the British and French began to relinquish their sovereignty in the rebellious region. Their success in this area led them to believe that they would have similar success in their second cause, which was the prevention of the restoration of the Jewish state of Israel. The widespread attacks of US embassies across much of the Middle East and North Africa in September of 2012, were further evidence ot the growing unity amongst the Islamists.

## "US Embassies Targeted in Protests Spanning 20 (Islamic) Countries"

*Newsmax 9/17/12*

Immediately upon the formation of the Jewish state in 1948, the surrounding Arab nations of Egypt, Jordan, Iraq, Syria, and Lebanon, supported by other Arabs, attacked the Jewish nation. They lost and the tents of Edom became a startling reality.

**Fig. 4. Palestinian refugee camp, 1949.**

(Reproduced by permission from UNRWA. UNRWA photo, "Palestinian Refugees—Historical Photos," Badil.org, http://www.badil. org/Photos/history/Archive1/Photogallery/photo9757/real.htm [accessed 12/20/07].)

**Fig. 5. Palestinian refugee camp, 1949.**

(Reproduced by permission from UNRWA. UNRWA photo, "Palestinian Refugees—Historical Photos," Badil.org, http://www. badil. org/Photos/history/Archive1/Photogallery/photo9757/real.htm [accessed 03/10/08].)

The twenty-first century stands upon this unsettled soil. The surrounding Arab nations empathize predominately with the Palestinian disposition of hatred for the reforming nation of Israel. Failed conventional Arab wars against the Jews have evolved into unconventional terrorist entities. These terrorists have extended their reach out of the region and into the international community. The world ponders the predicament, and proposes political solutions aimed at resolving this conflict.

The world cries out "heaven forbid" that a major war breaks out in the Middle East between the Arabs and Jews, but heaven foreknows that it will happen! War is prophesied to occur, as these Arabs will settle for nothing less than exclusive title to the fertile riches of the Promised Land.

## The Report

We begin with Jeremiah's assessment against Edom, which parallels closely that of Obadiah. Both prophets talk about the final judgments determined by God against Edom. There are two judgments that come against the territory of Edom in the latter years. This point was made in the chapter called, "The Final Palestinian Farewell." The first is by the Jews against the Palestinians and their confederate neighbors, and the other is by the Jew, Jesus Christ, against the Armageddonites (the armies assembled in the campaign of Armageddon allied with the Antichrist). Both judgments will extend into and thereby adversely affect the geography of Edom, which is modern-day Southern Jordan. Jeremiah and Obadiah chronicle both judgments with more emphasis on the first of these two judgments.

> Against Edom. Thus says the LORD of hosts: "Is wisdom no more in Teman? Has counsel perished from the prudent? Has their wisdom vanished? (Jer. 49:7, NKJV)

Since "the tents of Edom" references the lead member of the Psalm 83 confederacy, we will begin at Jeremiah 49:7, whereby the prophet declares, "Thus says the LORD of hosts" and then fires out three rhetorical questions "Against Edom." To decipher the significance of these three questions, one must first look at the context in which they apply, and secondly understand the history of the Edomites.

The context is the coming confederate war effort of the Arabs to destroy the nation Israel. In essence, the God of the Jews is asking the Edomite descendants, who can be linked to a contingency residing within the Palestinians of today, "What on Earth are you thinking? Is wisdom no more in Teman?" Teman was the grandson of Esau, and the Temanites who came from his loins were renowned in ancient times for their wisdom.[162]

Teman understood from his grandfather Esau, who is the father of the Edomites, according to Genesis 36:1, that the birthrights to the Abrahamic covenant, passed through to Isaac who was Esau's father. Furthermore, he was taught that this birthright passed over Esau and was afforded to Jacob, Esau's younger twin brother. Therefore when God has Jeremiah ask, "Is wisdom no more in Teman?" we are to glean the fact that what was understandably the most foundational understanding of Teman has been overlooked by his descendants currently existing within the Palestinians.

The God of Teman's great-great-grandfather Abraham made an everlasting, unconditional covenant that guaranteed the survival of the very people that the Palestinian descendants of Teman are attempting to annihilate. Esau's twin brother is Jacob, Jacob is Israel according to Genesis 32:28, and his descendants are the Jews!

Has counsel perished from the prudent? Apparently. Asaph informs us of the following: For they have consulted together with one consent; They form a confederacy against You: The tents of Edom and the Ishmaelites; Moab and the Hagrites; Gebal, Ammon, and Amalek; Philistia with the inhabitants of Tyre; Assyria also has joined with them; They have helped the children of Lot. *Selah.* (Psa. 83:5–8 NKJV)

Due to the fact that the wisdom of the Abrahamic covenant no longer exists within Teman's descendants, the counsel advanced by their contingency within the Palestinians at this future final Arab summit, whereby they all consult "together with one consent," is void of any reference to this eternal covenant. As such, in the absence of any such rhetoric, these rhetorical questions asked by Jeremiah against the Palestinians, are astoundingly rudimentary! "Has their wisdom vanished?" Indeed, it has vanished.

The answers to the three questions directed at Edom are given at the time of Edom's first judgment. Yes, wisdom is no more in Teman! Yes, counsel has perished from the prudent! Yes, wisdom has vanished! Obadiah 1:8–9 tells us that the vanishing of wisdom results in the military slaughtering of Edom.

The three questions above follow in line with the theme of rhetorical questioning throughout Jeremiah chapter 49.

1. Against the Ammonites [Northern Jordanians] Thus says the LORD: "Has Israel no sons? Has he no heir? Why *then* does Milcom inherit Gad, And his people dwell in its cities?" (Jer. 49:1, NKJV; emphasis added)

2. Why is the city of praise [Jerusalem], the city of My joy, not deserted? (Jer. 49:25, NKJV) This question is directed at Damascus, Syria.

In Ammon's case (Jer. 49:1) it is the inheritance of the land that is fore fronted. In Edom's case (Jer. 49:7) it is the wisdom of the birthright of Jacob and his descendants, right to exist in fulfillment of the Abrahamic Covenant. In Damascus's case (Jer. 49:25) it is the eternal throne to be established in Jerusalem its appropriate place, "the city of My joy."

What is being highlighted by this sequence of rhetorical questions in Jeremiah 49:1,7,25 is the Abrahamic Covenant. At the time of the Psalm 83 war effort, Ammon, represented by Northern Jordan, will be encroaching upon the Holy Land allotted to Israel. The descendant Jewish heirs of Abraham will come under attack by the tents of Edom, represented by Southern Jordan, and the Palestinians. The eternal city of Jerusalem will come under threat by Damascus.

## The Report Continued

> Flee, turn back, dwell in the depths, O inhabitants of Dedan! For I will bring the calamity of Esau upon him, The time *that* I will punish him. (Jer. 49:8, NKJV; emphasis added)

This is a warning to the Saudis to disengage from their confederate allegiance with the Palestinians. They are instructed to flee from the slaughter back into the depths of Saudi Arabia. The historical location of "Dedan" was in Northwest Saudi Arabia. Ezekiel tells us below, that the Saudis do not appear to heed Jeremiah's warning.

> Therefore thus says the LORD GOD: "I will also stretch out My hand against Edom, cut off man and beast from it, and make it desolate from Teman; *Dedan* shall fall by the sword." (Ezek. 25:13, NKJV; emphasis added)

This reference to Dedan, Arabia offers a connection to the confederacy of Esau/Edom found in Psalm 83:4–8 and Obadiah 1:7. In Psalm 83:6, the Saudi's are represented by their ancestor Ishmael, and are labeled as the "Ishmaelites." Esau is Edom, according to Genesis 36:1, much like his twin brother Jacob is also called Israel Genesis 32:28.

> If grape-gatherers came to you, Would they not leave some gleaning grapes? If thieves by night, Would they not destroy until they have enough? I have uncovered his secret places, And he shall not be able to hide himself. His descendants are plundered, His brethren and his neighbors, And he is no more. (Jer. 49:9–10, NKJV; emphasis added).

The descendants of Esau ultimately align themselves with their Arab neighbors in a confederate effort to come against Israel. Psalm 83:1–8. Israel defeats this confederacy, and thus "His descendants are plundered, His brethren and his neighbors." This theme of severe judgment is echoed by Obadiah 1:5–7. The plundering, which is the result of a military defeat, extends beyond Edom's borders into the borders of "his neighbors." One of the neighbors has already been identified in verse 8 as Saudi Arabia (Dedan). The others are Gaza, Jordan, Egypt, Lebanon, Iraq, and Syria, all of which are enlisted members of the confederacy of Esau. This defeat brings an end to Esau and all his enmity that was harbored by his descendants throughout the centuries "he is no more."

> Leave your fatherless children, I will preserve *them* alive; And let your widows trust in Me." (Jer. 49:11, NKJV; emphasis added)

The refugees left behind are the fatherless and the widows. The "mighty men" (soldiers) as they are called in Obadiah 1:9 are slaughtered in defeat, and the refugees left behind are instructed to trust in the LORD.

> Then your *mighty men*, O Teman, shall be dismayed, To the end *that everyone* from the mountains of Esau May *be cut off by slaughter.* (Obad. 1:9, NKJV; emphasis added)

According to Obadiah, these fatherless children and widows appear to be transported to internment camps.

> The captives of this host of the children of Israel Shall possess the land of the Canaanites [Israel] As far as Zarephath [Southwest Lebanon]. (Obad. 1:20, NKJV)

> For thus says the LORD: "Behold, those whose judgment *was* not to drink of the cup have assuredly drunk. And *are* you the one who will altogether go unpunished? You shall not go unpunished, but you shall surely drink *of it.*" (Jer. 49:12, NKJV; emphasis added)

In this passage, we get the first hint as to why the first of the two judgments against Edom is necessary. Edom and its confederacy are guilty of the unauthorized oppression of the Jewish people. The Jews had already adequately been served the cup of judgment as evidenced by the Holocaust for their apostate condition, which long ago had led to their rejection of Christ at His first coming. Ezekiel tells us that they were to be scattered and judged for their mistaken ways and misdeeds.

> So I scattered them among the nations, and they were dispersed throughout the countries; I judged them according to their ways and their deeds. (Ezek. 36:19, NKJV; emphasis added).

The dry bones vision of Ezekiel 37:1–13 pointed to the gravelike conditions of the Holocaust that would bring to end this Jewish judgment sequence. Thus when Jeremiah says "Behold, those whose judgment was not to drink of the cup have assuredly drunk, he is referencing the Jews being subsequently oppressed by the Palestinians and their Arab confederacy. They are operating "in Excess" of what was determined as the just judgment of the Jewish people for their rejection of Messiah. They are forcing another "cup" of judgment down the throat of the Jewish people. God has not prescribed this "cup" of bad medicine.

This causes Jeremiah to forewarn Esau as follows: "You shall not go unpunished, but you shall surely drink of it." Obadiah 1:16 also references this cup of judgment from which Esau and his Arab neighbors shall surely drink.

> For as you (Esau) *drank* on My holy mountain, So shall all the nations *drink* continually;Yes, they shall drink, and swallow, And they shall be as though they had never been. (Obad. 1:16, NKJV; emphasis added)

Obadiah's passage is useful in that it connects Esau's judgment with Israel ("My holy mountain") and that it determines the timing of this judgment as occurring before "all the nations drink." The judgment of all the nations of the world occurs at the second coming of Christ. Therefore, the judgment of Esau concludes sometime before the second coming of Christ. "For as you (Esau) drank; So shall all the nations drink." Obadiah further depicts the timing to be before the "day of the LORD."

> For the day of the LORD upon all the nations *is* near; [not yet] As you have done, it shall be done to you; Your reprisal shall return upon your own head. (Obad. 1:15, NKJV; emphasis added)

The reprisal against the Palestinian refugees and their Arab partners occurs before the day of the LORD comes. It happens in the end-times, just before the final seven years of tribulation on the Earth. The reprisal against the Psalm 83 confederates is to be fashioned in the similar method as their oppression against Israel: "As you (Arab confederates) have done (to the Jews), it shall be done to you." This prescription is in alignment with the curse-for-curse-in-kind clause contained in the Genesis 12:3 clause of the Abrahamic Covenant.

## The Report Continued

> "For I have sworn by Myself," says the LORD, "that Bozrah shall become a desolation, a reproach, a waste, and a curse. And all its cities shall be perpetual wastes." (Jer. 49:13, NKJV)

To emphasize further the scope of the pending judgments Jeremiah declares that the LORD personally has sworn that Bozrah, which is located in ancient Edom, will "become a desolation, a reproach, a waste, and a curse. And all its cities shall be perpetual wastes." This is a result of the two judgments destined to befall Edom: one by the Jews and the final by the Jew Jesus Christ at His Second Coming.

The first judgment executed by the Jews is the cup of judgment served to Esau and his neighbors, who "shall surely drink of it" for their violent confederate attempt to destroy the nation Israel.[163] The second judgment, executed by Jesus Christ at His second coming, is against the nations of the world who assemble with the Antichrist in his Armageddon campaign. ("So shall all the nations drink"). These nations are judged in Edom because that is where they arrive in their attempt to destroy the faithful Jewish remnant, which at that time will have fled to the area of Bozrah/Petra in Southern Jordan, which is located in ancient Edom.

It is important to make this distinction in order to disassociate any connections between these two judgments. The first judgment destroys the Arab confederacy listed in Psalm 83:6–8. This is a result of the Israeli Conquest at the hands of the exceedingly great army of the Jewish people prophesied about in Ezekiel 37:10. The second judgment destroys the Armageddon confederacy comprised of all the remaining nations of the world, conducted single handedly by the exceedingly great one-man army of Messiah Jesus Christ Himself. Isaiah puts it this way:

> Who *is* this who comes from Edom, With dyed garments from Bozrah, This *One who is* glorious in His apparel, Traveling in the greatness of His strength? "I who speak in righteousness, mighty to save." Why *is* Your apparel red, And Your garments like one who treads in the winepress? "I have trodden the winepress alone, And from the peoples no one *was* with Me." (Isa. 63:1–3, NKJV; emphasis added)

## The Report Continued

> I have heard [*shama*] a message [*shemuah*] from the LORD, *And* an ambassador has been sent to the nations: Gather together, come against her, And rise up to battle! (Jer. 49:14, NKJV; emphasis added)

Jeremiah makes two statements. He first declares he has "heard a message from the LORD," then makes the announcement that "an ambassador has been sent to the nations." The report Jeremiah has heard, also heard by Obadiah, is the response by God to the message that the ambassador sends out "to the nations." The nations rally around the battle cry "Gather together, come against her." Jeremiah uses the Hebrew word goy which can mean Gentiles, nations, heathen, or Gentile nations. In this context, it apparently refers to the Gentile Arab nations assembling against Israel in fulfillment of Psalm 83:1–8.

Some commentaries suggest that the message Jeremiah and Obadiah receive from the LORD is that "an ambassador has been sent to, or among the nations," and that "the nations" confederate together to "come against her," alluding to Edom. However, for the following four reasons it is more likely that Jeremiah is identifying Israel as "her." And an ambassador has been sent to the (Arab) nations: "Gather together (confederate), come against her (Israel), And rise up to battle (fulfilling Psalm 83)!"

1. Edom is referred to as "her" only one time in the entire Bible, in Ezekiel 32:29, whereas Israel is referred to in the feminine context over 100 times in the Old and New Testaments.[164]

2. According to Jeremiah 49:15 and Obadiah 1:2, Edom is among the nations the "ambassador" rallys into a confederacy. As such, it would not make sense that the members of this confederacy, which are assembled to destroy Israel, would "rise up to battle" to attack one of their own members.

3. The study of Edom's decline in the subsection entitled, "*The Migration of the Edomites,*" within the chapter called, "The Whodomites, Who are the Edomites Today," illustrates that at no time since the prophecies of Jeremiah, which spanned from approximately 627 BC to 587 BC and up until the present, has any confederacy of nations come against them. Nor, does one appear to be coming in the future, for the reason explained in in number 4 below.

4. The Bible only references two end-time judgments against Edom and the Edomites, and neither involves a confederacy of nations. The exceedingly great army of Israel against the Psalm 83 Arab confederacy executes the first judgment. Jesus Christ delivers the second judgment at the time of His return to the Earth. As previously stated, the second judgment serves to defeat the Antichrist and his armies assembled in the campaign of Armageddon.

Conversely, "The Report" Jeremiah heard from the LORD is most likely that "an ambassador has been sent to the nations" to "rise up to battle against her," Israel. This confederacy is identified in Psalm 83:5-8.

Jeremiah 49:15 announces a provision contained within "The Report" he has heard from the LORD that Edom will be made "least or small among the nations, despised by Mankind."[165] Through the process of time, Edom was indeed made "small among the nations." Today there is little to no acknowledged Edomite existence, apart from some Bedouins residing in the Southern Jordan area; however, if you follow the migratory path of the Edomites, they end up primarily in Israel. Contained amongst the Palestinians of modern times resides a remnant of the Edomites

The reference to the Palestinians in Psalm 83:6 as those assembled as the "tents of Edom," informs us that at the time the Arabs confederate to come against Israel, the descendants of Esau, who through time were "made small among the nations" will be the "least among the nations," referring to the Palestinians as the smallest in stature among the confederacy. None of the other confederating members is identified with the "tents of " condition.

Today we see this is the case, as the Palestinian refugees are without their own Arab state. Although the Arab League succeeded quickly in legitimizing autonomy for member nations like Saudi Arabia, Iraq, Lebanon, Syria, and Jordan, the Palestinians are still recognized by the international community as refugees. The world community is hard at work attempting to establish a Palestinian state; however, at the time of the authoring of this book, the Palestinians are yet stateless. Therefore, if the Psalm 83 prophecy were to be fulfilled in advance of the establishment of a Palestinian state, the most suitable title for the Palestinians would be "the tents of Edom," reflecting the current condition of the Palestinian refugees.

The Palestinian refugees enjoined within the Arab confederacy, as the star of the show, is the least in stature among them. This is because through time, they were "made small among the nations." However, Jeremiah further prophesies that they will also become, "despised by humankind." This results from the next events described in "The Report."

> "The terror you [Palestinians] inspire and the pride of your heart have deceived you, you who live in the clefts of the rock, who hold the height of the hill. Although you make your nest as high as the eagle's, from there I will bring you down," says the LORD. (Jer. 49:16, niv)

The Palestinians are guilty of inspiring terror! This terror has become a mushroom cloud, extending over the international community. As such, it is beginning to concern all of mankind. Terror as we understand it today is mainly associated with the Middle East. It is the unconventional method of warfare inspired by Arab nations coincidentally listed in the Psalm 83:6–8. Terrorism was the by-product of the failed Arab attempts to destroy the Jewish state. Who can forget the airline hijackings of the 1970s, which primarily occurred after the 1973 Yom Kippur war?

Terrorist entities like Hezbollah, Hamas, Al-Qaeda, and Islamic Jihad have several things in common: Islamic faith, Middle-Eastern origins, combative attitudes toward Israel, and encouragement from the Palestinian struggle for Arab statehood. Therefore, when Jeremiah declares of the Edomite descendants of Esau, the "terror you inspire," we can prophetically credit the world's newfound foe terrorism to its inspirational source, the Palestinians. A detailed prophetic study of the terror inspired by the Palestinians is contained in the chapter within my book called *Isralestine, The Ancient Blueprints of the Future Middle East* in a chapter entitled "The End of Terror: Another Bible Prediction."

Jeremiah 49:16 says that, "The pride of your heart has deceived you." The Palestinian refugees are deceived through prideful hearts into thinking that their plight is a worthy cause. The Hebrew word for deceived is nasha, which is also used in Obadiah

1:7. The Obadiah usage portrays the Palestinians as a beguiled member among their Arab allies.

> All your allies have deceived [*nasha*] you, they have driven you to the border [of Israel]; your confederates have prevailed against you; your trusted friends have set a trap under you— there is no understanding of it. (Obad. 1:7, RSV)

What Obadiah 1:7, in connection with Jeremiah 49:16, describes for us today in real-world application, is that the Palestinian refugees are beguiled by the pride of their hearts into thinking Palestinianism can become reality. This thinking enables their Arab allies strategically to keep them deployed at the borders of Israel in lieu of assimilating them into their own national borders. Collectively, the other confederate members of Psalm 83 have successfully convinced the Palestinian refugees into thinking they ultimately belong inside the borders of Israel, in full possession of the Holy Land.

Obadiah further discloses, "your trusted friends have set a trap under you." This trap is thoroughly explained inside *Isralestine, The Ancient Blueprints of the Future Middle East,* within the chapter called, "The Palestinian Confederacy." It will prove a grave mistake for the Palestinian refugees to conclude in their prideful hearts that they will someday inherit the Holy Land of Israel. These Edomite descendants of Esau elevate their cause of Palestinianism into the embrace of their Arab allies, who in turn unwittingly ensnare them at the borders of Israel.

Obadiah says, "There is no understanding of it." This statement alludes to the underlying dangerous misconception that incites the Arabs to unite, and ultimately will ignite the Arabs to fight in fulfillment of Psalm 83. Whereas Zionism has become a reality, Palestinianism will prove to be frivolity, a trap that ensnares the "tents of Edom" and their Arab cohorts.

Jeremiah 49:16 also says, "Though you make your nest as high as the eagle." Hand-in-hand with this inspired terror is the religious thinking that convinces Esau that his fierceness is invincible. Edom, inspiring terror supported by its confederate partners, believing itself invincible, is brought down from that deceived spiritual condition by the LORD. "I will bring you down from there," says the LORD.

## The Report Continued

> "Edom also shall be an astonishment; Everyone who goes by it will be astonished And will hiss at all its plagues. As in the overthrow of Sodom and Gomorrah And their neighbors," says the LORD, "No one shall remain there, Nor shall a son of man dwell in it." (Jer. 49:17–18, NKJV)

The result of the two judgments against Edom leaves it uninhabitable for humans. It will astonish everyone in the Messianic Kingdom that goes by it. It will serve as a reminder to them of the severe judgment that came against Sodom and Gomorrah, and their neighbors. The Bible suggests it will be only suitable for the habitation of the demons, and or fallen angels probably of Revelation 12:9. They are cast out of heaven with Satan and team up with the Antichrist in the campaign of Armageddon. Scripture tells us that the Antichrist and the false prophet end up in the Lake of Fire described in Revelation 19:20.

Revelation 20:1–13 declares that Satan finds himself in chains for 1000 years, returns to Earth, and ends up in the Lake of Fire. Furthermore, unsaved men and women end up in Hades for 1000 years until the White Throne Judgment, at which point they too are sent to the Lake of Fire. However, it does not specifically reference the whereabouts of the fallen angels.

Isaiah 34:1–17 and Isaiah 13:19–22, in association with Revelation 18:2, tells us that Babylon and most probably Edom will be their places of confinement during the kingdom period. The fallen angels are thought to possess the creatures that inhabit those areas during the Messianic Kingdom.

> Behold, he shall come up like a lion from the *floodplain of the Jordan* Against the dwelling place of the strong; But I will suddenly make him [Esau] run away from her [Israel]. And who *is* a chosen *man that* I may appoint over her [Israel]? For who *is* like Me? Who will arraign Me? And who *is* that shepherd Who will withstand Me?" (Jer.49:19, NKJV; emphasis added)

We must compare Jeremiah 49:19–22 to the counterpart passages found in Jeremiah 50:43–46. The depiction in both cases is a military effort staged at the "floodplain of the Jordan" against the Jews. The first campaign is by the Psalm 83 confederacy led by Edom, and the second is the campaign of Armageddon, led by the Antichrist. In both instances, the motivation is to destroy the client nation Israel.

The genocide of the Jewish people is a paramount goal of Satan within the angelic conflict. This is a topic for a different book; however, the point is that if there is no Jewish remnant to beckon the return of Christ, the word of God is breached; this has been the goal of the serpent since Genesis 3. Hosea 5:15 tells us that Christ returns when the Jewish remnant seeking refuge in Edom pleads for Him to come rescue them.

> I will return again to My place Till they [the Nation Israel) acknowledge their offense. Then they will seek My face; In their affliction they will earnestly seek Me. (Hosea 5:15, NKJV)

Both assaults against the Jews fail and the LORD causes the enemies to flee. As a result of the Jewish victory over the first assault, four rhetorical questions are asked.

1.  *Who is a chosen man that I may appoint over her?* This question causes the reader to remember that it is the LORD who sets up and takes down kings (Dan. 2:21). Whenever God used the Gentiles to discipline the Jewish people, it was because God empowered those Gentile nations to do so. In neither of these instances has God authorized the Psalm 83 confederacy or the Antichrist and his armies to commit genocide on the Jewish people.

2.  *For who is like Me?* This question emphasizes the sovereignty of God.

3.  *Who will arraign Me?* As the client nation, the Jewish people are likened to the apple of God's eye (Zech. 2:9, Deut. 32:10). Matthew 25:40,45 depicts the same concept, that whatever they do to the least of them, they do to Him, Christ.

4.  *Who is that shepherd Who will withstand Me?* God has reserved the role of shepherding for Christ (Isa. 40:10–11, Ezek. 34:12– 16, Matt. 2:6, John 10:11,14, Heb. 13:20, 1 Peter 5:4, Rev. 7:17). In the Messianic Kingdom, Christ will delegate this responsibility to the resurrected King David (Ezek. 34:23, 37:34).

No other shepherds will withstand the Messiah, Jesus Christ!

> Therefore hear the counsel of the LORD that He has taken against Edom, And His purposes that He has proposed against the inhabitants of Teman: Surely the least of the flock shall draw them out; Surely He shall make their dwelling places desolate with them. (Jer. 49:20, NKJV)

By now, "wisdom was no more in Teman," and good counsel had "perished from the prudent" (Jer. 49:7), so therefore Teman and the prudent of Edom will receive "the counsel of the LORD." This counsel is contained within "The Report" Jeremiah and Obadiah jointly heard from the LORD (Jer. 49:14, and Obad. 1:1).

"Surely the least of the flock shall draw them out," probably refers to the complete and exacting victory of Israel's exceedingly great army over the Psalm 83 Confederacy. There will be no mighty men left in Teman (Obad. 1:9), There will be no grapes to glean (Obad. 1:5, Jeremiah 49:9), Esau will be left bare (Jer. 49:10). The shepherd theme was introduced in Jeremiah 49:19, so the "least of the flock" would be all Jews.

To "draw them out," probably references the Jewish taking of Arab prisoners of war. This occurs in the aftermath of the first judgment against Edom. Jeremiah 49:20

closes with, "Surely, He shall make their dwelling places desolate with them." Ultimately, after the return of Christ, He will make the entire territory of Edom desolate. This occurs in the aftermath of the second judgment in Edom.

> "The Earth shakes at the noise of their fall; At the cry, its noise is heard at the Red Sea" (Jer. 49:21, NKJV).

The whole Earth is shaken by the soundness of the defeat of the Psalm 83 confederacy. The defeat itself extends to the Red Sea. The implication is that the confederate nations of Jordan, Egypt, and Saudi Arabia, which border the Red Sea, are also soundly defeated.

> Behold, He shall come up and fly like the eagle, And spread His wings over Bozrah; The heart of the mighty men of Edom in that day shall be Like the heart of a woman in birth pangs. (Jer. 49:22, NKJV)

The emphasis here is on the first judgment of Edom, which the prophet Ezekiel declares will be fashioned in this format: "I will lay My vengeance on Edom by the hand of My people Israel, that they may do in Edom according to My anger and according to My fury; and they shall know My vengeance," (Ezek. 25:14, NKJV).

The point here is that the exceedingly great army of Israel is divinely empowered by the LORD. It is likened to the spreading of the wings of an eagle over the prey, causing an alarming fear to the mighty men of the confederacy, particularly the mighty men of Teman Obadiah 1:9. The theme of a woman in birth pangs or fear is referenced in other passages relative to this defeat (Isa. 19:16, Egypt; Jer. 48:41, Moab; Jer. 49:24, Damascus). This study picks up again in the chapter called, "Obadiah's Mysterious Vision."

# SIXTEEN

# Obadiah's Mysterious Vision

**"Netanyahu says Palestinian unity government not a peace partner"**

*Reuters 5/16/11*

"Israel shall be a fire, But the Palestinians shall be stubble; The IDF shall kindle them and devour them, And no survivor shall remain of the Palestinians." (Obadiah 1:18; paraphrased by author).

The Jewish prophet Obadiah receives a mysterious vision, the contents are thoroughly outlined and described in this important chapter. In order to understand better his vision, it is important for the reader to review the chapters in this book entitled *The Who-domites?* and *The Psalm 83 Report*. These chapters contain the introductory content necessary to understand comprehensively Obadiah's mysterious vision.

To preface this chapter, remember that Obadiah identifies historical and future names, places and events using the Hebrew vernacular of his day. Furthermore, he presumes that his readers possess a basic understanding of Hebrew history at the time that his vision becomes discerned. Since this vision is to be deciphered in these present times, this historical consideration is inclusive of their exodus out of Egypt, the Babylonian captivity, their centuries of worldwide dispersion, on past the rebirth of the nation Israel in 1948, and on into these modern times. The most important facts to note as his mysterious vision opens up are:

- Esau settled in the territory of ancient Edom, which is modern- day Southern Jordan, and is the patriarchal father of the Edomite peoples.

- A remnant contingency of the Edomite population can be located within the modern-day Palestinians.

- This Palestinian generation will be judged for the historical crimes their Edomite fathers previously committed and the current crimes they presently perpetrate against the Jewish people. The execution of this judgment upon the Palestinians will be delivered through the military might of the nation Israel.

## The Commentary of Obadiah

A pastor once instructed his congregation to read the entire book of Obadiah before the next Sunday service. When the next Sunday arrived, he began the service by asking for a show of hands by everyone, who had read at least the first three chapters of Obadiah. He was humored to observe that several hands were raised. After letting out a laugh, he commented, "That's funny, there is only one chapter in the book of Obadiah; what Bible were you reading from?"

Obadiah is only one chapter consisting of 21 verses, which ranks it as the fifth shortest book in the Bible. Although it is a short book, it is packed with timely prophetic information for this final generation. Unless one understands the book of Obadiah, he or she will likely lack significant understanding about the missing Psalm 83 piece of the prophetic puzzle. Below is a list of the ten shortest books in the Bible:[166]

1. 3 John --- 1 chapter, 14 verses, 299 words

2. 2 John --- 1 chapter, 13 verses, 303 words

3. Philemon --- 1 chapter, 25 verses, 445 words

4. Jude --- 1 chapter, 25 verses, 613 words

5. Obadiah --- 1 chapter, 21 verses, 670 words

6. Titus --- 3 chapters, 46 verses, 921 words

7.  **2nd Thess.** ---3 chapters, 47 verses, 1042 words

8.  **Haggai** --- 2 chapters, 38 verses, 1131 words

9.  **Nahum** --- 3 chapters, 47 verses, 1285 words

10. **Jonah** --- 4 chapters, 48 verses, 1321 words

> The vision of Obadiah. Thus says the LORD GOD concerning Edom (We have heard a report from the LORD, *And* a messenger has been sent among the nations, *saying,* "Arise, and let us rise up against her for battle." (Obad. 1:1 NKJV; emphasis added)

Two things are declared in verse 1. First, the prophets (plural) have heard "a report from the LORD." Second, "a messenger has been sent among the nations." Note that the "report from the LORD" is not necessarily the message sent to the nations; rather, the message to the nations dictates the need for the report. The report is given through the prophets so that the Jewish people will know God's response to the battle-stirring message "sent among the nations."

We know what the message says: "And rise up to battle" (Jer. 49:14, NKJV). But who are the "We" to whom the report is given? Who are the nations "among the nations" to which the messenger has been sent? Lastly, who is "her" that these nations will attack? The prophets are Obadiah and Jeremiah. "We," Obadiah and Jeremiah, "have heard a report from the LORD." Obadiah echoes a report first heard by Jeremiah: "I have heard a message from the LORD, And an ambassador has been sent to the nations: 'Gather together, come against her, And rise up to battle!'" (Jer. 49:14, NKJV).

Who are the nations "among the nations?" There are three key ways to determine what nations are "among the nations." First, in verse 2 we are told that Edom is among these nations:

> Behold, I will make you [Edom] small *among the* [confederating] *nations;* You shall be greatly despised. (Obad. 1:2, NKJV; emphasis added)

Secondly, in verse 7 the other nations, in addition to Edom, are assembled along with these Edomites in a confederacy:

> All the men in *your confederacy* Shall force you [Palestinians] to the border; The men at peace with you Shall deceive you *and* prevail against you. (Obad. 1:7, NKJV; abbreviated with emphasis added)

Lastly, in verse 1 the mandate of the confederacy is to rise up to battle against some nation referred to as "her." Is Edom this "her?" Scripture generally references

Edom or Esau as "him" or "he," rather than "her" or "she." In addition, how could Edom be a member of a confederacy that was against him? Though verse 7 depicts Edom as a deceived member within the confederacy, he is still a known member of the confederacy. It is not probable that the Edomites, who are linked to the modern-day Palestinians, would rise up to battle among the confederating nations, with the nations, to extinguish their own existence.

More importantly, however, is to note that the report Obadiah hears concerns the final judgment against the Edomite peoples. Scripture points to the final judgment against the Palestinians as being leveled by one single nation—that nation is Israel.[167] There is no scriptural basis to assume that the final destruction of the Edomite people will be at the hands of Edom itself, assembled with a multiplicity of nations.

Presently residing within the modern-day Palestinian refugees is a contingency of Edomite descendants. Therefore, this yet unfulfilled prophecy is destined to find its association with a pending judgment against the Palestinians and their neighboring Arab cohorts that support them. These nations are identified further on in this study.

So then, who is the "her" of verse 1 destined to be attacked? She comes under attack by a group of confederating nations. Since Edom is among these attacking nations, "her" must be someone the Palestinians want to destroy. Obadiah 1:10–14 tells us it is Israel that Edom antagonizes. Psalm 83:1–8 tells us that the Palestinians involve themselves in a confederacy for rising up to battle against Israel. In addition, Israel is referred to as "her" within the Bible more times than any other nation.

Thus, in summary, God gives the Jewish people through their prophets, predominately Jeremiah and Obadiah, as prescribed in the prophetic formula of Amos 3:7 an important report, the contents of which will be spelled out in Obadiah 1:1–20 and Jeremiah 49:7–22. This report from the LORD serves as God's response to the petition of the Psalmist Asaph in Psalm 83:9-18.

Secondly, "a messenger has been sent among the nations." Though it singles out Edom, this response also incorporates the Psalm 83:6–8 confederated member nations of Lebanon, Syria, Iraq, Jordan, Saudi Arabia, and Egypt, and the Gaza; Edom is only one member "among the nations." We can restrict the "among the nations" grouping to those members who in Obadiah 1:7 are aligned in a confederacy with Edom.

"Arise, and let us rise up against her for battle." Among the confederated nations, the call to battle has sounded in Obadiah's vision of the future. The time has come for the Psalm 83:6–8 members to rise up against her, the nation Israel, for battle. The intent: They have said, "Come, and let us cut them off from being a nation, That the name of Israel may be remembered no more." (Psa. 83:4, NKJV; emphasis added)

## Onward with Obadiah's Vision

> Behold, I will make you [Edom] *small among the* [confederate] *nations*; You shall be greatly despised. (Obad. 1:2, NKJV; emphasis added)

The report from the LORD begins by making two prophetic assertions in verse 2 regarding Edom. First, they will be reduced in national stature among the nations, and secondly they will be greatly despised.

Among the confederate nations, Edom will be the least in stature. This condition is emphasized in Psalm 83:6, whereby the Palestinians are identified as "the tents of Edom." By the time the call to battle among the confederate nations arises, "Edom" will be "small among the nations." The Palestinians are identified as tent dwellers, likely referring to them as a displaced population, perhaps a people without their own state. Remember that biblically, "the tents of," typically refers to refugees, military encampments, or both.[168]

Many consider Obadiah to be a contemporary of Jeremiah, which means his prophetic ministry flourished about the time of the Babylonian captivity.[169] A study of the history of Edom from the time of the Babylonian captivity was given in the chapter called "The Whodomites, Who are the Edomites Today," but is worth encapsulating again. The quote below illustrates the process of the national reduction of Edom, i.e., "Behold, I will make you small among the nations." From the *International Standard Bible Encyclopedia:*

> "They [the Edomites] gave what help they could to Nebuchadnezzar, and exulted in the destruction of Jerusalem, stirring the bitterest indignation in the hearts of the Jews (Lam. 4:21; Ezek. 25:12; 35:3ff; Ob. 1:10ff). The Edomites pressed into the then evacuated lands in the South of Judah. In 300 BC, Mt. Seir with its capital Petra fell into the hands of the Nabateans. West of the Arabah the country they occupied came to be known by the Greek name Idumea, and the people as Idumeans. Hebron, their chief city, was taken by Judas Maccabeus in 165 BC (1 Macc 4:29, 61; 5:65). In 126 BC, the country was subdued by John Hyrcanus, who compelled the people to become Jews and to submit to circumcision. Antipater, governor of Idumaea, was made procurator of Judea, Samaria and Galilee by Julius Caesar. He paved the way to the throne for his son Herod the Great. With the fall of Judah under the Romans, Idumaea disappears from history."

Presently, there is a group of displaced Arabs in the region fighting for a homeland. They are commonly called Palestinians. Over the past one hundred years, the international community has at various times encouraged them to resettle into their ancestral Arab lands away from what is known as modern-day Israel. However, to date these peoples are still predominately residing as refugees and are generally unable to resettle in the Arab nations.

There are numerous Palestinian refugee camps located at various locations inside the borders of Israel and her neighboring Arab countries. These countries have generally refused to assimilate these refugees into their citizenry. These displaced peoples, at least in part, likely find their ancestry traceable to the ethnic group known as the Edomites. We might infer that these displaced peoples, have been "made small among the nations."

## Onward with Obadiah's Vision

> "The pride of your heart has deceived you, *You* who dwell in the clefts of the rock, Whose habitation is high; *You* who say in your heart, 'Who will bring me down to the ground?' Though you ascend *as* high as the eagle, And though you set your nest among the stars, From there I will bring you down," says the LORD. (Obad. 1:3–4, NKJV)

Though they are the least among the member nations of the confederacy, they are under the illusion that they are invincible. This is the result of their deluded religious thinking, "you ascend as high as the eagle; you set your nest among the stars." By his usage of "stars," Obadiah prompts us to recognize the Bible typology of angels. Numerous passages in the scriptures associate the angelic realm with the stars. Thus, there is a possible connection to be made between the deluded condition of the Palestinians, and their religious Islamic mindset.

Notice the decline of Edom. First they are reduced nationally in Obadiah 1:2, and then they are to be brought down spiritually in Obadiah 1:4. It is important to recognize the role of Islam as the embodiment of all the ancient hatred passed down through the ages, throughout the region, against Israel. Islam tends to encourage violence against the Jewish people.[170]

The Islamic suicide bomber notoriously utters the chant "Allah Akbar" just before he or she blows up their intended Israeli target. This chant means Allah, their Islamic god, is greater than everything. Furthermore, remember that the predominant attitude of the Arab countries in the Middle East is to hinder the worship of Jehovah, the Old Testament God of the Jews. They generally prohibit the establishment of Jewish synagogues on Arab soil.

## Onward with Obadiah's Vision

> If thieves had come to you, If robbers by night—Oh, how you will be cut off!—Would they not have stolen till they had enough? If grape-gatherers

had come to you, Would they not have left *some* gleanings? Oh, how Esau shall be searched out! *How* his hidden treasures shall be sought after! (Obad. 1:5–6, NKJV; emphasis added)

Up to verse 5, Edom has been described as a confederate member "among the nations," that would become "made small among them (the nations)," and "greatly despised," but now in verse 5–6 Edom "will be cut off," and "his (Esau's) hidden treasures shall be sought after." Obadiah warns of the severest form of judgment, thieves taking everything, grape-gatherers leaving no gleanings, and even hidden treasures sought after.

The prophet Amos tells us that there is a point whereby Edom's punishment cannot be postponed.

> Thus says the LORD: "For three transgressions of Edom, and for four, I will not turn away its *punishment*, Because he pursued his brother [Israel] with the sword, And cast off all pity; *His anger tore perpetually*, *And he kept his wrath forever.*" (Amos 1:11, NKJV; emphasis added)

Amos alludes to the historical hatred of the Jews by their Edomite brothers with "His anger tore perpetually," and informs us that it continued through the ages: "And he kept his wrath forever." From generation to generation, an enmity toward the Jews tore at the very core of Edomite existence. They never abandoned this feeling, which perpetuates even today through the Edomite remnant contingency residing within the modern-day Palestinians.

It is important to note that God does not levy punishment upon Gentile nations randomly. He judges Edom specifically for their continual assaults against the Jews. As such, they will provoke upon themselves the Genesis 12:3 clause contained within the Abrahamic Covenant, i.e., the curse-for-curse-in-kind.

The "him" that curses you in that important verse, has individual, national, and international applications. All who individually or collectively come against Israel beyond that point determined by God as acceptable will provoke the curse-for-curse-in-kind clause upon themselves.

There is a point whereby God used Gentile nations, such as in the Babylonian captivity, to serve out judgment against the Jews, and in these instances, those nations were "in exempt." However, the minute those nations crossed beyond the acceptable point and persecuted the Jews, they were determined to be operating "in contempt" or "in excess," and they provoked the Genesis 12:3 clause upon themselves.

> *All the men in your confederacy* Shall force you to the border; The men at peace with you Shall deceive you *and* prevail against you. *Those who eat your*

bread shall lay a trap for you. No one is aware of it. (Obad. 1:7, NKJV; emphasis added)

In verse 7 we gain the recognition that Edom, made small among the nations and greatly despised, is involved in a confederate effort, which is most likely the same confederacy described in Psalm 83:5–8.

These nations, supposedly having pledged a peaceful allegiance with the Edomites in support of the Palestinians plight, actually "force" them "to the border" (of Israel). Because the Edomites have their minds set upon their religious invincibility "Though you ascend as high as the eagle, And though you set your nest among the stars," the Palestinians become deceived. The deception encourages them toward the border of Israel, and serves the other nations purposes to use them as their pawns. This diabolical scheme uses the Palestinians as insulation between Israel and the other confederate nations listed above.

This deception predominately started in 1967 because of the Arab defeat in the Six-Day War. At that point, the Jews expanded their borders and the Arab leaders realized they could not cut off the nation Israel militarily. Henceforth, the Arab leaders in the region adopted the unconventional strategies of terror and propaganda. Terror enabled them to conduct an ongoing war against Israel, aimed at the continued disruption of Israel's national sovereignty. Terror also gave these Arab nations the ability to conduct this dirty war with somewhat clean hands. They found the displaced Palestinians to be great foot soldiers and human land mines, yet the Jewish blood would not blatantly appear as stains upon their national hands.

These nations opted to keep these displaced peoples deceptively deployed within the Gaza Strip, West Bank, and various border lying refugee camps. Note that all of these locations above are nearby the border of Israel. These Palestinians now breed profusely in these border- lying communities, and from their moment of birth are taught in textbooks to hate Israel.

With apparently clean hands, these nations go about the dirty business of promoting Palestinian propaganda within the international community. The three main issues that fuel the unrest in the Middle East are: Israel's right to exist as a sovereign nation, a Palestinian state within the borders of Israel, and the rights of the Arab-Palestinian refugees at the borders of Israel to return to Israel. What to do about Jerusalem is a byproduct of these three issues. These Arab nations refuse Israel the right to exist, they demand a state for the displaced Arabs—but only within the borders of Israel—and they demand the refugees be assimilated within the borders of Israel.

Numerous studies have shown that the Arab refugees could be easily assimilated into these bordering Arab nations, but these nations make it difficult for the refugees to become citizens. All of these issues are only issues, because these Arab nations are poised to confederate in an attempt to destroy the nation Israel. This effort will fail!

This confederacy is rising into formation for the specific purposes referenced in Obadiah 1:1: "Arise, and let us rise up against her for battle." They confederate to destroy Israel. They encourage the Palestinians toward the borders of Israel as their front line offensive, while they themselves protect their own borders.

Is this not the case today, with the Palestinians and the many refugee camps along the borders of Israel? These Palestinians have a plight, and their so-called Arab partners have fully propagandized it to their favor. For the most part, they discourage the thought that Israel has any right to exist, and encourage the thought that the Palestinians and refugees belong in Israel. They do not assimilate these peoples into their borders; rather, they promote the thought that they all belong in the land of Israel. They have encouraged the myth that Israel is the homeland of the Palestinians, whereas history suggests no such thing. The trap is that Israel has nowhere else to go and, as such, they have become a great army ready to protect the very borders at which this confederacy forces the Palestinians to remain. As quoted earlier from Obadiah 1:7: "Those who eat your bread shall lay a trap for you." No one is aware of it.

Ultimately, these nations will unite in a conventional military effort to destroy the nation Israel, but the "exceedingly great army" of Israel will decisively defeat these Arab nations.

## Onward with Obadiah's Vision

> "Will I not in that day," says the LORD, "Even destroy the wise *men* from Edom, And understanding from the mountains of Esau? Then your *mighty men*, O Teman, *shall be dismayed*, To the end that everyone from the mountains of Esau May be cut off by slaughter." (Obad. 1:8–9, NKJV; emphasis added)

Obadiah has previously stated the severity of the judgment in verse 5–6 to befall Edom, and in v8–9 he extends the scope even further to include the destruction of the "wise" and the "mighty men." These mighty men "shall be dismayed" because of the slaughter that will be inflicted upon them by the exceedingly great army of Israel.

> *For violence against your brother Jacob*, Shame shall cover you, And you shall be cut off forever. (Obad. 1:10, NKJV; emphasis added).

The reason for the slaughter is "For violence against your brother Jacob." As stated previously this behavior provokes upon the persecutor of the Jews the curse-for-curse-in-kind clause of the Abrahamic Covenant as prescribed in Genesis 12:3. Obadiah continues in verses 11 through 14 to outline and identify the historical crimes, whereby Esau's descendants, the Edomites committed "violence against Jacob." Their criminal rap sheet spans the scope of time from the Exodus to the present.

*In the day that you stood on the other side.* (Obad. 1:11a, NKJV; emphasis added)

The Exodus of the Jews via the route of Edom is referenced in verse 11. The Jews were disallowed by the Edomites to pass through the territory of Edom, as they were making their way into the Promised Land. The Edomite descendants of Esau "stood (their ground) on the other side" in opposition to the request of Moses to harmlessly pass through. This was the first serious offense they committed against the descendants of Jacob.

This was a slap in the face of the God of the Jews, Who had clearly evidenced His favoritism to the Hebrews. Jehovah, their God, had parted the Red Seas and conquered the Egyptian army single-handedly enabling the descendants of Jacob the freedom to migrate toward the Promised Land.

> Now Moses sent messengers from Kadesh to the king of Edom. "Thus says your brother Israel: 'You know all the hardship that has befallen us, how our fathers went down to Egypt, and we dwelt in Egypt a long time, and the Egyptians afflicted us and our fathers. When we cried out to the LORD, He heard our voice and sent the Angel and brought us up out of Egypt; now here we are in Kadesh, a city on the edge of your border. Please let us pass through your country. We will not pass through fields or vineyards, nor will we drink water from wells; we will go along the King's Highway; we will not turn aside to the right hand or to the left until we have passed through your territory.'" Then *Edom said to him, "You shall not pass through my land,* lest I come out against you with the sword." Thus *Edom refused to give Israel passage through his territory; so Israel turned away from him.* (Num. 20:14–18, 21, NKJV ; emphasis added)

> *In the day that strangers carried captive his forces, When foreigners entered his gates And cast lots for Jerusalem—Even you were as one of them.* (Obad. 1:11b, NKJV; emphasis added)

Obadiah 1:11b is most likely depicting the siege in 845 BC by the Philistines. The Edomites at that time behaved indignantly to the Jews, much like the Philistines did. "Even you were as one of them."

> But you should not have gazed on the day of your brother *In the day of his captivity;* Nor should you have rejoiced over the children of Judah *In the day of their destruction;* Nor should you have spoken proudly *In the day of distress.* (Obad. 1:12, NKJV; emphasis added)

Obadiah 1:12 testifies of the crimes committed by the Edomites during the Babylonian period. Jerusalem and the temple were destroyed, and the Jews were carted off into seventy years of Babylonian captivity. He references three events: "the day of his captivity," "day of their destruction," and "the day of distress." By ordering these episodes chronologically, Obadiah appears to identify for us the three Babylonian sieges that came against the Jewish people.

"The day of his captivity" The Babylonians, led by Nebuchadnezzar, first attacked Judah in 606 BC. This resulted in the first deportation wave of Jews into captivity. Some royal youths, including the prophet Daniel and some of his companions were relocated into Babylon. Additionally the king and his family along with many notable and skillful Jews were likewise transported out of Judah at this time.[171]

"The day of their destruction": In 586 BC there was a second general deportation of Jews by Nebuchadnezzar. Many more principal Jews were moved into Babylon. The first Jewish temple was destroyed, and the Babylonians confiscated many of the holy vessels at this time.

"The day of distress": In 582 BC, the last deportation occurred. Many of the heads of families, their wives and children were exiled to Babylon because of this third Babylonian siege. Because of these three deportations, a sizeable Jewish community was established in Babylon.

Ample forewarning of the pending "day of" Esau's twin "brother" Jacob had been given by the prophet Jeremiah, among others. The world was put on notice that the client nation Israel would be disciplined through captivity for a period of seventy years for their idolatrous practices and overall failure to honor and obey their Mosaic Law.[172]

The Edomites "gazed on the day of your brother." The crime of the Edomites was that rather than glean from the mistake of their cousins the Jews; they "gazed" upon them at the time of their first deportation, depicting their severe disdain toward the Jewish people. First, they "gazed" then they "rejoiced" at the events of the second deportation, and lastly they "spoke proudly" at the time of the third Jewish deportation.

Moreover, history tells us at that time that they capitalized on the captivity of the Jews by further migrating into Hebron and the surrounding areas of Israel, further homesteading the Holy Land.

> You should not have entered the gate of My people In *the day of their calamity*. Indeed, you should not have gazed on their affliction In *the day of their calamity*, Nor laid *hands* on their substance In *the day of their calamity*. (Obad. 1:13; NKJV, emphasis added)

Obadiah advances the clock to the time of the Roman Empire. The phrase "day of their calamity," used in this passage three times alludes to a completely calamitous period in Jewish history. Such was the case during the occupation of the Romans in the Holy Land. First the Edomites "entered the gate," as exemplified by Antipater, a fullblooded Idumean (Edomite), who was established by Julius Caesar as the procurator over Judea in 47 BC. Then, Antipater's son, Herod the Great reigned over Israel between 37 BC and 4 BC with the blessings of the Roman Empire.

Subsequently we see that the Edomites are again accused of gazing rather than gleaning: "you should not have gazed on their affliction." They gazed during the Babylonian period, and that led to rejoicing and prideful boasting, Obadiah foretells in the Roman episode, they will likewise gaze, and then possess things of value to the Jews. One of the things most esteemed by the Jews was their second temple and all of its priestly implements. This temple became known during the Roman era as the "Herodian Temple," named after Herod, who was not even a Jew. He was one-half Edomite, and one-half Nabatean. Herod and his court found themselves in a position to have "laid hands on their (Jewish) substance."

> You should not have stood at the crossroads To cut off those among them who escaped; Nor should you have delivered up those among them who remained In the day of distress. (Obad. 1:14, NKJV)

Obadiah identifies two groups of Jews, those who attempted to escape from the Roman destruction of AD 70 and those who remained in Israel during the destruction, "In the day of distress." In so doing, he concludes his list of historical war crimes committed by the Edomites against their Jewish kindred.

In verse 1:14 he accuses the Edomites of attempting to hinder the prescribed disciplinary dispersion of the Jews out of Israel, into the nations of the world. They "stood at the crossroads to cut off those (Jews) among them who escaped." The Romans destroyed Jerusalem and the second Jewish temple in AD 70. This provoked a majority of the Jewish population to scatter amongst the nations of the world. This dispersion was in fulfillment of numerous Old Testament Bible prophecies.

The irony is that the Edomites as a population were "among them who escaped." At that time, they were identified by their Greek name, the Idumeans. Idumea was a recognized region in Southeastern Israel. The Idumeans "stood at the crossroads to cut off " those Jews attempting to flee from Roman persecution.

> A study of Hebrew history between the time of AD 33 to about AD 135 evidences a period of time whereby many Jews began to exit out of Israel into the nations of the world. The Idumeans tended to present themselves more as an obstacle to, rather than a facilitator of, that migration process. Obadiah ranks that episode of Edomite/ Idumean history as being comparable to the other war crimes on his lengthy list.

Lastly in Obadiah 1:14, not only did the Idumeans attempt to hinder the exodus of the Jews out of Israel, they "delivered up those among them who remained." This behavior completely evidenced their adversarial attitude against the Jewish people. It served to prove that down through the ages the ancient hatred spawned by Esau against his twin brother Jacob, continued to filter on down through to his descendants, the Edomites, and Idumeans.

The pages of history authenticate and adjudicate Obadiah's accusations. Today it is as if those very damaging pages have been reopened and are being relived through the events of the Arab-Israeli conflict. The Palestinians, who have some traces of Edomite ancestry among their ranks, continue to harbor the same ancient attitude of hatred outlined out of the annals of their history.

The atrocities of their past, combined with the catastrophes of their present seal their fate for the future! They will soon experience their ethnical demise through divine judgment. Although many suggest that the end of the Edomites came in correlation with the conclusion of Obadiah's list of war crimes, Bible prophecy defeats that presumption. The Edomites resurface on numerous pages of end time's prophecy.

Though it would have appeared as though they sealed their judgment from their actions in the past, that judgment has not been officially executed as of yet. The Judgment of the Edomites, who became called the Idumeans, and can now be best referred to as the Palestinians, will be judged in the fashion described in Ezekiel 25:14 and Obadiah 1:18.

> "I will lay My vengeance on Edom by the hand of My people Israel, that they may do in Edom according to My anger and according to My fury; and they shall know My vengeance," says the LORD GOD. (Ezek. 25:14, NKJV)

> "The house of Jacob shall be a fire, And the house of Joseph a flame; But the house of Esau *shall be* stubble; They shall kindle them and devour them, And no survivor shall *remain* of the house of Esau," For the LORD has spoken. (Obad. 1:18, NKJV)

Make no mistake: by his usage of "the house of Esau," Obadiah refers to the ancient Edomites in the Hebrew language, later labeled the Idumeans in the Greek language, who are today known as the Palestinians, which is a derivative from the Hebrew word Pelesheth, the Arab term Filastin, the Latin word Palaestina, and the English word Palestine. The Palestinian trail can be traced in part back to the ancient Philistines, and the Edomite descendants of Esau.

Presently the Palestinians have picked up where the Idumean contingency of their ancestors left off. "Nor should you have delivered up those among them who remained In the day of distress." They are still delivering up their Jewish cousins to oppressive conditions. It is as if the Jews who have returned to their motherland, are still living under persecution as in the former times "In the day of distress."

## Onward with Obadiah's Vision

> For the day of the LORD upon all the nations *is* near; As you have done, it shall be done to you; Your reprisal shall return upon your own head. (Obad. 1:15, NKJV).

The curse-for-curse-in-kind reprisal against Edom will occur before "the Day of the LORD" occurs; it occurs when "the day of the LORD upon all the nations is near." "The day of the LORD" is defined by most as either the entire seven-year period of the tribulation (i.e., Daniels seventieth-week), or only the second half of that period, spanning 3.5 years.

> For as you drank on My holy mountain, *So* shall all the nations drink continually; Yes, they shall *drink*, and *swallow*, And they shall *be as though they had never been*. (Obad. 1:16, NKJV; emphasis added)

To "drink," "swallow," and "be as though they had never been," finds association with biblical illustrations of judgment. The picture is that of a people being forcibly handed a cup containing a poisonous content. God, insuring that the intended recipients will not possess the antidote, personally conjures up this highly toxic concoction. The affected population group has done something that has greatly disturbed God, and as such has provoked upon them a divine judgment. Pertinent examples to this study can be found in Jeremiah 25:17–26, and Jeremiah 49:12.

The judgment to befall Edom will serve as a precursor to the judgment within "the day of the LORD upon all the nations." Zephaniah 2 also makes clear that this judgment against Edom, which will also extend further into the other confederate member nations, is to serve as an example to the other nations, but more importantly it is a call to the "meek of the Earth" to get right before "the day of the LORD" occurs.

> Gather yourselves together, yes, gather together, O undesirable nation [Israel today in unbelief, gathering in the land], Before the decree is issued, *Or* the day passes like chaff, Before the LORD'S fierce anger comes upon you, Before the day of the LORD'S anger comes upon you! Seek the LORD, all you *meek of the Earth*, Who have upheld His justice. Seek righteousness, seek humility. It may be that you will be hidden In the day of the LORD'S anger. (Zeph. 2:1–3, NKJV, emphasis added)

Zephaniah 2 goes on to describe the conditions subsequent to the Israeli Conquest of the Psalm 83 confederacy. For more information on the details of Zephaniah 2, refer to the Psalm 83 and the Prophets chapter contained within this book.

## Onward with Obadiah's Vision

> But on Mount Zion there shall be deliverance, And there shall be holiness; The house of Jacob shall possess their possessions. (Obad. 1:17, NKJV)

Though we are told in verse 16, that the Psalm 83 confederate nations first, and then the remaining nations at large in the world "shall be as though they had never been," this will not be the case on Mount Zion! "On Mount Zion there shall be deliverance," and holiness.

> "The house of Jacob shall be a fire, And the house of Joseph a flame; But the house of Esau *shall be* stubble; They shall kindle them and devour them, And no survivor shall *remain* of the house of Esau," For the LORD has spoken. (Obad. 1:18, NKJV)

Obadiah encapsulates the theme scattered throughout his vision; I will bring you Palestinians down (v4), you will be cut off (v5), your treasures searched out (v6), a trap for you (v7), everyone will be cut off by slaughter (v9,) shame shall cover you (v10), the forced drinking from the cup of judgment (v16). Obadiah in v18 determines the defeat of Esau's descendants residing within the modern-day Palestinians will be at the hands of Israel's exceedingly great army. The use of stubble, which when lit burns entirely, evidences the theme earlier presented of the severity of this judgment against Edom.

> The South shall possess the mountains of Esau, And the Lowland shall possess Philistia. They shall possess the fields of Ephraim And the fields of Samaria. Benjamin *shall possess* Gilead And the captives of this host of the children of Israel *Shall possess the land* of the Canaanites As far as Zarephath. The captives of Jerusalem who are in Sepharad Shall possess the cities of the South. (Obad. 1:19–20, NKJV; emphasis added)

After reading this chapter, please feel free to read ahead to the Greater Israel, The Future Maps of Isralestine chapter contained within this book. More details into the profound prophesies of Obadiah 1:19–20 can be found within this chapter. In essence, Obadiah 1:19–20 implies that as a direct result of the Jewish conquest over the Palestinians alluded to in Obadiah 1:18, Israel will be significantly increased in both size and prosperity. The tiny Israel as we recognize it today will soon encompass a major portion of the Middle East, and become one of the wealthiest nations in the world.

> Then saviors [yasha] shall come to Mount Zion To judge the mountains of Esau, And the kingdom shall be the LORD'S. (Obad. 1:21, NKJV)

The Hebrew word yasha can mean deliverers, victors, avengers, or saviors. What Obadiah appears to be stating in verse 21a is that from Mount Zion, Jewish sovereignty will be exercised over the conquered territory of Edom. The phrase "the kingdom shall be the LORD'S" in v21b is a probable reference to the sovereignty over the region by the Jews, as they will be known at that future point once again as "My people Israel." Ezekiel 25:14 addresses this conquest and refers to the Jews again as "My people Israel."

> "I will lay My vengeance on Edom [the Palestinians] by the hand of *My people Israel*, that they may do in Edom according to My anger and according to My fury; and they shall know My vengeance," says the LORD GOD. (Ezek. 25:14, NKJV; emphasis added)

# SEVENTEEN

# Psalm 83

## *The Arab Confederacy*

**"Arab League refuses to recognize Israel as Jewish state"**

*Ma'an News Agency 9/17/10*

**"Arab states unanimously approve Saudi peace initiative"**

*Haaretz 3/28/07*

"Saudi king calls for end to international blockade on Palestinians; EU urges Arab states to be flexible on plan."

This chapter takes a close look at Psalm 83 and its prophetic relevancy to the end-times. It was written by Asaph, a Levite musician, and prophet appointed by King David to serve in the tabernacle until the first Jewish temple was completed.[173] Asaph wrote this Psalm when the nation of Israel was experiencing the blessings of the Abrahamic Covenant in an unprecedented manner; they were a people of prominence entering a period of prosperity and residing in their own land under the leadership of their God-ordained king David.

As a people, their focus was on the growth of the nation, and building God, His first house of worship on Earth, i.e., the Jewish Temple, but unexpectedly in Psalm 83:2-8 Asaph introduces a futuristic threat to the Covenant God made with their patriarchs Abraham, Isaac, and Jacob—a warning so severe that the survival of the thriving nation could be in question.

In his Psalm, Asaph identifies two groups: "Your enemies," and "those who hate You." Then in verses 6–8, he specifies the populations that fall into either of these two categories, both of which possess adversarial attitudes against Jehovah, the God of the Jews. Geographically, these peoples throughout time have most closely bordered the nation of Israel. Furthermore, they are the ones who have historically contested the Jewish claims of there being only one God, and they being His chosen people.

Asaph would not necessarily have known the timing destined for the final fulfillment of this prophecy, and today this event is still impending, however he should have been well aware of the disposition of hatred that already plagued the region. Long before his time the family members previously identified in the chapter called "The Ancient Arab Hatred," had become infected by the enmity established by Hagar, between herself and Sarah, by Ishmael between himself and Isaac, by Esau between himself and Jacob, and by the children of Lot (Moab and Ammon) between themselves and the children of Israel.

The individuals classified within the group of "those who hate You" in Psalm 83:6-8, are Hagar representing the "Hagarenes," Ishmael father of the "Ishmaelites," Esau who is also called "Edom," Moab and Ammon, who are the "children of Lot, and Amalek, the grandson of Esau. These six infamous characters are enlisted members of the ten-member confederacy that will ultimately seek to destroy the Jewish nation of Israel. These ancestors all coveted the contents of the Abrahamic Covenant. They felt in some way cheated, or in the case of "Moab," and "Ammon," threatened by the covenant, and As such, they outsourced through their descendants that followed a hatred of the Jews.

This adversarial attitude spread rapidly throughout the entire Middle East region and overtook the populations residing in "Gebal, Philistia, Tyre, and Assyria." These remaining four confederate members comprise the "Your enemies" group. Unlike Hagar, Ishmael, Esau, Moab, and Ammon of the "those who hate You" group, the "Your enemies" group, has only an indirect association to the contents of the Abrahamic Covenant. They were not the near relatives of Abraham, however, the contents of the Abrahamic Covenant threatened their own territorial claims as well.

In Genesis 15:18, we are told that all of the land between the river of Egypt, and the river Euphrates, was to be "Grant Deeded" to the Jewish heirs of the Abrahamic Covenant. This prescription put the generally Arab populations within those confines on official notice that they were trespassing on Jewish land, and would need to cooperate with Jewish sovereignty over the region, or else pay the consequences.

As you can imagine, these affected Arab populations considered the ancient hatred attitude, which had been well established within the "those who hate You" group, worthy of adopting for their own territorial purposes. As such, the "Your enemies" group became formed. Throughout history, each individual member within these two groups evidenced their enmity in one way or another toward the Jewish people. Collectively these two groups embraced a common concern over the contents of the Abrahamic Covenant.

## Striking Similarities

Since this prophecy appears destined for fulfillment in the near future, some striking similarities for today should be extrapolated from the historical facts just described. As it was during Asaph's time, the Jewish people are again experiencing a time of blessings. Today they are thriving in their homeland, under the leadership of a king, (Prime Minister) poised to experience a period of prosperity. Once again, they draft blueprints for the building of a Jewish Temple for Jehovah their God. Lastly, the descendants of the same two groups comprised of "those who hate You" and "Your enemies" are enjoined in an adversarial attitude antagonistic against the restoration of the nation Israel.

As it was in Asaph's time, the prosperity of the nation Israel, should serve to remind the neighboring nations of the contents of the Abrahamic Covenant. These Arab nations are settled on soil promised to Abraham and his descendants, the Jews. Rather than subscribing to the positive side of the Genesis 12:3 clause of the Abrahamic Covenant, whereby all those peoples who would bless the Jews, would in return receive blessings of like kind, they align themselves on the reverse side of the same clause. In contrast, curses are promised to those who oppress and oppose the Jewish people.

Whether the modern-day descendants of these two angered groups consider the consequences of their actions in relationship to the contents of the ancient Abrahamic Covenant or not, their act of confederating against Israel on any level operates under the "threat" of the covenant, rather than the "trust" of the covenant. The lesson to this Jewish generation is the same as it was for Asaph's generation. They are not to forget that Jewish prosperity provokes their neighbors into a precarious position. Either these neighbors can support the process and be accordingly blessed, or they can resist the process and become collectively defiant. Asaph's prophecy tells us that Israel's Arab neighbors will choose the latter.

What a powerful mandate these two distraught groups formulate in Psalm 83:4 "That the name Israel, may be remembered no more." The ramifications of this war effort are staggering, considering that then and now numerous promises and prophecies rely upon the eternal existence of the nation Israel and the Jewish descendants of Abraham. For these ten confederate members to believe that they can successfully nullify the final fulfillment of the yet unfulfilled promises and prophecies centered upon the Jews and Israel requires a powerful faith.

Interestingly today, all of these ten confederate members are united under one umbrella of common faith known as Islam. Apparently, they believe that their god Allah has the ability to void out the contents contained within the Abrahamic Covenant specifically, and the Bible generally. This unity of faith did not exist during the time of Asaph, back then these various populations worshipped their own different deities. Milcom, Chemosh, Asherah, Baal, and many more gods were worshipped, in contrast to the Jewish God Jehovah.

The teachings of their prophet Mohammed cleverly convinced these peoples to abandon their polytheistic practices, in order to embrace his religious package. Islam presents itself as a monotheistic religion. Regardless, the fact is that these ten populations, that are prophesied to attempt the future genocide of the Jews, are presently all predominately Islamic.

## Psalm 83—An Imprecatory Prayer

Psalm 83 is a prophecy formatted by Asaph into a petition; a prayer of lament, or another synonymous term is an "imprecatory prayer." As such, it is generally void of any resolution content, and yet due to the severity of the prophecy it demands a reaction from God. In order to discover the divine response one is required to look elsewhere into the scriptures, as guided by clues contained within Asaph's Psalm 83 petition. This was accomplished in the chapters called "Psalm 83 and the Prophets, and "The Psalm 83 Report."

What is of utmost importance to understand is that this prophecy, though it threatens the survival of the Jewish people, is primarily an assault against the character of the covenant making God of Abraham, Isaac, Jacob, and Jesus Christ! This first clue is given in the very beginning passages of the Psalm

> Do not keep silent, O God! Do not hold Your peace, And do not be still, O God!For behold, Your enemies make a tumult; And those who hate You have lifted up theirhead. (Psa. 83:1–2, NKJV)

We can arrive at the understanding that this is an assault targeted at God, in that if the client nation is exterminated and the name Israel remembered no more, then their covenant-making God, Jehovah, is not a covenant-keeping God, and is therefore nothing more than a promise breaking God. The problem therein lies in the fact that if the God of the Jews has a character flaw, and breaks His promises, then so is the God of the Christians, because Jesus Christ came as the "Seed" of Abraham,[174] in fulfillment of the unconditional covenant God made with Abraham, Isaac, and Jacob. Therefore, Salvation as taught in Christianity, which is by faith in Christ, would likewise be un-assured.[175]

Asaph used the pronouns "Your," and "You," evidencing that he recognized this was an assault against God personally: "Your enemies," "those who hate "You," "counsel against Your people," "against "Your sheltered ones," "they form a covenant against You!" Asaph appears extremely cognizant of the inference; that if the Jews were exterminated, their God Jehovah was a failure. This point is made perfectly clear in Jeremiah 31:35-37, which declares that it is virtually impossible to destroy the Jewish race.

Cemented in the Abrahamic Covenant, is the survival of the chosen Jewish people. The other important subsequent covenants, which were created to compliment this Covenant are the Promised Land, (Land Covenant), the Eternal Throne, upon which Jesus Christ will sit as King (Davidic Covenant), and the Eternal Relationship, whereby the Spirit of God indwells the heart of man, both Jew and Gentile, (New Covenant). All of these other facets, the "Land," "Throne," "King," and "Relationship" are based upon the survival of the Jewish people.

1. *Chosen People* – Genesis 22:17-18, 26:4, 28:14.

2. *Promised Land* – Genesis 15:18, Joshua 1:4, Genesis 13:15.

3. *Davidic Covenant / Eternal Throne* – 2 Samuel 7:12-13, Luke 1:32-33.

4. *New Covenant / Eternal Relationship* – Jer. 31:33, and John 14:16-17, 26

Therefore, in conclusion any offensive against God originating upon the Earth is best directed at His promises made through the Abrahamic Covenant. This Covenant was designed to be inclusive of the entirety of God's foreign policy regarding all of humanity. If the Covenant could be voided out on Earth, then the heavens would no longer be able to justifiably declare God's glory.[176] Asaph thus petitions God to uphold His glorified position in the heavens, by protecting his people on Earth.

## The Angelic Conflict

Hence, when Asaph discovered prophetically the pending confederate attack against the nation Israel, aimed at the genocide of the Jews, he probably realized that this was not an event confined to the reaches of Earth, rather it extended well into the heavens, from which the angelic conflict is outsourced. He therefore acknowledges that it is God's reputation at stake. Any attack against the descendants of Jacob (Israel) is an attack at God's head, as Jacob is the "Apple of God's eye."[177]

Thus concealed within the heart of this pending confederate effort comprised of the Arab states most closely bordering the nation Israel, aimed at the extermination of the Jews, is the scheming of Satan. He intends to pin Arabs against Jews in an attempt to spear God in the "Apple of His eye." Let us not forget a few important powerful characteristics about this enemy of God as pointed out in the scriptures:

1.  Satan is extremely cunning in this world, or in other words, powerfully influential over the direction of world affairs. (Gen. 3:1a)

2.  The entire world lies under his sway, or persuasiveness. (1 John 5:19)

3.  The Devil is a liar and a murderer. (John 8:44)

4.  Satan presently possesses the ability to travel between the geographies of heaven and Earth, and upon the Earth is able to travel the entire expanse of it. (Job 1:6)

5.  Satan, also known as Lucifer, is a fallen angel who has said in his heart that he seeks to be like the Most High God Jehovah. (Isa. 14:12–14)

Thus, it is safe to conclude that the prophecy of Psalm 83, is a holy war outsourced by Satan, who desires to be like the "Most High," aimed at the character of God? Though it will manifest someday as a war in the Middle East between the Arab and Jewish respective kingdoms, it has far greater reaches. Jeremiah prophesied of this pending event that: The Earth shakes at the noise of their fall; At the cry its noise is heard at the Red Sea (Jer. 49:21, NKJV). Yet even further, it reaches into the heavenly realm, whereby the righteous character of God is placed on trial by the angelic conflict.

Some time after Psalm 83 is over, a war will break out in heaven between Michael the archangel and his good angels against Satan and his fallen angels. Michael's team will prevail, and Satan and his troops will finally be cast out of heaven.[178] Remember that it is Michael the archangel, whose ministry incorporates the preservation of the Jewish people.[179] Satan will shortly thereafter be imprisoned for the period of 1000 years, which appears to coincide with the timing of the Messianic Kingdom. Ultimately, Satan ends up in the "Lake of Fire," whereby he will be tormented day and night forever and ever.[180]

## Advancing the Clock

Having prefaced the scope, roots, and motivation of the prophecy, let us advance the clock forward in time, from Asaph to the present. In so doing we skip over centuries of Middle East history, but none of which can be identified as the final fulfillment of the Psalm 83 prophecy.

The stage was set during the worldwide dispersion of the Jewish people out of their homeland Israel, between AD 70 and AD 1948 for Satan to make sinister preparations for their prophesied return. Satan realized that the restoration of the nation Israel would mean the return of the Jews into the region.[181] He also understood that this event would occur in the latter days, meaning that the time of his free passage between heaven and Earth would soon then after be coming to an abrupt end.[182]

What could Satan possibly contrive to insure that upon the return of the Jew into their Promised Land, they would meet with the most hostile welcoming committee? Indeed, such a hostile committee was in place at the time of their return. It was coincidentally, a committee comprised of several of the members listed in the Psalm 83 confederacy. Immediately upon their return in AD 1948 the nations of Egypt, Jordan, Syria, Lebanon, Iraq, as well as Palestinian guerillas, engaged them in a war conflict. Welcome home bullets and bombs replaced the well-deserved banners and balloons.

More of the same aggression followed in the Six-Day War, an armed conflict in June 1967 between Israel and the Arab states of Egypt, Jordan, and Syria. In six days, Israel conquered the Sinai Peninsula, Gaza Strip, West Bank, and Golan Heights. Then came the "Yom Kippur" War of October 1973 between Israel and the Arab countries of Egypt and Syria. Egypt and Syria initiated the conflict to regain territories that Israel had occupied since the Six-Day War of 1967. Although both sides suffered heavy losses during the 1973 war, Israel retained control of the territories.

How inconsiderate! How inhumane! How could these nations attack a people who had been dispersed out of their homeland for centuries, and ultimately reduced to the lowest of refugee conditions because of the Holocaust? What we see, is that the longstanding hatred of the Jews by the Arabs, did not disintegrate during the centuries of worldwide Jewish dispersion rather it was kept alive and well. It was formatted into a unified force just lying in wait, to be easily provoked by the return of the Jew into the Promised Land.

Satan, who was well aware of God's prophetic program, which strongly referenced the restoration of the nation Israel as the Jewish homeland, took the well-established hatred plaguing the region, and packaged it up into an instrument formed to prevent the successful return of the Jews into their Promised Land.

## Islam

The religion of Islam originated in the Middle East during that window period of time when the Jews were dispersed out of Israel and into the nations of the world. Muhammad, who lived between 570 and AD 632, founded Islam.[183] His new religion was cleverly designed to convert the worship of the peoples in the region from their various gods, into the worship of one god, his god, whom he labeled as Allah. An excerpt out of Encyclopedia Encarta, helps to give a basic understanding of this point.

"Around the year AD 570 Muhammad, the founding prophet of Islam, was born in Mecca, at the time the central city of the Arabian Peninsula. Some 40 years later Muhammad started preaching a new religion, Islam, which constituted a marked break from existing moral and social codes in Arabia. The new religion of Islam taught that there was one God, and that Muhammad was the last in a series of prophets and messengers. Through his messengers, God had sent various codes, or systems of laws for living, culminating in the Qur'an (Koran), the holy book of Islam. These messengers were mortal men, and they included among many others Moses, the Hebrew prophet and law-giver, and Jesus, whom Christians believe to be the son of God rather than a prophet."[184]

"Islam, which constituted a marked break from existing moral and social codes in Arabia." Indeed, Islam presented "a marked break" from the historical worship practices in Arabia, and the entire Middle East for that matter. For centuries, the region worshipped Jehovah, Milcom, Chemosh, Baal, Asherah, Dagon, Molech, and others. Scholars estimate that as many as 360 different gods had been worshipped in the region throughout the time leading up to the arrival of Muhammad.

He declared that he was the last prophet, and his supposed divine message, was to invite all the gods to submit to his god, Allah. This invitation was not restricted to the prevalent polytheistic Arab practices present at that time, but also reached out to the monotheistic religions of Judaism, and Christianity. Of course history informs us that the Jews and Christians did not buy into his propaganda at that time, however the predominant non-Jewish, and non-Christian Arab population in the region did.

"Within two centuries after its rise in the seventh century, Islam spread from its original home in Arabia into Syria, Egypt, North Africa, and Spain to the west, and into Persia, India, and, by the end of the tenth century, beyond to the east. In the following centuries, Islam also spread into Anatolia and the Balkans to the north, and sub-Saharan Africa to the south. The Muslim community comprises about 1 billion followers on all five continents."[185]

What Satan attempted to do through Muhammad, was to incorporate all religions into one. If this plan succeeded it would enable him to dismantle Judaism and Christianity through conversion, or more importantly if Jews and Christians did not convert, it enabled him to ostracize them for their failure to convert. The quote below out of the Koran (Quran) is an example of what Islam truly teaches about Jews and Christians.[186]

O you who believe [Muslims]! do not take the Jews and the Christians for friends; they are friends of each other; and whoever amongst you takes them for a friend, then surely he is one of them; surely Allah does not guide the unjust people.[187] (Surah 5:51, Shakir; emphasis added)

As of May 14, 1948, the predominant Jewish population in the world did not convert into Islam and, as such, they entered back into the Promised Land as non-Muslims. They were simply the Jews, who had been hated in the region by the Arab ancestors from time immemorial.[188] They were that ethnic group that Hitler was unable to exterminate successfully. In the eyes of the Arab-Muslim populations in the region they were coming back to dispossess the Arabs of the real estate they had swallowed up during the centuries of Jewish dispersion into the nations of the world.

To date the Jews still request favor from most of the surrounding Arab nations, for the mere right to exist in the nation Israel as their homeland. This demonstrates that the underlying dominant Arab attitude is, as Asaph prophesied, "Come, and let us cut them off from being a nation, That the name of Israel may be remembered no more." (Ps. 83:4).

The world at large is tired of the Middle East entanglement, and continues to put forward political solutions aimed at resolving the conflict, however there is very little real estate left in Israel, for the world to pressure the Jews to forfeit into Arab hands. These political attempts also play well into Satan's plan, which is to cut the Jews off from being a nation.

## Summary

In summary, Satan schemed up Islam forwarded through the man Muhammad, during the period of the worldwide Jewish dispersion, in an attempt to ignite the longstanding hatred of the Jews, by the Arabs, and unite them in common cause to oppose the return of the Jew back into the Promised Land. The devils ultimate goal is to cut the nation Israel off, that the name Israel will be remembered no more. If this can be done, and every Jew destroyed, then the unconditional covenant that their God made with their patriarch Abraham becomes rendered void and inoperative. If this covenant can be permanently disrupted as such, then God its Maker, is indeed a liar!

Remember that the genocide of the Jews is the campaign of Satan. If he can exterminate every last Jew, he can discredit God, before his angelic piers, and fulfill his desire to exalt his throne above the stars of God, and be like the most high. As quoted earlier in this chapter, Satan is cunning, a murderer, and the whole world presently lies under his sway.

## Islamic Arabs

The Psalm 83 confederates have several things in common, they are predominately of Arab descent, they all reign from Muslim dominated countries, they all generally border the modern-day nation of Israel, and they primarily hail from ancestors that were the notorious historical enemies of Israel. Could there be better candidates for Satan to fashion as a first-line offensive against the returning Jews?

I apologize if this material is offensive to some, but scripture tells us, which is also the theme of this book, that the exceedingly great army of Israel will mightily defeat these Islamic Arabs, and their Psalm 83 confederate attempt. It is not the intent of this author to upset Islamic Arabs, rather to enlighten them of the pending prophetic events relating to them. Their lives, and those of their future generation, are in jeopardy if they subscribe to the Psalm 83 confederate effort.

By faithfully adhering to the principles of Islam, they appear to have patterned their lives contrary to the true content of the Abrahamic Covenant. It is through this covenant, which God exercises his entire foreign policy toward all humankind. God fully intends at the time of the Psalm 83 confederate effort finally to dispose of the adversarial attitude established in ancient times by their ancestors, Hagar, Ishmael, Esau, Moab, and Ammon. These attitudes infected the region and the other localized enemies of Israel throughout time embraced them.

## The Stage is Set for the Showdown

Psalm 83 required the existence of the nation Israel, in order that the nation could be cut off, and the name Israel be remembered no more. Today this requirement is met. It also required that these Arab nations find common cause in order to unite in a confederate effort to exterminate the Jews. If there is ever a Jew on Earth, there is the potential of a nation Israel to be his or her homeland. Therefore, in order to achieve their goal, "that the name Israel be remembered no more," the Arab confederates must exterminate the Jews. They are presently united in such a common cause, under the umbrella of Islam.

It is interesting that the terrorist organizations confronting the Jewish people today come from the very nations listed in Psalm 83, some examples being the Hezbollah from Lebanon (primarily sponsored by Iran and Syria), and the Muslim Brotherhood sponsored Hamas from the Gaza Strip, the Philistia of old.[189] Al-Qaida, though they hail from Afghanistan, their former leader Bin Laden was from Saudi Arabia, the nation predominately formed out of Ishmael. If you study the origin of many of the numerous terrorist groups, they have arisen out of Egypt, Saudi Arabia, Jordan, Syria, Lebanon, the Palestinian territories of the Gaza Strip, and the West Bank. All of these nations are members of the Psalm 83 confederate effort. This evidences their unity of cause, which is to disrupt the further establishment of the nation Israel. Ultimately, this random terrorism will give way to the concerted confederate attack described by Asaph in Psalm 83.

As previously point out, terrorism as demonstrated in the Middle East is nothing more than the unconventional method of warfare that these above nations adopted and collectively embraced when their conventional methods failed in 1948, 1956, 1967, and 1973. These Arab nations realized that they lacked the military capability at the time to destroy Israel, but they possessed the radical Islamic constituency sufficient to disrupt the final establishment of the nation Israel, i.e., the terrorist organizations.

Each terrorist group grew as they gained sponsorships from these Arab nations. The greater the act of terror, the stronger the support for the sponsoring nation.

Each hell-bent attack composed of wars or acts of state-sponsored terror by these Arab nations against Israel has ultimately served to create an exceedingly great army within the Jewish state. This army was foretold to come in Ezekiel 37:10. Now the the stage is set for the final showdown between the Jewish Kingdom, represented by Israel, and the Arab Kingdom, represented by the ten-member confederacy, in fulfillment of a Bible prophecy.

> And you will hear of wars and rumors of wars. See that you are not troubled; for all *these things* must come to pass, but the end is not yet. For nation will rise against nation, and *kingdom against kingdom*. And there will be famines, pestilences, and Earthquakes in various places. All these *are* the beginning of sorrows. (Matt. 24:6–7, NKJV; emphasis added)

Nation rose against nation in the World War I and World War II. Subsequent to these wars, the nation of Israel was restored as the Jewish homeland on May 14, 1948. Whereas "nation will rise against nation" referred to war on the broader international scale, "kingdom against kingdom" refers to war on a more localized regional level. Christ appears to be drawing his disciples attention to events surrounding Isaiah 19:2, with this prophecy. This topic is also addressed in the chapter called, "The Three Judgments of Egypt."

More specifically, Christ was issuing prophecy concerning the Jewish people. He continued to prophesy in the next breath:

> "Then they will deliver you up to tribulation and kill you, and you will be hated by all nations for My name's sake." (Matt. 24:9, NKJV)

What Christ was apparently alluding to was the prophetic future of the Jewish people, first there would be world wars, then a Middle East war, and then the oppressive conditions of the seven-year Tribulation Period. World wars would affect the Jews, in that they were at the time a scattered people residing within those very nations warring against one another. The Middle East war would be more specific in relationship to the Jews, in that they would be restored in their homeland Israel and through time develop an "exceedingly great army," and in that condition would come under assault by the confederacy representing the "Arab kingdom" listed in Psalm 83:6–8. Lastly, the Tribulation Period would be a final attempt at the genocide of the Jewish people by the Antichrist and his armies.[190]

The kingdom-against-kingdom prophecy may also find application with other contemporary regional disputes, such as North and South Viet Nam, North and South

Korea, Bosnia, the Sudan, Russia against Afghanistan, Iran vs. Iraq, the breakaway republics of the former Soviet Union, Georgia and Chechnya, and others.

## The Motive

In Psalm 83:9–11, Asaph petitions God to format His divine response against the Arab confederacy in the manner of historical precedent.

Deal with them as *with* Midian, As *with* Sisera, As *with* Jabin at the Brook Kishon, Who perished at En Dor, *Who* became as refuse on the Earth. Make their nobles like Oreb and like Zeeb, Yes, all their princes like Zebah and Zalmunna. (Psa. 83:9–11, NKJV)

All of these instances above represented historical attempts by various enemies of Israel to take for themselves the pastures of God for a possession. In each instance, God had a hand in putting the effort to an end. By requesting God to respond in a similar fashion, he identifies for us the underlying motive of the Psalm 83 confederacy.

Who said, "*Let us take for ourselves The pastures of God for a possession.*" (Psa. 83:12, NKJV; emphasis added)

These Arab confederates desire to take possession of the Promised Land, i.e., the "pastures of God" for themselves. In essence, they covet the land content contained within the Abrahamic Covenant. They come together and formulate a covenant of their own, which for our purposes we will call The Arabic Covenant.

For they have consulted together with one consent; *Against thee* do they make a [Arabic] *covenant* [*berith*]. (Psa. 83:5, ASV; emphasis added)

Asaph tells of a time to come in his Psalm, whereby the majority of Arabs will make a covenant against God. The Hebrew word is berith and we can translate it as "league."[191] These particular Psalm 83:6–8 nations will formulate an Arab League of sorts, which mutually agrees upon the destruction of the nation Israel. In addition, the term berith is used in similar covenant context in Genesis Chapter 15:

In that day Jehovah made a covenant [*berith*] with Abram, saying, Unto thy seed have I given this land, from the river of Egypt unto the great river, the river Euphrates. (Gen. 15:18, NKJV)

In an apparent attempt to avoid the ancient, and still existing berith covenant, (the Abrahamic Covenant), these enemies assembled in an Arab League, form a covenant of their own. They do not intend to amend or supplement the land provision within the Abrahamic Covenant, nor do they seek only to supersede the current covenant operating successfully in the region; rather, by destroying the Jews and erasing the name of Israel forever, they seek to eradicate the entire covenant itself.

Interestingly, the nations aligned fall for the most part within the scope of the land of the covenant God made with Abraham. Apparently, deeply and religiously rooted within the minds of these confederating covenant-making Arabs, is the belief that it is in the best interest of their present real estate holdings, to extinguish the Jews. In essence, whether they realize it or not, their end intention is the expiration of the Abrahamic Covenant.

Thus, Asaph is correct in suggesting in the beginning of his Psalm, that these conspirators are the enemies of God, formulator of the eternal Abrahamic Covenant. In essence, these nations want to extinguish the Jews, take over their territory, erase the name of Israel forever, and thus re-scramble the letters of the Abrahamic Covenant in their favor to create "The Arabic Covenant."

# EIGHTEEN

# The Ezekiel 35—Psalm 83 Connection

## *The War Before Ezekiel 38*

**"Russia: Attack on Tehran is Attack on Moscow"**

*Israel National News 1/15/12*

**"Russia Sending Navy Ships to Syria Amid Uprising"**

*CBS News 6/18/12*

**"Middle East regional war more likely"**

*Conservative News and Views 8/17/12*

Ezekiel 34:13, 36:24, 37:12, 38:8, and 39:27-28 all talk about the Jews being re-gathered out from the nations of the world back into the Holy Land of Israel. By the time one reads through Ezekiel 34-39 they are left with the indelible impression that in the last days, the Jews will be re-gathered into Israel. There is absolutely no way to draw any other conclusion!

Therefore, it stands to reason contextually that because Ezekiel 35 is huddled in the midst of the above chapters, it must have some association with the Jews, Israel, and the end times. As already discussed in the chapter called, "The Ancient Arab Hatred of the Jews", Ezekiel 35:5 is talking about a hatred that prompts Arabs to shed Jewish blood in the end times. So with this presupposition in mind, a study of Ezekiel 35 should underscore the present Arab-Israeli predicament in the Middle East. Ezekiel 35 appears to describe a war that precedes the Gog of Magog invasion in Ezekiel 38. Below is an author commentary of Ezekiel 35.

## Ezekiel 35 and Author Commentary

(Ezekiel 35:1-4) Moreover the word of the LORD came to me, saying, "Son of man, set your face *against* Mount Seir and prophesy *against* it, and say to it, 'Thus says the Lord GOD:"Behold, O Mount Seir, I am *against* you; I will stretch out My hand *against* you, And make you most desolate; I shall lay your cities waste, And you shall be desolate. Then you shall know that I am the LORD. (emphasis added).

Ezekiel begins with the word "moreover," which implies a continuation from the previous chapter 34. Ezekiel 34, concluded with an end-times' depiction of the Jews being re-gathered into Israel, restored as God's people, and being blessed. From other Scriptures, we recognize that Israel becomes blessed during the messianic kingdom, but before this is re-gathered in a condition of unbelief in preparation for judgment.

Dr. Arnold Fruchtenbaum says the following in his book, The Footsteps of the Messiah, regarding this two-step process:

"The Bible…speaks of two distinct worldwide regatherings (of the Jews). First, there is to be a worldwide regathering in unbelief in preparation for judgment; specifically the judgment of the Tribulation. That is to be followed by a second worldwide regathering in faith in preparation for blessing, specifically, the blessing of the Messianic Kingdom."[192]

The passages Dr. Fruchtenbaum uses to support this conclusion about the re-gathering in unbelief in preparation for judgment are contained in Ezekiel 20:33-38 and Ezekiel 22:17-22. Therefore, we are to recognize that the re-gathering of Jews into Israel occurs over time, and involves a two-step process.

The inference from Ezekiel 35:1-4 is that at some point during the two-step restoration process of the nation Israel, Mount Seir does something to aggravate the Lord. Four times the prophet uses the word "against," evidencing the Lord is provoked to anger to act against Mount Seir. Two times he uses the word desolate. Far beyond a divine disciplinary hand-slap, Mount Seir will experience desolation. The severity of punishment points out the seriousness of Mount Seir's crime.

As discussed earlier, Mount Seir finds connection with Esau and his Edomite descendants. However, we find out later in Ezekiel 35:15 that Mount Seir represents more Arabs than just the Edomites. Who exactly is the Mount Seir of Ezekiel 35? What are they guilty of? Lastly, at what point in the two-step re-gathering process does Mount Seir experience desolation?

> (Ezekiel 35:5) Because you have had an ancient hatred, and have shed the blood of the children of Israel by the power of the sword at the time of their calamity, when their iniquity came to an end.

Fortunately, we don't have to look farther than the next verse to find out what Mount Seir is guilty of. Because of their historical hatred of the Jews, the Arabs spitefully shed Jewish blood. The spilt blood angers the Lord; not just any blood, but Jewish blood. Furthermore, Ezekiel declares "the power of the sword" is used to shed this blood. This means the Arabs' war against Israel. This passage also identifies the timing of the Arab war. It occurs during the calamitous end times, apparently sometime after the Holocaust. Alluding to this happening in the end times, below are several Bible translations of Ezekiel 35:5:

> Because you cherished an ancient enmity, and gave over the people of Israel to the power of the sword at the time of their calamity, at the time of their final punishment. (NRSV).

> Because you harbored an ancient hostility and delivered the Israelites over to the sword at the time of their calamity, the time their punishment reached its climax. (NIV).

> Because thou hast had a perpetual enmity, and hast given over the children of Israel to the power of the sword in the time of their calamity, in the time of the iniquity of the end. (ASV).

> (Ezekiel 35:6) therefore, as I live," says the Lord GOD, "I will prepare you for blood, and blood shall pursue you; [Arabs] since you have not hated [shedding Jewish] blood, therefore blood shall pursue you."

Arab blood for Jewish blood is the remedial requirement determined by the Lord. This is the curse-for-curse-in-kind specification in Genesis 12:3. The Arabs severely curse Israel, and in turn will be similarly severely cursed. The Lord preferred the Arabs would have abandoned their ancient hatred of the Jews. The inhumane treatment of the Jews by the Nazis during the Holocaust should have prompted empathy from the Arabs, but verse six informs they still hated the Jewish bloodline.

> (Ezekiel 35:7-9) Thus I will make Mount Seir most desolate, and cut off from it the one who leaves and the one who returns. And I will fill its mountains with the slain; on your hills and in your valleys and in all your ravines those who are slain by the *sword* shall fall. I will make you perpetually desolate, and your cities shall be uninhabited; then you shall know that I am the LORD. (emphasis added).

Again Ezekiel repeats the sentiment of verse three: Mount Seir will be "most desolate." The mountains, hills, valleys, and ravines will be filled with the slain and the cities will be abandoned. In the aftermath, the Arabs will realize that the Lord had His hand in the massive slayings. Ezekiel 35:3 declares the outstretched hand of the Lord causes the desolation, but here in verse eight we discover the Lord's weapon of choice is the "sword."

Ezekiel 25:14 may hold an important clue as to how the sword in the Lord's outstretched hand represents the IDF executing judgment upon Edom:

> "I will lay My vengeance on Edom by the hand of My people Israel [IDF] that they may do in Edom [Mount Seir] according to My anger and according to My fury; and they shall know My vengeance," says the Lord GOD. (Ezekiel 25:14).

This passage finds definite association with a military judgment upon the Edomites, who hailed from ancient Mount Seir. Esau's Edomite descendants will be forced to recognize the Lord's hand of judgment when the IDF takes vengeance against them.

It is important to note that the Edomites are listed first within the Psalm 83 Arab confederacy, as the "tents of Edom." In the chapter called Whodomites, Who are the Edomites Today, I carefully connect the Palestinian refugees, through several historical waves of migration, with the tents of Edom. Today the Edomites have ethnic representation within the Palestinians.

It is additionally important to note that the massive slaying of Edomites described in Ezekiel 35:7-9 by the IDF has not occurred yet. After Ezekiel wrote, many Edomites were slaughtered by the Seleucid king Antigonus around 312 BC. However, this episode did not involve the IDF at the time, disqualifying it as a fulfillment of Ezekiel 25:14.

Subsequently, around 126 BC, the Jewish high priest John Hyrcanus fought and killed many Edomites. But, his IDF victory did not fill the mountains, hills, valleys, and ravines with the slain and cause the abandonment of the cities. To the contrary,

Hyrcanus allowed the surviving Edomites, who were called Idumeans at the time, to remain and repopulate within their cities as long as they converted to Israel's religion of Judaism. In addition, neither of the Antigonus or Hyrcanus victories occurred in the end time's fulfillment of Ezekiel 35:5.

> (Ezekiel 35:10-13) "'Because you have said, "These two nations and these two countries shall be mine, and we will possess them," although the LORD was there, therefore, as I live,' says the Lord GOD, 'I will do according to your anger and according to the envy which you showed in your hatred against them; and I will make Myself known among them when I judge you. Then you shall know that I am the LORD. I have heard all your blasphemies which you have spoken against the mountains of Israel, saying, "They are desolate; they are given to us to consume." Thus with your mouth you have boasted against Me and multiplied your words against Me; I have heard them.'"

Ezekiel uses the word "because" three times in this chapter, and verse ten begins with the second usage. The first "because" dealt with the ancient hatred in verse five and the second now addresses the Arab motive. The Arabs seek to possess "two nations" and "two countries." Because the Arabs harbor an ancient hatred, they shed Jewish blood. The reason they shed this blood is to destroy the Israelis and possess Israel.

Ezekiel 35:10 says, "These two nations and these two countries shall be mine, and we will possess them." At the time Ezekiel wrote, approximately 2,600 years ago, Israel was a divided country. There was the northern kingdom, commonly referred to as Israel or Samaria, and a southern kingdom, commonly known as Judah. Prior to Ezekiel's time, in 722 BC, the northern kingdom was conquered by the Assyrians, and subsequently in 586 BC, the Babylonians conquered Judah.

The Hebrew word for nations is goy, and for countries is erets. Goy identifies Gentiles, nations, or peoples; whereas erets deals more specifically with the earth and its lands, territories, or regions. Ezekiel is probably declaring the Arabs seek sovereignty over the Jewish people and their divided lands.

Being omniscient and omnipresent, the Lord possesses the unique "fly on the wall" advantage of sitting in on all confidential Arab meetings, past, present, and future.

Ezekiel summarizes the Anti-Semitic gist of these meetings for us by revealing the Arabs declare blasphemies against the mountains of Israel. Ezekiel notates the Arabs are angry, envious, hateful, and boastful people in their hatred of the Jews and their God Jehovah. They believe Israel's desolation evidences Israel's God is weak, and the land (mountains) of Israel belongs to the Arabs.

Below are some specific Arab quotes taken from the Bible, regarded with destroying the Jews and possessing the land of Israel;

- "Because you have said, 'These two nations and these two countries shall be mine, and we will possess them.'" (Ezekiel 35:10)

- "They [mountains of Israel] are desolate; they are given to us to consume." (Ezekiel 35:12)

- "Aha! The ancient heights have become our possession!" (Ezekiel 36:2)

- "Come, and let us cut them off from being a nation, that the name of Israel may be remembered no more." (Psalm 83:4)

- "Let us take for ourselves the pastures of God for a possession." (Psalm 83:12)

Jordan, identified by the Psalm 83 members of Moab and Ammon, has also made troubling comments along these lines. Zephaniah 2:8 informs us of the following; I [the Lord] have heard the reproach of Moab, and the insults of the people of Ammon, with which they have reproached My people, and made arrogant threats against their borders.

This disposition of Arab hatred and desire to dispossess Israel of their land was prophesied in Psalm 83. The Psalm warns that the Arabs will confederate, form a crafty plan, and attack Israel. Their mandate is to destroy the Jews and erase the name of Israel forever. Psalm 83:12 informs us the goal of the confederacy is possession of the land of Israel. They don't want a two-state solution, wherein Jews and Arabs co-exist side-by-side in peace; rather, they want one more Arab State of Palestine. Since Ezekiel 35:5 suggests the Arab war occurs in the calamitous end times, it appears that it could occur in the near future.

> (Ezekiel 35:14-15) "Thus says the Lord GOD: 'The whole earth will rejoice when I make you desolate. As you rejoiced because the inheritance of the house of Israel was desolate, so I will do to you; you shall be desolate, O Mount Seir, as well as all of Edom—all of it! Then they shall know that I am the LORD.'"

These verses, like Ezekiel 35:6 above, come out of the Genesis 12:3 foreign policy. The Arabs rejoiced when the Jews dwelt outside of their homeland in the Diaspora and Israel lay desolate. In turn, mankind will rejoice at the conclusion of the Arab – Israeli conflict.

## Why the World Rejoices When Israel Wins

Ezekiel proclaims "The whole earth will rejoice when I make you [Mount Seir] desolate." When the Arabs, represented by Mount Seir, are made desolate, humanity will be extremely pleased. This is peculiar, considering this desolation is characterized by a massive Arab slaughter by the IDF, according to Ezekiel 35:8, 25:14, and Obadiah v. 18. Considering most of the world presently believes Israel occupies Arab lands illegally, it is hard to imagine humanity would accept, let alone be comforted by, the massive slaughter of Arabs by the IDF. Yet, that is what Ezekiel predicts will occur. How can this be?

Perhaps events leading up to the Psalm 83 Arab – Israeli War, and the war itself, creates a worldwide crisis that mankind is happy to have resolved once and for all. Much of mankind could be fearful of terrorism and oil-dependent world economies in dire straits, due to OPEC-induced oil shortages. Christians could certainly rejoice, because they will witness their God honor His foreign policy commitments in Genesis 12:3. But what about secular, unbelieving man?

Christians will be able to say the Arabs pursued Jewish blood and so Jewish blood retaliated according to Ezekiel 35:6. Believers will rejoice because fulfilled Bible prophecies reinforce their faith by proving the Bible is true, and the Lord remains in control of world events.

However, unbelievers won't see it that way. They will be more concerned with how Mideast events adversely affect their lives. The fact that they rejoice when the Arabs are desolated, indeed suggests that the Arab-Israeli War created severe problems for them. Exactly how humanity is aggravated by Mideast turbulence is speculation at this point; however, when the war is over and the Arabs defeated, the world rejoices. Apparently, a temporary regional stability of sorts occurs in the aftermath.

Somehow an IDF victory pleases the international community. Perhaps they fear a nuclear war might spill over into other places and are relieved the IDF victory eliminates that possibility. Or, perhaps the threat of international terror subsides, and Israel gets some OPEC oil flowing back into world markets as it mops up the war-zone. Somehow, Israel seems to strike it rich after Psalm 83, because Russia stops rejoicing shortly thereafter, and forms the Gog of Magog coalition, in fulfillment of Ezekiel 38-39. These invaders come to capture Israel's great spoil according to Ezekiel 38:13.

It appears that the Psalm 83 War is so devastating that the world rejoices when it ends. Maybe it has less to do with the world hating Arabs, and more to do with the world needing a respite from the past six decades of Mideast chaos.

## Who is Ezekiel 35 Identifying as Mount Seir?

Ezekiel 35:15 says "O Mount Seir, as well as all of Edom," and then repeats, "all of it," alluding to the entirety of Edom. This implies that Mount Seir represents more than Edom; something in addition to Edom. Ezekiel 36:1-5 identifies Mount Seir as the surrounding nations encircling Israel including "all Edom."

'Thus says the Lord GOD: "Because the enemy [Mount Seir] has said of you, 'Aha! The ancient heights have become our possession,'"'"therefore prophesy, and say, 'Thus says the Lord GOD: "Because they made you desolate and swallowed you up on every side, so that you became the possession of the rest of the nations, and you are taken up by the lips of talkers and slandered by the people"—'therefore, O mountains of Israel, hear the word of the Lord GOD! Thus says the Lord GOD to the mountains, the hills, the rivers, the valleys, the desolate wastes, and the cities that have been forsaken, which became plunder and mockery to the *rest of the nations all around*—'therefore thus says the Lord GOD: "Surely I have spoken in My burning jealousy against the rest of the nations and against all Edom, who gave My land to themselves as a possession, with wholehearted joy and spiteful minds, in order to plunder its open country."' (Ezekiel 36:2-5; emphasis added).

Ezekiel specifies, "the rest of the nations all around" with "all Edom," are the slanderous people that seek to make Israel desolate and possess it. The people all around Israel comprise the "inner circle" of Arab states and terrorist populations listed in Psalm 83:6-8, i.e. "the rest of the [Mount Seir] nations all around" with "all Edom."

Mount Seir seems to be the representative term for the Arab confederacy of Psalm 83. Although there was a literal Mount Seir that was home to the Edomites, the use of mount, or mountains, in Scripture can also identify rulers, governments, or hierarchies.[193]

## Why Ezekiel 35 is Not an Armageddon Event.

Verses connecting the powerful sword utilized to defeat the Arab confederacy of Mount Seir to the IDF have been provided above. However, during the Armageddon campaign, the Antichrist and his world armies wield a powerful sword, as well. How can we be certain that Ezekiel 35:8 is not identifying the Antichrist instead of the IDF? The answer is located in Daniel 11.

He [Antichrist] shall also enter the Glorious Land, and many *countries* shall be overthrown; but these shall escape from his hand: Edom, [Mount Seir] Moab, and the prominent people of Ammon. (Daniel 11:41; emphasis added).

Daniel declares the Antichrist enters into the "Glorious Land," and overthrows many countries. But, Edom escapes his siege. Edom is located in modern-day southern Jordan, where Mount Seir is located. Although Ezekiel 35:15 identifies Mount Seir as an Arab confederacy, Ezekiel 35:7-8 suggests the literal Seir mountain range becomes the host location of the multitude of slain Arabs. Therefore, it makes no sense that the Antichrist slays Arabs upon Mount Seir, if Edom, Moab, and Ammon escapes his end times exploits.

## *What is the Glorious Land of Daniel 11:41?*

The Glorious Land identifies a much larger area than modern-day Israel encompasses. Daniel says countries are overthrown inside the Glorious Land. The fact Daniel calls it the Glorious Land identifies it with the Holy or Promised Land.[194] Other countries and / or territories, including Israel, that are possibly incorporated at the time could include portions of Syria, Lebanon, Iraq, Saudi Arabia, the Sinai, West Bank, and Gaza Strip. Sizeable portions of these locations exist inside the land described in Genesis 15:18, that were formerly promised to Abraham and his descendants.

If so, this suggests that Israel might attempt to annex more territory after their IDF victory in Psalm 83. Obadiah v. 20, Isaiah 19:18, Jeremiah 49:2, and Zephaniah 2:4-9 lends credence to this possibility. I'm not suggesting that Israel acquires all of the Promised Land prior to the return of Christ, but perhaps a significant portion. This topic is explored in greater detail in the chapter called, "Egypt's Desolation, Deportation, and Conversion."

# NINETEEN

# The Three Egyptian Judgments

**"Holy Jihad' is the only way to deal with Israel, says Egypt's Muslim Brotherhood chief"**

*Times of Israel 10/11/12*

**"Egypt's Brotherhood heads urged jihad for Jerusalem"**

*France 24 International News 10/11/12*

**"Egypt protesters breach US embassy over 'insulting' film"**

*BBC News 9/11/12*

These are the days when the Bible is its own best commentary. Imagine Isaiah the prophet, whose ministry spanned between 740-701 B.C., [195] standing on the streets of Cairo during the Arab Spring of 2011, speaking in front of a mainstream news camera declaring:

> "The Arab demonstrations have swiftly moved from Tunisia eastward into Egypt! Egyptians are fighting other Egyptians, the military is being pelted with hundreds of Molotov cocktails as brothers are bludgeoning each other, and neighborhoods are riddled with

unrest. The streets of Cairo are filled with violence and civil strife! It's a very dangerous situation here in Tahrir Square."

It's seems eerily reminiscent of what the prophet predicted about twenty-seven centuries ago.

> "The burden against Egypt. Behold, the LORD rides on a swift cloud, And will come into Egypt; … And the heart of Egypt will melt in its midst. "I will set Egyptians against Egyptians; Everyone will fight against his brother, And everyone against his neighbor..." (Isaiah 19:1-2; emphasis abbreviated).

Is it possible that Isaiah was foretelling of a prophecy intended for modern times? Will more unrest befall the world's most densely populated powerful Arab state? This chapter will take a close look at the judgment prophecies concerning Egypt that were predicted from Isaiah's time forward in the Bible.

Isaiah's alluded to Egypt 36 times in his 66 chapters, but almost half of his prophetic references to Egypt are found in Isaiah 19. Subsequently, Jeremiah and his contemporary Ezekiel inscribed the word Egypt a combined 97 times. Jeremiah and Ezekiel prophesied during the Babylonian era approximately 150 years after Isaiah's time. All told the word Egypt is mentioned approximately 565 times within the Bible, and some of these usages are pertinent to prophecies that appear to be presently stage-setting.

Since the Hebrew exodus from Egypt took place around 1313 BCE,[196] which was about six centuries before Isaiah's ministry, we know that all of Isaiah's, Jeremiah's, and Ezekiel's prophecies were not regarded with this historic exodus episode. Although at that time the Egyptians experienced a sequence of ten severe plague judgments that ultimately led to the destruction of Pharaoh's army at the Red Sea, (Exodus 14:26-28), it seems that the Egyptians potentially have an even greater desolation looming in their not so distant future.

From Isaiah's time forward there were at least three devastating judgments identified in Bible prophecy. These judgments will be discussed throughout this chapter, and in the continuation chapter called "Egypt's Desolation, Deportation, and Conversion." These three judgments are as follows;

- PAST – The Babylonian Judgment, described in Jeremiah 42 – 44, Ezekiel 29:18-19, 30:10 and elsewhere,

- PRESENT – The Israeli Defense Forces identified in Psalm 83 and Isaiah 19,

- FUTURE – The Antichrist during the "Day of the Lord" referenced in—Ezekiel 30:3-4, Daniel 11:42-43, Joel 3:19 and elsewhere.

Among all of Egypt's prophecies the most important, spiritually speaking, for Egyptians is undoubtedly concerning their national conversion. When all is said and done there will be a remnant of Egyptians that survive to reside in the one-thousand year Messianic kingdom. This is great news for the Egyptians because as this chapter points out, events in Egypt probably take a severe swift turn for the worse in the near future. Egypt's national conversion will be explored in the chapter called "Egypt's Desolation, Deportation, and Conversion."

However, concerning Egypt's existence during the Messianic kingdom era, Ezekiel informs us that the nation of Egypt will be the lowliest of all the kingdoms present upon the earth at that time.

> "It shall be *the lowliest of kingdoms*; it shall never again exalt itself above the nations, for I will diminish them so that they will not rule over the nations anymore." (Ezekiel 29:15 NKJV; emphasis added).

It appears safe to say that this specific prophecy has not been fulfilled as of yet. Clearly, Egypt today is not the *lowliest of kingdoms* on earth. In fact, Egypt's army, which is ranked number 16 among world armies, is the most powerful among the Arab states. The next closest Arab army in the region would be Saudi Arabia located directly eastward across the Red Sea from Egypt, that is ranked at number 26. [197] Moreover, there is a famous saying concerning Egypt that is quoted, "*As goes Egypt, so goes the Middle East.*" There are nearly 83 million people living in Egypt and comparatively only about 27 to 28 million in the Arab state of Saudi Arabia.[198]

## Egypt's "PAST" Judgment

The past Babylonian judgment against Egypt occurred in 568 BC when King Nebuchadnezzar marched upon the country in order to replenish his military budget and arsenals. He had endured a tiring, but successful campaign against Tyre, which is located in modern day Lebanon. Ezekiel identifies the king's military motive for us.

> "Son of man, Nebuchadnezzar king of Babylon caused his army to labor strenuously against Tyre; every head *was* made bald, and every shoulder rubbed raw; yet neither he nor his army received wages from Tyre, for the labor which they expended on it. Therefore thus says the Lord GOD: 'Surely I will give the land of Egypt to Nebuchadnezzar king of Babylon; he shall take away her wealth, carry off her spoil, and remove her pillage; and that will be the wages for his army. I have given him the land of Egypt *for* his labor, because they worked for Me,' says the Lord GOD. (Ezekiel 29:18-20, NKJV).

Jeremiah chapters 42 – 44 brazenly warned the Jews at the time not to flee to Egypt to avoid this impending confrontation with King Nebuchadnezzar. However, many of his people refused to follow his instructions and migrated into Egypt. As a result, scores of them were killed during the Babylonian conquest of Egypt.

> "The LORD has said concerning you, O remnant of Judah, *'Do not go to Egypt!'* Know certainly that I have admonished you this day." (Jeremiah 42:19, NKJV; emphasis added).

Subsequently, over the centuries Egypt experienced powerful events as the Persian, Greek, Roman, and Ottoman Gentile empires emerged successively. Then in the aftermath of the collapse of the Ottoman Empire, which had dominated over the region from 1517 – 1917, and the conclusion of World War I in 1918, on February 28, 1922, Egypt regained its national independence.

## The NEW EGYPT

In preparation of exploring Egypt's two pending judgments, it's important to introduce what might rightfully be called, the "NEW EGYPT." The New Egypt was born out of the Arab Spring. The tens of thousands of Tahrir Square protestors were demanding change during the early months of 2011. And shortly thereafter, that change ultimately came in the format of the rise to political power of the Muslim Brotherhood in Egypt.

Hosni Mubarak, who had reigned over Egypt from 1981 to 2011 is now serving a life sentence in prison, and now it's the Muslim Brotherhood's turn to rule over Egypt. If this New Egypt is about to become the NEW NORMAL for the Middle East, then understanding who they are should assist in determining the who's, what's, when's, where's, why's, and how's of the impending Egypt related Bible prophecies.

It's important to note that within six years after Egypt gained its independence, the Muslim Brotherhood was founded by Egyptian Hassan al-Banna on March, 1928 as an Islamist religious and political movement. Hassan al-Banna was an acknowledged admirer of Adolph Hitler and frequently corresponded with him. During the 1930's the Muslim Brotherhood became a secretive arm of Nazi Intelligence. The Third Reich intended to develop the Muslim Brotherhood into a Nazi army inside of Egypt.[199]

On October 26, 1954 the Muslim Brotherhood was suspected in the assassination attempt of Egyptian president Gamal Abd al-Nasser. This justifiably began a period of repression of the Muslim Brotherhood by the Nasser government. Then on October 6, 1981 Nasser's successor, Anwar Sadat was assassinated, and the Muslim Brotherhood was strongly implicated with his death. But now, with Nasser, Sadat, and Hosni Mubarak out of the Egyptian presidency, the Muslim Brotherhood can finally attempt to attain their goals to implement Sharia law in Egypt, and to form a United Arab States with Jerusalem as its capital city, through Egypt's new president Mohammed Morsi.

On April 30, 2011, shortly after the deposing of Egyptian president Hosni Mubarak, the Muslim Brotherhood founded a political wing called "The Freedom and Justice Party." Mohammed Morsi successfully ran for president on "The Freedom and Justice Party" ticket. Founding political groups is nothing new for the Muslim Brotherhood; they founded the Hamas in the Gaza in 1987. As of 2012, the Freedom and Justice Party is the dominant political power presiding over Egypt, and Egyptian president Mohammed Morsi is its leading authoritative figure.

### "Morsi warns Israel will pay heavy price"

*YNET News 11/16/12*

*"Egyptian president (Morsi) sharpens his tone against Israel, threatening: 'If I see the homeland in danger, I won't hesitate to take unusual steps.' He vows that his country will 'stop this* (Israel's) *brutal aggression* (against the Hamas).*"*

In light of the new Muslim Brotherhood controlled Egypt, Israel is justifiably concerned about the longevity of their 1979 peace accord with Egypt. Promptly upon coming into power Mohammed Morsi began making unsettling statements concerning Egypt's obligation to this treaty. As an example, in an article published by the New York Times on September 22, 2012 called "Egypt's New Leader Spells Out Terms for U.S.-Arab Ties."[200]

'If Washington is asking Egypt to honor its treaty with Israel, he said, Washington should also live up to its own Camp David commitment to Palestinian self-rule. He said the United States must respect the Arab world's history and culture, even when that conflicts with Western values."

Morsi also argued that Americans "have a special responsibility" for the Palestinians because the United States had signed the 1978 Camp David accord and added, "As long as peace and justice are not fulfilled for the Palestinians, then the treaty remains unfulfilled."

Statements like these emanating out of the "New Egypt," along with several of the Muslim Brotherhood credos listed below also trouble Israel.

- Islam is the solution,

- Allah is our objective,

- The Quran is our law,

- The Prophet (Mohammad) is our leader,

- Jihad is our way,

- And, death for Allah is the highest aspiration.

Obviously Egypt still has powerful future events to undergo! How does the world's most prominent Arab state diminish into the world's lowliest of kingdoms? The answer to this question is contained in understanding the PRESENT and FUTURE judgments prophesied against Egypt. Egypt's PRESENT, or imminent judgment that seems to be described in Isaiah 19:1-18 is a good place to start.

## Egypt's PRESENT Judgment

Presently events in Egypt appear to be setting the stage for the fulfillment of prophecies of Isaiah 19 that will likely culminate in Egypt's participation in the Arab – Israeli war under the banner of the "Hagarenes" described in Psalm 83. As such, a study of Isaiah 19:1-18 will be undertaken at this point.

"The tents of Edom and the Ishmaelites; Moab, and the Hagarenes;" (Psalm 83:6, ASV).

## Isaiah 19:1-18 Commentary

(Isaiah 19:1, NKJV) The burden against Egypt. Behold, the LORD rides on a swift cloud, And will come into Egypt; The idols of Egypt will totter at His presence, And the heart of Egypt will melt in its midst.

The very first sentence speaks about a judgment intended against Egypt. The judgment is from the Lord, and it happens quickly like a swift cloud moves through the windy sky. Before addressing the typological significance of the swift cloud, it's important to understand that the Lord never renders random judgments upon the nations. In this case, Egypt has done something deserved of divine judgment. The clue to Egypt's guilt appears to be described in Isaiah 19:16-18, and is relative to something between Israel and Egypt. Egypt's foul-play toward Israel will be discussed in the commentary of those verses.

The significance of the swift cloud, that makes the idols of Egypt totter, is that when Egypt's judgment occurs, it doesn't appear to be a long drawn out process, and it adversely affects the spiritual bedrock of the entire country, which today is predominately Islam. Cloud cover creates darkness underneath it. Darkness, alluding to a nation's religious condition, depicts a country's spiritual blindness. Egypt's history at the time of the Hebrew exodus saw a similar scenario of the Lord riding into Egypt on a swift cloud.

> "And the Angel of God, who went before the camp of Israel, moved and went behind them; and the *pillar of cloud* went from before them and stood behind them. So it came between the camp of the Egyptians and the camp of Israel. Thus it was *a cloud* and *darkness to the one, (Egyptians)* and it gave light by night *to the other, (Hebrews)* so that the one did not come near the other all that night." (Exodus 14:19-20, NKJV; emphasis added).

In addition to this Exodus 14 usage, clouds in relationship to spiritual matters are found in 1 Thessalonians 4:17 describing Christians caught up into the clouds during the Rapture. Also, in Exodus 19:9 the Lord visited Moses via a cloud, and in Exodus 24:15-16 after six days of cloud cover over Mount Sinai, the Lord called out to Moses from the cloud on the seventh day.

These are just a few biblical instances among several others where clouds are used as a typological representation of a deep-seated spiritual matter.

> (Isaiah 19:2, NKJV) "I will set Egyptians against Egyptians; Everyone will fight against his brother, And everyone against his neighbor, City against city, kingdom against kingdom.

This is another prophetic verse that does not appear to have found fulfillment. Because the idols of Egypt are tottering, and the heart of the country is melting in its midst, severe civilian unrest begins to occur. This civil strife quickly burgeons into a civil war, but doesn't stop there. Ultimately kingdoms begin to clash with each other. In this instance "kingdom against kingdom" appears to allude to a regional conflict. Presently there are three predominate kingdoms in the region, the Jewish, Arab, and Persian, and observably they are all mostly at odds with each other.

- Iran (Persian) is threatening to wipe the Jewish kingdom off of the map.

- Most Arab countries don't recognize Israel's right to exist, and want the Jewish state to give up large portions of land for one more Arab state called Palestine.

- Most Arab countries are genuinely concerned that Iran wants to attain a nuclear weapons program in order to control the balance of power in the Middle East.

I believe in Matthew 24:7 that Christ was quoting Isaiah 19:2 as instructions to his apostles when He said;

> "For nation will rise against nation, and *kingdom against kingdom*. And there will be famines, pestilences, and earthquakes in various places. All these *are* the beginning of sorrows." (NKJV; emphasis added).

By this point of the Olivet Discourse teaching in Matthew 24, the apostles should have realized that the second temple would be destroyed (Matt. 24:2). Then it should have dawned on them that the destruction of the temple would trigger the commencement of the numerous Old Testament prophecies concerning the worldwide Jewish dispersion. The historic precedent for this was that the destruction of the first temple in 586 BC caused the deportation of the Jews into the seventy years of Babylonian captivity.

As Christ continued to prophesy in Matthew 24:4-8 the apostles should have recognized the following prophetic possibilities:

- The second temple would be destroyed. *(Matt. 24:2).*

- The worldwide Jewish Diaspora would commence as a result. *(Ezekiel 20:23, 22:15).*

- There would be false Messiah's and rumors of wars during the Diaspora. *(Matt. 24:6).*

- There would be world wars (*nation against nation*). *(Matt. 24:7).*

- World wars would probably put Jews residing in those nations during the Diaspora in Harm's way. *(Ezek. 37:11-12).*

- Jews in the Diaspora in Harm's way probably climaxed in the "Dry Bones" vision of Ezekiel 37, i.e. a grave holocaust condition. *(Ezek. 37:11-12).*

- The holocaust condition of the "Dry Bones" vision would mean the worldwide regathering would occur subsequently. *(Ezek. 37:11-13).*

- The Jewish kingdom would be reestablished as a result of the regathering. *(Ezekiel 36:23-24, 37:11-12, 39:25-27, Isaiah 11:11-12).*

- The Jewish kingdom would fight against the Arab kingdom, as the separate kingdoms would collide, which seems to be the point of the Psalm 83 prophecy. *(Matt. 24:7).*

Regardless of whether you agree with these above inferences of what should have been the thinking of the apostles, the point still remains that Isaiah 19:2 predicts a regional conflict in Egypt's future. We will see in Isaiah 19:16-18 that this conflict appears to be between the Arab and Jewish kingdoms.

> (Isaiah 19:3-4, NKJV) The spirit of Egypt will fail in its midst; I will destroy their counsel, And they will consult the idols and the charmers, The mediums and the sorcerers. And the Egyptians I will give Into the hand of a cruel master, And a fierce king will rule over them," Says the Lord, the LORD of hosts.

If this prophecy is for our time, then these verses imply that when the swift judgment comes, that the Egyptians will consult their Muslim clerics and imams to no avail. Their Islamic counsel fails in the midst of the deteriorating matters, which ultimately makes Egypt susceptible to the takeover of a cruel dictator.

Some commentaries suggest that this cruel master was Assyrian king Esarhaddon, who conquered Egypt in 671 B.C. Another candidate was Nebuchadnezzar in 568 B.C. The Antichrist is yet another possibility since he is involved in a FUTURE prophecy against Egypt in Daniel 11:42-43. I think it could even be an Egyptian leader like Mohammed Morsi, rather than a foreign national like Esarhaddon, Nebuchadnezzar, or the Antichrist. One thing for certain is that it's not Hosni Mubarak. He didn't meet the overall descriptions contained in Isaiah 19, and he is currently serving a life prison sentence.

> (Isaiah 19:6-10, NKJV) The waters will fail from the sea, And the river will be wasted and dried up. The rivers will turn foul; The brooks of defense will be emptied and dried up; The reeds and rushes will wither. The papyrus reeds by the River, by the mouth of the River, And everything sown by the River, Will wither, be driven away, and be no more. The fishermen also will mourn; All those will lament who cast hooks into the River, And they will languish who spread nets on the waters. Moreover those who work in fine flax And those who weave fine fabric will be ashamed; And its foundations will be broken. All who make wages *will be* troubled of soul.

These five verses can be commented upon collectively. At the time of Egypt's swift calamity, the economy entirely collapses. The fishing and textile industries that have historically been Egypt's mainstay will go bankrupt. Tourism could be added into these passages as well. Although tourism was not a big source of revenue for Egypt during Isaiah's time, it has been throughout the 20th and 21st centuries.

Isaiah concludes by saying that "All who make wages will be troubled of soul." This statement sums up Egypt's entire economic predicament. Egypt experiences an utter economic collapse. Egypt's economy is already heading in this direction quite rapidly.

They are reliant upon foreign aid from Saudi Arabia, America, Turkey, and elsewhere now more than ever before. The Arab Spring may have brought changes politically, but as of yet it has not improved Egypt economically.

> (Isaiah 19:11-15, NKJV) Surely the princes of Zoan *are* fools; Pharaoh's wise counselors give foolish counsel. How do you say to Pharaoh, "I *am* the son of the wise, The son of ancient kings?" Where *are* they? Where are your wise men? Let them tell you now, And let them know what the LORD of hosts has purposed against Egypt. The princes of Zoan have become fools; The princes of Noph are deceived; They have also deluded Egypt, *Those who are* the mainstay of its tribes. The LORD has mingled a perverse spirit in her midst; And they have caused Egypt to err in all her work, As a drunken man staggers in his vomit. Neither will there be *any* work for Egypt, Which the head or tail, Palm branch or bulrush, may do.

To understand Isaiah's chastisements in these verses it is important to note that in the ancient world Egypt was known for its superior wisdom. Concerning the commentary of these above five verses The Bible Knowledge Commentary of the Old Testament notates the following:

> "Egypt was well known in the ancient world for its wisdom writings and its wise men. But Isaiah warned Egypt not to count on her wise men to save the nation from the coming destruction. The officials of Zoan (vv. 11, 13; cf. Zoan, a city in Egypt's Delta, in Num. 13:22; Ps. 78:12, 43; Isa. 30:4; Ezek. 30:14), the wise counselors of Pharaoh (Isa. 19:11), and the leaders of Memphis (v. 13; cf. Jer. 2:16; 44:1; 46:14, 19; Ezek. 30:13, 16; Hosea 9:6) thought their wisdom might save them from their coming judgment. But their wisdom was foolishness compared with the wisdom of the Lord Almighty who was planning the onslaught. No one in Egypt could do anything to avert the destruction; they were like staggering drunkards before the Lord. Neither the leaders (the head and the palm branch) nor the populace (the tail and the reed; cf. Isa. 9:15) could hold back God's judgment. At one time Zoan was Egypt's capital city (ca. 2050-1800). Memphis, on the Nile about 20 miles north of Cairo, was the first capital of united Egypt (ca. 3200 b.c.) and one of the major cities during much of its long history."

These comments illustrate that at the time the Isaiah 19 prophecy was issued, the pinnacle people and places in Egypt would be affected by this judgment. "The head or tail, Palm branch or bulrush," referred to everyone one in Egypt no matter what their station of life was at the time. If this judgment occurred today it would adversely affect the Muslim Brotherhood on through to the Tahrir Square street sweepers in

Cairo. No Egyptian seems to escape the powerful grasp of Isaiah's burden against Egypt.

> (Isaiah 19:16-17, NKJV) In that day Egypt will be like women, and will be afraid and fear because of the waving of the hand of the LORD of hosts, which He waves over it. And the land of Judah will be a terror to Egypt; everyone who makes mention of it will be afraid in himself, because of the counsel of the LORD of hosts which He has determined against it.

Up until these telling verses we have only been able to ascertain the adverse effects of Isaiah's prophecy, but now we get a clue to the underlying cause of Egypt's judgment. Isaiah starts by attributing all the events of Isaiah 19:1-15 to the consequences of Isaiah 19:16-17 by saying, "In that day." In essence, at the time that Egypt's wisdom fails, religious leaders falter, economy collapses, and Egypt is ruled by a harsh dictator, the country will be likened to a fearful woman that has become terrorized by Israel (Judah).

This implies that Egypt has confronted Israel, and in the process provoked a powerful retaliatory response from the Jewish state. More than likely this confrontation finds association with Egypt's military participation in the Psalm 83 war. These verses inform that Egypt is not terrorized by Babylon, nor by the Antichrist, but by Judah. This implies that Isaiah 19:1-18 is not addressing the PAST Babylonian conquest, or the FUTURE Antichrist invasion of Daniel 11:42-43, rather it seems to speak to the PRESENT Arab – Israeli war prophecy of Psalm 83 that now appears to be imminent.

Recalling that the Lord doesn't render random judgments, it makes perfect sense that if Egypt seeks to disavow its current peace treaty with Israel, and instead confederate with the Psalm 83 Arab states and terrorist populations in order to destroy the Jewish state, that Egypt will be judged! Egypt seeking to curse Israel will provoke the curse-for-curse in kind clause of Genesis 12:3 to come back against Egypt.

If the nuclear equipped IDF that is presently ranked #10 among world armies gets provoked into a war with Egypt, then the odds are that Egyptians will be terrorized by Judah to the point that they resemble the fearful woman of Isaiah 19:16. Commenting on these two verses, Dr. Arnold Fruchtenbaum writes the following on page 506 of his must read book called the Footsteps of the Messiah;

> "Never in ancient history has this been true. Only since 1948, and especially since the 6-day war, have the Egyptian forces evidenced the fear portrayed in this passage. There has been fear and dread of Israel ever since. With Egypt having lost 4 wars against Israel with heavy casualties, the fear is deeply rooted. Prophetically, today is still the period of Isaiah 19:16-17."

As I often find myself doing, I agree again with my friend Dr. Fruchtenbaum. Egypt is concerned about their defeats in the wars against Israel in 1948, 1956, 1967, and 1973. This genuine fear purposed the need for the 1979 peace treaty with Israel. If the Muslim Brotherhood increases its Anti-Semitic innuendos and threats to shred the peace treaty, or worse yet, marches militarily against Israel, then this will probably displease many Egyptians. It is highly likely that harsh measures taken against Israel will concern many Egyptians that still possess this genuine fear toward the Jewish state.

This type of provocation could make the violent Arab Spring protests pale comparatively to the civil strife, and potential civil war that could result inside Egypt. Egyptians coming against Egyptians could be exactly what occurs if, and when, the Muslim Brotherhood marches Egypt closer toward a war with Israel.

> (Isaiah 19:18, NKJV) In that day five cities in the land of Egypt will speak the language of Canaan and swear by the LORD of hosts; one will be called the City of Destruction.

Again Isaiah prefaces his prophecy by informing that "In that day," five cities in Egypt will speak the language of Canaan, which is Hebrew. This implies that Israel will annex five cities that are presently under Egyptian sovereignty when the prophecies spelled out in Isaiah 19:1-17 take place. If the IDF defeats the Egyptian army, then it is possible that they will take more Arab territory. They have a precedent for doing this, and Genesis 15:18 gives them authority to do so. It is possible that the five cities Isaiah 19:18 identifies will be located east of the Nile, and will be acquired after Egypt's defeat in Psalm 83.

*(Due to the length of this chapter, the third FUTURE judgment of Egypt will be explored in the next chapter.)*

# Egypt's Desolation, Deportation, and Conversion

**"Egypt's Christians face mass slaughter by Islamists"**

*World Net Daily 9/12/12*

**"Egyptian Islamists rally for Shariah law"**

*AP News 11/11/12*

*"CAIRO (AP) -- Over 10,000 ultraconservative Muslims demonstrated Friday in downtown Cairo to demand that Egypt's new constitution be based on the rulings of Islamic law, or Shariah, in the latest tussle over the role of religion in the country's future."*

**"U.S. suspends mail service to Egypt"**

*USA Today 2/4/11*

It was the latter part of February in 2011 and the violent protests in Egypt were in full swing when I heard baffling news from a U.S. Postal clerk on duty. I happened to be at a local post office in the process of shipping out several cases of *Revelation Road* books to a ministry, when the person at the counter next to me was told that all letters and mail shipments to Egypt were suspended temporarily. She had planned to ship an important package to a relative in Cairo, and was shocked to hear the disturbing news.

The customer was informed that the political unrest in Egypt had disrupted the normal methods of transportation to the country, and that all U.S. post offices were holding international mail to Egypt until the necessary transportation could resume. It was one of those, "you learn something new every day" moments for me. Having shipped thousands of books to various parts of the world, the thought of mail being suspended to a foreign country caught me totally by surprise.

According to a couple of ancient prophecies this apparently won't be the last time that the U.S. Postal service suspends all mail to Egypt. These Bible prophecies inform us that a future time is coming where all carrier services from every nation could be suspended to Egypt for several decades. This is because they predict that the land of Egypt will undergo severe desolation. The text of these prophecies, listed below, make the Tahrir Square episode seem miniscule in comparison.

> "I will make the land of Egypt desolate in the midst of the countries *that are* desolate; and among the cities *that are* laid waste, her cities shall be desolate forty years; and I will scatter the Egyptians among the nations and disperse them throughout the countries." (Ezekiel 29:12, NKJV).

> "Egypt shall be a desolation, And Edom a desolate wilderness, Because of violence against the people of Judah, For they have shed innocent blood in their land." (Joel 3:19, NKJV).

This chapter picks up where the chapter called "The Three Egyptian Judgments" left off, and begins by addressing Egypt's FUTURE third judgment. This judgment appears to be the most treacherous of the three, because it temporarily decimates Egypt. So bad is this desolation that Egyptians are forced out of their homeland for a period of forty years.

> "Yet, thus says the Lord GOD: "At the end of forty years I will gather the Egyptians from the peoples among whom they were scattered." (Ezekiel 29:13, NKJV).

The key to understanding what leads up to and eventuates into Egypt's desolation and Egyptian deportation of forty years could be found in the FUTURE judgment of Egypt. This judgment is accomplished by the Antichrist and the primary verses that state this are in the book of Daniel.

> "He (Antichrist) shall stretch out his hand against the countries, and the land of Egypt shall not escape. He shall have power over the treasures of gold

and silver, and over all the precious things of Egypt; also the Libyans and Ethiopians *shall follow* at his heels." (Daniel 11:42-43, NKJV; emphasis added).

Much like Nebuchadnezzar did around 568 BC, as recorded in Ezekiel 29:18-20, the Antichrist will do when he conquers Egypt in the future. He will successfully invade Egypt and seize control over the nation's treasuries. Daniel 11:40-45 informs us that this happens in the end time's, and many Bible prophecy teachers believe that contextually, this occurs during the second half of the seven year tribulation period, i.e. the Great Tribulation.

One of the primary undertakings of the Antichrist during the Great Tribulation is a final genocidal attempt of the Jewish race. Zechariah 13:8 is one verse that references this by declaring that two-thirds of the Israelis are killed at the time. Christ warned about this in Matthew 24:15-22, and instructed Israelis to flee the area immediately when the Antichrist commits the "abomination of desolation" referenced by the prophet Daniel.

Although Daniel 11:42-43 predicts the Antichrist will obtain Egyptian treasures of gold, silver and assorted precious things, there is probably more than just Egyptian bounty that motivates the Antichrist to attack Egypt. If Isaiah 19:18 has been fulfilled by this future time, then there will be at least five Hebrew speaking cities in Egypt that are populated with Jews. If the Antichrist seeks Jewish genocide, and Jews reside in Egypt, then invading Egypt is a logical undertaking. This is what Adolf Hitler did during the Nazi genocide in Europe. He overthrew European countries and then proceeded to kill the Jews residing in those toppled nations.

Here is how the future Egyptian scenario might play out prophetically. Please note that this is the author's best educated guess, and it is entirely predicated upon the premise that Egypt is a confederate participant against Israel in Psalm 83. In the chapter called "The Three Egyptian Judgments" the case was made for connecting Isaiah 19:1-18 with Egypt's role in Psalm 83. Egypt's potential involvement in the Psalm war is also explored in the appendix called "Is Egypt in Psalm 83."

## *The End Time Egyptian Scenario*

Ultimately Egyptian leadership violates its 1979 peace treaty with Israel and wages war in Psalm 83 with the Jewish state. This seemingly creates a serious civil crisis within Egypt because not all Egyptians will be in favor of this aggression. Those not likely to support this war could comprise today about 10 million Coptic Christians, along with an untold amount of Egyptians, that maintain a healthy fear of Israel because of Egypt's war defeats in 1948, 1956, 1967, and 1973. Isaiah 19:17 spoke of this fear by stating "the land of Judah will be a terror to Egypt; everyone who makes mention of it will be afraid in himself."

Even though many Egyptians contest this war, it appears to take place. For Egypt's participation in this war the country experiences a bitter defeat. Subsequently as the victors, the state of Israel annexes at least five cities east of the Nile River that are presently located in modern day Egypt. This would potentially fulfill Isaiah 19:18, which predicts that five cities in Egypt will speak Hebrew. It is safe to suggest these cities are on the east side of the Nile because that land was promised to Abraham in Genesis 15:18.

As bitter as Egypt's defeat is, it probably doesn't entirely desolate the land for forty years in fulfillment of Ezekiel 29:12 because this would seem time prohibitive for Israel to takeover and populate these five Hebrew speaking cities. This is not to say that Egypt will escape destruction in Psalm 83, because one of the five Israeli cities is called "heres" in Hebrew, which translated means "destruction."[201]

Israel has proven that it can win wars in the region, and annex land in the aftermath without entirely desolating the countries of its enemies. This was the case in the 1948 War of Independence, and especially in the six day war of 1967.

As Egypt recovers from the Psalm 83 war, and Israel potentially acquires these five cities, the Jewish state eventually gets involved in the seven year peace treaty, which Daniel 9:26 declares is confirmed by the Antichrist with many. As a result of Israel's involvement in this treaty, the Jewish state assumes that it can dwell securely, and begins to let its guard down somewhat. This seems safe to suggest, because three and one-half years into the seven years of peace, Israel's militarily becomes so complacent that the Antichrist can easily enter into the Jewish temple, which exists at the time, in order to commit the "abomination of desolation." Upon committing this detestable act, the Antichrist embarks upon his campaign of Jewish genocide.

## The Declaration of Daniel

This campaign becomes a top priority of the Antichrist and apparently correlates with what Daniel 11:41-45 specifies below.

> "He (Antichrist) shall also enter the Glorious Land, and many *countries* shall be overthrown; but these shall escape from his hand: Edom, Moab, and the prominent people of Ammon. He shall stretch out his hand against the countries, and the land of Egypt shall not escape. He shall have power over the treasures of gold and silver, and over all the precious things of Egypt; also the Libyans and Ethiopians *shall follow* at his heels. But news from the east and the north shall trouble him; therefore he shall go out with great fury to destroy and annihilate many. And he shall plant the tents of his palace between the seas and the glorious holy mountain; yet he shall come to his end, and no one will help him." (Daniel 11:41-45).

These important Daniel passages break down as follows:

- The Antichrist enters into the Glorious Land.

- He overthrows many countries.

- Jordan (Edom, Moab, and Ammon) escapes from being overthrown.

- Egypt is one of the overthrown countries.

- Egypt's treasuries are overtaken by the Antichrist.

- Libya and Ethiopia are in the process of being overthrown.

- But, troubling news interrupts the Antichrist conquering campaign.

- The Antichrist is infuriated by events occurring to the Northeast of Egypt.

- The Antichrist deploys to Megiddo in preparation for the Armageddon battle.

At this point, it is important to understand what the prophet Daniel declared regarding Edom and the end-times faithful Jewish remnant. Understanding the Antichrist's attempt to destroy the Jewish people, and this treasured remnant hidden within Israel, assists in understanding how Egypt becomes desolated for forty years.

Daniel declares that the Antichrist enters into the "Glorious Land," likely referring to territories under Jewish sovereignty, which at that future time should encompass parts of what are modern day Lebanon, Syria, Jordan, and Egypt. The Jews could come into possession of these lands because of their successful defeat of the Psalm 83:1–8 confederacy, via the means of their "exceedingly great army."

> "He [the Antichrist] shall also enter the Glorious Land, and many *countries* shall be overthrown; but these shall escape from his hand: *Edom, Moab*, and *the prominent people of Ammon*." (Dan. 11:41, NKJV; emphasis added)

The Antichrist comes in heavy-handedly conquering many countries, but does not overthrow Edom, Moab, and Ammon. These three territories comprise what is today referred to as the nation of Jordan. Jordan became a nation in 1946, but in ancient times this land was referred to down through the generations as Edom, Moab, and Ammon. It is important to note what Isaiah 11:14 foretold about these three territories over a century before Daniel prophesied.

"They (the Jews) shall lay their hand on Edom and Moab; And the people of Ammon shall obey them." (NKJV).

Daniel declares that Jordan escapes the escapades of the Antichrist, yet Isaiah informs us that Jordanians do not escape the grasp of the "exceedingly great army" of Israel. In fact; the Jordanians become subservient to Israel and "shall obey them." The next paragraph orchestrates the chronological order of events prophesied over Edom, Moab, and Ammon.

First, the Jordanians align themselves as a member nation in the Psalm 83:6–8 confederacy. Second, this confederacy engages in a major war against Israel. Third, Israel exacts victory via the hands of its "exceedingly great army." Fourth, Israel establishes sovereignty over Jordan. Fifth, the Antichrist initiates a military campaign to overthrow the glorious land, which is so called because it is comprised of countries predominately under Israeli sovereignty, including Jordan. Sixth, the Antichrist avoids Jordan, and marches through Israel proper instead.

The reason this crazed individual comes into the glorious land is to overthrow it. Since much of this land will probably belong to Israel at the time; we can surmise that a top priority of the Antichrist is the killing of the Jews according to Zechariah 13:8 and elsewhere.

There are a couple probable reasons why the Antichrist does not initially overthrow "Edom, Moab, and the prominent people of Ammon." First all of these areas by then appear to be generally desolated because of the Psalm 83 war between the Arabs and Jews. By territories, the setting at the time of the genocidal campaign of the Antichrist should be as follows:

1. *Southern Jordan (Edom)*. This territory presently is desert and is minimally populated. In addition, the Mountain range of Seir traverses through Edom, making it generally undesirable for day-to-day living. Much of these mountains are impassable, making it an obstacle to the Antichrist in his campaign to overthrow this element of the Jewish kingdom. Lastly, it will have been hard hit by the Arab-Israeli war, meaning that very few Jews will find it desirable to migrate there. As such, Jews for the Antichrist to kill will be sparsely found there.

2. *Central Jordan (Moab)*. This terrain today is primarily desert, not extremely desirable for habitation. This territory may at that time also be the location of the valley of "Hamon Gog." The valley of "Hamon Gog" becomes the designated area of the mass burial grounds for millions of dead soldiers killed in association with the Russian-Iranian confederacy described in Ezekiel Chapters 38 and 39.[202] This prophetic episode, whereby Russia and its coalition form against Israel, occurs after the Israeli Conquest of the "Glorious Land,"

but before the Antichrist marches into the "Glorious Land." Due to the desolated desert environment, coupled with the possibility that Moab becomes burdened by the largest cemetery since the flood of Noah, the Antichrist will find few Jews there for the killing as well.

3. Northern Jordan (Ammon). Daniel stated "but these shall escape from his hand: "Edom, Moab, and the prominent people of Ammon." Who are these prominent people? In Isaiah 11:14 we were informed that They shall lay their hand on Edom and Moab; And the people of Ammon shall obey them. Both Isaiah and Daniel have listed these same three locations and in the same order.

By connecting the dots, we can determine that the people whom Isaiah says the Jordanians "shall obey," are those reigning over them. Since the events Daniel 11:41-45 describes occur subsequent to the events Isaiah describes, we can surmise "the prominent people of Ammon" referred to by Daniel are those governing Jordan at the time that the Antichrist marches into the glorious land. According to Isaiah, those sovereign over Jordan at that time appear to be the Jews.

Therefore, "the prominent people of Ammon," whom Daniel declares will escape the march of the Antichrist, would be either Jewish governors, or some form of a vassal Jordanian government subservient to Israeli sovereignty. Because the Antichrist is on a campaign to overthrow the "Glorious Land" and kill all the Jews, his primary focus should be on the supreme leadership headquartered in Israel, rather than their ambassadors stationed in Ammon. This could be the reason that "the prominent people of Ammon" escape.

> "He [the Antichrist] shall stretch out his hand against the countries, and the land of Egypt shall not escape. He shall have power over *the treasures of gold and silver, and over all the precious things of Egypt*; also the Libyans and Ethiopians *shall follow* at his heels. (Dan. 11:42–43, NKJV; emphasis added)

Following the trail of the Antichrist further, we see that he avoids Jordan, but moves through Israel proper, and then heads down into Egypt. Why does he set Egypt within his sights? Daniel says he gains power over the great wealth of Egypt "the treasures of gold and silver, and over all the precious things of Egypt." History demonstrates that many armies have sustained themselves through the spoils of war. This point was highlighted in the section concerning Egypt's PAST judgment that was executed by the Babylonian King Nebuchadnezzar.

Perhaps the Antichrist's invasion of Egypt is partially concerned with replenishing military supplies, payrolls, and weapons arsenals, but in addition the Antichrist appears to attack Egypt because at that time, there could be a significant population of Jews residing there. An IDF victory over Egypt might facilitate the establishment of "five Israeli cities in the land of Egypt." These cities could experience a migration of Jews into them. As a result, these Jews would establish their language, culture, and religion therein. Isaiah 19:18 states that they "will speak the language of Canaan (Hebrew) and swear by the LORD of hosts."

As mentioned earlier, Isaiah also predicts that one of these five cities "will be called the City of Destruction." Jewish tradition dating back to the biblical era of Joshua about 3500 years ago evidences the common historical practice of renaming a city or location in an attempt to identify a powerful epic event that occurred there. One of the reasons for this practice was so that future Jewish generations would be caused to learn and reflect upon the lessons of the significant episode.[203] This city will likely meet its destruction at the hands of the "exceedingly great army" of Israel, at which point the city will be aptly renamed "the City of Destruction."

> "But *news from the east and the north shall trouble him*; (Antichrist) therefore he shall go out with great fury to destroy and annihilate many [Jews]. And he shall *plant the tents of his palace between the seas and the glorious holy mountain*; yet he shall come to his end, and no one will help him." (Dan. 11:44–45, NKJV; emphasis added)

The Antichrist intercepts troubling news while he is basking in the glory of his victory over Egypt. The newsworthy information comes from the east and the north. In the Old Testament of the Bible, there are no translations using the word "Northeast" or "Eastnorth," but we can surmise that is where Daniel is directionally describing. Breaking news comes out of the territory directly "Northeast" of Egypt.

Some teach that the troubling news received by the Antichrist concerns the sixth bowl judgment of Revelation. They posit the possibility that the Chinese army represented by the "kings from the east," is crossing the Euphrates River in order to wage war with the Antichrist at Armageddon. This would certainly be troubling news, and the Euphrates River is east and north of Egypt.

> "Then the sixth angel poured out his bowl on the great river Euphrates, and its water was dried up, so that the way of the kings from the east might be prepared." (Revelation 16:12, NKJV).

Revelation 16:12-16 does specify that these kings are coming to Armageddon, but Revelation 16:14 informs us that in addition to the kings of the east, many other kings of the earth are also heading there. The world kings appear to be deploying to Armageddon with their armies to rendezvous with the Antichrist, rather than to war against him there.

"And I saw three unclean spirits like frogs *coming* out of the mouth of the dragon, out of the mouth of the beast, and out of the mouth of the false prophet. For they are spirits of demons, performing signs, *which* go out *to the kings of the earth and of the whole world,* to gather them to the battle of that great day of God Almighty. (Revelation 16:13-14; NKJV; emphasis added).

"And they gathered them together to the place called in Hebrew, Armaged-don." (Revelation 16:16, NKJV).

All these kings appear to be mobilizing to Armageddon in fulfillment of Joel 3, which refers to the final battle during the day of the Lord when the Antichrist, and his world armies wage war against the Lord, and they are defeated. Joel 3:2, 12, 14 identifies the location of the epic biblical battle as the "Valley of Jehoshaphat," and the "Valley of Decision." The location of this valley is generally taught to be in the Jezreel Valley.

*"Armageddon" comes from the Greek Harmagedoôn, which transliterates the Hebrew words for Mount (har) of Megiddo. That mountain is near the city of Megiddo and the plain of Esdraelon, the scene of many Old Testament battles."*[204]

There is no apparent clue in these Revelation 16 passages quoted above that the kings of the east are marching against the Antichrist. Moreover, Daniel 11 mentions king or kings fifteen times but never any emerging from the east. Therefore what I believe Daniel is describing about the troubling news is concerned with the fleeing of the faithful Jewish remnant into Petra, Jordan.

Daniel 11:44 says, "But news from the east and the north shall trouble him," this also points directionally to the location of modern-day Southern Jordan, which is ancient Edom. This is the territory directly, and more immediately to the "Northeast" of Egypt than the Euphrates River. What news could possibly disturb the Antichrist, who at that time will be exalted in his recent victory over Egypt? Perhaps this will be the headline, and opening paragraph from the Jerusalem Post, or its equivalent during that period:

### "ISRAELIS ESCAPE TO EDOM"
"A multitude of Jews have fled Israel in an emergency mass exodus into Southern Jordan. The Jews are taking refuge in the protective cliff fortresses of ancient Bozrah, Edom. Known today as Petra, its rugged mountain terrain offers the Jews a form of temporary protection from the ongoing slaughter taking place in the Glorious Land."

Possibly, the troubling news is that a massive exodus of Jews has been occurring under his nose directly northeast of his location in Egypt. This would be the faithful

Jewish remnant referenced earlier in this chapter. The Antichrist then moves to "plant the tents of his palace between the seas and the glorious holy mountain." This move by the Antichrist sets the stage for the heavily prophesied campaign of Armageddon. The targets of this campaign are the Jewish faithful who have fled into Edom, or modern Southern Jordan. They will hide in the cliff fortresses of the mountain ranges of ancient Seir. Remember that Edom along with Moab and Ammon had escaped the overthrowing of countries taking place in the glorious land by the Antichrist.

Ultimately, according to Hosea 5:15, the Jewish refugees residing in Petra become the faithful remnant that realizes Jesus Christ is the Messiah during the Great Tribulation period. They repent as a nation, and beckon the return of Christ. This motivates Christ to come to the Earth again. During this visit, He rescues the faithful Jewish remnant, and defeats the Antichrist. Daniel foretells the destruction of the Antichrist in Daniel 11:45 quoted earlier: "he [the Antichrist] shall come to his end, and no one will help him." The Antichrist meets his end through the crushing might of Jesus Christ, in fulfillment of Genesis 3:15.

> "And I will put enmity Between you [Satan] and the woman, And between your [Satan] seed [the Antichrist] and her Seed [the Messiah]; He [Jesus Christ the Messiah] shall bruise your head [destroy the Antichrist], And you shall bruise His heel. (Genesis 3:15, NKJV).

## Egypt's Desolation and Conversion

Fortunately, the Egyptian people don't experience as crushing a defeat as the Antichrist, who ultimately spends eternity in the Lake of Fire according to Revelation 19:20. As stated in a previous chapter, there is some good news for Egypt. There will be a remnant of Egyptians that survive the Psalm 83 war, the Antichrist's invasion of their homeland, and the perilous judgments that occur during the tribulation period. But coinciding with Egypt's conversion to Christ, which renders it as a saved nation within the Messianic kingdom, the country does experience a severe forty years of desolation, which turns Egypt into the lowliest of kingdoms throughout the kingdom period.

Remember that Ezekiel 29:15 says That Egypt "shall be the lowliest of kingdoms; it shall never again exalt itself above the nations, for I will diminish them so that they will not rule over the nations anymore."

The remainder of the chapter will explore Egypt's desolation and conversion through various prophecies contained in Isaiah 11, 19, and Ezekiel 29.

> "The LORD will utterly destroy the tongue of the Sea of Egypt [Red Sea]; With His mighty wind He will shake His fist over the River [The Nile River], And

strike it in the seven streams, *And make men cross over dryshod* (dry land). (Isa. 11:15, NKJV; emphasis added)

In keeping with the possible establishment of a Jewish presence in Egypt, Isaiah 11:15 declares that the geography of Egypt will be re-shaped through a series of what appears to be natural disasters. The result would better facilitate Jewish migration into Egypt. The tip of the Red Sea will experience a devastation of sorts that serves to dry it up.[205]

Furthermore, the Nile River seems to undergo tornado-like conditions, which will establish dry land over "the seven streams," which probably refers to tributaries of the Nile River. All of the above will enable Jews to "cross over" into Egypt on "dryshod" as part of the IDF victory, and the capturing of the five cities of Isaiah 19:18. If this affected territory remains as "dryshod" when the Antichrist invades Egypt, then he may also opt to deploy his forces to "cross over" on this transformed land.

The geographical change predicted in Isaiah 11:15 could not have been fulfilled during the exodus era because it was prophesied about eight hundred years afterward. However, similarities exist between this future crossover into Egypt on dry land, and the historical Hebrew exodus out of Egypt, which fit the same description. Waters miraculously converted into dry land should also remind Egyptians of their ancient history when Pharaoh's army was swallowed up, and destroyed by the converging waters of the Red Sea. (Exodus 14:26-31).

> "Then Moses stretched out his hand over the sea [Red Sea]; and the LORD caused the sea to go *back* by a strong east wind all that night, and made the sea into *dry land,* and the waters were divided. So the children of Israel went into the midst of the sea on the *dry ground,* and the waters *were* a wall to them on their right hand and on their left. (Exod. 14:21–22, NKJV; emphasis added).

A possible point of comparison would be that "the tongue of the Sea of Egypt" referred to in Isaiah 11:15 might be close in proximity to the location of the historical miracle whereby the waters parted, facilitating the ancient Hebrew exodus out of Egypt. Remember that according to the covenant made between God and the Jewish patriarch Abraham in Genesis 15:18, the Jews are entitled to a landmass that extends to the Nile River.

Perhaps, as a result of the Israeli Conquest over Egypt, and in light of the Promised Land given to Abram, later renamed Abraham, the Jews will feel justified in their mass migration campaign into Egypt.[206] As they populate Egypt, the potential for the final fulfillment of Isaiah 11:15 and Isaiah 19:18 could occur.

"There will be a highway for the remnant of His people Who will be left from Assyria, As it was for Israel In the day that he came up from the land of Egypt. (Isaiah 11:16, NKJV).

Isaiah concludes his Chapter 11 by referencing "a highway for the remnant of His people who will be left from Assyria." This highway is opened for unrestricted travel between Assyria and Israel sometime after Israel's conquest over its Arab enemies. This highway appears to further facilitate the return of Jews who have remained outside the land of Israel until after the coming Middle East war.

The opening of this highway appears to be made possible by the fact that Israel will gain supremacy of the region. This highway seems to offer safe passage to the Jews who would like to emigrate from the north into what will then be referred to as the Glorious Land. Furthermore, in the context of Egypt's national conversion, Isaiah Chapter 19 also appears to describe this highway.

"In that day there will be *a highway* from Egypt to Assyria, and the Assyrian will come into Egypt and the Egyptian into Assyria, and the Egyptians will serve with the Assyrians. In that day Israel will be one of three with Egypt and Assyria—a blessing in the midst of the land, whom the LORD of hosts shall bless, saying, "Blessed *is* Egypt My people, and Assyria the work of My hands, and Israel My inheritance." (Isaiah 19:23–25, NKJV; emphasis added)

If the highway described in Isaiah 19:23 is the same as that described in Isaiah 11:16, it appears to remain accessible from the time of its opening after the Israeli Conquest into the Messianic Kingdom period. This can be deduced from the fact that the final fulfillment of these Isaiah 19 passages, whereby "Israel will be one of three with Egypt and Assyria—a blessing in the midst of the land," occurs in the Messianic Kingdom period. Some scholars teach that the ancient "Kings Highway" becomes extended into Syria and becomes the highway described here.

## Summary of Egypt's Prophetic Future

As this chapter and the "The Three Egyptian Judgments" chapter illustrates, Egypt has a very busy future ahead of itself. And, if it wasn't for the fact that an Egyptian remnant maintains the lowliest of kingdoms within the Messianic kingdom, Egypt's outlook would be terrible from this point forward. But at the very least, the world atlases will reflect and entirely different Egypt during the Messianic kingdom. This is because every aspect of Egypt's present existence is essentially devastated. Below is a summary list of perilous prophetic events about to befall Egypt.

- *Government* – Egypt becomes a dictatorship, ruled by a cruel master *(Isaiah 19:4)*.

- *Wisdom* – Egypt notorious for ancient wisdom, becomes foolish *(Isaiah 19:11-13)*.

- *Religion* – Islam totters and Sharia Law fails the Muslims *(Isaiah 19:1, 3)*.

- *Economy* – Egypt experiences entire economic collapse *(Isaiah 19:8-10, 14-15)*.

- *Population* – Egyptians kill each other, and get deported *(Isaiah 19:2, Ezekiel 29:12-14)*.

- *Military* – Egypt's army is defeated twice *(Isaiah 19:16-17, Daniel 11:42-43)*.

- *Geography* – Egypt experiences desolation *(Isaiah 19:5-7, Ezekiel 29:10-11)*.

- *Culture* – Egypt becomes the lowliest of kingdoms *(Ezekiel 29:15)*.

In his book The Footsteps of the Messiah, Dr. Arnold Fruchtenbaum explains how Ezekiel 29:1-16 generally sums up Egypt's overall prophetic fate.

> "Ezekiel is commanded to prophesy against Egypt (vv.1-2) and predict the coming dispersion of the Egyptians from their land (vv. 3-5) because of their long history of mistreatment of Israel (vv.6-7). The land of Egypt will suffer a period of total desolation (vv. 8-10), which will last for forty years (vv. 11-12a), and the Egyptians will be scattered all over the world like Israel was before her (v. 12b). But after the end of the period of forty years, the Egyptians will be regathered (v.13) and brought back into their land (v.14). Though Egypt will become a kingdom again, it will never be a powerful one (v. 15). Nor will Israel ever again be guilty of placing her confidence in Egypt (v 16), but will trust in the Lord their God."

> "In summary, peace will come between Israel and Egypt by means of conversion. Only when the Egyptians worship the same God as Israel, through Jesus the Messiah, will peace finally come. For the first forty years of the Kingdom, the land of Egypt will be desolate and the Egyptians will be dispersed all over the world. But afterwards, the Egyptians will be regathered, becoming a kingdom again."[207]

Dr. Fruchtenbaum believes that the forty years of desolation will overlap into the thousand year Messianic kingdom. This means he believes it's a future prophecy. It also implies Egypt's desolation occurs at the end of the tribulation period. This suggests that it is brought about by Egypt's FUTURE judgment at the hands of the Antichrist. If so, then I would concur with him.

With all of this discernment in hand, then who is Egypt's cruel master of Isaiah 19:4? It's probably not Nebuchadnezzar, since the time of the cruel master is "in that day" when Egypt is terrorized by Judah according to Isaiah 19:16-17. It's likely not the Assyrian king Esarhaddon who conquered Egypt in 671 B.C., as some suggest, for the same reason above. It's not Hosni Mubarak, or any of his presidential predecessors, like Gamal Nasser, or Anwar Sadat, because they are all either dead or deposed, and Isaiah 19 is still a prophecy pending fulfillment. Lastly, it's not the Antichrist, because his invasion of Egypt seemingly causes forty years of desolation and dispersion, leaving the country without the need for any governance. And, according to Revelation 19:20 the Antichrist will be dwelling in the Lake of Fire, and not Egypt during those forty years of desolation.

Perhaps it could be an Israeli leader that cruelly governs the Egyptians when five cities in Egypt speak Hebrew as per Isaiah 19:18, but I believe it could be the Egyptian leader that moves Egypt into the Psalm 83 war. If this war were to happen at the time of the publication of this book, it could be Mohammed Morsi who became Egypt's president on June 24, 2012.

### "The return of pharaoh? The 'power grab' by Egypt's Mohamed Morsi"

*Washington Post 11/26/12*

"Calling someone a "pharaoh" in Egypt is not a compliment; it is a condemnation of the absolute political rule that held sway in Egypt for millennia under dynasty after dynasty of kings who were considered gods, and who oppressed the people."[208]

# TWENTY-ONE

# The Destruction of Damascus

**"If NATO attacks Syria, we'll fire missiles at Tel Aviv"**

*Jerusalem Post 10/4/11*

"Syria's Assad says Damascus can call on Hezbollah to launch rocket attack on Israel if western countries take "crazy measures,""

**"IDF fires warning shot into Syria after shell hits Golan"**

*Jerusalem Post 11/11/12*

"Israel says further attacks from Syria will "elicit a vigorous response" from IDF, sends letter to UN warning Syrians to avoid spillover; Incident marks first time IDF has fired at Syria since 1973 Yom Kippur War."

**"Bashar Assad: I will 'live and die' in Syria"**

*CBS News 11/8/12*

"Syria's embattled President Bashar Assad says he will not leave his country. Speaking hypothetically about Western military action to help Syrian rebels oust him, Assad "the price of this invasion, if it happens, is going to be more than the whole world can afford."

This chapter contains an exhaustive verse by verse commentary of Isaiah 17. Isaiah 17:1 predicts that Damascus will someday be reduced to a ruinous heap of rubble. Some, like my friend and widely respected Bible scholar Dr. Mark Hitchcock, believe that this prophecy was historically fulfilled by the Assyrian conquest of Damascus in 732 B.C. Concerning the destruction of Damascus according to Isaiah 17:1 Dr. Hitchcock writes the following in his book called Middle East Burning:

> "I believe it makes more sense to hold that Isaiah 17 was fulfilled in the eighth century BC when both Damascus, the capital of Syria, and Samaria, the capital of Israel, were hammered by the Assyrians. In that conquest, both Damascus and Samaria were destroyed, just as Isaiah 17 predicts."[209]

I respectfully disagree with this assessment, that Isaiah 17:1 found final fulfillment at that time in history, and herein point out that Isaiah mentions Assyria, Assyrian, or Assyrians at least 41 times in his 66 chapters, but never once mentions any of the above in Isaiah 17. To the contrary, I point out in this chapter that Isaiah 17:9 seems to suggest that Israel is responsible, in self-defense, for the destruction of Damascus.

Additionally, Jeremiah 49:23–27 written approximately fifteen hundred years after Isaiah 17 also talks about a burden against Damascus. If Damascus was literally destroyed in 732 B.C. by the Assyrians, this means that it had to become restored subsequently for Jeremiah's prophecy to find a future fulfillment. I think it is more logical to read Isaiah 17 and Jeremiah 49:23-27 in connection with each other to glean more prophetic details of the destruction of Damascus.

Lastly, the prophet Amos says the following;

Thus says the LORD: "For three transgressions of Damascus, and for four,

> I will not turn away its *punishment,* Because they have threshed Gilead with implements of iron. But I will send a fire into the house of Hazael, Which shall devour the palaces of Ben-Hadad. (Amos 1:3-4 NKJV).

Some, like me, believe this can be interpreted as follows; the three transgressions of Damascus were fulfilled in the Arab – Israeli wars of 1948, 1967, and 1973. Syria was among the most prominent enemy nations in all these wars. Their involvement under the banner of Assyria in the soon coming Psalm 83 war would then become the fourth and final straw that brings about its punishment prophesied by Amos.

(Isaiah 17:1-2)—The burden against Damascus. "Behold, Damascus will cease from *being* a city, and it will be a ruinous heap. The *cities of Aroer are forsaken*; they will be *for flocks* which lie down, and no one will make *them* afraid." (emphasis added)

These first two verses inform us that the Syrian capital city of Damascus will be destroyed, causing it to cease from being a city. Since Damascus exists today, this prophecy remains unfulfilled. Additionally other cities "of Aroer" are adversely affected, causing them to be "forsaken." The Hebrew word used for forsaken is azab, and means abandoned, withdrawn, left behind, released, or neglected.[210]

Since these cities eventually become agriculturally zoned "for flocks," the best understanding is probably that the destruction of Damascus necessitates the withdrawal of the surrounding city populations, which ultimately leads to their release and rezoning. Whichever government is sovereign over this area at that time, will reevaluate the highest and best use of the territory to be agricultural.

Parson's Bible Atlas lists three possibilities for Aroer: Aroer Judah, Aroer Sihon, and Aroer Gad.

- *Aroer Judah* was located about twelve miles southeast of Beersheeba, which places it as the furthest away from Damascus of the three options.

- *Aroer Sihon* was a city situated on the northern banks of the Arnon River, which was formerly located inside the tribal territories of Reuben. This places Aroer Sihon in ancient Moab (central Jordan), which is still fairly far south from Damascus.

- *Aroer Gad* becomes the likely option, because it was located in the area of ancient Ammon, (northern Jordan).[211]

Damascus is located in southern Syria, and Amman (Aroer Gad), the capital of Jordan, is in northern Jordan, where most Jordanians live. Only 109 miles separates the two Arab capitals, which is a shorter distance than the distance between the two most populated California cities of Los Angeles and San Diego. Approximately 120 miles, less than a two hour drive, separate these two US cities.

Aroer Gad was part of the tribal territory of Gad. Numbers 32 informs us that the tribe of Gad was generally agriculturalists and as such, Gad requested this territory because it was suitable for his sizable flocks. Thus, the destruction of Damascus apparently spills over into northern Jordan. Jeremiah 49:1-2, seems to give more detail about these northern Jordanian cities.

Against the Ammonites [northern Jordanians today]. Thus says the LORD: "Has Israel no sons? Has he no heir? Why *then* does Milcom inherit [Aroer] Gad, And his people dwell in its cities? Therefore behold, the days are coming," says the LORD, "That I will cause to be heard an alarm of war In Rabbah of the Ammonites; It shall be a desolate mound, And her villages shall be burned with fire. Then Israel shall take possession of his inheritance," says the LORD. (Jeremiah 49:1-2)

The sequence of events should be as follows. Damascus and Rabbah are destroyed, probably in the same war effort. In the aftermath, Israel takes possession of northern Jordan including ancient Aroer, and rezones much it for agricultural purposes. Milcom was the Ammonite god when Jeremiah wrote. Since Milcom and all the other pagan Arab gods have all since been replaced by Allah, Jeremiah likely alludes to Islam in his prophecy. Jeremiah asks why do Arabs, (Jordanians today); dwell in the cities bequeathed to one of Jacob's twelve sons? This is a very fitting question considering that the Nazi's attempted to kill all of Jacob's posterity. However, since their genocidal attempt failed, leaving Jacobs some descendants, Jordan is accountable to answer Jeremiah's rhetorical question.

Ultimately, in the aftermath of a war, Israel possesses "his inheritance," represented by the cities of Aroer Gad. Ammon is a participant in the Psalm 83 Arab confederacy. Thus, the war in question is probably Psalm 83. If this is so, then the destruction of Isaiah's Damascus and Jeremiah's Rabbah are probably closely related Psalm 83 events. Assyria, which comprised part of modern day northern Syria when Psalm 83 was written, is also part of the Arab confederacy.

(Isaiah 17:3)—"The fortress also will cease from Ephraim, The kingdom from Damascus, And the remnant of Syria; They will be as the glory of the children of Israel," Says the LORD of hosts.

Assyria conquered Aram, the location of Damascus, around 732 BC and the "fortress" of Ephraim ceased to exist, when the Assyrians conquered the northern kingdom of Israel in 722 BC. Isaiah, whose ministry spanned between 740–701 BC, appears to have authored chapter 17 prior to the Assyrian conquests.[212]

This could explain the first part of Isaiah 17:3, but fails to address the latter part, which identifies the remnant of Syria with the glory of the children of Israel. At the time of the Assyrian conquest of Damascus and Ephraim, there was no Syrian "remnant" under Israeli rule, "as the glory of the children of Israel."

Therefore a dual fulfillment of the prophecy may be coming. What Isaiah could be warning about is that strongholds in northern Israel (Ephraim) will become wartorn at the time of Damascus's destruction. The Syrian refugees (remnant) thereby, become captured by the IDF (children of Israel). Isaiah 17:9 below suggests Israel is responsible for the downing of Damascus. Isaiah concludes verse 3 by informing us, even though Damascus will cease to exist, a remnant of Syrians will survive.

> (Isaiah 17:4-6)—"In that day it shall come to pass *That* the glory of Jacob will wane, And the fatness of his flesh grow lean. It shall be as when the harvester gathers the grain, And reaps the heads with his arm; It shall be as he who gathers heads of grain In the Valley of Rephaim. Yet gleaning grapes will be left in it, Like the shaking of an olive tree, Two *or* three olives at the top of the uppermost bough, Four *or* five in its most fruitful branches," Says the LORD God of Israel.

These verses open with "In that day." Isaiah uses this expression four times throughout the chapter. The fact that he first uses this in verse four suggests that the preceding three verses all serve as the antecedent to the phrase. In other words, "In that day":

- Damascus ceases to be a city (v. 1),

- The cities of Aroer are forsaken (v. 2),

- The fortress of Ephraim, and kingdom of Damascus ceases (v. 3), and

- The Syrian remnant becomes subservient to the glory of the children of Israel (v. 3).

If so, than at the time all the above occurs, Isaiah 17:4-6 finds fulfillment. These verses picture Israel in an undesirable condition, suggesting the Jewish nation comes under attack at that time. Some believe these verses occur at the time of Armageddon, because Israel will suffer severely at that time. The problem with aligning the "in that day," with Armageddon at the end of the tribulation period is that verse nine clues us otherwise. Isaiah 17:9 informs us that the cities that become forsaken are abandoned because of the Jews. Any cities abandoned during the campaign of Armageddon will be abandoned because of the Antichrist's war related activities, not Israel's.

In conjunction with Israel's suffering, Isaiah 17:4-6 mentions terms, idioms, and locations, like heads of grain, Valley of Rephaim, gleaning grapes, olive tree, olives, uppermost bough, and fruitful branches. These usages suggest there could be casualties in Israel. The Valley of Rephaim, is located in Israel, and is now called el-Bukei'a.[213] This valley was the site of two historic wars the Israelites successfully waged under King David against their arch enemy the Philistines.

Coincidentally, Philistia is listed in Psalm 83. Perhaps Isaiah is telling us that, like David defeated the Philistines in the Valley of Rephaim, so will a lean and waning war-torn Israel bring about the destruction of Damascus before or during the Psalm 83 war episode.

But, Jewish genocide will be averted as Jews will survive in northern Israel (uppermost bough), and even more will survive in the more populated cities (fruitful branches).

> (Isaiah 17:7-8)—In that day a man will look to his Maker, And his eyes will have respect for the Holy One of Israel. He will not look to the altars, The work of his hands; He will not respect what his fingers have made, Nor the wooden images nor the incense altars.

These verses teach that the overwhelming events "in that day," cause humanity to question the power of its false gods of religion, technology, and materialism. The events surrounding the destruction of Damascus adversely affect all of mankind, prompting some to consider their creator, and his protection over the nation Israel. Zephaniah 2:11 points out that someday all false gods will be destroyed and everyone will worship the Lord.

The American Standard Version translates Isaiah 17:8 as follows:

> And they shall not look to the altars, the work of their hands; neither shall they have respect to that which their fingers have made, either the Asherim, or the sun-images.

The Hebrew word used for Asherim is Asherah. The Holman Bible Dictionary defines Asherah as,

> "A fertility goddess, the mother of Baal, whose worship was concentrated in Syria and Canaan and the wooden object that represented her."

By using Asherah, Isaiah seems to emphasize that the false god of Syria will suffer disrespect. Asherah, like most other Mideast gods, gave way to Allah worship around the seventh century, when Islam was officially conceived. Allah is the would-be Syrian god today, that will suffer dishonor and shame when Damascus is destroyed.

> (Isaiah 17:9)—In that day his strong cities will be as a forsaken bough And an uppermost branch, Which they left because of the children of Israel; And there will be desolation.

In this verse Damascus is personified by the pronoun "his." In that day, that the destruction of Damascus and "his" strong cities (of Aroer, v. 2) are forsaken; it will be a scene of "desolation." At the time Damascus meets its doom, it is characterized by "strong cities" about it. It is not a picture of weakness, but of a militarily strong Syria.

The "children of Israel" are responsible for this desolation and these forsaken cities. This verse implies that the IDF may have something to do with the destruction of Damascus. The devastation appears to also extend into cities north of Damascus, identified as "an uppermost branch."

> (Isaiah 17:10-13)—Because you have forgotten the God of your salvation, And have not been mindful of the Rock of your stronghold, Therefore you will plant pleasant plants And set out foreign seedlings; In the day you will make your plant to grow, And in the morning you will make your seed to flourish; But the harvest will be a heap of ruins In the day of grief and desperate sorrow. Woe to the multitude of many people Who make a noise like the roar of the seas, And to the rushing of nations That make a rushing like the rushing of mighty waters! The nations will rush like the rushing of many waters; But God will rebuke them and they will flee far away, And be chased like the chaff of the mountains before the wind, Like a rolling thing before the whirlwind.

Isaiah 17:9 previously informed Damascus that his strong cities will be desolated apparently because of Israel. Isaiah 17:10-13 foretells why this desolation comes. Damascus, identified by the pronoun "you" in this instance, is not mindful of God.[214] But in addition to that, the Syrians are amongst a multitude of mighty waters that are rushing like roaring seas. This suggests that Syria, represented by Damascus, comes against Israel forcefully in a confederate effort with other nations.

Seas typically represent the Gentile nations, and in this instance they are noisily roaring and rushing like mighty waters.[215] This pictures a massive military invasion. We can safely assume this invasion is targeted at Israel, because verse 9 implies that Israel retaliates. The fact that they come against Israel evidences they have forgotten the "God of their salvation." The God of Israel is the God of salvation, and he promised in several Scriptures that Israel could never be destroyed.[216]

Isaiah says the war campaign results in a "heap of ruins," and characterizes the whole episode as a "day of grief and desperate sorrow." Isaiah 17:13 seems to connect with Psalm 83:13-15. In Psalm 83, Asaph petitions the Lord to do what Isaiah 17:13 says occurs to this confederacy. This implies that the destruction of Damascus and desolation of the surrounding cities could be related in some way to the Psalm 83 scenario. They both use the same six Hebrew words of galgal, paniym, ruach, har, radaph, and suphah, as comparatively highlighted below.

> O my God, make them like the whirling dust, [galgal] Like the chaff before [paniym] the wind! [ruach] As the fire burns the woods, And as the flame sets

the mountains [*har*] on fire, So pursue [*radaph*] them with Your tempest, And frighten them with Your storm [*suphah*]. (Psalm 83:13-15)

Compared to Isaiah 17:13 below:

The nations will rush like the rushing of many waters; But God will rebuke them and they will flee far away, And be chased [*radaph*] like the chaff of the mountains [*har*] before [*paniym*] the wind, [*ruach*] Like a rolling [*galgal*] thing before [*paniym*] the whirlwind [*suphah*].

If this is the case, then the nations that rush mightily like many waters are the Psalm 83:6-8 Arab States. If the destruction of Damascus occurs in a related Psalm 83 event, this would help explain why Syria, under the banners of either Aram or Assyria, doesn't appear listed in the Ezekiel 38:1-6 coalition of Magog invaders. This would imply that the destruction of Damascus occurs prior to the fulfillment of Ezekiel 38.

As stated above, the destruction of Damascus seems to occur at the hands of the IDF, according to Isaiah 17:9. This suggests that the "day of [Damascus's] grief and desperate sorrow" is a pre-tribulation event for the following reasons:

- The first three and one-half years are characterized by Israel dwelling in a false peace.

- The second three and one-half years are characterized by attempted Jewish genocide.

- The day of the Lord is never specifically mentioned in Isaiah 17, or in the connecting prophecy about Damascus in Jeremiah 49:23-27.

During the first half of the tribulation, Israel is dwelling in a false sense of national security. The covenant confirmed with them by the Antichrist in Daniel 9:27 creates this period of deceptive calm. The IDF appears to let its guard down, as a result.

At the mid-point of the tribulation, the Antichrist enters into the third Jewish temple and abominates it, as Christ prophesied in Matthew 24:15. This violation of the temple commences an unprecedented Jewish genocidal attempt by the Antichrist, which characterizes the last three and one-half years of "great tribulation."

Regarding the Israel Defense Forces' inability to prevent the "abomination of desolation" discussed above, Dr. Arnold Fruchtenbaum points out that the IDF can't even curtail the event. He suggests this evidences a weakness, or complacency, characterizing the IDF during the first half of the tribulation period. You can read the highlights of Dr. Fruchtenbaum's interview with me, called Is Psalm 83 a Great

Tribulation Event?, at this link: http://prophecydepot.blogspot.com/2009/12/is-psalm-83-great-tribulation-event.html

Conversely, the second half of the tribulation period is not characterized by IDF complacency, but by IDF catastrophe. Israelis and their soldiers appear to be on the run from the perils plaguing that period. Zechariah 13:8 says that two-thirds of the Israelis in the land will be killed. The Antichrist and his troops are on the rampage to annihilate the Jews. Both Dr. Fruchtenbaum and I concur, that this will probably prompt the IDF to flee, rather than fight.

Interestingly, Isaiah 17:13 speaks of mighty rushing nations, but the prophet doesn't use the usual Hebrew word for nations, which is goy. Goy is the Hebrew word utilized in the classic Armageddon passages like, Joel 3:2, Zechariah 12:3, 9, Isaiah 34:1-2, and Psalm 2:1. Goy is found approximately 512 times in Scripture, evidencing it as the typical word to describe the "Gentile nations." Isaiah uses the term goy sixty-six times throughout his sixty-six prophetic chapters, but never uses it once in Isaiah 17.

Instead, to describe the mighty rushing nations, Isaiah opts for the Hebrew word leom. This word appears approximately thirty-one times in Scripture and Isaiah 17 repeats it twice in the same context. The word means "to gather, a community:—nation, people."[217] The plural use of the word is leummim, and it is translated as "communities; an Arabian, or a descendent from Dedan, which was formerly located in modern day Saudi Arabia."[218] The usages of leom in the passage below identifies populations that ultimately appear to participate in Psalm 83.

The first biblical usage of leom is found in Genesis 25, describing two peoples whose descendants end up in Psalm 83; the Israelites and the Edomites.

> And the LORD said to her: "Two nations [goy] are in your womb, Two peoples [leom] shall be separated from your body; One people [Israelites of Jacob—leom] shall be stronger than the other, [Edomites from Esau - leom] And the older shall serve the younger." (Genesis 25:23).

The first and only biblical usage of the word leom in the plural, as leummim, is also found in Genesis 25, as an Arab descendent of Dedan. Dedan formed an area in what is today Northwest Saudi Arabia. Saudi Arabia is also in Psalm 83 under the banner of the Ishmaelites.

> Jokshan begot Sheba and Dedan. And the sons of Dedan were Asshurim, Letushim, and Leummim. (Genesis 25:3)

These two above passages identify Edomites, which have ethnical representation in the Palestinians today, and descendants of Dedan, which are modern-day Saudis. Both Palestinians and Saudis are involved in Psalm 83. For the above reasons, it is reasonable to presume that the destruction of Damascus, the desolation of the surrounding strong cities, and the disrespect toward Allah, all find a correlation to the events prophesied in Psalm 83.

> (Isaiah 17:14)—Then behold, at eventide, trouble! And before the morning, he is no more. This is the portion of those who plunder us, And the lot of those who rob us.

Isaiah concludes his oracle against Damascus by describing the length of time it takes for the city to become reduced to rubble. Overnight, this historic city is destroyed. One evening Damascus flourishes, but by the next morning it's obliterated. This occurs as the penalty portion of Genesis 12:3. Syria's capital city is reduced to ruins, because Syrians attempted to plunder Israel, probably in Psalm 83.

The bottom line is that Damascus can presently be destroyed overnight by the weapons technologies Israel presently possesses. Unless Syria changes its hateful disposition toward the nation of Israel soon, humanity could wake up one nearby morning to a flood of Syrian refugees exiting out of the Damascus rubble.

# TWENTY-TWO

# The Destruction of Damascus Continued

**"Syria Chemical Weapons: Israel Would Strike To Secure Syrian Arsenal"**

*Huffington Post 7/22/12*

**"US Concerned About Israeli Strike On Damascus"**

*Yeshiva World News 6/22/12*

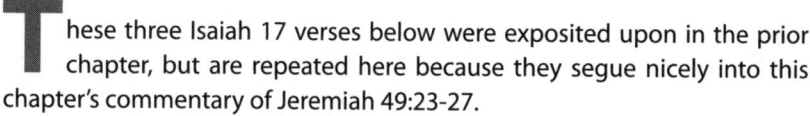

These three Isaiah 17 verses below were exposited upon in the prior chapter, but are repeated here because they segue nicely into this chapter's commentary of Jeremiah 49:23-27.

> The burden against Damascus. "Behold, Damascus will cease from *being* a city, And it will be a ruinous heap." (Isaiah 17:1)

> In that day his [Damascus] strong cities will be as a forsaken bough And an uppermost branch, Which they left because of the children of Israel; And there will be desolation. (Isaiah 17:9)

Then behold, at eventide, trouble! *And* [overnight] before the morning, he *is* no more. This *is* the portion of those who plunder us, [Israel] And the lot of those who rob us. (Isaiah 17:14)

Isaiah 17:1, 9, and 14, seemingly teach that Damascus will someday be reduced to a heap of rubble (verse 1) overnight, between some sunset and sunrise, because Damascus attempts to "plunder" and "rob" "the children of Israel," (verse 14) who in return retaliate (verse 9). The Hebrew word used for both plunder and rob is bazaz. This dual usage infers that Syria, represented by its capital city Damascus, will be guilty of plundering and pillaging Israel.

In direct alignment with the mandatory cursing aspects defined in Genesis 12:3, Syria's punishment is formatted similar to its aggression. Genesis 12:3b can be understood, "I must curse those who curse you." The pronoun "you" refers to the Israeli descendants of Abraham, Isaac, and Jacob. Simply stated, those seeking to curse the Israelis, must be cursed. Syria someday seeks to plunder Israel; therefore, Israel someday is empowered to plunder Syria in retaliation.

The Isaiah 17:9 verse informs us that Syrians from "strong cities" are displaced, inferring Syria is guilty of attacking populated or strong cities inside Israel. Isaiah 17:6 refers to these heavily populated Israeli cities as "fruitful branches," and announces there will be some survivors. The bottom line, according to Isaiah 17, is that Syria will experience widespread desolation, seemingly because they preemptively attempt to create desolation inside Israel.

Damascus will be destroyed, leaving Syria with no capital city, because Syria will apparently attempt to destroy Israeli claims to Jerusalem as its future capital city. This theme against Jerusalem seems to collaborate with the Damascus verses found in Jeremiah 49:23-27.

Against Damascus [southern Syria]. "Hamath [northern Syria] and Arpad [northern Syria] are shamed, For they have heard bad news. They are faint-hearted; There is trouble on the [Mediterranean] sea; It cannot be quiet. Damascus has grown feeble; She turns to flee [Syrian refugees], And fear has seized her. Anguish and sorrows have taken her like a woman in labor. Why is the city of praise [Jerusalem] not deserted, the city of My joy? Therefore her young men shall fall in her streets [civilian casualties], And all the men of war shall be cut off in that day [military casualties]," says the LORD of hosts. "I will kindle a fire in the wall of Damascus, And it shall consume the palaces of Ben-Hadad [Syrian capital buildings]." (Jeremiah 49:23-27).

The prophet points out that events inside Syria digress dramatically from bad to worse. The following tabulated bullet points below illustrate the gloomy destiny awaiting Damascus;

1. Bad News – becomes fainthearted,

2. There is trouble on the sea; It cannot be quiet,

3. The city has grown feeble,

4. She turns to flee,

5. Fear has seized her, like a woman in labor,

6. Her young men shall fall in her streets, (resulting in civilian casualties),

7. All the men of war shall be cut off, (resulting in military casualties),

8. The lord will kindle a fire and consume the palaces of Ben Hadad.

By connecting Jeremiah's passage to Isaiah's we get a grander picture surrounding the destruction of Damascus. Although some expositors teach that Jeremiah 49:23-27 found fulfillment during Jeremiah's time through the Babylonian conquest over Damascus, clues in Jeremiah's passage suggests otherwise. For instance, Jeremiah asks Damascus, "Why is the city of praise not deserted, the city of My joy?" This alludes to Jerusalem, which was destroyed and deserted during Jeremiah's lifetime. Therefore, Jeremiah's rhetorical question to Damascus about Jerusalem would prove pointless at the time. (For more information read the appendix called the Oracle of the Rhetorical in my book called Isalestine, The Ancient Blueprints of the Future Middle East).

Additionally, Jeremiah says Damascus becomes fainthearted because "there is trouble on the sea," which "cannot be quiet." The Babylonian conquest of Damascus was by land, rather than by any surrounding sea. Unless Jeremiah wants us to view the term "sea" allegorically to mean the Gentile world, like it does in Revelation 13:1 and elsewhere, or figuratively as a manner of speaking to a point, we must conclude Jeremiah's prophecy about Damascus was not fulfilled at the time of the Babylonian captivity.

Conversely, Jeremiah's passage makes complete sense when aligned with Isaiah 17. For instance Hamath and Arpad, two northern Syrian locations, are shamed because they receive troubling news. They become distressed along with Damascus, because they are all about to become battle zones.

These ancient cites, mentioned dozens of times in the Bible, historically ranked among the more important cities of Aram (modern-day Syria). Hamath is approximately 120 miles north of Damascus, and Arpad over 200 miles northeast of Damascus, about twenty-five miles north of today's Aleppo. Therefore, when Isaiah 17:9 predicts Syria's "strong cities will be as a forsaken bough And an uppermost branch," we presume from Jeremiah's descriptions the IDF's retaliation against Syria will cause the abandonment of several formidable "strong" Syrian cities in addition to Damascus.

The trouble on the disquieted sea is a literal threat today, since Israel suppos-edly has nuclear weapons concealed in Dolphin class submarines off the Middle East coastline of the Mediterranean Sea. Perhaps some surface to air missiles containing nuclear warheads could be launched toward Damascus by Israel from the Mediter-ranean. Could this be why Jeremiah says Damascus is seized by fear, grows feeble, and turns to flee as if anguished like a woman in labor? Is this why "young men shall fall in her streets, And all the men of war shall be cut off in that day?"

Notice Jeremiah predicts all the men of war, not a just a few troops, will be destroyed in this coming war. Presently the Syrian army is ranked 35th among world armies, and includes many "young men" 18 and older.[219] Jeremiah's prophecy causes us to consider the depths of Syria's defeat. Furthermore, the young men he alludes to may include both civilians and military personnel. Certainly, an assault that devastates an entire city like Damascus will cause much civilian loss of life. Consider the following information contained in the Encyclopedia of the Nations.[220]

> The population of Syria in 2003 was estimated by the United Nations at 17,800,000, which placed it as number 55 in population among the 193 nations of the world. In that year approximately 3% of the population was over 65 years of age, with another 41% of the population under 15 years of age. There were 102 males for every 100 females in the country in 2003. According to the UN, the annual population growth rate for 2000–2005 is 2.38%, with the projected population for the year 2015 at 23,018,000. The population density in 2002 was 95 per sq km (245 per sq mi), but most of it was concentrated in a small area; 70% of Syria's people live in Damascus and the six western provinces.

Damascus is the capital of one of Israel's main enemies and is a strategic target for Israel, in the event of a multi-front war with Iran, Hezbollah, Hamas, and Syria. Syria is among the Arab countries that refuses to recognize Israel's right to exist. They have warred against Israel in 1948, 1967, and 1973. Unlike Jordan and Egypt, Syria has refused to make peace with Israel because it wants the Golan Heights returned, which Israel captured in 1967. Technically, Syria is still at war with Israel, and tensions between the two countries remain high.

On September 6, 2007, Israel attacked a suspected nuclear reactor in the Deir ez-Zor region of Syria, as part of Operation Orchard. Threats and rumors of war have characterized the standoff between the two countries. In an interview with BBC TV on June 17, 2010, Syrian president Assad accused the reigning Israeli administration of Benjamin Netanyahu of being a "pyromaniac government," and stated that there was no way to achieve peace with such a government.[221] His comments came on the heels of the Mavi Marmara incident, where nine Turkish activists died on a flotilla bound for Gaza.

A few months prior, in February of 2010, Israel's blunt-talking foreign minister, Avigdor Lieberman, warned Syria's president, Bashar al-Assad, that the Assad family would lose power in any war with Israel. In a speech at Bar-Ilan University, near Tel Aviv, Mr. Lieberman said: "I think that our message must be clear to Assad. In the next war, not only will you lose, you and your family will lose the regime. Neither you will remain in power, nor the Assad family."[222]

Syria's arsenal includes the most advanced scud missiles in the world.[223] Additionally, Damascus is one of the closest major cities to Israel's borders and could be used as a staging ground for a ground and air attack into Israel, due to its ideal location between Iran to the east and Lebanon to the northwest. Reportedly, many Middle East terrorist organizations are headquartered in, or at least affiliated with Damascus, further heightening IDF concerns about humanity's oldest continuously inhabited city in recorded history. Damascus is thought to be between 4,000 to 5,000 years old.

Logically, if Israel comes under a multi-front attack from enemies possessing weapons of mass destruction, it will have to act aggressively, expeditiously, and decisively. Israel is the approximate size of the state of New Jersey, meaning a couple nuclear bombs could wipe the Jewish state off of the map. Israel doesn't have the luxury of waging a war of attrition. It's a matter of survival for the Jewish state and the destruction of Damascus by the IDF would indicate to its enemies that the war has become an all-or-nothing proposition.

# TWENTY-THREE

# Ezekiel 38-39 Overview

**"Anti-Putin protesters show their strength in Russia"**

*ABC News 9/16/12*

"Tens of thousands of demonstrators marched though Moscow under streaming banners, flags and balloons on Saturday to demand an end to President Vladimir Putin's long rule and show their protest movement remains strong."

This chapter is intended to compliment the earlier chapter called "Psalm 83 or Ezekiel 38: What's the Next Middle East News Headline?" It only presents a basic overview of certain parts of Ezekiel 38-39. Although a couple of paragraphs may seem somewhat repetitive to other parts of *this book*, they are included because they enhance the author's ability to paint an overview picture of these Ezekiel prophecies. The text of Ezekiel 38-39 can be read in the appendix called, "The Text of Psalm 83 and Ezekiel 38:1-39:20."

A cruel Russian leader appears to be presiding at the time Ezekiel 38 occurs. Some ponder the possibility that he could be Russian President Vladimir Putin, but whoever he is, we are informed he devises a maniacal plan against Israel.

"Thus says the Lord GOD: "On that day it shall come to pass *that* thoughts will arise in your [Russian] mind, and you will make an *evil plan*: You will say, 'I will go up against a land of unwalled villages; I will go to a peaceful people, who dwell safely, all of them dwelling without walls, and having neither bars nor gates'—to take plunder and to take booty, to stretch out your hand against the waste places *that are again* inhabited, and against a people gathered from the nations, who have acquired livestock and goods, who dwell in the midst of the land. Sheba, Dedan, the merchants of Tarshish, and all their young lions will say to you, 'Have you come to take plunder? Have you gathered your army to take booty, to carry away silver and gold, to take away livestock and goods, to take great plunder?"''" (Ezekiel 38:10-13; emphasis added)

These verses clearly evidences that the Russian leader forms an evil plan, which is to assemble a formidable strategic coalition in order to invade Israel for the sake of material gain. Ezekiel 38:12-13 points out that the invaders seek to take a spoil. I point out the strategic aspect of his evil plan in the chapter entitled "Russia Forms an Evil Plan to Invade Israel," in my book called *Revelation Road, Hope Beyond the Horizon*. For those of you not familiar with the official Old Testament identity of this Russian leader, he is referenced early on in Ezekiel's prophecy.

> Now the word of the LORD came to me, saying, "Son of man, set your face against Gog, of the land of Magog, the prince of Rosh, Meshech, and Tubal, and prophesy against him, and say, 'Thus says the Lord GOD: "Behold, I *am* against you, O Gog, the prince of Rosh, Meshech, and Tubal.""'' (Ezekiel 38:1-3)

Gog, is the lead figure who hails from the land of Magog. Some scholars debate whether or not Gog is an individual or a location within the greater territory of Magog; however, Ezekiel calls Gog a prince and uses the pronoun "he" to identify him. The opinion among some scholars, which I favor, is that Gog represents a title of an individual, rather than a specific name or place. Gog, would be likened to a Caesar from ancient Rome, or a Czar from the former Soviet Union, or the Kaiser from Germany, prior to the Nazi era.

The connection between Magog and Russia runs partially through the Scythians. This association was made centuries ago, by the secular Jewish historian Josephus. He called them an "invading horde from the north."[224] During Ezekiel's time, Magog existed in the proximity of where Russia is today. Wikipedia states, "In the 17th and 18th centuries, foreigners regarded the Russians as descendants of Scythians. It became conventional to refer to Russians as Scythians in 18th century poetry."[225]

Because the name Russia only dates back to around the eleventh century AD, it makes the Magog-to-Russia connection a bit difficult, but most scholars point out that Ezekiel 38:15 declares that Gog personally comes out from the far north, which directionally to Israel is the location of Russia. Many scholars, including Dr. Arnold Fruchtenbaum, Chuck Missler, Dr. Ron Rhodes, Dr. David Hocking, Dr. David Reagan, and Joel Rosenberg, subscribe to Russia being identified by Ezekiel.

Regarding Iran's involvement in the Ezekiel (or Gog of Magog) invasion, refer to Ezekiel 38:5, where Iran is identified as Persia. The Iranian-Persian connection is easily made, considering Persia was renamed Iran in 1935 AD.

For an exhaustive look at Ezekiel 38-39, I have footnoted my recommended readings on the subject.[226] Below is a nutshell outline of the Ezekiel 38-39 prophecies.

Ezekiel 38:1-7 lists the nine-member coalition of Gog's hordes, consisting of armies from Magog, Rosh, Meshech, Tubal, Persia, Ethiopia (Cush), Libya (Put), Gomer, and

Togarmah. To discover their modern-day identities, please refer to the Ezekiel 38 Invaders image below.

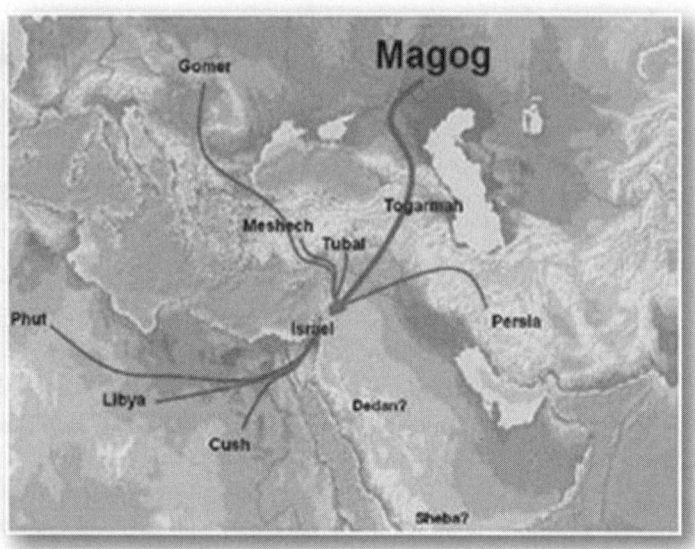

**Fig. 6. Ezekiel 38 Invaders** *(Map obtained from Chuck Missler's Koinonia House Ministries. Text imposed by the author. Some people believe Gomer represents Germany, but many others teach that Gomer settled in Asia Minor.)*

Ezekiel 38:8-10 appropriates the general timing and battlefield location of the invasion. The prophecy occurs in the latter years, upon the land of Israel. Prerequisites of the invasion require that the nation of Israel be reestablished, that the worldwide re-gathering of the Jews be underway, and that the Israelis live in a condition of national security.

It is safe to assume that the first two requirements have been met. Israel was restored as the Jewish State on May 14, 1948, and Jews have been returning steadily ever since. However, the last prerequisite does not presently exist, in my estimation. Israelis are not dwelling safely in their homeland. They live under constant threat by multiple surrounding enemies. This point was previously presented in the chapter called, "Psalm 83 or Ezekiel 38: What's the Next Middle East News Headline?"

Ezekiel 38:11-13 informs us that Russia's leader prepares an evil plan to invade Israel and capture great plunder. The plunder consists of agricultural and commercial goods, as well as gold and silver. At least four more populations are introduced into the prophecy, apparently as protestors. These are Sheba (Yemen), Dedan (Saudi Arabia), the Merchants of Tarshish, (Britain or Spain, or both), and all their Young Lions. (United States of America, and / or Central and South America).

Ezekiel 38:14 through 39:6 informs us the attackers will be many, and they come against Israel primarily from the north. We are reminded the event finds fulfillment in the "latter days," and that the Lord warned of the event well in advance. Moreover, these verses confirm that the invaders are destroyed by the Lord, through an Old Testament type of fire and brimstone battle. This is important to note, because it reminds us that the Israel Defense Forces (IDF) of today, are apparently not a factor in this battle.

Ezekiel 39:7-8 provides the Lord's purpose for personally defeating this massive Mideast invasion.

> "So I will make My holy name known in the midst of My people Israel, and I will not *let them* profane My holy name anymore. Then the nations shall know that *I am* the LORD, the Holy One in Israel. Surely it is coming, and it shall be done," says the Lord GOD. "This *is* the day of which I have spoken." (Ezekiel 39:7-9)

It is vital to recognize the significance of what the prophet Ezekiel declares in these verses. They represent the summation of the divine purpose surrounding this prophetic event. He is emphasizing that the God of his people, the Jews, is upholding His Holy Name in the end times through the nation of Israel. This beckons the question:

Where on Earth is the Church, God's People Presently, at the Time of this Event?

Perhaps more importantly, it notifies the world that the God of the Jews is a promise keeper. The Magog invaders seek to annihilate the race that the Lord appointed virtually impossible to eradicate. One point made in other parts of this book that bare repeating, is that genocidal attempts of the Jews are all doomed to failure unless they meet the stringent requirements specified in Jeremiah 31:35-37.

Ezekiel 39:9-10 clues us in to the types of weaponry the invaders possess. Israel will be able to convert the enemy weapons into fuel for at least seven years. The picture is of energy provision for the entire nation, rather than a few isolated households. Verse 9 says "those who dwell in the cities" utilize this converted weapons-grade fuel. The widespread use and lengthy seven year span suggests that the weapons must be far more sophisticated than wooden bows and arrows, which would undoubtedly only last a short while. I mention this because some expositors today limit the weapons to wooden ones. I doubt nuclear non-proliferation will reduce Russian arsenals to wood between now and then.

There may actually be more than seven years' worth of fuel provided by these weapons, but the possibility looms large that the events occurring at the mid-point of the tribulation period interrupts the continued usage of the weapons. At this critical mid-trib point on the end-time's timeline, three-and-one-half years into the tribulation period, Israelis come under genocidal attack by the Antichrist. Thus, they are preoccupied with survival and probably not weapons conversion. If so, then there could be eight-plus years of weapons fuel, but no Jews taking time to harness the additional energy.

These missiles and rockets probably include the ABCs of weaponry—atomic, biological, and chemical. We can presume this because these types of weapons already exist inside the arsenals of Russia and some of their cohorts. Additionally, the dead soldiers appear to require Hazmat (Hazardous Materials) teams to assist with their burial according to Ezekiel 39:14-16. The fascinating fact is that whatever the weapons configuration, Israel will possess the technological know-how to convert them into national energy. Today, whether it is cell phones or irrigation techniques, Israel is on the cutting-edge of technological advances.

Ezekiel 39:11-16 describes the location of the mass burial grounds of the destroyed armies of Gog. A valley east of what is probably the Dead Sea is renamed the Valley of Hamon Gog, which means the "hordes or multitudes" of Gog, in Hebrew. Why I believe it refers to a valley in modern-day Jordan is explained in the chapter called "Greater Israel."

In this section, we also find that the Israelis will be burying the dead in order to cleanse the land. This could imply two things. One, that the hordes of Gog's dead soldiers are contaminated, requiring a professional quarantine burial and two, that the Jews are adhering to their ancient Levitical Law. Concerning the latter, Dr. Ron Rhodes writes in his book Northern Storm Rising:

> "From the perspective of the Jews, the dead must be buried because exposed corpses are a source of ritual contamination to the land (Numbers 19:11-22; Deuteronomy 21:1-9). The land must therefore be completely cleansed and purged of all defilement. Neither the enemies nor their belongings (their weapons) can be left to pollute the land!"[227]

Ezekiel 39:17-20 is an invitation "to every sort of bird and to every beast of the field" to partake of the sacrificial meal of the "flesh" and "blood" of the invaders. This passage is not for the faint of heart. I remember hearing expert Joel Rosenberg, teach this topic at a Calvary Chapel Chino Hills prophecy conference and he brought tears streaming down from my eyes.

Additionally foretold, the creatures are instructed, "to drink the blood" of the defeated "princes." This implies that not only the Magog infantry, but their governments are destroyed. Two questions come to mind when reading these three sobering verses: "How can the hordes of Gog's dead soldiers be contaminated," and "How can every sort of bird and beast get to Israel?"

Regarding the first question, we will have to assume that if some of the dead soldiers are contaminated, the birds and beasts will detect this and ingest those that aren't. Regarding the migration of every sort of vulture-type bird, the fact is they are already beginning to nest in Israel. Whereas, through the years they would make Israel a mere migratory pit-stop, they are now setting up shop in the Jewish state by the thousands. The anomaly is so intriguing that several Israeli tour guides have been known to make mention of this on their excursions.

Ezekiel 39:21-29 concludes the chapter with a recap of some Jewish history and a promise to the faithful remnant of Israel that the Lord will pour out His spirit upon them in the end.

# TWENTY-FOUR

# Iran's Double Jeopardy in the End Times

## The prophecies of Elam and Persia

"Iran condemned after over claim 'cancerous tumor' Israel has no place in Mideast"

*NBC News 8/18/12*

"Israel Has Until Week's End to Strike Iran Nuclear Facility, Bolton Says"

*Fox News 8/17/10*

The prophet Jeremiah issued and interesting prophecy that seems to remain unfulfilled, and could involve Iran's nuclear program. The subject of Jeremiah's prophetic utterances is Elam . During the prophet's time, Elam comprised what is today considered the central western portions of Iran. Elam basically hugged much of the northeastern coastline of the Persian Gulf. Persia, spoken of by Jeremiah's contemporary Ezekiel, in Ezekiel 38:5, encompassed most of today's northern Iran at their time. The following Scriptures from Jeremiah 49 and commentary below it, suggests that Iran could be involved in dual end time prophecies, a double jeopardy of sorts. This would include the prophecies of Elam by Jeremiah and those regarding Persia in Ezekiel 38-39.

Below is a study of Jeremiah's prophecy concerning Elam. Jeremiah 49:34-39

The word of the LORD that came to Jeremiah the prophet against Elam, in the beginning of the reign of Zedekiah king of Judah, saying, "Thus says the LORD of hosts: 'Behold, *I will* break the bow of Elam, The foremost of their might. Against Elam *I will* bring the four winds From the four quarters of heaven, And scatter them toward all those winds; There shall be no nations where the outcasts of Elam will not go. For *I will* cause Elam to be dismayed before their enemies And before those who seek their life. *I will* bring disaster upon them, My fierce anger,' says the LORD; 'And *I will* send the sword [*military* campaign] after them Until I have consumed them. *I will* set My throne in Elam, And [I] *will* destroy from there the king and the princes,' says the LORD. 'But it shall come to pass in the latter days: *I will* bring back the captives of Elam,' says the LORD." (emphasis added)

## *Jeremiah 49:34-39 Commentary*

The most important declaration to note in this passage is that Elam has done something that has fiercely angered the Lord, "My fierce anger." As a result, the Lord has Jeremiah declare eight times, "I will" bring about a judgment against Elam. Nine related prophecies result as listed below. "I will:

1. Break the bow of Elam, the foremost of their might,

2. Bring the four winds from the four quarters of heaven,

3. Scatter them [Elamites] toward all those winds [worldwide],

4. Cause Elam to be dismayed before their enemies and before those who seek their life,

5. Bring disaster upon them, my fierce anger,

6. Send the sword after them until I have consumed them,

7. Set My throne in Elam,

8. Destroy from there the king and the princes, and

9. [in the latter days] bring back the captives of Elam."

Items #1-3 above appear to result from the expressed intentions described in #4-6. As stated above, the key to grasping the why's and wherefore's of Jeremiah's utterances against Elam is in recognizing that the Elamites have done something to anger the Lord as per #5. Because they have aroused the Lord, they will be "dismayed" in #4 as "disaster" in #5 befalls them. The nature of the disaster is by the "sword," suggestint that it is militarily related, in #6.

The disaster is severe in #6, "until I have consumed them." And, it is witnessed by Elam's "enemies" and those who "seek their life" in #4. If the event were to happen in the near future, the enemies seeking to end Iran's quest for regional power, and dispossess the rogue state of nuclear weapons would be: America, Israel, and / or some predominately Sunni Muslim countries like Saudi Arabia, Egypt, and the United Arab Emirates. Additionally, several other countries have levied sanctions against Iran because of its nuclear program.

## Historical Overview of Jeremiah's Elamite Prophecy

Elam was a son of Shem, Noah's oldest son. His descendants settled in what is today central western Iran, east of the Tigris River. Their capital city was Susa. Today, Susa's city ruins are located in Southwest Iran, about 150 miles north of the Persian Gulf.[228]

The Elamites were a war-like people, according to Genesis 14:1-9. Jeremiah issued this prophecy regarding Elam about 597 BC, one year prior to Nebuchadnezzer's conquest over Elam around 596 BC.[229] There is some evidence that the Babylonian king put Elamites under his subjugation, but as a whole the Elamite culture and language remained intact and the Elamites were not dispersed worldwide, as called for in the prophecy.

Subsequently, Cyrus of Persia conquered Babylon about 539 BC, beginning the Persian Empire period, which lasted until around 330 BC.[230] The Persian Empire extended throughout most of the Middle East and parts of northern Africa, and encompassed Elam. However, Ezra 4:9 reveals the Elamites still had political representation during the time. And, Ezra 2:7, 31 states that the Elamites returned to their homeland after the Babylonian captivity.

Even though power shifts occurred after the Persian period, the Elamites still survived in Elam. Acts 2:9, written several centuries afterward, around the time of Christ's first advent, informs us that the Elamites and their language still existed. Furthermore, Jeremiah 25:17-29 and Isaiah 11:11 evidence the existence of an end time's Elam.

The above historical tracking, aligned with the nine prophetic requirements of Jeremiah, suggests that the pertinent Elamite prophecies remain unfulfilled. Importantly, none of the above indicates that Elam aroused the fierce anger of the Lord, also suggesting an event in waiting.

We are told that the "bow" of Elam will be broken. Iran will be struck at the "foremost of their might." The Hebrew word used as foremost is reshith, and can also be translated at the chief, choicest, or finest point of its might. Additionally, we're informed that Iranian refugees will flee into the nations of the world. Importantly, we are informed: "it shall come to pass in the latter days." This infers the following:

## Come to pass in the latter days

Since this prophecy does not appear to have been fulfilled historically and applies to the "latter days," the foremost of Iran's power may include its nuclear facilities. Along the lines of this being an end-time's event, Dr. Arnold Fruchtenbaum, founder of Ariel Ministries, records the following in his book The Footsteps of the Messiah:[231]

> "Although Persia or Iran (ancient Elam) is not an Arab state but a Persian one, its future will be examined here because it shares the same religion (Islam) with Moslem Arabs. Peace will come between Israel and Iran by means of destruction, according to Jeremiah 49:34-39. In verses 34-38 Jeremiah described the destruction of Elam, with the inhabitants being completely dispersed all over the world. But then verse 39 declares: 'But it shall come to pass in the latter days, that I will bring back the captivity of Elam, says Jehovah.'
>
> The destruction of Iran will be partial, and the dispersion will be temporary. Eventually the inhabitants will return and resettle Iran. The future of Iran is similar to that of Egypt, but the length of time they will be in dispersion is not revealed. So peace will come between Israel and Iran via destruction, dispersion, and then a conversion and a return. There will be a saved nation of Elam (Persia or Iran) in the (Millennial) Kingdom."

Dr. Fruchtenbaum points out that these Jeremiah verses represent a forthcoming event. He acknowledges, "The destruction of Iran will be partial, and the dispersion will be temporary."

## Break the bow

Isaiah 22:6 tells us that the Elamites were experts in archery. Jeremiah appears to pick up on this theme in his prophecy. The prophet utilizes the Hebrew word for an archer's bow, which is qesheth. Without a functional bow, an archer is unable to launch arrows at his target. This implies Iran may be unable to launch rockets or nuclear warheads as a result of being struck militarily, by the "sword," at its place of foremost might.

## Foremost of their might

This suggests Iran will be strategically targeted at the pinnacle point of its power, which today includes its developing nuclear program. This could also include its military installations, headquarters, and armories One of Iran's chief nuclear site is in the area of Bushehr, and is located today inside the boundaries of ancient Elam. It is possible that Jeremiah predicted an attack upon Iran's nuclear site(s) approximately 2,600 hundred years ago.

> ### "Attack against Bushehr nuclear reactor could kill hundreds of thousands"
>
> *Examiner 9/6/12*

Could such an attack create a Chernobyl-effect inside part of Iran, causing many to evacuate into various nations of the world? Is that what Jeremiah 49:36 alludes to below?

> "Against Elam I [the Lord] will bring the four winds from the four quarters of heaven, And scatter them toward all those winds [away from the radiation fallout]; There shall be no nations where the outcasts of Elam will not go."

Jeremiah uses the Hebrew word kol, which rather than being translated as a scattering toward, or into, the four winds, means a thorough dispersion into everywhere, or throughout. In essence, it suggests that an event happens in Elam predicating a massive evacuation in all geographic directions. Presently, at the time of authoring this section, the Bushehr nuclear plant is loaded with nuclear fuel rods, and if struck militarily, could cause radiation fallout to occur.

It is doubtful that Jeremiah's prediction of an Iranian worldwide dispersion has occurred historically, meaning it probably remains a pending prophetic event. Furthermore, Iran's involvement in the Ezekiel 38-39 prophecy prohibits the possibility that all Iranians experience a worldwide dispersion prior to the fulfillment of Ezekiel's prophecy. Iran appears to be one of Russia's primary allies in Ezekiel's prophecy, meaning Iran maintains an army, although it may be weakened, at the time.

Thus, if the breaking of Elam's bow and the worldwide dispersion of Elamites has not occurred historically, then Jeremiah 49:34-39 and Ezekiel 38-39 could be separate, or the same event(s). Perhaps the breaking of Elam's bow occurs before Ezekiel 38 and temporarily adversely affects Iran's military prowess, but does not permanently eliminate it. Then the worldwide dispersion occurs separately as a result of Ezekiel 38.

There is another possibility: maybe the broken "bow" (nuclear weapons or nuclear facilities like Bushehr) is broken, causing some isolated geographical contamination. This could force the affected populations to disperse out of Iran into uncontaminated neighboring nations. As stated earlier, ancient Elam represents only a portion of modern-day Iran. Thus, it is plausible the Iranian exodus is not nationwide, but limited to the affected populations. This would enable Iran to muster up an army in the gap-period, between the breaking of its bow and the joining in with the Ezekiel invasion.

## Iran Fiercely Angers the Lord

### "Wipe Israel 'off the map' Iranian says"

New York Times 10/17/05

*"Iran's conservative new president, Mahmoud Ahmadinejad, said Wednesday that Israel must be "wiped off the map" and that attacks by Palestinians would destroy it."*

As stated in #5 above, disaster befalls Elam because they provoke the Lord to fierce anger. Since the Lord is not easily angered, what might Elam, or Iran today, be guilty of? Perhaps the fact that Iran's apocalyptically-minded leadership threatens to wipe Israel off the map, and that they are developing a nuclear program to accomplish that dastardly deed, could have something to do with it. Iran publicly denounces the Jewish state's right to exist, and is guilty of antagonizing Israel through its proxies, Hezbollah, Syria, and Hamas. Additionally, Iran has fomented terrorism and violence since the Iranian Revolution in 1979.

According to Zechariah 2:8, Israel is the "apple of God's eye." Additionally, Ezekiel 39:7 declares the Lord intends to uphold His holy name through Israel, and according to Ezekiel 38:8, 16 this occurs in the end times. The fact that the Lord loves Israel, and still has end time plans in place for the Jewish state, provides sufficient grounds for Him to be upset if Iran attempts to thwart those plans by decimating Israel. In fact, throughout all of Elam's history since Jeremiah's time, it doesn't appear until recently that Elam, apart from being religiously pagan, has done anything to provoke the Lord to such a fierce anger.

## The Future of Iran

Since Jeremiah 49:34-39 appears to remain unfulfilled, the nine prophecies described could occur as follows:

## The Military Option

Iran's present enmity toward Israel has fiercely angered the Lord. As the Lord sits on His heavenly throne presently, He is extremely upset with the rogue state of Iran. This puts Iran in jeopardy of the severe judgments the prophet predicts. The reprobate state is about to be invaded militarily, by the sword, at the foremost center of its might. The target area is restricted to only the western central region of the nation; i.e., ancient Elam, Persia is seemingly not included. The attack will be disastrous, witnessed and / or caused by Iran's enemies, and result in much dismay in Iran. As a result of the military invasion and wind patterns, the affected Iranians disperse outside of the area into other nations. This suggests that nuclear fallout from Bushehr's nuclear facility occurs at the time.

Items listed in #7-9 above foretell that the Lord will set His throne in Elam, destroy their king and the princes, and in the latter days bring back their captives. This means the presiding Iranian leadership in the affected area is destroyed at the time of the breaking of the bow at the foremost of Elam's might. Since Persia of Ezekiel 38:5 is not affected by the events in Elam, it remains in place to join up with Russia's coalition in the Gog of Magog invasion. This is regionally possible because when Ezekiel prophesied, Persia had not yet become a world empire and did not include Elam territorially. Thus, modern-day Iran was comprised of both Persia and Elam when the prophets wrote.

## The Natural Disaster Option

This option finds potential merit by chronologically ordering the events described in Jeremiah 49:34-38. It would probably play out similar to the military option above, but the military aspect comes after Elam's bow is broken, rather than before. The military option suggests that some sword invasion targets Elam's foremost point of might, but chronologically Jeremiah lists the sword subsequent to the breaking of the bow. Items #1-5 occur prior to the reference in #6 to a sword. In the natural disaster option the sword is a by-product of the disaster. The passage reads, "'For I will cause Elam to be dismayed before their enemies And before those who seek their life. I will bring disaster upon them, [Elamites] My fierce anger,' says the LORD; 'And [subsequently] I will send the sword [military campaign] after them Until I have consumed them.'"

Iran has a history of seismic activity. It has experienced a multitude of significant earthquakes, dating back as far as the 7.3 Silakhor quake on January 23, 1909, with an estimated 6,000 fatalities. At least 40,000 were killed in the 7.4 Mangil-Rudbar quake of June 20, 1990. Iran has experienced about ten 6.0 or greater quakes already in the twenty-first century.

Wikipedia states the following:

> Iran is one of the most seismically active countries in the world, being crossed by several major fault lines that cover at least 90% of the country. As a result, earthquakes in Iran occur often and are destructive.[232]

In light of Japan's Fukushima nuclear disaster, that resulted from the 8.9 quake and subsequent tsunami in March of 2011, it is possible that Iran could experience a natural disaster brought on by an earthquake, as well. Jeremiah says; "I will bring disaster upon them, My fierce anger," says the LORD." Matthew 24:7 predicts earthquakes will occur worldwide in the end times. Luke 21:11 declares that there will be many great earthquakes.

## The Ezekiel 38 - 39 Option

Since the Jeremiah 49:34-39, and Ezekiel 38 prophecies appear to be end-time's events, they could be part of the same episode. Ezekiel 38:18-39:7 clearly shows that the Lord is angry with the Magog invaders, which includes Iran (Persia), and as a result destroys them all. Perhaps the Jeremiah 49:34-39 prophecies simply add more detail to the fifty-two descriptive verses contained in Ezekiel 38-39. This would make sense and demonstrate a pattern in Scripture that other prophets have followed. Details of a prophecy are often given by more than one prophet. However, this option doesn't address the logical question; "Why did Jeremiah allude to Elam, but Ezekiel to Persia?"

## The Lord Establishes Authority over Elam

Personally, I suspect Jeremiah and Ezekiel identify for us two differing last day's unfulfilled prophetic events, that are regionally specific to the time of their authorship. Perhaps addressing Jeremiah 49:38a, which declares "I will set My throne in Elam," holds a clue to our better understanding of his prophecy. This is an interesting statement for two reasons. First, Elam is outside the Promised Land described in Genesis 15:18, which stops westward of Elam at the Euphrates River. This beckons the question: why would the Lord position His throne outside the Promised Land? Second, Isaiah 66:1 declares the Lord's literal throne is in heaven. This beckons the question: why would the throne be moved anywhere on Earth prior to the Messianic reign of Christ?

Jeremiah 49:38 does not describe an event characteristic of the messianic kingdom. It discusses the destruction of an Elamite king and his princes. The messianic kingdom is biblically presented to be a time of peace wherein swords are converted into plowshares, and the knowledge of the Lord covers the expanse of the earth.[233] Most of the killing of the world's bad kings and princes occurs prior to the establishment of the messianic kingdom at the end of Armageddon. Thus, Jeremiah 49:38

appears to happen before the return of Christ to establish His 1,000 year kingdom on Earth.[234]

Therefore, for these above reasons it is difficult to view this "throne" Jeremiah 49:38 alludes to as literal. The Hebrew word Jeremiah uses for throne is kisse, and it means a seat of honor, a throne, or authority.[235] Jeremiah 49:38 states the throne gets set up in Elam, and then from that throne the king and princes are destroyed. Thus, who or whatever destroys the king and princes of Elam, probably occurs antecedent and is likely related to the throne in Elam. Jeremiah 49:37 talks about the sword used to consume the Elamites. Therefore, the sword and the throne seemingly find connection. The same prior verse notates that there are those who seek to kill the Elamites.

Hence the connection could be as follows: Because Iran has angered the Lord in that they plot the destruction of Israel, in turn the Lord gives authority (throne) and military empowerment (sword) to those who seek to destroy Iran. Listed above was an assortment of Iran's enemies, and any one of them could be empowered militarily to execute the Lord's will against Iran. It could be America, Israel, Saudi Arabia in conjunction with several other Sunni Arab States; or less likely, other members of the international community. It could be a combination of any of the above.

*Caveat to Jeremiah 49:34-39: Unlike Ezekiel 38-39, Jeremiah's Elamite prophecies are less commonly taught. All of the author comments in this chapter are interpretive suggestions only of Jeremiah's prophecy regarding Elam. These interpretations are the result of a modicum of study performed by the author. Some possibilities border on classic newspaper exegesis, which the author attempts to avoid. Readers are encouraged to thoroughly research Jeremiah 49:34-39 carefully on their own for greater understanding of the text. If the prophecy can be proven to have found historical fulfillment then some of the author's comments regarded with the subject matter should be ignored.*

# Why Iran's Absent from Psalm 83

**"Iran "concerned" over "Saudi Arabia's recent violent measures"**

*Iran Daily Brief 7/13/12*

**"Iranian plot to kill Saudi ambassador thwarted, U.S. officials say"**

*CNN Justice 10/11/11*

This chapter picks up where the prior chapter left off concerning Iran's potential double jeopardy in the end times. It is difficult to know whether or not Jeremiah 49:34-39 foretells of an Israeli air-strike upon Iran's nuclear sites resulting in nuclear fallout. However, if the prophets' predictions are about to find a modern-day fulfillment, then that could be exactly what he describes. Jeremiah says Elam gets attacked at the foremost of its might, and that the Elamites subsequently evacuate their homeland, and scatter amongst various world nations.

A strategic IDF / IAF strike is a plausible scenario because Israel has a history of attacking the nuclear sites of its enemies. Israel struck the Osirak nuclear plant in Iraq on June 7, 1981, and on September 6, 2007 struck the suspected Syrian nuclear site in the Deir ez-Zor region. Iran possesses several such sites, and Israel considers Iran to be an enemy.

It is interesting that Iran's modern day proxies, Syria, Hezbollah, and Hamas all appear to be members of the Psalm 83 Arab confederacy. Surprisingly, Iran does not! Why not, considering the rogue nation is presently considered by many to be Israel's number one existential threat, and Psalm 83 appears imminent?

The news headlines of this chapter illustrate that there is mounting tension between Sunni Muslim countries, like Saudi Arabia, and Iran, which is primarily comprised of Shiite Muslims. Saudi Arabia is part of Psalm 83, along with other Sunni states like Egypt and Jordan. Maybe the friction between the Sunni and Shia factions factors into Iran's absence in Psalm 83, but there could be other reasons to consider.

In Psalm 83, Syrians and Iraqis are identified under the banner of Assyria, Hezbollah via Tyre, and Hamas connects with Philistia. However, there is no observable mention of Iranians by their three primary historical names, Elamites, Medes, or Persians. This is puzzling, considering Iran reportedly formed bona fide war-pacts in December, 2009, with this troublesome Muslim trio.[236] Some suggest Iran may be included in Psalm 83 as part of the Assyrians. The Assyrians seem to be among the stronger members in the psalm, because they support the Jordanian army referred to as the children of Lot (Moab and Ammon) in Psalm 83:8.

> Assyria also has joined with them; they have helped the children of Lot [Jordanians]. *Selah* (Psalm 83:8)

The pitfall of connecting modern-day Iran with Assyria is that during the psalmist's time, Assyria only comprised much of what is today northern Syria and part of Iraq. In order for Iran to be mentioned in Psalm 83, the psalmist would need to have included, Elam, Media, or Persia in the confederate lineup. At the time, Elam existed in what is now west-central Iran, Media existed in eastern Iran and far beyond, and Persia occupied primarily the northerly parts of today's Iran, a few centuries after the psalm was penned.[237] Thus, it is reasonably safe to exclude Iranians, which are primarily of Persian descent, from the predominately Arab confederacy of Psalm 83.

## Iran is Persian and Psalm 83 is Arab

The Persian verses Arab distinction made in the previous sentence may be part of the reason Iran doesn't participate alongside their Arab proxies in Psalm 83. The confederacy is dominated by Arab populations. Arabs and Persians have a longstanding history of warring against each other, dating as far back as the Persian conquest of the Babylonians around 539 BC. In modern history, Iraq and Iran fought against each other from 1980-1988.

Saudis, as the Ishmaelites, and Egyptians, as the Hagarenes, are members of Psalm 83 and they may feel threatened by any Iranian meddling in the Arab-Israeli war. Both of these Arab countries are deeply concerned about Iran's present nuclear aspirations, and fear Iran's greater goal is to subdue their respective nations in order to form a Shiite Crescent throughout the Middle East.

The Arab verses Persian argument is not the only possible reason Iran refrains from participating in the Psalm 83 War. Possibility number two is that part of Iran may be temporarily incapacitated at the time, according to a generally overlooked prophecy issued by Jeremiah.

## The Dual End-Time Prophecies of Iran

(*Although some of this portion of commentary may seem repetitive from the previous chapter, it is included because it is germane to the understanding of why Iran might be excluded from the Psalm 83 confederacy.*)

Even though Iran appears absent from the climactic, concluding Arab-Israeli War, they are not excluded from two other significant end-time's events. The one most widely taught among eschatologists is the Ezekiel 38, Gog of Magog invasion of Israel. Persia is clearly identified militarily in Ezekiel's invasion "with shield and helmet."

Persia, Ethiopia, and Libya are with them, all of them *with* shield and helmet; (Ezekiel 38:5)

Perhaps Persia's utter destruction in Ezekiel's prophecy prohibits Iran from fighting in Psalm 83. Although this would satisfactorily answer the question about Iran's apparent absence in the Arab war, the problem is that Psalm 83 seems to precede Ezekiel 38. If this is the case, then Iran's "shield and helmet," could still exist when the Arabs come against Israel.

The prophecy that may precede Ezekiel 38, and partially answer the question about Iran's mysterious absence in Psalm 83, is located in Jeremiah 49:34-39. As previously discussed, Jeremiah 49:35 predicts Iran gets struck at the foremost of its might, which could allude to its nuclear program. Then, the next two verses inform us that the affected Iranians will be scattered out of the immediate area into world nations. Apparently, this dispersion is the direct result of this disastrous strike.

Against Elam I will bring the four winds From the four quarters of heaven [potentially causing the spread of nuclear fallout], And scatter them toward all those winds; There shall be no nations where the outcasts of Elam will not go. For I will cause Elam to be dismayed before their enemies And before those who seek their life. I will bring disaster [potentially nuclear] upon them, My fierce anger," says the LORD; (Jeremiah 49:36-37a)

Jeremiah and Ezekiel were contemporaries of each other. They both wrote around 2,600 years ago. Why did Ezekiel prophesy about Persia, and Jeremiah about Elam? Geographically, they occupied two adjoining territories at the time, and were distinct civilizations. Presently, Persia and Elam comprise greater Iran. A careful study suggests both Ezekiel's and Jeremiah's Iranian prophecies appear to be end time events, awaiting fulfillment.

The possible explanations of Jeremiah's prophecy given in the prior chapter, makes one wonder if Iran's nuclear program comes under attack soon, rendering Iran of little military utility when Psalm 83 takes place. Additionally, perhaps nuclear fall-out causes Iranians from the central west coast to evacuate into other nations, which would still potentially leave Persia, (northern Iran) with some remaining shields and helmets to fight with in Ezekiel 38.

It is critically important to note that Ezekiel intentionally omits Elam from the Gog of Magog invasion. This probably means that not all of modern-day Iran participates in the infamous Gog of Magog invasion of Israel. This conclusion can be drawn by recognizing that Ezekiel 32 identifies Elam and Meshech and Tubal. Meshech and Tubal are listed in the Magog invasion, but Elam is not. Why not? Why didn't Ezekiel list Elam alongside Persia to identify the entirety of modern-day Iran in his predicted invasion?

> "There *is Elam* [Iran] and all her multitude, All around her grave, All of them slain, fallen by the sword, Who have gone down uncircumcised to the lower parts of the earth, Who caused their terror in the land of the living; Now they bear their shame with those who go down to the Pit. They have set her bed in the midst of the slain, With all her multitude, With her graves all around it, All of them uncircumcised, slain by the sword; Though their terror was caused In the land of the living, Yet they bear their shame With those who go down to the Pit; It was put in the midst of the slain. "There *are Meshech* and *Tubal* [Turkey] and all their multitudes, With all their graves around it, All of them uncircumcised, slain by the sword, Though they caused their terror in the land of the living. (Ezek. 32:24-26, NKJV; emphasis added).

The fact that Ezekiel lists Persia in Ezekiel 27:10 and Ezekiel 38:5, and Elam in Ezekiel 32:24, implies that he recognized the territorial and ethnic distinctions between these two populations during his time. He probably omits Elam for the same reason that he omits the Arab populations identified in Psalm 83:6-8, which is because Elam and the Arabs of Psalm 83 do not participate in the Ezekiel 38 invasion.

The probable reason the Psalm 83 Arabs abstain is because they are dealt with in a prior separate war, won by the IDF. The reason Elam isn't listed is because Jeremiah 49:34-39 tells us the Elamites are also involved in their own separate prophecy. Thus, there appear to be three distinct end time Mideast prophecies identified: Psalm 83 (Arabs), Ezekiel 38-39 (Persians), and Jeremiah 49:34-39 (Elamites).

In summary, it is important to note that clear territorial distinctions existed between Elam and Persia when Jeremiah and Ezekiel prophesied. It is doubtful that all of modern-day Iran participates in the Magog invasion of Israel in Ezekiel 38. More likely is the possibility that only northern Iran joins in with Magog (Russia); otherwise Ezekiel should have included both Persia and Elam in his prophecy. Since Elam is not part of Ezekiel 38, it suggests that Jeremiah's prophecy regarding Elam is a separate prophetic event. If Elam is struck at the foremost of its might prior to the fulfillment of Ezekiel 38, then this could be the reason Ezekiel omitted Elam from his prophecy.

## The Bleak Future of Islam

Psalm 83, Jeremiah 49:34-39, and Ezekiel 38 all involve predominately Muslim populations. The ten Arab populations of Psalm 83, one in Jeremiah 49, and eight of the nine in Ezekiel 38 are unquestionably today Islamic. The one exception in Ezekiel 38 is Russia. Although Russia's Muslim population remains a minority, that's expected to change by the year 2050. Vladimir Dergachyov, an advisor to Russian Prime Minister Vladimir Putin, said in 2007,

> Differences in growth rates of Christian and Muslim groups in Russia along with the arrival of Muslim immigrants from abroad will boost the percentage of Muslims there from 10 percent now to 50 percent by 2050.[238]

Regardless, if this boost occurs, the coming invasions of Israel are characterized by Muslim attempts to destroy Jews, and the Jews win! Enmity toward Israel already existing in Iran, and rapidly incubating presently in Turkey, should mature into a fully-grown hatred for the Jewish state in the aftermath of the IDF defeat of the Arab Muslims in Psalm 83. Russia should have no problem coercing these two cohorts into its Ezekiel 38 coalition, subsequently.

When nineteen of Islam's most devout nations and terrorist populations are obliterated by the IDF in Psalm 83, and subsequently by the God of the Jews in Ezekiel 38, the public outcry of all remaining Muslims worldwide should be shouts of "Death to Israel!"—that is, the initial shouts.

It can be anticipated that sometime shortly after the Muslims digest the brevity of the two prophetic events, they will begin to question the power of their god Allah. First, they will be forced to wonder how a tiny state like Israel can defeat the Arabs. Many Muslims today are already asking that question in light of the fact that Israel still exists after repeated Arab attempts to destroy the Jewish state in 1948, 1967, and 1973 all failed.

Additionally, when world Muslims witness Israel receiving international esteem, which occurs when they bury the Muslim hordes of Gog, they will inevitably be caused to question how the Jehovah of the Jews could successfully destroy the much more formidable Islamic forces.

"For seven months the house of Israel will be burying them [the Muslim hordes of Gog], in order to cleanse the land. Indeed all the people of the land [a national Israeli effort] will be burying, and they will gain renown for it on the day that I am glorified," says the Lord GOD. (Ezekiel 39:12-13)

Zephaniah 2:8-11 suggests contextually that Allah's best days are behind him. His decline appears to be triggered by Psalm 83, and his final undoing appears to occur early in the tribulation period.

"I have heard the reproach of Moab [central Jordan, a member of Psalm 83], And the insults of the people of Ammon [northern Jordan, a member of Psalm 83], With which they have reproached My [Jewish] people, And made arrogant threats against their borders. Therefore, as I live," Says the LORD of hosts, the God of Israel, "Surely Moab shall be like Sodom, And the people of Ammon like Gomorrah— Overrun with weeds and saltpits, And a perpetual desolation. The residue of My people [IDF] shall plunder them, And the remnant of My people shall possess them. This they shall have for their pride, Because they have reproached and made arrogant threats Against the [Jewish] people of the LORD of hosts. The LORD will be awesome to them, For He will reduce to nothing all the gods of the earth [Allah is the present god of these afore mentioned peoples]; People shall worship Him, Each one from his place, Indeed all the shores of the nations." (Zephaniah 2:8-11)

Zephaniah says the "Lord will be awesome to them," and that the gods of the earth will be "reduced to nothing." Who is "them," and what specific "gods," are in question? Consider that the previous passage refers to Moab and Ammon, who happen to be members of Psalm 83. And, they are threatening the Israelis and their borders; they must be "them." The Lord will be awesome to Moab and Ammon, which are primarily Jordanians today.

The Lord will prove He is awesome (in modern vernacular, "shock-and-awe") to the Jordanians by reducing their gods and ultimately "all the gods of the earth" to nothing. At Zephaniah's time, the god of Moab was Chemosh, and the god of Ammon was Milcom. Jeremiah, Zephaniah's contemporary, addresses the Jordanians and these two gods in the respective prophecies below.

For because you [Moab] have trusted in your works and your treasures, You also shall be taken. And Chemosh shall go forth into captivity, His priests and his princes together. (Jeremiah 48:7)

Woe to you, O Moab! The people of Chemosh perish; For your sons have been taken captive, And your daughters captive. "Yet I will bring back the captives of Moab In the latter days," says the LORD. (Jeremiah 48:46-47)

Against the Ammonites. Thus says the LORD: "Has Israel no sons? Has he no heir? Why then does Milcom inherit Gad, And his people dwell in its cities? Therefore behold, the days are coming," says the LORD, "That I will cause to be heard an alarm of war [probably Psalm 83] In Rabbah [near Amman Jordan] of the Ammonites; It shall be a desolate mound, And her villages shall be burned with fire. Then Israel shall take possession of his inheritance," says the LORD. "Wail, O Heshbon, for Ai is plundered! Cry, you daughters of Rabbah, Gird yourselves with sackcloth! Lament and run to and fro by the walls; For Milcom shall go into captivity With his priests and his princes together... But afterward I will bring back The captives of the people of Ammon," says the LORD. (Jeremiah 49:1-3,6)

These above verses point out that the Jordanians and their gods go into captivity. But, in the "latter days" the captive Jordanians will be restored. This signals that these are end time events. Chemosh and Milcom are no longer the Jordanian gods. They, like most other Arab gods, submitted to Allah around the seventh century AD. Jeremiah wrote about 1,200 years earlier, before Islam came into existence. Thus, he appears to be suggesting the Jordanians will realize how awesome the Lord is when their current god, Allah, is reduced to nothing.

In my estimation, Psalm 83 is the punch to the gut of Islam. Subsequently, Islam receives an uppercut to the jawbone by Ezekiel 38-39. These two blows should decrease the world Muslim population dramatically, and begin the decline of Islam. By the time the Antichrist arrives on the scene, in the aftermath of the above, Islam should be in a serious state of disarray. The Muslim demographics below suggest about one-third of the Muslim population will be affected by these two wars.

Islam is the world's second largest religion after Christianity. According to a 2009 demographic study, Islam has 1.57 billion adherents, making up 23% of the world population.... Approximately 50 countries are a Muslim-majority. Around 62% of the world's Muslims live in Asia, with over 683 million adherents in such countries as Indonesia, Pakistan, India, and Bangladesh. About 20% of Muslims live in Arab countries in the Middle East. The non-Arab countries of Turkey and Iran are the largest Muslim-majority countries; in Africa, Egypt and Nigeria have the most populous Muslim communities.[239]

Some suggest that the Antichrist will be a Muslim. However, it is my view that by the time of his arrival Islam won't provide a very stable platform from which he can arise. Punched silly by these two pre-tribulation wars, by the time the first-half of the tribulation period begins, Islam should be knocked-out for the ten-count!

If you want more information about the pros and cons of the Muslim Antichrist theory, I suggest the following books for your research.

1. *The Man of Lawlessness,* by Dr. David Reagan.

2. *Mideast Beast, The Scriptural Case for an Islamic Antichrist*, by Joel Richardson.

# TWENTY-SIX

# Greater Israel

## The Future Maps of Isralestine

**"Politicians urge Israel government to annex West Bank"**

*Saudi Gazette 1/3/13*

Although approximately 6000 years of recorded history has emanated from the Middle East, today's maps of the area are primarily composed of countries that have relatively recently gained or regained their independence. The Ottoman Empire had ruled over the area from 1517 until 1917, but with its collapse at the conclusion of World War I, the empire was forced to forfeit its holdings, primarily into British and French hands. Within decades, the Middle East as we presently recognize it, formed as follows:[240]

| Country | Year of Independence | Total Area SQ. Miles | Approximated Population |
|---------|----------------------|----------------------|-------------------------|
| Afghanistan | 1919 | 251,826 | 29,117,000 |
| Egypt | 1922 | 386,660 | 81,731,000 |
| Saudi Arabia | 1932 | 829,995 | 27,137,000 |
| Iraq | 1932 | 169,234 | 30,400,000 |
| Iran | 1935 | 636,368 | 75,330,000 |
| Lebanon | 1943 | 4,015 | 4,224,000 |
| Syria | 1946 | 71,498 | 22,717,500 |
| Jordan | 1946 | 34,495 | 6,407,000 |

**Fig. 7.**

As Britain and France began relinquishing control over the region, one-by-one, these Arab and Persian population groups became autonomous. Territory was generally allotted in alignment with ancestral boundaries. The region was reshaping itself in a relatively orderly fashion, with the exception of the inklings of the international community to appropriate territory for a Jewish state.

In 1917, the Balfour Declaration was introduced to the world. It was designed to transfer a substantial portion of the former Ottoman Empire into a Jewish state. In its initial draft, it offered up the territory of Palestine and was to include about 46,000 square miles, extending from the Mediterranean Sea in the west, eastward to the western borders of modern-day Iraq. The Arabs in the region desired sovereignty over this land, and promptly protested this international proposal. Continued Arab agonizing over the matter postponed the issue.

Then, with the conclusion of the Holocaust, the International community arguably forced the Arabs to expect a Jewish State to surface in their neighborhood. The Palestine Partition Plan, UN Resolution GA 181 of 1947, emerged and appropriated 8,000 to 9,000 square miles from the Mediterranean Sea to the Jordan River for the re-creation of Israel. Since Jordan had become a nation in the year prior and consumed most of what the Balfour Declaration intended as territory for the Jewish State, the nation Israel was formed on the little bit of unclaimed land left in the region.

| Country | Year of Independence | Total Area SQ. Miles | Approximated Population |
|---------|---------------------|---------------------|------------------------|
| Israel  | 1948                | 8,019               | 7,836,000              |

*Fig. 8. (Includes the Gaza Strip, and West Bank)*

The purpose of this chapter is to redefine the Middle East territorially in accordance with the prophetic content contained within the Bible. In the near future, we can expect another facelift in the Middle East. Publishers will soon be busy reproducing entirely new *Isralestine* atlases of the area. It is helpful to list the pertinent passages sequentially, and to map them out territorially to better understand how that region will be reshaped.

(Isralestine is an author neologism, and refers to the foretold expansion of the modern-day Jewish State of Israel over the formerly recognized territory of Palestine, and is not suggesting that the name Isralestine is destined to become the literal name for the future area).

Up to this point, this book has clearly hypothesized that the Bible tells us, that the decades of regional unrest between the Arabs and Jews, will upgrade itself soon into a war of epic biblical proportion in the Middle East. The Psalm 83 Arabs will confederate in an attempt to extinguish the nation Israel. Israel will defeat them, and subsequently expand their national borders well into these Arab territories. This expansion will bear some resemblance to the former borders of the ancient territories allotted to the Twelve Tribes of Israel. Additionally, Arab exiles are destined for detention camps within the described areas.

*(Please note that the author is not saying that Israel will possess all of the Promised Land specified in Genesis 15:18 after Psalm 83. However, scripture does suggest that modern-day Israel expands incrementally after the Psalm 83 war).*

## The Confederacy

The (The Psalm 83 "Arab Confederacy") map, depicts a pentagon shaped border around the confederate nations. These are the nations most closely bordering Israel today. They are listed in Psalm 83:6–8, and can be viewed alongside their modern day equivalents in the image. The pentagon shape inside the map represents the "inner circle"[241] of Arab territories in Psalm 83. The ancient names of these lands are superimposed upon their modern day equivalents. [242]

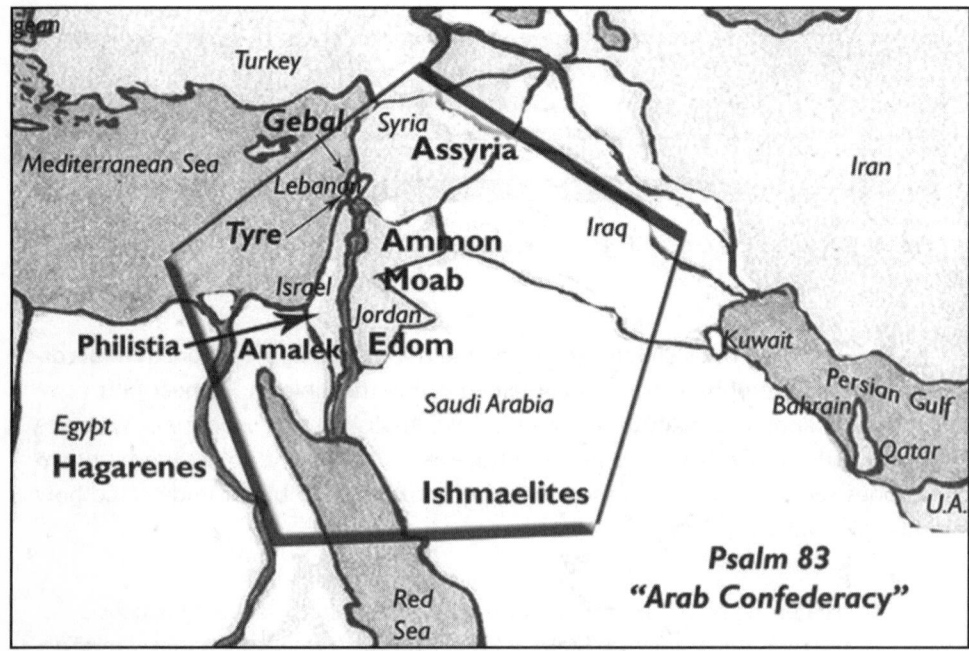

**Fig. 9. Inner Circle of Psalm 83.** *The Psalm 83 Arab nations and/or terrorist populations are located inside the pentagon figure on the map.*
*(Map provided by Lani Harmony Salhus)*

## The Psalm 83 Confederates

| | |
|---|---|
| *Tents of* **Edom** | Palestinians & Southern Jordanians |
| **Ishmaelites** | Saudis (*Ishmael father of Arabs*) |
| **Moab** | Palestinians & Central Jordanians |
| **Hagarenes** | Egyptians – (*Hagar Egypt Matriarch*) |
| **Gebal** | Hezbollah & Northern Lebanese |
| **Ammon** | Palestinians & Northern Jordanians |
| **Amalek** | Arabs of the Sinai Area |
| **Philistia** | Hamas of the Gaza Strip |
| **Tyre** | Hezbollah & Southern Lebanese |
| **Assyria** | Syrians and Northern Iraqi's |

*Fig. 10. The Psalm 83 Confederates*
*(Provided by the Prophecy Depot Ministries)*

The above Psalm 83 nations present the first confederate attempt at destroying the reforming nation of modern-day Israel. Foretold are three confederacies that will conspire, for differing motives, but for the same general cause, which is the genocide of the Jewish race.

The second such confederacy is prophesied in Ezekiel Chapters 38 and 39. For this book, we will call those nations the "Outer Ring,"[243] and they are on the following (Magog Invasion) map. None of the outer ring countries share a common border with Israel. At the time of the formation of their coalition, the inner circle of nations should have been decisively defeated by the "exceedingly great army" of Israel. In victory, Israel seems to extend its territorial embrace into some portions of those inner circle nations on the (Psalm 83 Arab Confederacy) map. As such, the expanding nation of Israel will become a slightly closer neighbor in proximity to the outer ring of nations.

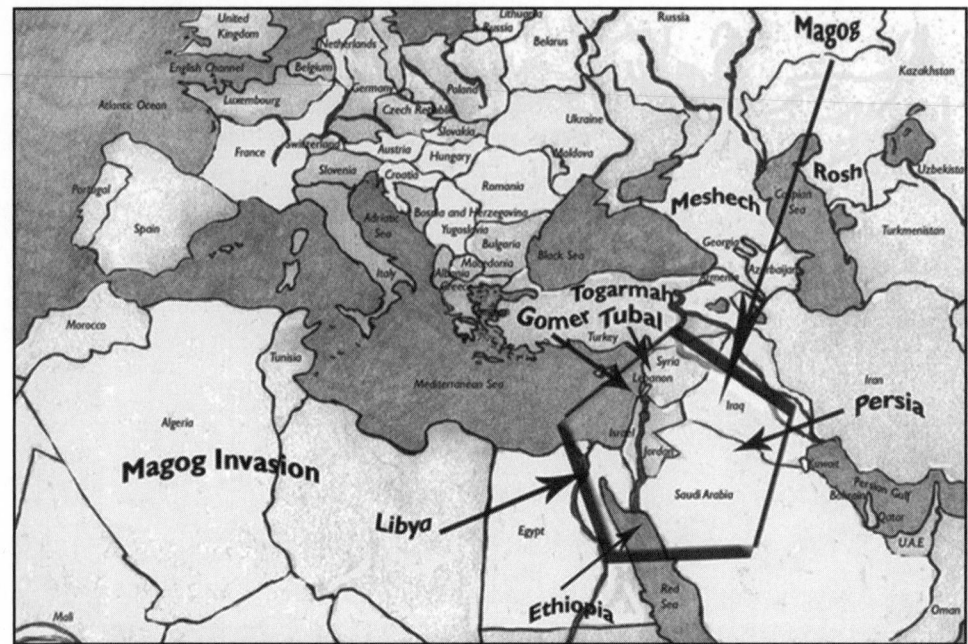

**Fig. 11. Outer Ring of Ezekiel 38.** *The Psalm 83 Arab nations and/or terrorist populations are located inside the pentagon figure on the map and are part of the "inner circle." The arrows pointing toward the pentagon represent the Ezekiel 38:1-5 Gog of Magog invaders.* (Map provided by Lani Harmony Salhus)

The outer ring of nations will not welcome Israel into their neighborhood; rather, they will formulate an attempt to seize the wealth acquired by Israel resulting from their conquest over the inner circle of nations. As the (Magog Invasion) map displays, the second confederacy of Ezekiel 38 enlists those nations that border the primary bodies of water surrounding Israel. (The Mediterranean Sea, Red Sea, and Persian Gulf). This appears, in part, to be done in an attempt to challenge Israel's ability to distribute its increased commerce capacity into the International community.

The (Magog Invasion) map displays the nine confederate members and their approximate historical locations, of the outer ring of nations. These nations are identified by their ancient names in Ezekiel 38:1-6 in the New King James Version as: Magog, Rosh, Meshech, Tubal, Persia, Ethiopia, Lybia, Gomer, and Togarmah. Unlike the inner circle, which experiences defeat at the hands of the "exceedingly great army" of Israel, the outer ring of nations meet their defeat via divine intervention. Israel becomes a powerful entity because of these two victories over the inner circle and outer ring.

As such, the third confederacy, spearheaded by the world leader at the time, will act promptly to neutralize Israel's enormously grown international esteem. This world leader, more commonly referred to as the Antichrist, will accomplish this by confirming a seven-year covenant with the nation of Israel.

> Then he [Antichrist] shall confirm a covenant with many for *one week;* But in the middle of the week He shall bring an end to sacrifice and offering. And on the wing of abominations shall be one who makes desolate, Even until the consummation, which is determined, Is poured out on the desolate. (Dan. 9:27, NKJV; emphasis added)

As this passage states, the Antichrist breaches this covenant at the midway point of the seven-year covenant and commences his campaign to destroy the nation Israel and extirpate the Jewish race once and for all. He enlists the remaining nations of the world, which at that time will be conspicuously void of the inner circle and outer ring of nations. Not all inhabitants of the world will join his effort; some will support the Jewish race; however, his effort concludes all attempts to annihilate the Jews.

Considering all the above prophetic information, what should soon begin to happen in the Middle East? How will Israel become a greater and safer place, which is what appears to be predicted in Ezekiel 38:8-13? How does Israel expand incrementally into what the prophet Daniel calls the "Glorious Land?"

> "He [the Antichrist] shall also enter the Glorious Land, and many *countries* shall be overthrown; but these shall escape from his hand: Edom, Moab, and the prominent people of Ammon." (Daniel 11:41, NKJV; emphasis added).

Ultimately, the tiny Israel of today seemingly burgeons into sizeable "Glorious Land," but how?

## The Post-Psalm 83 Greater Israel

In the aftermath of their decisive IDF victory over the Psalm 83 Arab confederacy, Israel temporarily becomes a safer place. Temporarily, because looming in the shadows of Psalm 83 appears to be an even more formidable offensive foretold to follow in Ezekiel 38-39. Ezekiel 38:11-13 informs us that Israel is extremely prosperous at the time of this subsequent invasion. These verses seem to describe a "Greater Israel" than presently exists. For the purposes of this book, Greater Israel identifies a safer, wealthier, and larger nation than the modern-day Jewish State.

How Israel amasses its great wealth prior to the Ezekiel 38 invasion is a subject of some debate. Israel's increased prosperity is also addressed in the appendix called "Israel Strikes it Rich Someday!" Many believe that Israel strikes it rich someday from its own commercial endeavors and natural resources. In addition to the relatively recent sizable natural gas and shale oil discoveries, many believe Israel soon locates a significant surplus of crude oil under its soil.

Most of the proponents of this theory don't include Psalm 83 into the greater Israel equation. Factoring out the Arab threats, riches, and lands, they gravitate toward thinking that Israel already dwells securely and its coming prosperity is entirely self-made.

Additionally, they generally believe that the lesser Israel of today, which measures under 9,000 square miles, becomes extremely wealthy within its modern-day (pre-Psalm 83) borders. The menu of reasons that they don't include Arab spoils into the national treasures of Israel, include the following:

- Psalm 83 is only an imprecatory prayer and not a *bona fide* Bible prophecy.

- Psalm 83 found historical fulfillment according to 2 Chronicles 20.

- Psalm 83 occurs at the same time as the Ezekiel 38 Gog of Magog invasion.

- Psalm 83 occurs during the battle of Armageddon.

The second reason listed above is refuted in the appendix called Psalm 83—Has it Found Final Fulfillment. The third reason is debated in the chapter called, "Psalm 83 or Ezekiel 38: What's the Next Middle East News Headline?" The chapter called "Psalm 83 and the Prophets," explains why Psalm 83 is much more than a prayer.

Regarding the fourth reason, it is doubtful that either Psalm 83 or Ezekiel 38 are part of the Armageddon nations of the Antichrist. Prophecies in Joel 3:2, Zechariah 12:3, 9, and elsewhere inform us that "all (world) nations" are part of Armageddon. However, the caveat is that not "all nations" as we know them today, may remain intact by the time Armageddon unfolds. Psalm 83 involves only ten populations, and Ezekiel 38 lists nine entirely different ones. Neither the Psalm 83 or Ezekiel 38 prophecies alludes to "all nations," in their prophetic description. There are approximately 195 recognized nations in the world, and presently they include those spoken of in Psalm 83 and Ezekiel 38. However, by the time Armageddon comes, the Psalm and Ezekiel invasion should be concluded, and these nineteen predominately Muslim countries, will probably not participate due to their defeats.

In essence, the world as we presently identify it will not likely be the same at that time. The fact that neither Psalm 83 nor Ezekiel 38 allude to "all nations," along with other reasons given throughout this book, strongly suggests that Psalm 83, Ezekiel 38, and the battle of Armageddon, are three different prophetic events.

Moreover, the fact that Armageddon occurs during the seven-year Tribulational Period, further negates the probability that Psalm 83 takes place at that time. This argument was previously explained in the chapter called, "The Destruction of Damascus," within the Isaiah 17 commentary. However, the same rationale for the timing of the destruction of Damascus applies for the timing of Psalm 83. Below is the quote from the Isaiah 17 commentary that is slightly revised for this chapter:

1.  The first three and one-half years are characterized by Israel dwelling in a false peace. During the first half of the tribulation, Israel is dwelling in a false sense of national security. The covenant confirmed with them by the Antichrist in Daniel 9:27 creates this period of deceptive calm. The IDF appears to let its guard down, as a result. This statement is supported by the understanding, that the IDF is unable to prevent the Antichrist from entering the third temple in the middle of the Tribulational Period, and committing his sacrilegious act, the "abomination of desolation."

2.  The second three and one-half years are characterized by attempted Jewish genocide. Subsequently, at the mid-point of the tribulation, the Antichrist enters into the third Jewish temple and abominates it, as Christ prophesied in Matthew 24:15. This violation of the temple commences an unprecedented Jewish genocidal attempt by the Antichrist, which characterizes the last three and one-half years of "great tribulation."

    Contrariwise, the second half of the tribulation period is not characterized by IDF complacency, but by IDF catastrophe. Israelis and their soldiers appear to be on the run from the perils plaguing that period. Zechariah 13:8 says that two-thirds of the Israelis in the land will be killed. The Antichrist and his troops are on the rampage to annihilate the Jews. This killing campaign will probably prompt the IDF to flee for safety, rather than fight the Psalm 83 Arabs.

3.  The "day of the Lord," (Tribulational Period), is not specifically mentioned in Psalm 83.

## Israel's Great Booty Includes Arab Spoils of War

Conversely, concerning the prosperous Israel Russia someday invades, many others, myself included, believe a greater Israel becomes a reality in the aftermath of Psalm 83. We believe that Israel, in addition to its own resources, captures Arab spoils of war through Psalm 83. The appendix called, "Israel Strikes it Rich Someday," points out that the Hebrew word for the spoil Russia comes for, is actually despoil. Ezekiel 38:13 could be translated as, "Have you (Russia) come to plunder the great spoil of the despoilers." In this instance, the spoil would be the booty from the defeated Psalm

83 Arabs, and the despoiler would be Israel. Additionally, the Jewish nation seems to capture more of their Promised Land identified in Genesis 15:18, which extends between northeast Egypt and portions of Iraq and Syria.

The Jews have both an ancient and a modern history of expanding their borders in the aftermath of achieving military victories over the Arabs. Joshua started this trend about 3,400 years ago, King David followed suit about 500 years later, and Israel continued this precedent in June 1967 after the IDF victory in the infamous "Six Day" war against primarily Egypt, Syria, and Jordan.

## Jordan Surrenders Sovereignty to Israel

Listed below are a few passages which teach that the modern-day nation of Jordan surrenders sovereignty to Israel. In each instance the IDF appears to be involved in the conquest that leads to Jordan's surrender.

> "Therefore behold, the days are coming," says the LORD, "That I will cause to be heard an *alarm of war* In Rabbah of the Ammonites [northern Jordan]; It shall be a desolate mound, And her villages shall be burned with fire. Then *Israel shall take possession* of his inheritance," says the LORD. (Jeremiah 49:2; emphasis added)

> But *they shall fly down upon* the shoulder of the Philistines [Gaza] toward the west; *Together they shall plunder* the people of the East; They shall *lay their hand on* Edom [southern Jordan] and Moab [central Jordan]; And the people of Ammon [northern Jordan] *shall obey them*. (Isaiah 11:14; emphasis added)

> "Therefore, as I live," Says the LORD of hosts, the God of Israel, "Surely Moab shall be like Sodom, And the people of Ammon like Gomorrah— Overrun with weeds and saltpits, And a perpetual desolation. The residue of *My people shall plunder them*, And the remnant of *My people shall possess them*." (Zephaniah 2:9; emphasis added)

Today Jordan, represented in these passages as, Ammon, Moab, and Edom, rests within the Promised Land that was allotted to Abraham in Genesis 15:18. Many eschatologists believe that Jordan, along with the rest of the Promised Land, will be given to the Jewish descendants of Abraham by Christ at His second coming. I respectfully disagree with this assessment, and suspect that the Jews capture parts of Jordan prior to this, as a result of winning in Psalm 83. For the following two reasons, I believe the Jews annex Jordan before Ezekiel 38 occurs:

1. The Valley of Hamon Gog is probably located in central Jordan.

2. The faithful remnant of Israel flees to southern Jordan.

## The Valley of Hamon Gog is probably located in Central Jordan

Hamon Gog in Hebrew means the multitudes or hordes of Gog. It is a place that presently doesn't exist, and won't exist until it becomes necessary. It is necessitated when the Lord destroys the Ezekiel 38 invaders. As mentioned earlier, the Lord destroys the Ezekiel invaders through an Old Testament fire, hailstone, and brimstone episode.

> And I will bring him to judgment with pestilence and bloodshed; I will rain down on him [Gog of the land of Magog], on his troops, and on the many peoples who *are* with him, [the other Ezekiel invaders including Iranians, Turks, and more] flooding rain, great *hailstones, fire,* and *brimstone.* (Ezekiel 38:22; emphasis added)

*(On a side note, please recognize that the IDF does not appear to serve an instrumental military role in the defeat of the Ezekiel invaders, described in Ezekiel 38:18-39:6. This is another issue that separates Psalm 83 from Ezekiel 38).*

In the aftermath of the Lord's victory, there will likely be death and destruction second only to the flood of Noah. These dead must be buried promptly, in order to prevent the plague potentials associated with the decomposition of dead soldiers. In Ezekiel 39:11-16, we are given a detailed account of the burial instructions.

The process begins with seven months of burial in a designated location, in order to cleanse the land. The cemetery is in a valley east of some sea. The valley is called Hamon Gog. As stated earlier, no such place presently exists. However, it will when the multitudes of Gog's dead soldiers lay stricken dead across parts of the Middle East.

What sea could the prophet be alluding to, that has a large enough valley on its east side to accommodate the burial of potentially millions of dead contaminated soldiers? There are only four primary choices to choose from: the Mediterranean, the Sea of Galilee, the Red Sea, or the Dead Sea.

## The Mediterranean Sea

The Mediterranean Sea can probably be ruled out because the candidate valleys in Israel, like the Jezreel, Kidron, Hula, Beit Netofa, Beracah, and Valley of the Cross are inside of modern-day Israel. Logically, since Ezekiel 39:14 declares the Jews are "cleansing the land," it doesn't make sense that they would contaminate their own fertile Israeli soil, given other options.

Contamination is an appropriate term in this instance, considering Ezekiel 39:14-15 appears to involve the resemblance of a hazmat (hazardous materials) team. Additionally, some of us believe the Jews are cleansing the land in compliance with requirements specified in the Mosaic Law. (Numbers 19:11- 22; Deuteronomy 21:1-9). If so, this implies the supernatural defeat of the Magog invaders inclines the Jews to revert to orthodoxy, and resulting in their seeking to rebuild their temple, reinstate Levitical Law, and resume their animal sacrifices.

## The Sea of Galilee

The Sea of Galilee is likewise unlikely, because candidate valleys to the east are located primarily in southern Syria or northern Jordan. Occasional southwesterly wind patterns blow through these areas into Israel, which could cause the contamination referenced above to spread into the world's most heavily populated Jewish area of Gush Dan, which encompasses Tel Aviv and some surrounding metropolitan areas.

Another negative is that presently both Syria and Jordan are under Arab rule. The Syrians and Jordanians would prohibit Israel from burying the multitudes of Gog under their sovereign soil. However, if Israel captured these valleys during Psalm 83 prior, perhaps they would gain the option of someday burying the dead in one of their valleys.

But, what about Damascus, the capital city of Syria, which is approximately sixty miles northeast of the Sea of Galilee? Isaiah 17:1, 9, 14 predicts it will someday be destroyed (v. 1), probably overnight (v. 14), and probably by the IDF(v. 9). Damascus may be a desolate and contaminated place, due to its possible prior destruction. This could also dissuade the use of some valley east of the Sea of Galilee.

For these above reasons the Sea of Galilee drops low on the list of choices. However, even if it is the referenced Sea, eastward Arab valleys can only be used by Israel for mass burial purposes if Israel negotiates either politically or militarily, the use of the land. Politically, this is improbable, but as a result of an IDF military victory in Psalm 83, it becomes possible.

## The Red Sea

The Red Sea option is unfeasible due to the logistics of transporting multitudes of dead and probably contaminated soldiers so far southward. Remember that Ezekiel 38:15 informs us that the Magog invaders attack from the north. The Red Sea is over 400 miles to the south of Israel's capital city of Tel Aviv. Valleys east of the Red Sea are currently under Saudi sovereignty, inhibiting Israel's ability to bury the dead there, as well. Additionally, Saharan winds that could potentially blow contaminants into Israel should be considered.

## The Dead Sea

The Dead Sea presents the best option for the creation of a place called the Valley of Hamon Gog. Satellite topography shots of the Middle East clearly picture central Jordan as the perfect location for the mass burial site of the multitudes of Gog. Unlike northern Jordan, where most Jordanians live, and portions of southern Jordan that are mountainous, much of central Jordan is flat, barren, and home to Bedouins.

Regional wind patterns favor this location as well. For instance, the hot, dry, dusty desert wind called a "Sirocco," an Arab word for "easterly," often blows in the eastward direction of Europe. Sirocco is also known as the Sharkiye in Jordan, Sharav in Israel, and Simoom in Arabia.

If the central Jordanian land, formerly called ancient Moab, becomes captured by the IDF during Psalm 83, then Israel would possess the unrestricted ability to establish the Valley of Hamon Gog there. Thus, when the hordes of Gog need a burial location, one already exists, requiring Israel to simply use it and rename it.

Moab is one of the ten members listed in the Psalm 83 Arab confederacy. Because the Valley of Hamon Gog is probably going to exist in Jordan, and Ezekiel 38 precedes Christ's second coming, this is one reason I believe Israel annexes all or part of Jordan in the aftermath of Psalm 83 and prior to Christ's return.

It was previously mentioned, that the Balfour Document of 1917 intended to create a Jewish state inclusive of modern-day Israel and Jordan, but in 1922 the League Nations passed the Transjordan memorandum, which essentially excluded modern-day Jordan from the proposed Jewish territory. On May 25, 1946, the United Nations recognized Jordan as an independent sovereign Arab kingdom. Two years later, on May 14, 1948, Israel was officially established as the Jewish State. It is my opinion, fashioned from Jeremiah 49:2, Zephaniah 2:8-9, and several other verses which I connect with the Psalm 83 prophecy, that after the Psalm 83 war Israel captures all, or part of Jordan. This would enable Israel to establish the valley of Hamon Gog in Jordan, east of the Dead Sea.

## The Faithful Jewish Remnant of Israel Flees to Southern Jordan

Zechariah 13:8-9 informs us that a remnant of Israelis emerges from out of the Antichrist's final genocidal attempt of the Jews. This horrific holocaust episode takes place during the final three-and-one-half years on the earth's timeline, in a period commonly called the "great tribulation" (great-trib). Zechariah says this remnant will ultimately become believers and say, "The Lord is my God." (Zechariah 13:9). Thus, they are often referred to as the "faithful remnant of Israel." They are the saved Israel, described in Romans 11:26-27.

> "And so all Israel will be saved, as it is written: "The Deliverer will come out of Zion, And He will turn away ungodliness from Jacob; For this is My covenant with them, When I take away their sins."" (NKJV)

In Matthew 24:15 Christ instructs this group of survivors to flee to the mountains without delay, when they witness the "abomination of desolation" spoken of by the prophet Daniel (Daniel 9:27, 12:11). We glean from connecting passages in Isaiah 63 and elsewhere that the specific mountains Christ alludes to are located in ancient Edom, which is modern-day southern Jordan.

According to Hosea 5:15, this Jewish remnant recognizes Christ as their Messiah during their great tribulation. Subsequently, they plead for Him to return and rescue them from the onslaught of the Antichrist. Isaiah 63:1 tells us that He first touches down at their location in Edom. Isaiah's verses go on to declare that Christ's garments are stained with the blood of Antichrist and his Armageddon armies. Christ wins the war and then makes His victory ascent up to the Mount of Olives, as per Zechariah 14:3-4.

The point of all the above is that no faithful remnant would presently be permitted unrestricted passage into Jordan, as southern Jordan is under Arab rule. Thus, should a remnant of Israelis numbering in the hundreds of thousands, perhaps millions, attempt to cross the Israeli borders for refuge in the Jordanian mountains, the Jordanian government would undoubtedly protest. Under current pre-Psalm 83 conditions the historical account inscribed in Numbers 20, would likely repeat itself.

> Then Edom said to him, "You [Moses and the Hebrews at the time of their exodus out of Egypt] shall not pass through my *land,* lest I come out against you with the sword." So the children of Israel said to him, "We will go by the Highway, and if I or my livestock drink any of your water, then I will pay for it; let me only pass through on foot, nothing *more.*" Then he said, "You shall not pass through." So Edom came out against them with many men and with a strong hand. Thus Edom refused to give Israel passage through his territory; so Israel turned away from him. (Numbers 20:18-21)

However, unrestricted passage could come under future conditions when Edom, a member of Psalm 83, is conquered by Israel. This is the second reason I believe Jordan surrenders sovereignty in advance of Christ's second coming. The faithful remnant, refuged in Edom, crying out, "Blessed is He who comes in the name of the Lord," in fulfillment of Matthew 23:39, is a prerequisite requirement of Christ's return.

For I say to you, you shall see Me no more till you say, "Blessed is He who comes in the name of the Lord!" (Matthew 24:39).

## Israel Expands Territorially Into Arab Lands

About 4,000 years ago, recorded in Genesis 15, the Lord promised Abraham an enormous amount of land. This land extended from the Nile River in Egypt to the Euphrates in modern- day Iraq and Syria. Through his son Isaac, rather than Ishmael, and through his grandson Jacob instead of Esau, the Promised Land became the heritage of the Israelites. Jacob was renamed Israel in Genesis 32:28 and 35:10. Thus, the Israelites, or Jews today, are named after their patriarch Jacob / Israel.

However, Abraham was informed, as recorded in the passage below, that at least 400 years stood between the promise and the possession of the land.

> Then He [the Lord] said to Abram [Abraham]: "Know certainly that your [Hebrew] descendants will be strangers in a land [Egypt] that is not theirs, and will serve them, [Egyptians] and they will afflict them [Hebrews] four hundred years. And also the nation [Egypt] whom they serve I will judge; afterward they shall come out with great possessions. Now as for you, you shall go to your fathers in peace; you shall be buried at a good old age. But in the fourth generation they shall return here, [to the Promised Land] for the iniquity of the Amorites is not yet complete." (Genesis 15:13-16)

After the 400 years of exile elapsed and the exodus of the Hebrews out of Egypt ensued, Joshua brought the Israelites into some of the Promised Land. The division of the land is described in the book of Joshua chapters 13-21. At the time, the Israelites possessed more land than their modern-day equivalents.

About 400 years later, around 3,000 BC, King David and subsequently his son King Solomon, expanded into an even greater Israel. For the first time, Israel annexed lands to the northeast extending to the River Euphrates in Syria, as promised in Genesis 15:18. Unfortunately, King Solomon's reign was followed by "two bums..." (Reho-bum) Rehoboam, and (Jero-bum) Jeroboam. Their struggle for power split the Israelite kingdom in two. Rehoboam was Solomon's son, but Jeroboam was not kin to the king; Solomon appointed him to be the superintendent over his vast labor forces. Jeroboam used this position of authority to gain support for eventual quest for ruler-ship over Israel.

That was as good as the Israelite land-grab got, because Jeroboam took ten of the twelve tribes into the northern kingdom, and Rehoboam ruled over the remaining two in the southern kingdom. Assyria conquered the northern kingdom in 722 BC, and Babylon conquered the southern kingdom in 586 BC.

The Jews began returning to their homeland over a period of time after the Babylonian captivity, but they never grew back into the landmass Solomon previously possessed. Then in 70 AD, the Romans conquered Israel, sacked Jerusalem, and destroyed the second Jewish temple. The Romans brought down the Jewish rebellion at that time, and in 135 they defeated the final rebellion, led by Bar Kokhba.

The Jewish leadership at the time had reached a condition of irreversible apostasy. According to Leviticus 26:31-34, this required a desolation of the land and a dispersion from the land. The Roman Empire was empowered to execute this disciplinary duty of the Mosaic Law. At the time, the world thought the God of the Jews was a weak god, because He couldn't sustain His chosen people in the land. However, they didn't understand this disciplinary clause in Leviticus.

If they'd read on further to Leviticus 26:44-45, they would have realized that the Diaspora of the Jews and the desolation of the Promised Land was only a temporary scenario. Albeit 1,878 years elapsed between Israel's desolation in 70 AD and her restoration on May 14, 1948, Israel's existence today proves their God is anything but weak. In fact, part and parcel with the prophesied return of the Jews into Israel is the promise to expand the borders of Israel to accommodate their massive aliyah. Someday, the Jews will occupy all of the territory defined in Genesis 15:18. But when?

Many eschatologists believe the full spectrum of the land will be deeded over to the faithful Jewish remnant upon the return of Christ during the 1,000- year messianic kingdom period. However, I believe Scripture supports the premise that some of the land will be captured by the IDF, prior to the second coming of Jesus Christ.

The Promised Land includes parts of Jordan, the Gaza Strip and the West Bank, and portions of Egypt, Saudi Arabia, Lebanon, Syria, and Iraq. Coincidentally, all of these Arab populations are listed in the Psalm 83:6-8 confederacy that someday seeks to destroy the Jews and rob them of their homeland. As pointed out in the chapter called, "Israel's Exceedingly Great Army," the IDF wins this war!

Like they did during the time of Joshua, King David, and in June of 1967, the Jews will probably repeat the pattern of capturing portions of conquered Promised Land. Listed below are several Scriptures that suggest this could be the case. These passages appear to find association with the Psalm 83 war scenario. Some of this section has been previously explained in this book.

## Jordan

Below are the pertinent passages relating to Israel's capture of Jordan.

Jeremiah 49:1-2. Jeremiah seems to predict the surrender of Jordanian sovereignty to Israel after a devastating Arab – Israeli war in these verses.

Isaiah 11:14. Isaiah says Israelis will lay their hands on Jordan, and Jordanians will obey them. (Jordan is represented by Edom, Moab, and Ammon in this passage.)

Isaiah 17:2. Isaiah possibly predicts the cities of Aroer Gad become rezoned as agricultural lands by Israel, after the destruction of Damascus, Syria. These cities could be located in between modern-day northern Jordan and southern Syria. It is interesting to note that, although Isaiah 17:1 predicts the destruction of Damascus, Ezekiel 47:16-18 uses Damascus as a future boundary line for dividing the tribal territories for the Jews.

Zephaniah 2:9. Zephaniah clearly evidences the plundering of Jordan by the IDF leads to its annexation by Israel.

## Egypt

Isaiah 19:16-18. Isaiah declares that after Egypt becomes terrified of Israel, five cities inside Egypt begin speaking the language of Hebrew. One of these cities is named the "City of Destruction." This implies Egypt surrenders at least five cities to the Jews upon destruction. For more commentary on these verses refer to the appendix called Is Egypt in Psalm 83?

Isaiah 11:15 Isaiah points out the men will walk over dried-up streams connected to the Nile River. Contextually, it appears as though these are Israelis, when compared to Isaiah 11:14-16.

## Gaza

Obadiah v. 19. Obadiah suggests the lowland inhabitants of Judah will possess the coastal areas near Gaza. The preceding verse 18 discusses an Arab–Israeli conflict between the house of Jacob (Israel) and the house of Esau (Arabs).

Zephaniah 2:4. Zephaniah correlates with Obadiah v. 19 and emphasizes that the seacoast of the Mediterranean near Gaza will be designated for the flocks of Judah.

## Saudi Arabia

Jeremiah 49:8. Jeremiah warns the Saudis to abandon the area once called Dedan. Dedan was located in what is today northwest Saudi Arabia and appears to be located within the Promised Land parameters. Ezekiel 25:13. Ezekiel says the Saudis will experience casualties of war apparently for their involvement in Psalm 83.

## Lebanon

Obadiah v. 20. Obadiah prepares us to recognize that Israel will expand its borders at least up to Zarephath, in the aftermath of the Arab – Israeli war in Obadiah v. 18. Zarephath was located in what is today part of southern Lebanon.

## West Bank

Obadiah v. 19. Obadiah says the Jews will possess the fields of Ephraim and fields of Samaria, in addition to Gilead. These are all areas associated with today's West Bank and slightly beyond.

## Syria

Obadiah v. 19. Similar to the West Bank, Obadiah says Gilead becomes the possession of the tribe of Benjamin. According to Parson's Bible Atlas there are several candidates for Gilead, including, Gilead (Transjordan), Gilead (Jezreel), and Gilead (City). Gilead (Transjordan) was a territory east of the Jordan River, which places it in modern-day Jordan, and possibly a small portion of southern Syria.

Isaiah 11:16. Isaiah points out there will be a remnant of Jews in Assyria. At the time Isaiah wrote, approximately 2,850 years ago, Assyria encompassed much of modern-day Syria. Although there are a few Jews still residing in Assyria today, the point Isaiah seems to make is that there will eventually be a route running between Assyia and Israel for future travel into Israel.

## Summary

This chapter points out that the modern-day nation of Israel is but a mere fragment of its appointed size. Soon, Israel will likely grow territorially to approximately ten to fifteen times its present size. This territorial expansion likely engulfs portions of the Gaza, West Bank, Lebanon, Syria, Jordan, Egypt, and parts of Saudi Arabia. The Jews will feel justified in stretching out their hand in sovereignty over all of these lands for two primary reasons. First, they will have conquered these nations militarily and, secondly, they will remember their patriarchal father Abraham was promised this land.

To understand the size and scope of the coming Greater Israel, try to imagine one of the following scenarios:

- The United States of America, enlarged territorially, to the extent that she possesses all of the landmass that currently composes, North,Central, and South America, Australia, and the entirety of Europe.

- New Jersey winning a major war against all the Eastern and Midwestern states, and subsequently annexing about one-third of the country from the Atlantic Ocean to the Mississippi River.

Proportionately speaking, this appears to be what happens between the time of Psalm 83 until the return of Christ to set up the Messianic Kingdom.

In essence, it seems preposterous for the international community to preclude that the propensity of what was promised to the Jews territorially is adequately appropriated presently. The inhabitants of this world are in store for a shocking revelation when they witness the transformation of Israel today into the Isralestine of tomorrow.

# TWENTY-SEVEN

# Preparing for Psalm 83

**"Threats of war cloud hopes for Middle East"**

*Washington Post 2/11/12*

**"U.S. Is Preparing for a Long Siege of Arab Unrest"**

*New York Times 9/15/12*

It is my sincere hope that by the time you come to this final chapter, that you have read the entire book and gleaned greatly from its timely and informative content. The Bible speaks volumes about these uncertain times. Inside its pages lie the secrets to successful living in the last days.

## The Purpose of Bible Prophecy

Prophecy is invaluable predictive information given to us by a loving God, with 100% accuracy. In addition to equipping us for the days in which we live, prophecy authenticates God's sovereignty, spares human lives, and ultimately saves lost souls. The primary goal of prophecy is to inform us, rather than impress us. God is not someone with too much time on His hands; He holds all time in His hands. This enables Him to share and declare the end from the beginning.[244] His plan is to pronounce hope, rather than announce harm. However, He won't denounce truth when He foreknows it's about to overtake the world.

How God knows what He knows, only He knows. But, we can be thankful that He does, and that He is willing to share His knowledge with us. "God so loves us that he wants us to know what's headed our way. And, in turn, our natural response should be to worship him for caring."

## Caveat to Bible Prophecy

My friend Jonathan Cahn, the author of the bestselling book called *The Harbinger* humors, "When you put two Jews together to discuss a topic you end up with three differing opinions, but when you pin two Bible prophecy experts together to discern a prophecy, you end up with five different interpretations."

Although Jonathan's comments were humorous, they also indicate the complexities of understanding Bible prophecies in advance. As pointed out prior in this book, there are opposing interpretations of Psalm 83 from respected scholars. Why is this?

It's because anticipating the coming of a prophecy by understanding its biblical description, and discerning its stage setting signs, is like looking through a drinking glass; no matter how clear the glass, perfect vision is impossible. Describing a coming prophecy or ordering it chronologically, tends to be an imperfect science. Therefore, the sequential outline of prophecies in this book, represents the educated estimate of the author, and cannot be chronologically guaranteed! Only when a prophecy becomes history, can its exact details be known. The generation that experiences the fulfillment of a specific prophecy is the one that will be able to pen its epic details with precise accuracy.

Another good friend is Bible prophecy expert Dr. Chuck Missler. Chuck makes it a point to let his audience know that they need to conduct their own scriptural research by following the Berean model in the book of Acts, when attempting to understand eschatological matters.

> "These (Bereans) were more fair-minded than those in Thessalonica, in that they received the word with all readiness, and searched the Scriptures daily *to find out* whether these things were so." (Acts 17:11, NKJV; emphasis added).

The prophecies explored in this book all represent earth-shattering events, and like every other Bible prophecy, are intended to be generally discerned in advance of their arrival. That is what this book attempts to accomplish; the basic presentation of what to expect when Psalm 83, Isaiah 17, Ezekiel 38, and more find fulfillment.

The eyewitnesses of these coming prophecies had better hope that they are not caught off guard by their overpowering effects. Everyone has the opportunity to prepare for the fulfillment of a prophecy. This is because the numerous Bible prophecies that were issued through the Old Testament prophets, the New Testament apostles and disciples, and Jesus Christ, were generation sensitive; intended for those needing the relevant information.

For example, understanding Psalm 83 in the fourteenth century several hundred years before Israel was rebirthed as a nation on May 14, 1948 would be difficult to do, because there was no Israel in existence. But, now that Israel is surrounded by the very existential threats described in Psalm 83, discerning this prophecy is most crucial!

Another case in point is contained in my answers to an inquiry from my friend Dr. David Reagan. David is a widely respected author of Bible prophecy, and he presented the following questions to me as part of one of his prophetic forums. Below are his questions and my interpretive responses.

*Dr. Reagan Question:* How do you interpret Daniel 12:4?

Author Answer: When interpreting Daniel 12:4, I find it helpful to split the verse into two sections as follows;

> "But you, Daniel, shut up the words, and seal the book until the time of the end; (Daniel 12:4a) many shall run to and fro, and knowledge shall increase." (Daniel 12:4b)

Daniel 12:4a informs us that the prophetic information of Daniel 12:1-3 would find fulfillment in a future generation, rather than his. Daniel 12:1-3 contained both good and bad news. The bad news was that Daniel's people, the Jews, would experience an unprecedented period of travail as a nation. The good news was that through that tribulation a faithful remnant of Jews would emerge.

Moreover, Daniel 12:2-3 informs of a future resurrection of the dead that will be followed by a divine judgment. The resurrected righteous would be rewarded with everlasting life, but the unrighteous would be escorted to everlasting shame and contempt.

The instruction issued to Daniel in 12:4a to "shut up the words, and seal the book until the time of the end," essentially orders him to let these specific prophetic matters rest, because their full discernment would be accomplished by a future generation, which is identified in Daniel 12:4b.

Daniel 12:4b provided comforting news to Daniel by informing him that some future generation would greatly glean from his prophecies. Those discerning his prophecies and benefiting from them in the time of the end, would be traveling to and fro, and knowledge would be readily available to them, as is the case now, with resources like the Internet.

Today's eschatologists have the advantage of understanding the intended ramifications of Daniel 12:4b. With the advent of planes, trains and automobiles, prophecy buffs can get access to any teaching venue they desire expeditiously. Moreover, present technologies enable the flow of information via a plethora of media sources, including the Internet and TV. Knowledge began to increase with the invention of Gutenberg's printing press around 1439. This enabled the Bible and other related readings to reach the masses.

Above all, I believe that Daniel 12:4b teaches that his prophecies would be discerned at the appropriate time; when they made sense, and were needed to inform and equip the final generation. What was important for Daniel to know was not that people would be able to scoot around all over the world, or be able to get information at the touch of a button, but that his prophecies would be understood and applied at the necessary time. Presently, Bible prophecy teachers like Dr. David Reagan, Dr. Arnold Fruchtenbaum, Dr. Mark Hitchcock, and a host of others are discerning Daniel's important prophecies, and at just the right time, in the time of the end.

## Rich Revelation for the Rough Road Ahead

So then, how do these coming prophecies play out in the end times? It is one thing to study them, but another to experience them first-hand. This concern prompted me to author a book series in a very unique format. In an attempt to paint the end time's picture into a story line, I wrote *Revelation Road, Hope Beyond the Horizon*. It is a combination novel and extensive biblical commentary all rolled up into one book.

*Revelation Road* is the first book in a series that is intended to escort the reader through the prophecies between now and the second coming of Jesus Christ. Below are the book's back cover synopsis and an outstanding World Net Daily review that compares *Revelation Road* to the popular "*Left Behind*" series authored by Tim LaHaye and Jerry Jenkins.

## Revelation Road Synopsis

George Thompson believes his grandson Tyler lives in the final generation. Lovingly, he prepares the lad for the treacherous road ahead.

All young Tyler wants is a chance to join his sister at Eastside Middle School in the fall, but the burgeoning Arab Spring leads to an apocalyptic summer, disrupting his plans. Middle East war and nuclear terror in America turn Tyler's world upside down.

Once upon a time, the Bible predicted the end of time, and now the Thompsons need revelation about the road ahead. Join them on their journey and discover how their gripping story uncovers the silver lining of hope against the backdrop of global gloom and doom.

*Revelation Road, Hope Beyond the Horizon*, puts you in the center of the end times calendar. You are invited to enjoy a one-of-a-kind reading experience. This unique book is designed with appeal for both fiction and non-fiction audiences. Enjoy a novel and a biblical commentary at the same time!

Storyline events could easily happen during your lifetime, and the commentary explains why and when!

## World Net Daily—WRITER'S BLOC BOOK REVIEW[245]

## Bible's Revelation comes to life

*Exclusive: Jim Fletcher reviews sizzling novel ripped from today's headlines*

*By* JIM FLETCHER

*(Jim Fletcher has worked in the book publishing industry for over 15 years, and is now director of the apologetics group Prophecy Matters.)*

> Many publishing moons ago, when I was a snot-nosed acquisitions editor, I was thumbing through a trade journal and saw the first ads for Tyndale's soon-to-be-blockbuster series, "Left Behind."
>
> Having seen a fair number of "end times novels," I actually laughed. I took counsel with myself and decided the book would be a huge failure, both for Tyndale and the co-authors, Tim LaHaye and Jerry Jenkins.

Isn't honesty refreshing?

Of course, the book took off like a rocket and was followed by the series, which became a juggernaut.

I was careful not to pass judgment after that!

In the intervening years, I've seen another fair number of such novels, some good and some not-so-good.

I've just read another terrific one.

Bill Salus got on the publishing radar a few years ago with his debut book, "Isralestine." I remember thinking at the time, here is a great title, cover and compelling Bible prophecy offering. In short, Salus's writing and marketing combined to knock one out of the park.

Now, he has tried his hand at fiction—but that term is not quite accurate, given the current headlines!

"Revelation Road" is a truly unique novel, presenting a gripping story with an actual commentary, explaining terms and concepts that might be unfamiliar to many. This is one of the chief assets of "Revelation Road," since I've long thought that Bible prophecy teachers fail to explain those terms and concepts that are now archaic to modern audiences.

Salus pens the story of a young man and his grandfather. As the world spins out of control—bringing into shape age-old biblical prophecies—the grandfather mentors his young grandson, explaining to him what is unfolding before their eyes. It's one of the best fiction efforts I've ever read in the genre.

Salus weaves a story of a "suddenly" crumbling society, with the growing awakening of young Tyler and Grandpa George.

The Thompson family realizes that the world has changed permanently, and their chief priority now is survival. I somewhat identify with Tyler, since I came of age during the convulsions of Vietnam, Watergate, the Cold War, etc. I would argue we are now living in scarier times, and "Revelation Road" camps out on this premise.

Nonetheless, just one of the reasons I love Salus' new novel is that he offers real, biblical hope.

He also, I think, has a flair for fiction; a sample: "Stuffing the classified dossier hastily into his brown leather attaché case, Mikhail Trutnev whisked suspiciously toward the back exit door of his office, startling his secretary. The middle-aged, silver-haired Russian receptionist that seldom wore a smile had set nearly every one of his appointments over the past decade, and Alena Popov was unprepared for his peculiar departure."

Yet, as I wrote earlier, Salus doesn't leave it to the reader to unwrap the sometimes confusing world of Bible prophecy. He provides a commentary section that identifies concepts and terms that would normally frustrate the "uninitiated."

For example, here is a snippet from the commentary: "Lately the realization has set in among many teachers and students of prophecy that the Bible teaches the trib-period begins by the confirmation of a false covenant confirmed by the Antichrist with the nation of Israel, rather than the Rapture. Isaiah 28:15,18 and Daniel 9:27 are the scriptures providing details regarding this agreement. Because of Daniel's prophecy the trib-period is more appropriately called Daniel's Seventieth Week."

The nice thing about the combined novel and commentary is that readers can devour the novel portion, then travel through the commentary at leisure. Being able to go back and re-read the commentary ensures that "Revelation Road" will have "legs," as readers refer to it again and again. I must say, Salus is one of the best and most thorough researchers I've run across, and this project and its readers are the beneficiaries of that singular skill. I learned a ton.

The historical detail Salus provides in the commentary is rich and extensive. It's not often one can purchase a book and get at least two books in the process!

Agree with him or not (Salus has bravely dived into a cauldron of debate and fierce disagreement among prophecy teachers and students), the author has fashioned an end times novel that will grip the reader and, thankfully, also instruct and exhort.

It's the kind of triple play most authors couldn't pull off. Bill Salus and "Revelation Road" have done it with room to spare.

A thrilling ride!

## What is the Hope Beyond the Horizon?

In these perilous end times, many believers and unbelievers alike, are buying gold as an investment hedge or a bartering tool, guns and ammunition for protection, and storing up goods like food and water. In fact, I can remember attending a Bible study at Desert Springs Church in Palm Desert California around 2009 and hearing world renown Bible prophecy scholar Hal Lindsey, the author of The Late Great Planet Earth, advise that people should try to have about $20,000 cash on hand, if possible, in case of an emergency crisis.

Personally, I concur that it is better to be prepared and to be safe, rather than sorry, in the event of an emergency. What if an electro-magnetic pulse (EMP) weapon was detonated over the heartland of America and the preponderance of the countries electronic systems were downed indefinitely? Russia and several other countries have EMP weapons capabilities. Some experts have warned that a strategically detonated EMP could send America back to the 18th century! Are you prepared to go without using your ATM or debit cards?

### "Russian Attack Submarine Sailed in Gulf of Mexico Undetected for Weeks"

*Fox Nation 8/14/12*

### "'Revolution' Depicts America After an EMP Blast: But Is It Plausible?"

*Forbes 9/19/12*

Since these powerful, prophetic events contained inside this book are forthcoming, it's prudent to prepare for them in advance. There is biblical precedent for prophetic preparedness. It's smart to fill the storehouses with food in advance of a pending famine—that's what Joseph did in the Genesis 41 historic account. Joseph possessed invaluable insights into the future, and took the necessary measures to provide for the Egyptians. In the process, his Hebrew posterity was also preserved. Joseph's actions were blessed, because they glorified God, and were in alignment with the Lord's plan for that time.

If a Christian exemplifies the lessons of Joseph by preparing for prophetic events, his or her actions, if rightly motivated and appropriately understood, can serve as a testimony to an unbelieving spectator. The goal is to temper the survival efforts with a clear demonstration of whole-hearted faith in Christ, and a wholesome understanding of Bible prophecy.

The believer's behavior should resemble that of Noah's.[246] While his ark was being constructed, he used the opportunity to preach to those curious about his foreknowledge of the flood. Although only his immediate family heeded his warnings, the inaction of those in denial did not deter him from taking the necessary survival measures. In the process, his posterity was also preserved. Noah's actions were also blessed because they glorified God, and were in alignment with the Lord's plan for that time.

Additionally, stockpiling some cash, gas, and goods, in advance of the fulfillment of a Bible prophecy, can insulate the believer from the predictable panic and hysteria that could follow. Long gas lines, food shortages, and inaccessible ATM machines for instance, can be temporarily avoided. This buys time for some resemblance of normalcy to resume. In the process, the believer's posterity can also be preserved.

## Jesus Christ is Hope Beyond the Horizon

Although the preparatory remarks above are important for the material well-being of the reader, the crux of the matter is the individual soul. These coming prophetic wars are deeply rooted in the angelic conflict. Satan wants to destroy the Jewish people and steal their homeland in order to stain the promise–keeping character of the Lord. Set aside the smokescreen illusion that peace and safety can be had apart from Christ.

There were many Christians that went down when the twin towers toppled on September 11, 2001. There may be many more Christians that will likewise experience adversity from the existential threats of Iran's nuclear program and the coming prophetic Mideast wars. Christ imparted very important information to humankind when He said.

> "And do not fear those who kill the body but cannot kill the soul. But rather fear Him who is able to destroy both soul and body in hell. Are not two sparrows sold for a copper coin? And not one of them falls to the ground apart from your Father's will. But the very hairs of your head are all numbered. Do not fear therefore; you are of more value than many sparrows." (Matthew 10:28-31).

Christ warned of a second death that involves the human soul. These verses demonstrate how important the individual soul is to the Lord. The IVP Bible Background Commentary of the New Testament explains these verses this way;

*"Sparrows were one of the cheapest items sold for poor people's food in the marketplace, the cheapest of all birds. Two were here purchased for an assarion, a small copper coin of little value (less than an hour's work); Luke 12:6 seems to indicate that they were even cheaper if purchased in larger quantities. This is a standard Jewish "how much more" argument: If God cares for something as cheap as sparrows, how much more does he care for people!"[247]*

Another commentary correlates Christ's two - sparrows comparison to a symbol of sacrifice;

*"Jesus told the leper to offer a sacrifice to the priest as Moses had commanded. In Leviticus 14, if a person was cured of leprosy, they were to bring two sparrows to the priest. One was to be cut open and killed. Running water was to be poured over the first sparrow, and the water and blood mingled together would run over the living bird. The living bird was then allowed to go free. The blood of the sparrow was put on the cleansed leper's thumbs and on his big toe, and the person was then allowed to go free. This is symbolic of the work of Jesus Christ on the cross. The first sparrow represents Jesus, the other sparrow represent us. Since Jesus took our place on the cross, we have been redeemed by His blood and are now allowed to go free."[248]*

In both interpretations above it is clear that Christ is alluding to the importance of the individual soul. The human soul is so precious to the Lord that He even knows the number of hairs on one's head.[249] Studies in this area suggest that the average healthy head of hair can contain over 100,000 strands. Even the world's best hair stylist doesn't know the number of hairs on their favorite customer's scalp.

Bible prophecy is extremely important for us to understand, and so much the more so in these last days, but according to the apostle Paul prophecy is not the end of the story. Paul points out in 1 Corinthians 13 that the all-important bottom line is love. The Bible is one of the primary methods that the Lord designed from the very beginning to express His long–suffering love for the lost.

Love never fails. But whether *there are* prophecies, they will fail; whether *there are* tongues, they will cease; whether *there is* knowledge, it will vanish away. For we know in part and we prophesy in part. But when that which is perfect has come, then that which is in part will be done away. (1 Corinthians 13:8-10, NKJV).

## Time to Prepare for Psalm 83

Therefore, in the end analysis the decision on how to make final preparations to weather the prophetic storms of Psalm 83 and the other coming prophecies is to make the ultimate decision for the wellbeing of your individual soul. If you are ready to make the most important decision you can make in your lifetime, then promptly read the attached appendix called, "The Sinner's Salvation Prayer.

# Appendix 1

## *The Text of Psalm 83 and Ezekiel 38:1-39:20*

### *The Text of Psalm 83:1-18*

(New King James Version)

1. Do not keep silent, O God! Do not hold Your peace, And do not be still, O God!

2. For behold, Your enemies make a tumult; And those who hate You have lifted up their head.

3. They have taken crafty counsel against Your people, And consulted together against Your sheltered ones.

4. They have said, "Come, and let us cut them off from being a nation, That the name of Israel may be remembered no more."

5. For they have consulted together with one consent; They form a confederacy against You:

6. The tents of Edom [Palestinians refugees including West Bank Palestinians] and the Ishmaelites [Saudis]; Moab [central Jordanians] and the Hagrites [or Hagarenes— Egyptians];

7. Gebal [Lebanese], Ammon [northern Jordanians], and Amalek [Arabs of the Sinai area]; Philistia [Palestinians of the Gaza, including Hamas] with the inhabitants of Tyre [Lebanese, including Hezbollah];

8. Assyria [Syrians and northern Iraqis] also has joined with them; They have helped the children of Lot. Selah

9. Deal with them as with Midian, as with Sisera, as with Jabin at the Brook Kishon,

10. Who perished at En Dor, who became as refuse on the earth.

11. Make their nobles like Oreb and like Zeeb, Yes, all their princes like Zebah and Zalmunna,

12. Who said, "Let us take for ourselves The pastures of God [Promised Land] for a possession."

13. O my God, make them like the whirling dust, like the chaff before the wind!

14. As the fire burns the woods, and as the flame sets the mountains on fire,

15. So pursue them with Your tempest, and frighten them with Your storm.

16. Fill their faces with shame, that they may seek Your name, O LORD.

17. Let them be confounded and dismayed forever; Yes, let them be put to shame and perish,

18. That they may know that You, whose name alone is the LORD, are the Most High over all the earth.

## The Text of Ezekiel 38:1-23

(New King James Version)

1. Now the word of the LORD came to me, saying,

2. Son of man, set your face against Gog, of the land of Magog, the prince of Rosh, Meshech, and Tubal, and prophesy against him,

3. and say, 'Thus says the Lord GOD: "Behold, I *am* against you, O Gog, the prince of Rosh, Meshech, and Tubal.

4. I will turn you around, put hooks into your jaws, and lead you out, with all your army, horses, and horsemen, all splendidly clothed, a great company *with* bucklers and shields, all of them handling swords.

5. Persia, Ethiopia, and Libya are with them, all of them *with* shield and helmet;

6. Gomer and all its troops; the house of Togarmah *from* the far north and all its troops—many people *are* with you.

7. "Prepare yourself and be ready, you and all your companies that are gathered about you; and be a guard for them.

8. After many days you will be visited. In the latter years you will come into the land of those brought back from the sword *and* gathered from many people on the mountains of Israel, which had long been desolate; they were brought out of the nations, and now all of them dwell safely.

9.    You will ascend, coming like a storm, covering the land like a cloud, you and all your troops and many peoples with you."

10.   'Thus says the Lord GOD: "On that day it shall come to pass *that* thoughts will arise in your mind, and you will make an evil plan:

11.   You will say, 'I will go up against a land of unwalled villages; I will go to a peaceful people, who dwell safely, all of them dwelling without walls, and having neither bars nor gates'—

12.   to take plunder and to take booty, to stretch out your hand against the waste places *that are again* inhabited, and against a people gathered from the nations, who have acquired livestock and goods, who dwell in the midst of the land.

13.   Sheba, Dedan, the merchants of Tarshish, and all their young lions will say to you, 'Have you come to take plunder? Have you gathered your army to take booty, to carry away silver and gold, to take away livestock and goods, to take great plunder?'"'

14.   "Therefore, son of man, prophesy and say to Gog, 'Thus says the Lord GOD: "On that day when My people Israel dwell safely, will you not know *it?*

15.   Then you will come from your place out of the far north, you and many peoples with you, all of them riding on horses, a great company and a mighty army.

16.   You will come up against My people Israel like a cloud, to cover the land. It will be in the latter days that I will bring you against My land, so that the nations may know Me, when I am hallowed in you, O Gog, before their eyes."

17.   Thus says the Lord GOD: "Are *you* he of whom I have spoken in former days by My servants the prophets of Israel, who prophesied for years in those days that I would bring you against them?

18.   "And it will come to pass at the same time, when Gog comes against the land of Israel," says the Lord GOD, "*that* My fury will show in My face.

19.   For in My jealousy *and* in the fire of My wrath I have spoken: 'Surely in that day there shall be a great earthquake in the land of Israel,

20.   so that the fish of the sea, the birds of the heavens, the beasts of the field, all creeping things that creep on the earth, and all men who *are* on the face of the earth shall shake at My presence. The mountains shall be thrown down, the steep places shall fall, and every wall shall fall to the ground.'

21. I will call for a sword against Gog throughout all My mountains," says the Lord GOD. "Every man's sword will be against his brother.

22. And I will bring him to judgment with pestilence and bloodshed; I will rain down on him, on his troops, and on the many peoples who *are* with him, flooding rain, great hailstones, fire, and brimstone.

23. Thus I will magnify Myself and sanctify Myself, and I will be known in the eyes of many nations. Then they shall know that I *am* the LORD."'

## The Text of Ezekiel 39:1-20

(New King James Version)

1. And you, son of man, prophesy against Gog, and say, 'Thus says the Lord GOD: "Behold, I *am* against you, O Gog, the prince of Rosh, Meshech, and Tubal;

2. and I will turn you around and lead you on, bringing you up from the far north, and bring you against the mountains of Israel.

3. Then I will knock the bow out of your left hand, and cause the arrows to fall out of your right hand.

4. You shall fall upon the mountains of Israel, you and all your troops and the peoples who *are* with you; I will give you to birds of prey of every sort and *to* the beasts of the field to be devoured.

5. You shall fall on the open field; for I have spoken," says the Lord GOD.

6. And I will send fire on Magog and on those who live in security in the coastlands. Then they shall know that I *am* the LORD.

7. So I will make My holy name known in the midst of My people Israel, and I will not *let them* profane My holy name anymore. Then the nations shall know that I *am* the LORD, the Holy One in Israel.

8. Surely it is coming, and it shall be done," says the Lord GOD. "This *is* the day of which I have spoken.

9. "Then those who dwell in the cities of Israel will go out and set on fire and burn the weapons, both the shields and bucklers, the bows and arrows, the javelins and spears; and they will make fires with them for seven years.

10. They will not take wood from the field nor cut down *any* from the forests, because they will make fires with the weapons; and they will plunder those who plundered them, and pillage those who pillaged them," says the Lord GOD.

11. "It will come to pass in that day *that* I will give Gog a burial place there in Israel, the valley of those who pass by east of the sea; and it will obstruct travelers, because there they will bury Gog and all his multitude. Therefore they will call *it* the Valley of Hamon Gog.

12. For seven months the house of Israel will be burying them, in order to cleanse the land.

13. Indeed all the people of the land will be burying, and they will gain renown for it on the day that I am glorified," says the Lord GOD.

14. "They will set apart men regularly employed, with the help of a search party, to pass through the land and bury those bodies remaining on the ground, in order to cleanse it. At the end of seven months they will make a search.

15. The search party will pass through the land; and *when anyone* sees a man's bone, he shall set up a marker by it, till the buriers have buried it in the Valley of Hamon Gog.

16  *The* name of *the* city *will* also *be* Hamonah. Thus they shall cleanse the land.'"

17. "And as for you, son of man, thus says the Lord GOD, 'Speak to every sort of bird and to every beast of the field:

18. "Assemble yourselves and come; Gather together from all sides to My sacrificial meal Which I am sacrificing for you, A great sacrificial meal on the mountains of Israel, That you may eat flesh and drink blood.

19. You shall eat the flesh of the mighty, Drink the blood of the princes of the earth, Of rams and lambs, Of goats and bulls, All of them fatlings of Bashan.

20. You shall eat fat till you are full, And drink blood till you are drunk, At My sacrificial meal Which I am sacrificing for you.

21. You shall be filled at My table With horses and riders, With mighty men And with all the men of war," says the Lord GOD.

# Appendix 2

## Psalm 83: Has It Found Final Fulfillment?

*(Appendix based upon an article from the author written on 3/18/2009 . Linked at: http://prophecydepot.blogspot.com/2009/03/psalm-83-has-it-found-final-fulfillment. html)*

Currently many prophecy buffs are discussing the Psalm 83, petition-formatted prophecy written by the seer Asaph approximately 3,000 years ago. This prophecy enlists a ten-member population whose goal is nothing short of wiping Israel off of the map. Their confederate mandate is:

> They have said, "Come, and let us cut them off from being a nation, That the name of Israel may be remembered no more." (Psalm 83:4)

My book, *Isralestine—the Ancient Blueprints of the Future Middle East*, has caused many eschatologists to rethink their end-time model. However, not all the experts agree with my end-time equation that Psalm 83 precedes Ezekiel 38-39. There are those who still sweep the prophecy into the catchall closet of the seven-year tribulation or simply deposit the event into the file thirteen trash bin of historical fulfillment.

The three primary reasons that Psalm 83 doesn't belong in the seven-year tribulation period, has already been addressed in the chapter called "Greater Israel The Future Maps of Isralestine," however, this appendix is intended to pull the prophecy out of the annals of historical fulfillment, and place it back into the pending event category.

## The 2 Chronicles 20 Argument:

Eschatologist, Nathan Jones, the webmaster for Dr. David Reagan's Lamb and Lion Ministries, and co-host for the "Christ in Prophecy" television show, asked me to participate in an ongoing blog. The argument was raised by some gentleman identified as Don, that 2 Chronicles 20:1-37 likely describes the final fulfillment of the Psalm 83 prophecy. You can read my blog comments and review some of the other assorted blogs made by others at the following link: http://www.lamblion.us/2009/01/gaza-conflict.html.

*Here is my comment on the subject:*

"Nathan and Don- 2 Chronicles is not likely the episode Asaph describes in Psalm 83. The 2 Chronicles account primarily describes only three, possibly four, of the ten-member populations enlisted in the prophecy of Psalm 83. These are the Psalm 83:6-8 confederates: The tents of Edom and the Ishmaelites; Moab and the Hagrites (Hagarenes); Gebal, Ammon, and Amalek; Philistia with the inhabitants of Tyre; Assyria also has joined with them; They have helped the children of Lot.

Now compare all of the above to 2 Chronicles 20:1-37 in your Bible.

> 2 Chronicles 20:1—It happened after this that the people of Moab with the people of Ammon, and others with them besides the Ammonites, came to battle against Jehoshaphat. (Following *Masoretic Text* and *Vulgate*; *Septuagint* reads Meunites see 2 Chronicle 26:7)

> 2 Chronicles 20:1; ASV—And it came to pass after this, that the children of Moab, and the children of Ammon, and with them some of the Ammonites, came against Jehoshaphat to battle. (Verse 1 enlists Moab and Ammon, and possibly the Meunites.)

The NKJV suggests that "others" were involved besides them, but that likely refers to the Meunites, a much smaller grouping than those of Psalm 83:6-8. The Meunites, if that is who verse 1 references, were an Arab tribe that dwelt about twelve miles southeast of Petra, which still puts them in modern-day southern Jordan. I cited the American Standard Version in addition to the New King James Version to illustrate that it only identifies Ammon, and Moab. Verse 2 references Syria, according to some Masoretic Text, Septuagint, and Vulgate; some Hebrew manuscripts and Old Latin read Edom.

Edom or Syria, or both—this still is only a portion of the ten populations of Psalm 83. Verses 10, and 22-23 of 2 Chronicles 20 lists Moab, Ammon, and Mt. Seir. Mt. Seir identifies primarily with the people of Edom. Thus, the populations referenced primarily would be modern-day Jordan, with a slight possibility of Syria having been involved. Moab is today central Jordan, Edom is southern Jordan, and Ammon is northern Jordan. Petra, Mt. Seir, and the Meunites, would also be clustered in and around southern Jordan today.

Due to the fact that less than half of the required ten Psalm 83 populations are referenced, it is not possible that 2 Chronicles 20 could be considered as the source of Psalm 83 fulfillment. In addition, several scholars like Dr. Arnold Fruchtenbaum, Chuck Missler, Hal Lindsey, Dr. David Reagan, Jacob Prasch, David Dolan and many others believe that Psalm 83 has yet to find its final fulfillment."

## The 1948 and 1967 Arab-Israeli War(s) Argument:

There are those who believe that the Six-Day war of 1967 occasioned the final fulfillment of the prophecy. I have this suggestion presented to me often, and below is a recent email I sent to a friend in response to his concern that this could be the case.

"I have recently been informed that you believe Psalm 83 may have found its fulfillment in the Six-Day war of 1967. Interestingly Dr. David Reagan and I discussed this possibility recently, while visiting together at a Calvary Chapel Chino Hills conference hosted by Pastor Jack Hibbs, in February 2009. We concurred that the better argument for fulfillment was the 1948 war commonly considered by the Israeli's as "The War of Independence;" however neither of these truly meets the description in our estimation. There are ten populations involved in Psalm 83:6-8 and not all of them were involved in 1967; and more than all of them, at least peripherally, were involved in 1948.

Additionally it is important to note that the "tents of Edom" are the first population listed in the Psalm 83:6-8 grouping, and a careful study demonstrates that the Edomite descendants became tent-dwellers only in the aftermath of the 1948 Arab – Israeli War. This abrogates the possibility that Psalm 83 found fulfillment in the 1948 "War of Independence."

Biblically the "tents of" condition alludes to either refugees or military encampments. In the Edomite instance their refugee condition became a troubling reality in 1949, when the Palestinian refugee crisis commenced. Up until that time, they were known as the Arabs of Palestine; ever since they have been referred to as refugees.

This book devotes an entire chapter to this topic called, "Whodomites"—Who are the Edomites Today. Inside the "Whodomite" chapter the Edomite – Palestinian refugee connection is clearly made. The chapter traces several historical waves of Edomite migration out from their original homeland into Israel. They generally settled in and around Hebron, which today exists in the modern-day West Bank. Ultimately they became known as the Idumeans, which is the Greek word for Edomites. The territory they developed inside of Israel assumed the name Idumea.

It appears that from 1949 to the present day the Palestinian refugees, the apparent antagonistic star of the Psalm 83 show, have a descendant Edomite contingency residing within their ranks.

However, the additional argument against either of these two Arab – Israeli wars being the fulfillment is the fact that Asaph is petitioning God to utterly destroy this confederacy as per Psalm 83:17, an event that has not yet occurred. He petitions God to fashion their demise in the similar format of the historic examples he lists in Psalm 83:9-11 and the allegorical illustrations of Psalm 83:13-16. The fact that these populations still exist, seek possession of the Promised land in Psalm 83:12, and continue to collectively possess the antagonistic attitude toward Israel of Psalm 83:4 conclusively evidences, in my estimation, that this prophecy has yet to find fulfillment."

## Conclusion:

The two arguments listed above are the primary ones forwarded by today's top scholars who believe that Psalm 83 has already found its fulfillment. Having previously deposited Psalm 83 into the historical fulfillment file thirteen, these advocates tend to then center their focus upon Ezekiel 38-39 as the next Mideast Bible prophecy set to find fulfillment. I disagree with this thinking and express my opinions in the chapter called Psalm 83 or Ezekiel 38: What's the Next Middle East News Headline?

We must consider the fact those mere rumblings today between Russia and Iran in the epicenter of the Middle East, as Joel Rosenberg aptly refers to them, does not constitute, but rather simply suggests the nearby fulfillment of the Ezekiel 38-39 invasion. Oddly, many military experts are predicting just the opposite, that Israel may be forced to invade Iran in order to forestall their nuclear aspirations. This could temporarily sideline Iran and render them of little immediate utility to Russia, and may be one of the reasons Iran (ancient Persia) is not listed among the Psalm 83 confederates.

Anyway you "prophe-size" it up, some big, world-changing Middle East event is certainly about to happen, just like the Bible predicted it would. The fact that the Psalm 83 confederates live on today and embrace the ancient hatred of Israel, signals the likelihood that Psalm 83 is the next Mideast prophecy to find fulfillment.

# Appendix 3

## Those Surrounding Israel to be Devoured!

*(Appendix drawn from an article written by author on 6/9/11. Linked at: http://prophecynewsstand.blogspot.com/2011/06/those-surrounding-israel-to-be-devoured.html)*

The prophet Zechariah informs us in chapter 12 that those peoples surrounding Israel will someday be devoured by Israel. The key to understanding portions of his prophecy rests in recognizing the direct correlation between Zechariah 12:2, and Zechariah 12:6.

> Behold, I will make Jerusalem a cup of drunkenness to all the surrounding peoples, when they lay siege against Judah and Jerusalem. (Zechariah 12:2)

Someday Jerusalem will become a cup of raal in the Hebrew, which is commonly translated as reeling, trembling, or drunkenness. This occurs when the surrounding peoples lay siege against both Judah and Jerusalem. This cup of raal should not be confused with the "heavy stone" classification of Jerusalem in the following passage.

> And it shall happen in that day that I will make Jerusalem a very heavy stone for all peoples; all who would heave it away will surely be cut in pieces, though all nations of the earth are gathered against it. (Zechariah 12:3)

Jerusalem becomes a heavy stone for all peoples, from all nations, rather than a cup of trembling to the surrounding peoples sharing common borders with Israel. Certainly, Jerusalem will feel like a burdensome stone and a cup of trembling to Israel's bordering nations, when they lay siege upon Judah and Jerusalem, but the heavy stone application applies to a much broader worldwide audience.

Zechariah 12:6 informs us that the Israel Defense Forces devour those sharing common borders with them like a fiery torch consumes sheaves or rows of fallen grain.

> In that day I will make the governors of Judah like a firepan in the woodpile, and like a fiery torch in the sheaves; they shall devour all the surrounding peoples

on the right hand and on the left, but Jerusalem shall be inhabited again in her own place—Jerusalem. (Zechariah 12:6)

The differing imageries of a cup of trembling verses a burdensome stone seems to represent different prophetic events. Although they are somewhat interrelated due to their connection with Jerusalem, the first event describes the IDF causing their surrounding enemies to tremble because they retaliate against them for laying siege upon Judah and Jerusalem. As a result of a decisive IDF victory, Jerusalem is inhabited again by Israelis.

Continued Israeli claims of exclusive sovereignty over Jerusalem meet with ongoing resistance throughout the world. From Joel 3:2, Psalm 2:1-3, and elsewhere we realize anti-Semitism spreads throughout the world and ultimately causes all peoples from all nations to assemble against Israel in the final stages of the Armageddon Campaign.

## Clues

The main clues given to separate the two Jerusalem-centered prophecies are:

- The Surrounding Peoples

- The Fiery Torch

- The Heavy Stone

The Surrounding Peoples—appears to identify those sharing common borders with Israel at the time Jerusalem becomes a cup of trembling. The Hebrew word used for the surrounding peoples is sabiyb. This same word is used to describe the enemy Arab nations encircling Israel in Ezekiel 36:3, 4, and 7. It is doubtful Zechariah was loosely identifying all peoples, from all nations, by using this specific Hebrew word. If he was, why didn't he repeat the same word again in Zechariah 12:3? Instead the prophet uses the Hebrew word "erets" in verse 3. This word describes all people upon the earth. It is a much broader reference.

The Fiery Torch—the illustration of a torch devouring a swath of sheaves is a clear picture of a military conquest. Since it is the governors (also translated as clans or captains) of Judah that wield the torch, rather than the Lord single-handedly, like in Isaiah 63:3 and Ezekiel 38:18-39:6, it should be regarded with a prophecy involving the Israeli military.

Ezekiel 25:14, Obadiah v. 18, Isaiah 11:13-14, Zephaniah 2:9 and elsewhere describes the IDF in end-times military actions. However, the IDF is not instrumental in Isaiah 63:3 or Ezekiel 38:18-39:6. These events involve the destruction of Israel's enemies solely by the Lord. In Isaiah's prophecy it is the Messiah that is "mighty to save" that fights against the Antichrist and his armies. In Ezekiel's account, it is the Lord that destroys the Ezekiel 38 invaders. In neither Isaiah's nor Ezekiel's scenarios does the IDF seem influential in the battle.

Thus, there appears to be at least three end-time battles over Israel; two of which the IDF apparently plays no decisive role. If Zechariah 12:2 and 12:6, which both identify surrounding peoples, is not part of Armageddon or Ezekiel's Gog of Magog invasion, then what battle remains? The only logical conclusion is that described in the Psalm 83 prophecy. The Psalm identifies the surrounding peoples, sharing common borders with Israel, that want to destroy Israel.

The Heavy Stone—although some allegorical correlation to the stone of Daniel 2:34-35, 45 could be made with Zechariah 12:3, the illustration appears to deal with disputed territory. Sovereign Israeli claims over Jerusalem become a burden to all peoples from all nations, and Jerusalem is pictured as an immovable stone. Due to its weight it can neither be heaved away nor cut into pieces, to be removed fractionally. Even though the international community continuously attempts to heave it out of Israel's real estate portfolio, it falls back in its same location, injuring those attempting to cast it away.

The prophet Joel predicts this matter's final resolution as an end time event occurring after the Jews return from the nations of the world into the reestablished State of Israel.

> For behold, in those days and at that time, When I bring back the captives of Judah and Jerusalem, I will also gather all nations, And bring them down to the Valley of Jehoshaphat; And I will enter into judgment with them there On account of My people, My heritage Israel, Whom they have scattered among the nations; They have also divided up My land. (Joel 3:1-2)

The nations of the world are guilty of attempting to divide the land of Israel, including Jerusalem. This is occurring now, and will probably continue to occur after the Psalm 83 conflict. Ultimately, the Lord gathers all the nations to a final battle against the Jews, which appears to be when Zechariah 12:3 finds its final, literal fulfillment. Partial geopolitical fulfillment has been occurring since Israel was reestablished on May 14, 1948.

# Appendix 4

## *Is Ezekiel's Army About to Face-Off with the Arabs?*

*(Appendix is based upon an article from the author written on 5/19/2011 Linked at: http://prophecynewsstand.blogspot.com/2011/05/psalm-83-icegesis.html)*

Approximately 2,500 years ago the prophet Ezekiel envisioned a future valley filled with dry bones and is described in Ezekiel 37:1-13. It appears the dry bones represent the Jews in a holocaust condition, dispersed throughout the nations of the world. This conclusion can be safely suggested, because Ezekiel 37:11-12 says,

> Then He said to me, "Son of man, these bones are the whole house of Israel. They indeed say, 'Our bones are dry, our hope is lost, and we ourselves are cut off!'" Therefore prophesy and say to them, " Thus says the Lord GOD: 'Behold, O My people, I will open your graves and cause you to come up from your graves, and bring you into the land of Israel.'"

These verses clearly evidence that these bones represent the "whole house of Israel." Furthermore, it pictures the Jews in a desperate condition. Their "hope is lost," and they "are cut off." Lastly, they are being restored "into the land of Israel," meaning they were outside of the land of Israel during the vision.

Ezekiel's dry bones vision pictures the Jews during the Diaspora; therefore, the Nazi holocaust would be the root cause of their condition of hopelessness. Thus, Ezekiel sums up the metric of time that the Jews would be without a homeland; not in years, decades, or centuries, but in their helpless concluding condition. History testifies to the accuracy of Ezekiel's prediction, because shortly after the Holocaust the reestablishment of the nation Israel officially occurred on May 14, 1948. It is important to note that Ezekiel 37:10 prophesied that the Jewish people would arise from their hopeless condition as refugees and emerge into an "exceedingly great army."

> "So I prophesied as He commanded me, and breath came into them, and they lived, and stood upon their feet, an exceedingly great army." (NKJV)

The ongoing Arab – Israeli conflict has forced Israel to form a great army. The Israel Defense Forces (IDF) have had to become the superior military in the Middle East as a matter of national survival. In addition to Ezekiel 37:10, prophecies written in verse 18 of Obadiah, Ezekiel 25:14, Zechariah 12:6, and elsewhere also seem to identify today's IDF.

Based upon the above premises, the remainder of this article discusses the debate among scholars as to whether or not Ezekiel 37:10 describes an exceedingly great army. Some scholars believe Ezekiel describes an army; whereas others believe Ezekiel is predicting a great multitude or host will emerge out of the dry bones.

## Point 1

The Hebrew word Ezekiel uses in verse 10 for army is chayil and it is used twelve times elsewhere by Ezekiel, and over 225 times throughout the Old Testament. All of Ezekiel's usages, and many Old Testament renderings clearly depict it as either an army, or riches acquired via the spoils obtained by an army, in the aftermath of a war. Nowhere else in the book of Ezekiel can it possibly be translated as a multitude or host. This establishes precedent that an army, rather than a multitude, is being described by Ezekiel.

Ezekiel's twelve specific usages of the word *chayil* are as follows:


- Ezekiel 17:17 – describing Pharaoh's army,

- Ezekiel 26:12 – depicting the Babylonian army taking "riches" or spoil from victory over Tyre,

- Ezekiel 27:10-11 – alluding to the armies of Tyre,

- Ezekiel 28:4-5 – picturing the riches acquired by the ruler of Tyre,

- Ezekiel 29:18-19 – describing Nebuchadnezzar's Babylonian army,

- Ezekiel 32:31 – alluding to Pharaoh's army,

- Ezekiel 37:10 – describing Israel's "exceedingly great army,"

- Ezekiel 38:4, 15 – predicting the coming armies of Gog of Magog.


## Point 2

Further supporting the proper interpretation being an army, the following Bible translations interpret chayil to be an "army": King James Version, New King James

Version, American Standard Version, New American Standard Bible, New International Version, New Living Translation, New Century Version, and The Living Bible. Conversely, the Revised Standard Version translates the word as "host." The New Revised Standard Version calls it a "multitude."

Conclusion—Obviously the above reasons overwhelmingly favor the interpretation of Ezekiel 37:10 as an army, rather than a host or multitude. *Isralestine* points out that the purpose of this army is to protect Israel from its surrounding enemies, who someday confederate in a final attempt to destroy the Jewish State of Israel, according to Psalm 83.

# Appendix 5

## *Ezekiel: Israel's Dry Bones Can Fight*

Lining bookstore shelves today are numerous books foretelling the coming invasion of Israel by a nuclear equipped, Russian – Iranian led coalition. Relations between Russia and Iran have never been stronger, causing the serious spectator to wonder if this assault is about to commence. Prescribed in Ezekiel 38:18 - 39:6 is Israel's survival and the confederacy's demise.

Turning a few pages back to Ezekiel 37:10, we discover that Israel someday produces an "exceedingly great army." This army, the Israel Defense Forces (IDF), exists today. Although it would appear this army has emerged to engage in the coming Russian – Iranian led conflict, IDF participation in the battle is minimal, if at all. Instead, as per Ezekiel 38:18-39:6, divine events collapse this Russian led coalition. Justifiably, this beckons the question: what future military event earns the IDF "exceedingly great" esteem?

Clues deposited in Ezekiel 37:1-9 help us to discover what necessitated the existence of the IDF. These passages inform us that about 2,600 years ago the Hebrew prophet was fast-forwarded in time to the 1940s, wherein he envisioned the Holocaust. He saw a valley full of dry bones, which represented the Jewish people in a horrifically grave condition. He was asked, "Can these bones live?" or simply put, can the Jewish race survive? Not only will they survive, he was told, but they would be restored to their ancient homeland of Israel, and emerge into an "exceedingly great army." By alluding to this army, he causes humanity to ponder its purpose. Why would the surviving Jews need to graduate from refugees to soldiers? Amazingly, we see that one failed Arab war upon another has caused the creation of the IDF. The enemies of Israel have quickly learned that Ezekiel's "dry bones" can fight!

By strategically inserting the prophecy of Psalm 83 somewhere between the events of Ezekiel 37:1-13 and Ezekiel 38, we come to recognize the primary purpose of Ezekiel's emerging army. Psalm 83 tells us that the Arabs are going to follow on the heels of the Germans with a genocidal attempt of their own. This Psalm foretells the future development of a predominately Arab confederacy that will soon seek to destroy the Jewish state and erase the name of Israel from the map forever.

Although the IDF does not play a major role in Ezekiel 38-39, they will face-off with an Arab confederacy apparently comprised of Hezbollah, Hamas, Muslim Brotherhood, Saudis, Palestinians, Jordanians, Egyptians, Iraqis, Syrians, and Lebanese.

Coincidentally these populations are not listed in the Russian – Iranian coalition of Ezekiel 38. As a modern-day map of the Middle East depicts, they have Israel surrounded. According to numerous Scriptures, Israel will go ballistic and soundly defeat this confederacy. In victory, the Jewish army achieves the title of becoming "exceedingly great"!

Destiny designed the emergence of the IDF to prevent the destruction of modern-day Israel. Ezekiel foretold the arrival of these Israel Defense Forces. Now the only thing that stands between Ezekiel's dry bones army and its "exceedingly great" title is the Israeli conquest over the Psalm 83 Arab confederacy.

# Appendix 6

## *Israel Strikes it Rich Someday!*

The Bible predicted the coming of a reestablished and extremely prosperous Israel. Ezekiel 36:24 and elsewhere foretold that the Jews would be re-gathered from the nations of the world into their own homeland. What had begun as a trickle around the turn of the century, began accelerating in the aftermath of WWII, and shortly thereafter; the prophesied return of the Jews into the rebirthed nation of Israel became official on May 14, 1948.

Ezekiel 36:8-12 informed that upon their return, the land of Israel would be tilled, sown, and become extremely fruitful. Ezekiel declares the historic ruins would be rebuilt and the ancient cities repopulated. In these verses, he predicts the Jews will be more prosperous than at any prior time in their history. This is a startling prediction considering the land of Israel lay mostly desolate between AD 70 and May, 1948, when Israel was restored as the Jewish state.

Equally as impressive is that Israel's abundance appears to proportionately exceed the national treasures King Solomon accumulated nearly 3,000 years ago. According to 1 Kings 10, King Solomon was the wealthiest king on Earth during his reign over Israel.

> So king Solomon exceeded all the kings of the earth in riches and in wisdom. (1 Kings 10:23; ASV)

1 Chronicles 22:14-16 informs that Solomon owned a seemingly limitless supply of gold, silver, bronze, and iron. The International Standard Bible Encyclopedia says Solomon possessed "A sum greater than the national debt of Great Britain." We are told in 2 Chronicles 9:13, that one year Solomon's estimated income was 666 talents, which is the approximate equivalent today of $708,400,000.21 These earnings represented a monumental amount of annual wealth at that time. Presently, the cities are being rebuilt and repopulated and Israel is becoming very prosperous, but have they accumulated all the riches predicted?

Relatively recently, Israel gained acclaim for their two large discoveries of natural gas resources. In 2009, approximately ninety kilometers due west of the port of Haifa, in the Mediterranean Sea, Israel discovered a large supply of natural gas. The drilling site is called Tamar-One, and the gas supply is estimated to be worth about $15 billion.[250] Subsequently in 2010, Israel located another sizable natural gas supply near Tamar-One, called Leviathan. This gas field reserve is estimated at $90 billion.[251]

Some eschatologists believe the Israelis will also someday discover crude oil underneath their fertile soil. Natural gas and crude oil could certainly become contributors toward Israel's foretold fortunes, but what does Scripture point to, possibly in addition to these resources?

Ezekiel 38:1-13 informs that a major alliance will form to invade Israel to confiscate Israel's riches. Ezekiel 38:13 specifically states this confederacy comes for Israel's great spoil. This prophecy, commonly referred to among scholars as the Gog of Magog invasion, remains unfulfilled. Should no unforeseen circumstances prohibit, this means Israel has more time to amass an even greater fortune beforehand.

The Hebrew words utilized for the Magog invaders goal to capture great spoil are shalal gadol shalal. According to the definitions given in the New America Hebrew and Greek Dictionaries, these words can be translated successively to read, "Plunder the great spoil of the despoilers." Despoil means to deprive someone of something valuable by force. It suggests that the invaders are coming to plunder the spoils Israel previously captured from another. Please don't mark my words, but I believe the respected eschatologist, Dr. Arnold Fruchtenbaum, teaches that the Magog invaders are coming to, "To take a spoil of a spoil."

In the prior verse, Ezekiel 38:12, the prophet says the Magog invaders are coming after acquired, or gotten, cattle and goods. The Hebrew word is asah and suggests that Israel has acquired livestock and commercial goods externally, perhaps more-so than developed them from their own natural resources and / or commercial endeavors.

If the enticing great spoil spoken of is acquired, in addition to potentially being homegrown, then where does it originate? Zechariah 14:14 appears to hold an important clue in this regard. Apparently Israel acquires it from the Arab nations round about them.

> And Judah also shall fight at Jerusalem; *and the wealth of all the* (Arab) *nations round about shall be gathered together*, gold, and silver, and apparel, in great abundance. (Zechariah 14:14, ASV; emphasis added)

Zechariah declares that Israel gathers great abundance from the neighboring Arab nations "round about." Zechariah 14:14 appears to find connection with Zechariah 12:2, 6. To get a greater understanding of this connection, compare this appendix with the attached appendix called Those Surrounding Israel to be Devoured!

Zechariah chapters 12 and 14 find connection in that, portions of each chapter address the wars between Israel and its hostile Arab neighbors, and the subsequent conflict fought by Jesus Christ against the Antichrist and his armies during the campaign of Armageddon. These are two distinct wars, that are intricately interwoven between Zechariah's chapters 12 and 14. Zechariah 12:6 below, and 14:14 above, specifies that the IDF, represented as Judah, fights the Arab nations round about for possession of Jerusalem.

> In that day will I make the chieftains of Judah like a pan of fire among wood, and like a flaming torch among sheaves; and they shall devour all the peoples round about, on the right hand and on the left; and *they of* Jerusalem shall yet again dwell in their own place, even in Jerusalem. (Zechariah 12:6; ASV)

The IDF is instrumental in Israel's fight against the Arab confederacy of Psalm 83, but does not appear to get involved in the war waged between Christ and the armies of the Antichrist. Isaiah 63:1-6 informs us that the Messiah, as the one who is mighty to save, goes into battle alone. The absence of the IDF in the battle of Armageddon is reinforced by Zechariah 13:8, which points out that two-thirds of the Jewish population in the land of Israel will not survive. Zechariah's prophecy infers the IDF will flee from the armies of the Antichrist, rather than fight against them.

## Conclusion

According to Bible prophecy, Israel is enroute to striking it rich someday. Their blossoming portfolio appears to include Arab spoils of war. Once obtained, the Ezekiel 38 Magog invaders are enticed to coalesce in an attempt to capture Israel's new national livelihood, which should by then include the acquired Arab resources, including oil and natural gas, plundered by Israel after their decisive victory over the Psalm 83 Arab nations round about.

Psalm 83 is a prophecy formatted into an imprecatory prayer. It foretells the coming of a climatic concluding conflict between the IDF and the Arab nations that share common borders with Israel. Presently those Arab nations are using the Palestinians as pawns in their ongoing war against Israel. This plight of the Palestinians also appears to have been predicted. This is discussed in the chapter called, "Obadiah's Mysterious Vision."

# Appendix 7

## Is the Church Identified in Psalm 83?

In August of 2010, I received an email asking a very interesting church-related question regarding the *hidden ones* of Psalm 83:3. Some translations use the word "hidden" instead of sheltered.

> "They [Arab confederates] have taken crafty counsel against Your people [national Israel], And consulted together against Your sheltered [hidden] ones." (Psalm 83:3, NKJV).

> *Question: "I have a question concerning Psalm 83:3 and its link with Isaiah 26:20. The last section of the Psalm verse reads, "and consulted against thy hidden ones," and Isaiah explains who these are that are hiding. I understand these passages refer to the Saints/Church. That being the case would not the inference in the Psalm be that the Church has already been taken before the fulfillment of that prophecy?"* Kindest Regards Garry M.

Author's Answer: Brother Garry, I don't believe the church is identified anywhere in Psalm 83. Furthermore, since the rapture is an imminent event, Psalm 83 is about to occur, and the church is still present, it is very possible that Christians may witness the final fulfillment of Psalm 83.

In Psalm 83:3, the Hebrew word for "hidden" in "hidden ones" is tsaphan. This word does not appear in Isaiah 26:20 or anywhere else in the book of Isaiah. The first usage of tsaphan is in Exodus 2:2-3, alluding to the baby Moses being hidden by his mother from Pharaoh's edict of death in Egypt. At the time, all Hebrew males were being killed at birth in order to keep the Hebrew ethnicity weak and enslaved. However, a remnant led by Moses ultimately survived and departed for the Promised Land.

Typologically, from an end-time perspective, the mother of Moses likely represents national Israel, and Moses the faithful end-time remnant that eventually emerges from within it. Similarly, the next usage of tsaphan is found in Joshua 2:4, wherein Rahab was hiding the two spies. These two also typologically signify a select sub-group or remnant of Israel.

I believe that Psalm 83:3 alludes to both national Israel (Your people), which exists today in a condition of unbelief, and the faithful remnant (hidden ones) that comes out from national Israel in the end times in a condition of belief. Although the faithful remnant hasn't emerged yet from within Israel, one will in the tribulation period. Today, they are tsaphan within national Israel. Presently, they remain unidentified, but probably exist on the world scene somewhere unknowingly. However, omniscient God knows who, and where they are.

Psalm 83 represents a genocidal attempt of the Jews and the final destruction of the Jewish state, that the name Israel be remembered no more (Psalm 83:4). Geopolitically, the Arab confederates want to destroy Israel and confiscate the Promised Land. We see this stage-setting in the Middle East today. Geo-prophetically, Satan wants to destroy all Jews worldwide, especially the infamous coming faithful remnant, to prove God is not a covenant-keeper. In Genesis 13:15, 22:17 and elsewhere, God unconditionally promised Abraham, Isaac, and Jacob, descendants forever. In Genesis 15:18 these patriarchs were promised land from the Nile River in Egypt to the Euphrates in Iraq and Syria. The Psalm 83 Arabs dwell upon a majority of this "Holy Land" today. They want to destroy the Jews and possess the land (Psalm 83:12).

Psalm 83 represents the first of three end-time genocidal attempts against the Jews. Ezekiel 38-39 appears to follow soon and sequentially on the heels of Psalm 83. In Ezekiel's prophecy, Russia, Iran, Turkey, and several other nations will confederate to kill the Jews and confiscate the plunder and booty that Israel will possess after they defeat the Psalm 83 confederacy.

Lastly, the Antichrist will muster up his Armageddon forces in the tribulation period in a final Jewish genocidal attempt. This is when the tsaphan, the faithful remnant, of Israel will emerge. They become the saved remnant of Romans 9:27 and 11:26. They are also the "sons of the living God" in Hosea 1:10 and Romans 9:26. I believe the Psalmist Asaph was informing us that Israel's Arab enemies will attempt to kill all Jews, even the hidden faithful, the end time's remnant, so that God's promises to Abraham, Isaac, and Jacob would be broken.

Although the church may be here to witness Psalm 83, it does not appear to be identified anywhere in the Psalm. Psalm 83 is Satan's attempt to inspire the Islamic Arabs, that hate and surround Israel, to destroy the Jews and the Jewish state in order to prove God is a promise-breaker. In fact, the church needs to come out of hiding regarding Psalm 83 and preach the possibility that it's about to find final fulfillment.

# Appendix 8

## The Treasured Ones of Psalm 83

*Comment*—"Dear Mr. Salus—I regularly receive emails concerning Bible Prophecy and as a matter of fact, I pray Psalm 83 every night for the total defeat of Israel's satanic enemies. Regarding your article *"Is the Church Identified in Psalm 83?"* I would like to bring the following to your attention. In my Bible Ps.83.3 reads as follows: "They are making secret plans against your people; they are plotting against those you protect." I feel that this translation of vs. 3 is far more descriptive, especially in light of current events that are leading up to Psalm 83, which I believe will be the next "happening" in the prophetic Mideast calendar. It never ceases to amaze me how much different Bible translations differ." *Yours in Christ – J.M. - South Africa*

Author's Response—Dear J.M., thanks for your comment. In 2010, Chuck Missler and I discussed this topic at a southern California prophecy conference we were speaking at. Chuck is studying the possibility that the "hidden" or "treasured" ones in Psalm 83:3 could represent true, born-again Christians. He presented a couple arguments in support of this view. However, for the reasons expressed in (refer to the appendix called, Is the Church Identified in Psalm 83?) and those listed below, I believe the "hidden ones" probably represent the faithful remnant inside national Israel.

- To make the "hidden ones" the church implies the confederacy of Psalm 83:6-8 wages a multi-front war against Israel and true Christian believers. It seems that geography alone would defeat this plan. The Psalm 83 confederacy is centered in the Mideast, but true believers are scattered throughout the world. The confederates surround Israel, making it an easy target. However targeting Christians would require a worldwide campaign headquartered in the Middle East, which is unlikely.

- The mandate of Psalm 83:4 is to destroy the Jewish state, "that the name Israel be remembered no more." This mission is very specific regarding Israel.

- The motive of Psalm 83:12 is the capture of the Promised Land of Israel. Thus, the mandate and motive of the Psalm 83 confederacy are entirely regarded with the Jewish people and the land of Israel.

- The Hebrew word for "hidden" is *tsaphan* and is first used in Exodus 2:2-3, identifying Moses being hidden in the basket from Pharaoh's persecution.

- The second usage is in Joshua 2:4 describing Rahab hiding the two spies.

In these initial usages the Hebrew word tsaphan best represents the faithful inside national Israel. Therefore, I suggest the "hidden ones" of Psalm 83:3 represent the faithful remnant that will surface out of today's national Israel and survive both Psalm 83 and ultimately the tribulation. The caveat is that if there is a significant generational gap between Psalm 83 and the tribulation, which I doubt, then the hidden ones in Psalm 83 probably represent the Messianic Jewish community dwelling inside Israel when Psalm 83 occurs.

# Appendix 9

## Is Egypt in Psalm 83?

**M**ost modern-day equivalents of the Psalm 83:6-8 participants are easily iden-
tifiable today. Clearly, the territories of Edom, Moab, and Ammon represent
modern-day Jordan. Furthermore, Tyre still exists in Lebanon and the Gaza Strip is
located in ancient Philistia. However, Egypt is more difficult to identify, causing some
scholars to question its existence in the Psalm. Among them is the respected broad-
cast journalist David Dolan. He authored a book in 2001 entitled *Israel in Crisis, What
Lies Ahead*. Dolan's book, along with Dr. Arnold Fruchtenbaum's *Footsteps of the Messiah*, were among the first books published that addressed Psalm 83 as a future war
between Israel and its bordering Arab enemies. Dolan excluded, but Fruchtenbaum
included, Egypt in the Psalm 83 confederacy.[252] Probably motivated by the February,
2011 crisis in Egypt, David Dolan wrote the following.

> "*Will Egypt eventually break its peace treaty with Israel? I suspect that in the end,
> the American-funded and trained army will not allow this to take place. I noted
> in my latest book, Israel in Crisis, that Egypt is not listed in Psalm 83 as being
> among a host of regional Arab powers that will attempt to destroy Israel in the
> prophesied end days, while Jordan, Lebanon and Syria are mentioned, along
> with the Palestinians.*" David Dolan 2/7/11

As much as I respect Dolan's work, I respectfully disagree with his assessment on
Egypt's non-participation in Psalm 83. Here is what the Psalm says:

> "O God, keep not thou silence: Hold not thy peace, and be not still, O God.
> For, lo, thine *enemies make a tumult*; And they that *hate* thee *have lifted up
> the head*. Thy take crafty counsel against thy people, And consult together
> against thy hidden ones. They have said, Come, and let us cut them off from
> being a nation; That the name of Israel may be no more in remembrance. For
> they have consulted together with one consent; Against thee do they make a
> covenant: The tents of Edom and the Ishmaelites; Moab, and the Hagarenes;
> [Hagar, the mother of Ishmael] *Gebal*, and Ammon, and Amalek; *Philistia* with
> the inhabitants of *Tyre*: *Assyria* also is joined with them; They have helped the
> children of Lot. Selah! "(Psalm 83:1-8, ASV; emphasis added)

## The Enemies vs. The Haters

Asaph seems to identify two distinct groups inside the ten-member confederacy. He says "thine enemies make a tumult; And they that hate thee have lifted up the head." The New American Standard Version translates; "Your enemies make an uproar, And those who hate You have exalted themselves."

Who are the *enemies* and *haters* of God listed inside the Psalm? I cover this extensively in the chapter called "The Ancient Arab Hatred of the Jews."

The Psalmist says the Lord has those who hate Him, but unlike the general carnal hatred characteristic of sinful humanity described in Romans 8:7, it is a deeply rooted hatred dating back almost 4,000 years. These haters listed by Asaph include the Egyptian matriarch Hagar, alongside the ancient patriarchs: Ishmael, Edom (Esau), Moab, Ammon, and Amalek. These all had familial relations with Abraham and histories of aggression against Abraham, Sarah, Isaac, Jacob, and their Hebrew descendants.

Hagar mothered Abraham's first son Ishmael. Esau was Abraham's grandson from Isaac. Moab and Ammon were the children of Abraham's nephew Lot. Lastly, Amalek was Abraham's great-great grandson through the line of Esau.[253] Esau fathered the Edomites according to Genesis 36:1.

These individuals coveted the rich contents of the Abrahamic Covenant and entered into family feuds with the true Hebrew recipients of the covenantal promises. These individuals, along with their Hebrew counterparts, would be likened to, Israeli Prime Minister Benjamin Netanyahu, Jordan's King Abdullah II, and Egyptian President Mohammad Morsi if they were living today; from their loins nations were formed.[254]

These jealous "haters" incubated an enmity against the Lord that manifested throughout the region against the Israeli descendants of Abraham, Isaac, and Jacob. The Bible calls it an "ancient hatred," also translated as a "perpetual enmity." Ezekiel 35:5 tells us it was spawned by Esau.

The two Hebrew words used by Ezekiel are olam ebah, which when used together can be translated as, "a condition stemming back long ago in ancient times, perpetuated throughout time, manifesting into hostility with no apparent end in sight." As time progressed, the Hebrews staked their covenantal claims throughout the Middle East. These claims included:

- Our God is the only God and you shall have no others before Him, (Exodus 20:3)

- We will be a "great nation" above all others, (Genesis 12:2)

- Arabs must bless Hebrews or be cursed, (Genesis 12:3)

- You Arabs are trespassing on our Hebrew lands. (Genesis 15:18)

Suffice it to say the other four members of Psalm 83, Gebal, Philistia, Tyre, and Assyria, found it favorable to their religious, real estate, and cultural needs to resist these Hebrew claims and embrace the ancient hatred, well established throughout the region. Thus, these four populations probably represent the your enemies group in Psalm 83. The family feuds that developed can be studied in the chapters depicted in the image. *(Refer to figure 3, page 133 ).*

Hagar's jealous behavior toward Sarah is one of the reasons we can include her among the Psalm 83 haters. Considering Hagar was an Egyptian, according to Genesis 16:1, and had her son Ishmael marry an Egyptian bride in Genesis 21:21, we can safely conclude the Hagarenes represent Egypt in Psalm 83, through her and Ishmael's family tree. However, it's not quite that simple. Some Bible translations list Hagarites or Hagrites, rather than Hagarenes. This has caused many to believe Psalm 83 is describing another ethnicity than Egyptians. This is because the Hagrites or Hagarites show up in 1 Chronicles 5:10,19-20 and elsewhere as a tribe dwelling approximately 300 miles northeast of Egypt, east of Gilead.

The Hebrew word used by the Psalmist to identify the Hagarenes was Hagri. Both the Strong's Hebrew and Greek Dictionaries, and the New American Standard Hebrew and Greek Dictionaries suggest Hagri has a possible matronymic relationship to "Hagar," the Egyptian matriarch.

Additionally, listed below are other reputable quotes supporting the Psalm 83 Hagar - Egyptian connection:

### Holman Bible Dictionary —

HAGARITE (Hag' ahr ite) Name of nomadic tribe whom the tribe of Reuben defeated east of the Jordan River (1 Chron 5:10, 19-20). Reuben won because they called on and trusted in God. The tribal name is apparently taken from Hagar, Sarah's maid and mother of Ishmael (Gen. 16).[255]

### International Standard Bible Encyclopedia—

Hagarenes / Hagarites / Hagrites

An Arab tribe, or confederation of tribes (1 Ch 5:10, 19, 20 the King James Version "Hagarites"; 1 Ch 27:31 the King James Version "Hagerite"; Ps 83:6 "Hagarenes"), against which the Reubenites fought in the days of Saul. In Gen. 25:12-18 are recorded the descendants, "generations," of Ishmael, "whom Hagar the Egyptian Sarah's handmaid, bare unto Abraham."[256]

### *New Commentary on the Whole Bible: Old Testament—*

Ps. 83:6-8 tabernacles—i.e., tents. Edom—Esau's descendants; they were located southeast of the Dead Sea and repeatedly attacked Israel (Psa. 137:7; Obadiah). Ishmaelites—descendants of Hagar and Abraham (Gen. 25:12ff.) as are the "Hagarenes."[257]

### *Barnes, Notes on the Old Testament – Ps. 83:6-8—*

And the Hagarenes—The Hagarenes were properly Arabs, so called from Hagar, the handmaid of Abraham, the mother of Ishmael. Gen. 16:1; 25:12. As connected with the Ishmaelites they would naturally join in this alliance.[258]

Due to the confusion caused by the Hagarene verses Hagrite translation in Psalm 83, I emailed my friend Dr. Arnold Fruchtenbaum of Ariel Ministries in 2008. Dr. Fruchtenbaum, a graduate of Dallas Theological Seminary, ranks among today's most respected eschatologists. I asked him how certain he was that Psalm 83 identified Egypt through the Hagarenes. His email response to me confirmed that he felt comfortable that Egypt is identified through the Hagarenes in Psalm 83.

Lastly, those who omit Egypt from Psalm 83 need to explain Egypt's apparent future confrontation with Israel in Isaiah 19:16-18. Isaiah 19:16 declares Egypt will someday greatly fear Israel. From Isaiah's time until now, this fear has only been in place since Israel's defeat of Egypt in the wars of 1948, 1967, and 1973. It is this fear that drove former Egyptian President Anwar Sadat to make peace with Israel in 1979. This topic is thoroughly detailed in the chapters called "The Three Judgments of Egypt," and "Egypt's Desolation, Deportation, and Conversion."

Some suggest Isaiah 19 deals with the Antichrist's invasion of Egypt, specified in Daniel 11:42-43. Although portions of Isaiah 19 may find partial association with Daniel 11:42-43, it is doubtful that Isaiah 19:16-18 finds any association.

Isaiah 19:18 predicts that someday five cities in Egypt will speak the language of Canaan, but this beckons the question, "Why would the Antichrist take over five Egyptian cities and allow Hebrew to become the spoken language?" It is commonly understood the Antichrist will be attempting Jewish genocide at the time. If this is the case, it would be contrary to his overall purposes to allow five cities in Egypt to promote the language of Hebrew.

For the above reasons I strongly believe that Egypt is identified in Psalm 83. Therefore, unlike David Dolan, I believe Egypt will someday break its peace treaty with Israel and join the Psalm 83 confederacy.

# Appendix 10

## *The Sinner's Salvation Prayer*

"In an acceptable time I have heard you, And in the day of salvation I have helped you." Behold, now *is* the accepted time; behold, now *is* the day of salvation. (2 Corinthians 6:2).

The most important life decision one can make is to receive Christ as his personal Lord and Savior. It is the sinner's passport to a forgiven and changed life, so that they can enter paradise. However, sin is not allowed in heaven; therefore, Christ came to remedy the sin problem confronting mankind. He was sent because God so loved the world that He wished none would perish, but all would inhabit eternity.

> For God so loved the world that He gave His only begotten Son, [Jesus Christ] that whoever believes in Him should not perish but have everlasting life. (John 3:16).

> And this is eternal life, that they may know You, the only true God, and Jesus Christ [Begotten Son of God] whom You have sent. (John 17:1-3).

These passages point out that people are perishing, to the great displeasure of God, Who loves them immeasurably. He wishes that none would perish, but that everyone would inhabit eternity with Him and His only begotten Son, Jesus Christ. Of the utmost importance to eternal life is the knowledge of these two.

## *Sin Separates Us from the Love of God*

The apostle John reminds us in 1 John 4:8, 16 that God is love; but, man lives in a condition of sin, which separates him from God's love. Romans 8:5-8 explains how sin manifests into carnal behavior, that creates enmity between God and man. So then, those who are in the flesh cannot please God. (Romans 8:8).

The book of Romans also instructs us that sin entered into the world through Adam, and spread throughout all mankind, thereafter. Additionally, Romans informs us that sin is the root cause of all death, but through Jesus Christ eternal life can be obtained.

> Therefore, just as through one man [Adam] sin entered the world, and death through sin, and thus death spread to all men, because all [men] sinned. (Romans 5:12).

> All we like sheep have gone astray; We [mankind] have turned, every one, to his own way; And the LORD has laid on Him [Jesus Christ] the iniquity of us all. (Isaiah 53:6).

> For the wages of sin *is* death, but the gift of God *is* eternal life in Christ Jesus our Lord. (Romans 6:23).

If this makes sense to you, and you:

- Will humble yourself and recognize you are a sinner, separated from your Creator and living under the curse of sin,

- Believe that Jesus Christ took your punishment for sin so that you could be pardoned, as the only way to be saved

- Want to repent and start letting God make changes in your life, to be in right relationship with Him,

- And, want to do it right now,

Then you have come to a right place spiritually. It is the place where millions before you, and many of your contemporaries alongside you, have arrived.

By the grace of God, you have only one final step to take to complete your eternal journey. This is because salvation is a gift of God. Christ paid the full price for all sin, past, present, and future, when He sacrificed His life in Jerusalem about 2,000 years ago. Your pardon for sin is available to you through faith in the finished work of Jesus Christ completed upon His bloodstained cross. His blood was shed for us. He paid sins wages of death on our account.

You must now take the final leap of faith to obtain your eternal salvation. It is your faith in Christ that is important to God.

> But without faith *it is* impossible to please *Him*, [God] for he who comes to God must believe that He is, and *that* He is a rewarder of those who diligently seek Him. (Hebrews 11:6; emphasis added).

> In this you [believer] greatly rejoice, though now for a little while, if need be, you have been grieved by various trials, that *the genuineness of your faith, being much more precious than gold that perishes*, though it is tested by fire, may be found to praise, honor, and glory at the revelation of Jesus Christ, whom having not seen you love. Though now you do not see *Him,* yet believing, you rejoice with joy inexpressible and full of glory, receiving the end of your faith—the salvation of *your* souls. (1 Peter 1:6-9; emphasis added).

Before the necessary step to salvation gets introduced, it is important to realize and appreciate that salvation is a gift provided to us through God's grace. We didn't earn it, but we must receive it. If you are one who has worked hard to earn everything you have achieved in life, then you are to be commended. However, there is nothing you as a sinner could have done to meet the righteous requirement to cohabit eternity with God. In the final analysis, when we see our heavenly Father in His full glory, we will all be overwhelmingly grateful that Christ's sacrificial death bridged the chasm between our unrighteousness, and God's uncompromising holiness.

> But God, who is rich in mercy, because of His great love with which He loved us, even when we were dead in trespasses, [sin] made us alive together with Christ (*by grace you have been saved*), and raised *us* up together, and made *us* sit together in the heavenly *places* in Christ Jesus, that in the ages to come He might show the exceeding riches of His grace in *His* kindness toward us in Christ Jesus. *For by grace you have been saved* through faith, and that not of yourselves; *it is the gift of God,* not of works, lest anyone should boast. (Ephesians 2:4-9; emphasis added).

## The Good News Gospel Truth

The term gospel is derived from the Old English "god-spell," which was understood to mean "good news" or "glad tidings." In a nutshell, the gospel is the good news message of Jesus Christ. Jesus came because God so loved the world that He sent His Son to pay the penalty for our sins. That's part of the good news, but equally important is the "Resurrection."

This is the entire good news gospel:

> For I delivered to you first of all that which I also received: that Christ died for our sins according to the Scriptures, and that He was buried, and that He rose again the third day according to the Scriptures (1 Corinthians 15:3-4).

> Christ resurrected, which means He's alive and able to perform all of His abundant promises to believers. The Bible tells us that He is presently in heaven, seated at the right hand side of God the Father, waiting until His enemies become His footstool.

> But this Man, [Jesus Christ became a Man, to die a Man's death] after He had offered one sacrifice for sins forever, sat down at the right hand of God, from that time waiting till His enemies are made His footstool. For by one offering He has perfected forever those who are being sanctified. (Hebrews 10:12-14).

The resurrection of Christ overwhelmingly serves as His certificate of authenticity to all His teachings. He traveled through the door of death, and resurrected to validate His promises, prophecies, and professions. This can't be said of the claims of Buddha (Buddhism), Mohammed (Islam), Krishna (Hinduism), or any of the other host of deceased, human, non-resurrected, false teachers. All the erroneous teachings they deposited on the living side of death's door were invalidated when they died and lacked the power to conquer death itself, as Jesus had done. One of Christ's most important claims is:

> Jesus said to him, "I am the way, the truth, and the life. No one comes to the [heavenly] Father except through Me." (John 14:6)

This is a critical claim, considering eternal life can only be obtained by knowing the heavenly Father, and Christ, whom He (the Father) sent, according to John 17, listed at the top of this appendix. Most importantly, the resurrection proves that death has an Achilles heel. It means that its grip can be loosed from us, but only by Christ who holds the power over death.

> "O Death, where is your sting? O Hades, where is your victory?" The sting of death is sin, and the strength of sin is the law. But thanks be to God, who gives us the victory [over Death and Hades] through our Lord Jesus Christ. (1 Corinthian 15:55-57)

## How to be Saved —You Must Be Born Again

> Jesus answered and said to him, [Nicodemus] "Most assuredly, I say to you, unless one is born again, he cannot see the kingdom of God."(John 3:3)

Jesus told Nicodemus, a religious leader of his day, that entrance into the kingdom of God required being born again. This is a physical impossibility, but a spiritual necessity, and why faith plays a critical role in your salvation. You can't physically witness your new birth; it is a spiritual accomplishment beyond your control, that happens upon receiving Christ as your Lord and Savior. God takes full responsibility for your metamorphosis into a new creation at that point.

> Therefore, if anyone *is* in Christ, *he is* a new creation; old things have passed away; behold, all things have become new. (2 Corinthians 5:17)

You must trust God to perform on His promise to escort you through the doors of death into eternity, and to process you into the likeness of Christ meanwhile. This is the ultimate meaning of being born again; and alongside Christ, it is a responsibility undertaken by the third member of the Trinity, the Holy Spirit. Christ holds the power over Death and Hades, but the Holy Spirit is your "Helper" that participates in your spiritual processing.

> I *am* He [Jesus Christ] who lives, and was dead, and behold, I am alive forevermore. [Resurrected] Amen. And I have the keys of Hades and of Death. (Revelation 1:18)

> "If you love Me [Christ], keep My commandments. And I will pray the Father, and He will give you another Helper [Holy Spirit], that He may abide with you forever— the Spirit of truth, whom the world cannot receive, because it neither sees Him nor knows Him; but you know Him, for He dwells with you and will be in you. (John 14:15-17)

> "These things I have spoken to you while being present with you. But the Helper, the Holy Spirit, whom the Father will send in My name, He will teach you all things, and bring to your remembrance all things that I said to you. (John 14:25-26)

In order for you to successfully cross over from death to eternal life, at the appointed time, God has to work His unique miracle. Christ's resurrection demonstrated He possesses the power to make your eternity happen. Death wasn't eliminated in the resurrection, it was conquered. Death still serves its purpose on Earth by providing the sinner his due wage. Death continues to serve its purpose even in the Messianic Kingdom, where Christ reigns over a restored Earth for 1,000 years.[259]

> "No more shall an infant from there *live but a few* days, Nor an old man who has not fulfilled his days; For the child shall *die* one hundred years old, But the sinner *being* one hundred years old shall be accursed. (Isaiah 65:20; emphasis added)

This is why the full gospel involves both God's love and power. His love for us would be of little benefit if it ended with our deaths. His love and power are equally important for our eternal assurance. Therefore, we see in Romans 10, the following:

> But what does it say? *"The word is near you, in your mouth and in your heart"* (that is, the word of faith which we preach): that if you confess with your mouth the Lord Jesus and believe in your heart that God has raised Him from the dead, you will be saved. For with the heart one believes unto righteousness, and with the mouth confession is made unto salvation. For the Scripture says, *"Whoever believes on Him will not be put to shame."* For there is no distinction between Jew and Greek, for the same Lord over all is rich to all who call upon Him. For *"whoever calls on the name of the Lord shall be saved."* (Romans 10:8-13)

These Romans verses sum it up for all who seek to be saved through Christ. We must confess that Jesus Christ is Lord, and believe in our hearts that God raised Him from the dead.

## The Sinner's Prayer for Salvation

Knowing that confession of Christ as Lord, coupled with a sincere faith that God raised Him from the dead, are salvation requirements, the next step is customarily to recite a sinner's prayer in order to officiate one's salvation.

### Definition of the Sinner's Prayer

A sinner's prayer is an evangelical term referring to any prayer of humble repentance spoken or read by individuals who feel convicted of the presence of sin in their life and desire to form or renew a personal relationship with God through His son Jesus Christ. It is not intended as liturgical like a creed or a confiteor. It is intended to be an act of initial conversion to Christianity, and also may be prayed as an act of recommitment for those who are already believers in the faith. The prayer can take on different forms. There is no formula of specific words considered essential, although it usually contains an admission of sin and a petition asking that the Divine (Jesus) enter into the person's life.[260]

## Example of the Sinner's Prayer

Below is a sample Sinner's Prayer taken from the Salvation Prayer website. If you are ready to repent from your sins, and to receive Jesus Christ as your personal Lord and Savior, read this prayer will all sincerity of heart to God.

Dear God in heaven, I come to you in the name of Jesus. I acknowledge to You that I am a sinner, and I am sorry for my sins and the life that I have lived; I need your forgiveness.

I believe that your only begotten Son Jesus Christ shed His precious blood on the cross at Calvary and died for my sins, and I am now willing to turn from my sin.

You said in Your Holy Word, Romans 10:9 that if we confess the Lord as our God and believe in our hearts that God raised Jesus from the dead, we shall be saved.

Right now I confess Jesus as the Lord of my soul. With my heart, I believe that God raised Jesus from the dead. This very moment I receive Jesus Christ as my own personal Savior and according to His Word, right now I am saved.

Thank you Jesus, for your unlimited grace which has saved me from my sins. I thank you Jesus that your grace never leads to license for sin, but rather it always leads to repentance. Therefore Lord Jesus transform my life so that I may bring glory and honor to you alone and not to myself.

Thank you Jesus, for dying for me and giving me eternal life.

Amen.[261]

*Congratulations and welcome into the household of God!*

Below are the congratulatory words and recommendations also taken from the Salvation Prayer website. If you just prayed the Sinner's Prayer please be sure to read this section for further guidance.

> "If you just said this prayer and you meant it with all your heart, we believe that you just got saved and are born again. You may ask, "Now that I am saved, what's next?" First of all you need to get into a Bible-based church, and study God's Word. Once you have found a church home, you will want to become water-baptized. By accepting Christ you are baptized in the spirit, but it is through water-baptism that you show your obedience to the Lord. Water baptism is a symbol of your salvation from the dead. You were dead but now you live, for the Lord Jesus Christ has redeemed you for a price! The price was His death on the cross. May God Bless You!"[262]

Remember, being born again is a spiritual phenomenon. You may have felt an emotional response to your commitment to Christ, but don't be concerned if fireworks didn't spark, bands didn't march, sirens didn't sound, or trumpets didn't blast in the background at the time. There will be plenty of ticker-tape for us in heaven, which is where our rewards will be revealed. If you meant what you said, you can be assured God, Who sent His Son to be crucified on our behalf, overheard your every word. Even the angels in heaven are rejoicing.

> "Likewise, I say to you, there is joy in the presence of the angels of God over one sinner who repents." (Luke 15:10).

## *Welcome to the family…!*

# Endnotes

1. Quote taken from the Internet on 10/25/12 at this link: http://news.bbc.co.uk/2/hi/europe/5216320.stm

2. 2 Chronicles 29:30 identifies Asaph, the author of Psalm 83, as a seer. The Hebrew word used is *chozeh* and can also be translated as, a prophet, or a beholder in vision, according to *Strong's Hebrew and Greek Dictionaries* as per H2374.

3. The Rapture is primarily written about in 1 Corinthians 15:51-52 and 1 Thessalonians 4:15:18.

4. The Gog of Magog alliance is described in Ezekiel 38 and 39.

5. Revelation 20:4 informs of the 1000 year kingdom period.

6. The restoration of Israel's fortunes is predicted in several scriptures like: For the LORD their God will be mindful of them and restore their fortunes. (Zeph. 2:7). "Then Israel shall take possession of his inheritance," says the LORD. (Jer. 49:2).

7. The Prophet Ezekiel had a vision, described in Ezek. 37:1-13, which represented the Jewish people outside the Holy Land in a worldwide dispersion scenario. Furthermore, it foretells the horricially grave circumstances that occur to the whole house of Israel that climactically concludes their dispersion sequence. In essence, the prophet envisioned the Holocaust centruies ago.

8. The Psalmist Asaph is identified as a "seer" in 2 Chronicles 29:30

9. The definition of the word Hebrew was taken from the Easton Bible Dictionary.

10. Dr. Reagan's article can be accessed at www.lamblion.com

11. These eight specifications have been paraphrased by the author, but generally provide the gist of the important points made by Israeli Prime Minister Netanyahu at the time.

12. Information about Syrian President Assad's threats against Tel Aviv were obtained over the Internet on 10/16/11 at this link: http://www.ynetnews.com/articles/0,7340,L-4131259,00.html

13. Internet accessed on 6/15/2011 at http://www.washingtontimes.com/news/2010/apr/22/hezbollah-may-have-scud-type-missiles/

14. Information accessed on the Internet on 11/25/12 at this link: http://www.timesofisrael.com/defected-syrian-general-damascus-planned-to-send-chemical-weapons-to-hezbollah/

15. Internet accessed on 6/15/2011 at http://www.haaretz.com/news/report-chemical-weapons-in-hezbollah-arms-cache-blast-1.8552.

16. Georges Sada writes about Iraq's chemical weapons being transported into Syria in his book called "Saddam's Secrets, How An Iraqi General Defied And Survived Saddam Hussein."

17. 195 countries in the world as per this internet site that was accessed on 11/3/12 http://geography.about.com/cs/countries/a/numbercountries.htm

18. Examples of typological usages in the Bible of mountain or mountains Dan.2:45, Ezek. 37:22, Ezek. 19:9.

19. Mark Twain quote gathered from the Internet on 11/3/12 at this site: http://zionismandisrael.wordpress.com/2008/08/28/mark-twain-in-the-holy-land/

20. New American Standard Hebrew and Greek dictionaries. *Yashab*: to dwell. *Betach:* securely.

21. Other biblical use examples of Yashab Betach in tandem are Deut. 12:10, Ezek. 28:26.

22. Holman Bible Dictionary says that Solomon became the third king of Israel and reigned forty years about 1000 BC.

23. Curse-for-curse-in-kind is a phrase I first heard from Dr. Arnold Fruchtenbaum of Ariel Ministries. The phrase aptly describes the curse component of Gen. 12:3.

24. Aliyah (Hebrew "ascent" or "going up") is a term widely used to mean "Jewish immigration to the Land of Israel." *Wikipedia Encyclopedia.*

25. Ezekiel 35:5. Ezekiel 25:15.

26. The topic of Edomite sponsored terrorism being fulfilled through the Palestinians is covered in *Isralestine*, within the chapter called "The End of Terror."

27. Gen. 4:1-13, 1 John 3:12.

28. Jer. 31:31-34 foretlls a New Covenant that God would make with the Jews.

29. Matthew 25:40

30. Genesis 4:13-14 NKJV

31. Hosea 1:9-10 foretells of a time when the Jewish people would be reclassified as "not My people."

32. Daniel 9:27 describes this seven-year period, and divides it in half. It speaks of one week, but scholars understand this is to represent one week of years; in essence, seven years.

33. Zechariah 13:8

34. Gen. 36:1. Now this *is* the genealogy of Esau, who is Edom.

35. Jer. 49:2 says modern-day Jordan will be a desolate mound (NKJV).

36. Primary supporting passages are Ezek. 28:24-28, Ezek. 38:8, 11, 14.

37. Hosea 5:15.

38. NKJV verse is abbreviated

39. Exodus 1:22

40. Several verses to reference would be 1 Kings 16:13, 16; 1 Kings 21:26, and Ezek. 8:10, 12.

41. Hosea 1:9.

42. Romans 9:3-5.

43. Isaiah 42:6, 49:6, 60:3.

44. Gen. 13:14-16, 17:3-8.

45. Wiersbe's expository outlines on the New Testament quotation "the fullness of the Gentiles" refers to the number of Gentiles that will be saved during this church age. When the body of Christ is completed, He will catch it away in the air; then will begin the seven-year Tribulation here on earth, "the time of Jacob's trouble."

46. Dan. 9:27, Isa. 28:15.

47. This event has not yet occurred, almost 2000 years after. That centuries have passed since the destruction of the Jewish genealogical records further evidences the supernatural orchestration of the emergence of these pure-bred Jewish witnesses. Only a God, who knows the beginning from the end, would be able to trace their tribal origins.

48. Regarding the mystery: Romans 11:25, Ephesians 3:3-6. Regarding the grafting in: Romans 11:17-24

49. John 1:29, 36 refers to Christ as the sacrificial Lamb of God.

50. Holman Bible Dictionary.

51. WND article accessed from the Internet on 7/26/11 at this link: http://www.wnd.com/?pageId=123758#ixzz1TEQE1McS

52. The DOHS operating budget for 2011 was $98.5 billion according to this Internet link accessed on 7/27/11: http://en.wikipedia.org/wiki/United_States_Department_of_Homeland_Security

53. "NYPD Pioneers New Dirty Bomb Detection System" article accessed on the Internet on 7/29/11 at this link: http://apnews.myway.com/article/20110729/D9OP0RTG0.html

54. "Dirty bomb threat reported on the Internet by CBS New York on September 9, 2011" at this link: http://newyork.cbslocal.com/2011/09/09/times-square-could-be-target-of-dirty-bomb-sources-say-police-on-heightened-alert/

55.   Read more about CDC and WHO concerns about the Swine Flu of 2009 at this internet link accessed on 7/26/2011 at: http://www.cdc.gov/h1n1flu/

56.   Information gathered over the Internet on 7/26/11 at this link: http://news.sky.com/skynews/Home/UK-News/Swine-Flu-Vaccines-Hampton-School-Closes-As-Govt-Orders-90-Million-Vaccines-To-Fight-H1N1-Virus/Article/200905315282480

57.   The UK has approximately 61,838 million residents, according to this Internet website accessed on 7/26/11 at: http://www.google.com/publicdata/explore?ds=d5bncppjof8f9_&met_y=sp_pop_totl&idim=country:GBR&dl=en&hl=en&q=population+of+britain

58.   Japanese Trend Shop information collected from the Internet on 7/26/11 at this link: http://www.japantrendshop.com/japanese-face-mask-protect-against-swine-flu-in-fashion-p-503.html

59.   List of top ten deadly diseases can be accessed on the internet as of 7/26/11 at this link: http://www.toptenz.net/top-10-deadly-viruses.php.

60.   Khomeini coined the term for America as the Great Satan. Information gathered from the Internet on 7/26/11 at this link: http://en.wikipedia.org/wiki/Great_Satan

61.   More information on the fundamental tenets of Islam can be obtained from the Internet at this link, which was accessed by author on 7/26/11. http://www.vexen.co.uk/religion/islam_unbelievers.html

62.   Quote taken from Internet on 7/26/11 at this link: accessed by author on 7/26/11. http://www.vexen.co.uk/religion/islam_unbelievers.html

63.   Regarding Jeroboam's superintendent position appointed by Solomon see 1 Kings 11:26-28.

64.   Jeremiah 25:10-11, and 29:10 predicted that seventy-years of Babylonian captivity would burden the Jews.

65.   Chuck Missler writes about the subject of Christopher Columbus's possible Jewish heritage at this Internet link, which was author accessed on 7/30/11 here: http://www.khouse.org/articles/1996/109/print/

66.   This information was gathered from the Internet on September 14, 2011 at this link: http://www.jewishfederationpittsburgh.org/page.aspx?id=148359

67.   Dr. David Reagan comments copied from an article accessed on 7/30/11 from the Internet at this site link: http://www.raptureready.com/featured/reagan/dr10.html

68.   Obama quote taken from the Internet on 11/25/12 at this link: http://www.wnd.com/2008/06/67735/

69.   DOMA definition taken from the Internet on 10/22/11 at this link: http://en.wikipedia.org/wiki/Defense_of_Marriage_Act

70.  *Huffington Post* quote about DOMA was taken from the Internet on 10/22/11 at this link: http://www.huffingtonpost.com/2011/02/23/obama-doma-unconstitutional_n_827134.html

71.  World Jewry population estimates were taken from the Internet on 10/24/12 at this website http://en.wikipedia.org/wiki/Jewish_population_by_country

72.  Morsi quotes taken from the Internet on 10/24/12 at this website http://www.jpost.com/DiplomacyAndPolitics/Article.aspx?id=285906

73.  Footsteps of the Messiah by Dr. Arnold Fruchtenbaum in Chapter 20 pages 498-499 of the hard cover book.

74.  Herzl quote gathered from the Internet on 10/26/12 at this link: http://www.mideastweb.org/thejewishstate.htm

75.  England and UK population totals gathered over the Internet on 3/31/12 at this website: http://wiki.answers.com/Q/What_is_the_population_of_people_in_England_2012

76.  Information quoted was gathered over the Internet on 3/31/12 at this link: http://en.wikipedia.org/wiki/British_Empire.

77.  300 of Gideon's men destroyed 120,000 Midianites, according to Judges 8:1-10.

78.  Kenite information gathered from the Holman Bible Dictionary.

79.  Scripture points to ancient Bozrah, now called Petra, located in Southern Jordan, as the place whereby Christ returns to save the faithful Jewish remnant from the destruction of the Antichrist and his armies. Isaiah 34:5-13, 63:1-8.

80.  Esau is the founder of the terrirtory of Edom. Gen. 36:1, 19. Gen. 25:25-26 regarding the brothers.

81.  Gen. 32:28 regarding Jacob to Israelites, and Gen. 36:9, 43 concerning Esau to Edomites.

82.  http://www.peacefaq.com/palestinians.html. Accessed 2/28/2008. Partially quoted from this web link.

83.  Zechariah 13:8.

84.  134–104 BCE John Hyrcanus, Ethnarch & High Priest of Jerusalem, "Age of Expansion", annexed Trans-Jordan, Samaria, Galilee, Idumea. Forced Idumeans to convert to Judaism, hired non-Jewish mercenaries, etc. http://en.wikipedia.org/wiki/History_of_ancient_Israel_and_Judah. Accessed 2/28/08.

85.  The Works of Josephus: Book of the Wars 6, Chapter 8.

86.  Refer to The Bar Kokhba Revolt map at http://en.wikipedia.org/wiki/Bar_Kokhba_revolt. Accessed 2/28/08.

87.  Hos. 1:9–10. Regarding "My people Israel," Ezek. 25:14, 36:12, 38:14,16, 39:7.

88.   Jer. 49:15, Obad. 1:2

89.   "Previous to the arrival of the British, the Arabs in Palestine had thought of themselves as Arabs rather than as Palestinians." Quotation from http://www.fsmitha.com/h2/ch17jeru.html. Accessed 2/28/08.

90.   http://www.kinghussein.gov.jo/his_nabateans.html . Online office of King Hussein I. Accessed 2/28/08.

91.   *International Standard Bible Encyclopedia*, "Asmonians."

92.   *The Wars of the Jews*, Book 4, Chapter 4.

93.   *The Wars of the Jews*, Book 4, Chapter 4:1.

94.   *The Wars of the Jews*, Book 4, Chapter 4:2 and Chapter 5:1–4.

95.   *The Wars of the Jews*, Book 4, Chapter 5:5.

96.   *The Wars of the Jews*, Book 5, Chapter 9:2.

97.   *The Wars of the Jews*, Book 6, Chapter 8:1

98.   From *Time Immemorial* by Joan Peters. Chapter 8, 2nd page.

99.   http://masada2000.org/ in the *Palestine?* section.

100.  From *Time Immemorial* by Joan Peters. Chapter 8, 5th page.

101.  From *Time Immemorial* by Joan Peters. Chapter 8, 11th page (600,000 Jews estimated).

102.  From *Time Immemorial* by Joan Peters. Chapter 8, 5th page.

103.  http://en.wikipedia.org/wiki/Palestine_%28region%29. Accessed 2/28/08.

104.  http://en.wikipedia.org/wiki/Palestine_%28region%29. Accessed 2/28/08.

105.   Matt. 24:7, Mark 13:8, Luke 21:10.

106.  Jordan gained its statehood in 1946. http://en.wikipedia.org/wiki/Jordan. Accessed 2/28/08.

107.  *New American Standard* Hebrew and Greek dictionaries.

108.  http://lexicorient.com/e.o/abraham.htm regarding the age of Abraham.

109.  *New American Standard* Hebrew and Greek dictionaries. *Olam* meaning "long duration," ancient, ancient times, days of old, everlasting, long ago, long time, without end, permanent, perpetual, and ebah enmity, hostility, hatred.

110.  Gen. 36:1

111.  Gen. 22:17

112.  Quotation from the Bible Knowledge Commentary, Old Testament.

113.  Gen. 17:17, 18:12.

114.  Gen. 17:17.

115. Gen. 21:17–20.

116. Gen. 21:21.

117. Surah's 2.125, 2.127, 2.133, 2.136, 2.140, 3.84, 4.163, 6.86, 14.39, 19.54, 21.85, 38.48.

118. Gen. Chapter 14 records a historical conflict during the time of Abraham's life. He joins the conflict in an attempt to rescue his relative, Lot. Abraham successfully accomplishes his mission, and in the process gains broader notoriety in the region. The presumption is that the numerous kings referenced in Gen. 14 must have known of Abraham due to his victory in the conflict.

119. Psalm 83:6.

120. *Strong's Exhaustive Concordance of the Bible* (King James Version).

121. Heb. 12:16–17.

122. Gen. 25:23.

123. Gen. 36:1.

124. Gen. 19:37.

125. Amos 1:13, Jer. 49:1.

126. Gen. 12:4-5.

127. Gen. 15:18.

128. Gen. 11:27.

129. Gen. 19:37.

130. Numbers 22:2-4.

131. Num. 22:2–6.

132. Gen. 13:5–16.

133. Judges 3:12–14.

134. Judges 3:28–30.

135. Gen. 25:24–26.

136. . Gen. 36:1. Also read the *Who-domites? Who Are The Edomites Today?* chapter contained in this book.

137. Deut. 1:8, Deut. 29:13.

138. Find further commentary on the crimes against Israel listed by Obadiah in the *Obadiah's Mysterious Vision* chapter within this Book.

139. http://en.wikipedia.org/wiki/1948_Arab-Israeli_War. Accessed 3/2/08.

140. Obad. 1:7. All the men in your (Esau's) confederacy Shall force you to the border; The men at peace with you Shall deceive you and prevail against you.

Those who eat your bread shall lay a trap for you. No one is aware of it.

141.   Bedouin Tribes information on the web as of 11/7/12  http://en.wikipedia.org/wiki/Bedouin

142.   The PLO's "Phased Plan" quotes were taken on 11/7/12 from this Internet site. http://www.iris.org.il/plophase.htm

143.   The PLO's "Phased Plan" quotes were taken on 11/7/12 from this Internet site. http://www.iris.org.il/plophase.htm

144.   Obadiah 1:15

145.   *Holman Bible Dictionary* suggests the ministry of Malachi to be sometime after 450 BC, whereas Easton's Bible Dictionary sets the timing around 420 BC

146.   Edom was prophesied to be made small among the nations by Jer. 49:15, and Obadiah 1:2.

147.   Hitchcock Quote is found on page 165 and 167 of his book called Middle East Burning.

148.   Quote taken from *Revelation Road, Hope Beyond the Horizon*, page 248 under the subtitle of "Why Ezekiel 38 is Probably Pre-Trib."

149.   World army rankings on the Internet as of 11/8/12 at this link http://www.globalfirepower.com/

150.   This section is located in chapter 20 of the Footsteps of the Messiah book, pages 497-515.

151.   Strong's Hebrew and Greek Dictionary.

152.   Edomite descendants exist within the Palestinian ethnicity, as do descendants from Moab, Ammon, and Philistia, among many others. Though Zephaniah doesn't specifically reference Edom in chapter two of his book, their current existence within the Palestinian ethnicity of today should not be discounted as his theme describes events relative to the peoples and territories inclusive of both Jordanians and Palestinians.

153.   *Holman Bible Dictionary* states PENTAPOLIS a league of five Philistine city-states which banded together to oppose the Israelite occupation of Canaan. See Philistines.

154.   http://en.wikipedia.org/wiki/Ashkelon.

155.   Rabbah is the ancient title of the modern-day capitol city of Jordan, which is Amman.

156.   Deut. 2:8-9 "And when we passed beyond our brethren, the descendants of Esau who dwell in Seir, away from the road of the plain, away from Elath and Ezion Geber, we turned and passed by way of the Wilderness of Moab. Then the LORD said to me, 'Do not harass Moab, nor contend with them in battle,

for I will not give you any of their land as a possession, because I have given Ar to the descendants of Lot as a possession.'" Deut. 2:16-19 "So it was, when all the men of war had finally perished from among the people, that the LORD spoke to me, saying: 'This day you are to cross over at Ar, the boundary of Moab. And when you come near the people of Ammon, do not harass them or meddle with them, for I will not give you any of the land of the people of Ammon as a possession, because I have given it to the descendants of Lot as a possession.'"

157.   New American Standard Hebrew and Greek Dictionaries.

158.   Among the Palestinian refugees is a contingency of the descendants of Esau, who were known as Edomites. Further explanation of this connection is delivered in the *Who-domites?* chapter.

159.   Bat Yeor. http://en.wikipedia.org/wiki/Bat_Yeor.

160.   Zionism. http://www.channel4.com/history/microsites/H/history/browse/glossary.html.

161.   Psa. 83:6 refers introduces the term the "tents of Edom." Psa. 83 foretells a confederacy that will come against Israel, and the "tents of Edom" are listed as one of the members.

162.   Teman was a grandson of Esau, one of the "dukes of Edom." Gen. 36:11, 15, 42. *Easton's Bible Dictionary*: The Temanites were renowned for their wisdom Job 2:11; compare Jer. 49:7. *Holman's Bible Dictionary*.

163.   Obad. 1:18, Ezek. 25:14, Psa. 83:1–8.

164.   Many Psalms depict Israel as "her." Psa. 48:12–13, 87:5. Also see Jer. 3:8, 3:20, Ezek. 36:17, and Rev. 12:1–6.

165.   The King James, New King James, American Standard, New American Standard, Revised Standard, and New International Versions translate the word "least" as "small." The New Living Translation says "cut you down to size."

166.   10 shortest books of the bible information taken from the Internet on 11/8/12 at this link: http://www.kneeholedesk.com/Pages/Did_You_Know/Books_of_the_Bible.html

167.   IDF in prophecy Ezek. 25:14, 37:10, and Obad. 1:18.

168.   Dan. 11:45, Zech. 12:7.

169.   The *Ryrie Study Bible NASB Expanded Addition* suggests Obadiah existed in either 841 or 586 BC. Also, an excerpt from the New Commentary on the Whole Bible: Old Testament Volume. In the book, it is clear that Jerusalem has already been overthrown (1:11–16, 20), and the prophet refers to the cruelty of the Edomites toward the Jews on that occasion (cf. also Lam. 4:21, 22; Ezek. 25:12–14; Psa. 137:7). This would seem to indicate the book was written some-

time soon after Jerusalem's fall to the Babylonians in 587/86 BC.

170. Surah 5:51 in the Koran discourage Muslims from befriending Jews and Christians because it considers them unjust people.

171. Dates and notes regarding the three sieges were obtained from *Easton's Bible Dictionary*.

172. Jer. 25:1–12 and Jer. 29:10.

173. 1 Chron. 6:39,48–2 Chron. 29:30.

174. Gen. 22:18, 26:4, 28:14, Gal. 3:16.

175. Eph. 2:8–10, John 3:16.

176. Psa. 19:1.

177. Deut. 32:8–10, Zec.2:8.

178. War in heaven Rev. 12:7-9.

179. Daniel 12:1 Michael the angelic prince over Israel.

180. Rev. 20:1–3, 7–10.

181. Ezek. 38:8,16.

182. Rev. 12:7–10, Job 1:6.

183. http://encarta.msn.com/encyclopedia_761553918/Muhammad_(prophet).html. Accessed 3/5/08.

184. http://encarta.msn.com/encyclopedia_761579171/Islam.html (emphasis added above). Accessed 3/5/08.

185. http://encarta.msn.com/encyclopedia_761579171/Islam.html. Accessed 3/5/08.

186. http://etext.virginia.edu/etcbin/toccer-new2?id=HolKora.sgm&images=images/modeng&data=/texts/english/modeng/parsed &tag=public&part=5&division=div1. Accessed 3/5/08.

187. http://islamawakened.com/Quran/5/51/. Accessed 3/5/08.

188. Book written about the Middle East in modern times by Joan Peters *From Time Immemorial*.

189. "Iran and Syria are linked by more than an alliance. They are linked by their patronage of a terrorist organization: Hezbollah, which is sponsored by Iran, supported by Syria and operates out of Lebanon." Quote from Tom Fenton. http://www.cbsnews.com/stories/2005/02/22/opinion/fenton/main675330.shtml. Accessed 3/5/08.

190. Zec. 13:8.

191. *Strong's Exhaustive Concordance of the Bible*, and the *New American Standard*

Hebrew and Greek dictionaries. This Hebrew term is also found in Obad. 1:7, and likely refers to the same Psa. 83:5–8 Arab League.

192. Quote taked from the Footsteps of the Messiah by Dr. Arnold Fruchtenbaum of www.ariel.ort on page 99.

193. Jordan gained its statehood in 1946. http://en.wikipedia.org/wiki/ Jordan. Accessed 2/28/08. Biblical examples of mount, mountain, or mountains alluding to leaders, governments or hierarchies: Daniel 2:35, 45, Micah 4:7, Zechariah 4:7, Revelation 17:9-10.

194. Other references to the Glorious Land are located in Daniel 8:9, 11:16.

195. Holman Bible Dictionary says Isaiah's ministry was between 740-701 BC.

196. The Seder Olam Rabbah (ca. 2nd century CE) determines the commencement of the Exodus to 2448 AM (1313 BCE). This information was accessed on the Internet on 10/11/12 here- http://en.wikipedia.org/wiki/The_Exodus

197. Army rankings accessed over the Internet on 10/10/12 at this site, http://www.globalfirepower.com/

198. Internet sources on 10/10/12 http://www.google.com/publicdata/ explore?ds=d5bncppjof8f9_&met_y=sp_pop_totl&idim=country:SAU&dl=en &hl=en&q=population+of+saudi+arabia, and http://www.google.com/public-data/explore?ds=d5bncppjof8f9_&met_y=sp_pop_totl&idim=country:SAU&dl=en&hl=en&q=population+of+saudi+arabia

199. Information about the Muslim Brotherhood / Nazi connection obtained over the Internet on 10/12/12 at this link: http://www.educationnews.org/breaking_news/106849.html

200. The NY Times article was accessed on the Internet on 10/13/12 at this link - http://www.nytimes.com/2012/09/23/world/middleeast/egyptian-leader-mohamed-morsi-spells-out-terms-for-us-arab-ties.html?pagewanted=all

201. "heres" translation taken from the Strong's Hebrew and Greek Dictionaries.

202. . . Ezek. 39: 11. "It will come to pass in that day that I will give Gog a burial place there in Israel, the valley of those who pass by east of the sea; and it will obstruct travelers, because there they will bury Gog and all his multitude. Therefore, they will call it the Valley of Hamon Gog."

203. Exod. 17:7, Num. 11:3, Josh. 5:9.

204. Quote taken from the Bible Knowledge Commentary of the New Testament by Walvoord and Zook in the commentary section of Revelation 16:16.

205. Isa. 11:15a Following Masoretic Text and Vulgate; Septuagint,

Syriac, and Targum read dry up.

206. Gen. 17:5.

207. Footsteps of the Messiah, by Dr. Arnold Fruchtenbaum on page 509.

208. Pharaoh quote about Mohammad Morsi taken from the Washington Post on 11/26/12 at this internet link: http://www.washingtonpost.com/blogs/guest-voices

209. Quote from Middle East Burning by Dr. Mark Hitchcock on page 176 of the chapter called, "Will Syria Be Destroyed Soon."

210. Definition of *azab* gathered from *New American Standard Hebrew and Greek Dictionaries*.

211. *Parsons Bible Atlas* – Aroer (GAD) A town near Rabbah, capital of Ammon, that was assigned to Gad. (Numbers 32:1) "Now the children of Reuben and the children of Gad had a very great multitude of livestock; and when they saw the land of Jazer and the land of Gilead, that indeed the region *was* a place for livestock. Also the *Holman Bible Dictionary* says, "GAD At the conclusion of the period of wilderness wandering, when the Israelites were preparing to occupy Canaan, the tribe of Gad requested permission, along with the tribe of Reuben and half the tribe of Manasseh, to settle east of the Jordan. Their reason was that they owned large numbers of livestock and the territory east of the Jordan was particularly suitable for raising livestock (Num. 32). This territory became known as Gad (Jer. 49:1)."

212. *Holman Bible Dictionary* gives the span of Isaiah's ministry.

213. Valley of Rephaim – is the location of two historic battles fought between King David and the Philistines. 2 Samuel 5, 1 Chronicles 11, and 14. The Philistines are listed in Psalm 83 as a member of the Arab confederacy. They would appear to be partially represented by Hamas today. It is remotely possible that the Valley of Rephaim, the Philistines, and Psalm 83 have some association here.

214. John 14:6, and Acts 4:10-12, informs us that Jesus is the only way of salvation.

215. Revelation 13:1 an example of sea connecting with Gentile nations.

216. Jeremiah 31:35-36, teach that Israel cannot be destroyed.

217. Definition of *Leom* taken from the *Strong's Hebrew and Greek Dictionaries*.

218. The definition of *Leummiym* was taken from two sources. 1) Arabian: *Strong's Hebrew and Greek Dictionaries*, and 2) as Dedan in the *New American Standard Hebrew and Greek Dictionaries*. The latter spells the word *Leummim*.

219. World army rankings taken as of 9/15/12 at this website on the Internet http://www.globalfirepower.com/

220. http://www.nationsencyclopedia.com/Asia-and-Oceania/Syria-POPULATION.html Information accessed over the Internet on 12/14/2010.

221. BBC interview with Syrian president Assad can be read on the Internet as of

9/4/11 at this link: http://www.bbc.co.uk/news/10337041

222.  Lieberman quote gathered from the internet on 9/4/11 at this link: http://www.informationclearinghouse.info/article24599.htm

223.  Syrian Scud Missile potential gathered from a *Prophecy Update Radio* interview between white house correspondent Bill Koenig and the author, and can be heard as of 7/14/11 at this Internet link: http://isralestine-blog.blogspot.com/2011/07/big-squeeze-against-israel.html

224.  Information about Josephus connecting Magog with the Scythians was collected from "The Old Testament Volume" of the *New Commentary on the Whole Bible*—Based on the classic commentary of Jamieson, Fausset, and Brown. It can be located in the commentary regarded with Ezekiel 38.

225.  Information accessed from the Internet on 7/8/11 at this link: http://en.wikipedia.org/wiki/Scythians

226.  Author recommended books and / or articles, and / or videos presentations covering Ezekiel 38 are *Northern Storm Rising* by Dr. Ron Rhodes; *Epicenter* by Joel Rosenberg; *The Magog Invasion and the The Alternative View to the Magog Invasion* by Dr. Chuck Missler; and *The Footsteps of the Messiah* by Dr. Arnold Fruchtenbaum.

227.  *Northern Storm Rising* – Russia, Iran, And the Emerging End-Times Military Coalition Against Israel - Page 159 under "The Burial of Enemy Bodies for Seven Months (Ezekiel 39:11-12,14-16) Published by Harvest House - Copyright 2008. Authored by Dr. Ron Rhodes.

228.  Information gathered from Parson's Bible Atlas under "Susa" (Quickverse Bible Software 6.0).

229.  Notes taken from Jeremiah 49 in The Bible Knowledge Commentary of the Old Testament, written by John Walvoord and Roy Zuck.

230.  Information gathered from Parson's Bible Atlas under "The Persian Empire." (Quickverse Bible Software 6.0).

231.  *The Footsteps of the Messiah* book, section C-6 pages 510-511. By Dr. Arnold Fruchtenbaum

232.  Quote taken from the Internet on 7/18/2011 at this link: http://en.wikipedia.org/wiki/List_of_earthquakes_in_Iran: all the earthquake information was gathered at this web link.

233.  Isaiah 2:4, Micah 4:3, and Isaiah 11:9

234.  Matthew 24:30-31, Revelation 20:4

235.  *New American Standard Hebrew and Greek Dictionaries*

236.  More on the war pacts between Iran, Hezbollah, Syria, and Hamas can be accessed over the Internet as of 7/10/11 at this link: http://www.worldview-

weekend.com/worldview-times/article.php?articleid=7021

237.  It is difficult to know if Persia technically occupied modern-day northern Iran at the time of the Psalm, about 3000 years ago. The Persian Empire was at its height around 500 BC. By the time Ezekiel included Persia in his Ezekiel 38 prophecy, Persia existed in this location. Ezekiel wrote about 500 years after the Psalm was penned.

238.  Information about Russia's growing Muslim population accessed from the Internet on 7/10/11 at this link: http://windowoneurasia.blogspot.com/2007/08/window-on-eurasia-russia-to-have-muslim.html

239.  Quote from Wikipedia and was accessed from the Internet on 7/11/11 at this link: http://en.wikipedia.org/wiki/List_of_countries_by_Muslim_population

240.  Atlas information obtained over the Internet on 11/10/12 at this link: http://www.worldatlas.com/

241.  "Inner Circle" is a name created by the author for the Psalm 83 countries. This term was first used in *Isralestine, The Ancient Blueprints of the Future Middle East.*

242.  Psalm 83 map created by Lani Harmony Salhus.

243.  "Outer Ring" is a name created by the author for the Ezekiel 38 countries. This term was first used in *Isralestine, The Ancient Blueprints of the Future Middle East.*

244.  Isaiah 46:9-10

245.  *Revelation Road* book review by Jim Fletcher was posted on the Internet on 1/31/12 at this link: http://www.wnd.com/2012/01/bibles-revelation-comes-to-life/

246.  Noah's testimonial actions are described in Hebrews 11:7, 1 Peter 3:20, 2 Peter 2:25.

247.  IVP Bible Background Commentary New Testament *by* Craig S. Keener (Matthew 10:29-31**).**

248.  Quote accessed from the Internet on 9/28/12 under "Symbolisms of Sacrifice" at this link: http://www.precepts.com/StudyMaterials/Outlines/Healing/Leave_the_Crowd.html

249.  Matthew 10:30, Luke 12:7.

250.  *Tamar One* value estimate obtained from the Internet on 9/14/11 at this link: http://www.businessweek.com/globalbiz/content/jan2009/gb20090119_996007.htm.

251.  Estimated value of *Leviathan* natural gas reserves was obtained from the Internet on 9/14/11 at this link: http://www.haaretz.com/print-edition/news/leviathan-natural-gas-reserve-said-worth-90-billion-1.334143.

252. Fruchtenbaum, Arnold, *The Footsteps of the Messiah* (San Antonio, TX: Ariel Ministries, Revised Edition, 2003), p 498.

253. Esau grandfathered Amalek according to Genesis 36:12.

254. Nations promised to Abraham Genesis 12:2, to Ishmael Genesis 17:20, to Jacob and Esau Genesis 25:23.

255. Parson's Technology Software, *Quickverse Version 6.0, Holman Bible Dictionary*, under "Hagarite," (Austin, TX; n.d.).

256. Parson's Technology Software, *Quickverse Version 6.0, International Standard Bible Encyclopedia*, under "Hagarenes/Hagarites/Hagrites," (Austin, TX; n.d.).

257. Parson's Technology Software, *Quickverse Version 6.0, New Commentary on the Whole Bible, Old Testament,* under "Ps. 83:6-8 tabernacles," (Austin, TX; n.d.).

258. Parson's Technology Software, *Quickverse Version 6.0, Barnes, Notes on the Old Testament,* under "And the Hagarenes," (Austin, TX; n.d.).

259. The Messianic Kingdom was the high-point of Old Testament prophecy. Revelation 20:4 informs that is lasts for 1,000 years.

260. Sinner's Prayer quote taken from Wikipedia over the Internet on 8/13/11 at this link: http://en.wikipedia.org/wiki/Sinner's_prayer

261. Sinner's prayer example was copied from the Internet on 8/13/11 at this website link: http://www.salvationprayer.info/prayer.html (slight emphasis was added in this appendix).

262. Quote welcoming those who prayed the sinner's prayer into the family of God copied over the Internet on 8/13/11 at this link: http://www.salvationprayer.info/prayer.html.

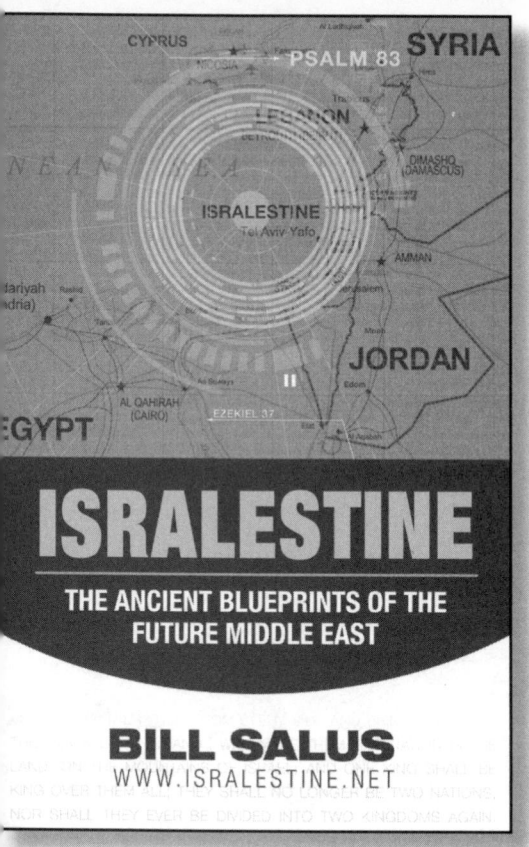

## Also by Bill Salus...

Set to explode in the not so distant future, is a devastating war in the Middle East. The Jews will fight off Arab aggression and end terrorism once and for all! *ISRALESTINE; The Ancient Blueprints of the Future Middle East*, boldly unveils significant Bible prophecy that has eluded the discernment of today's great scholars.

Bill Salus's first book, released in the summer of 2008, created quite a stir in prophetic circles. It discusses Psalm 83, Ezekiel 38, and many more prophecies and serves as an excellent prequel to his new book *Revelation Road*.

Here are a few endorsements from the experts:

*"Invaluable New Insights"* – Dr. David Reagan, the founder of Lamb and Lion Ministries and host of Christ in Prophecy Television

*"I wish I would have written it"* – Dr. David Hocking, the founder of Hope for Today Ministries.

*"Groundbreaking"* – Dr. Thomas Horn, bestselling author and founder of Raiders News Network.

*"Passionate and Believable"* – Terry James, bestselling author and co-founder of Rapture Ready.

*"Valid Arguments"* – Dr. Arnold Fruchtenbaum, founder of Ariel Ministries

Find out what the Bible predicts will happen next in the Middle East. Buy your copy of Isralestine at ***www.prophecydepot.com***

*Publisher: Highway – A division of Anomalos Publishing, Crane Missouri*